Experimentation in 5G and beyond Networks: State of the Art and the Way Forward

Experimentation in 5G and beyond Networks: State of the Art and the Way Forward

Editors

Giuseppe Caso
Özgü Alay
Anna Brunstrom
Harilaos Koumaras
Almudena Díaz Zayas
Valerio Frascolla

Basel • Beijing • Wuhan • Barcelona • Belgrade • Novi Sad • Cluj • Manchester

Editors

Giuseppe Caso
Department of Mathematics
and Computer Science
Karlstad University
Karlstad
Sweden

Özgü Alay
Department of Informatics
University of Oslo
Oslo
Norway

Anna Brunstrom
Department of Mathematics
and Computer Science
Karlstad University
Karlstad
Sweden

Harilaos Koumaras
Institute of Informatics and
Telecommunications
NCSR "Demokritos"
Agia Paraskevi
Greece

Almudena Díaz Zayas
Department of Electronics
Technology
University of Malaga
Malaga
Spain

Valerio Frascolla
Intel Deutschland GmbH
Neubiberg
Germany

Editorial Office
MDPI
St. Alban-Anlage 66
4052 Basel, Switzerland

This is a reprint of articles from the Special Issue published online in the open access journal *Sensors* (ISSN 1424-8220) (available at: www.mdpi.com/journal/sensors/special_issues/5G_beyond_networks).

For citation purposes, cite each article independently as indicated on the article page online and as indicated below:

Lastname, A.A.; Lastname, B.B. Article Title. *Journal Name* **Year**, *Volume Number*, Page Range.

ISBN 978-3-7258-0046-9 (Hbk)
ISBN 978-3-7258-0045-2 (PDF)
doi.org/10.3390/books978-3-7258-0045-2

Cover image courtesy of Sabino Colucci

© 2024 by the authors. Articles in this book are Open Access and distributed under the Creative Commons Attribution (CC BY) license. The book as a whole is distributed by MDPI under the terms and conditions of the Creative Commons Attribution-NonCommercial-NoDerivs (CC BY-NC-ND) license.

Contents

About the Editors vii

Preface ix

Giuseppe Caso, Özgü Alay, Anna Brunstrom, Harilaos Koumaras, Almudena Díaz Zayas and Valerio Frascolla
Experimentation in 5G and beyond Networks: State of the Art and the Way Forward
Reprinted from: *Sensors* 2023, 23, 9671, doi:10.3390/s23249671 1

Almudena Díaz Zayas, Giuseppe Caso, Özgü Alay, Pedro Merino, Anna Brunstrom and Dimitris Tsolkas et al.
A Modular Experimentation Methodology for 5G Deployments: The 5GENESIS Approach
Reprinted from: *Sensors* 2020, 20, 6652, doi:10.3390/s20226652 6

Victor Sanchez-Aguero, Ivan Vidal, Francisco Valera, Borja Nogales, Luciano Leonel Mendes and Wheberth Damascena Dias et al.
Deploying an NFV-Based Experimentation Scenario for 5G Solutions in Underserved Areas
Reprinted from: *Sensors* 2021, 21, 1897, doi:10.3390/s21051897 31

Adriana Fernández-Fernández, Carlos Colman-Meixner, Leonardo Ochoa-Aday, August Betzler, Hamzeh Khalili and Muhammad Shuaib Siddiqui et al.
Validating a 5G-Enabled Neutral Host Framework in City-Wide Deployments
Reprinted from: *Sensors* 2021, 21, 8103, doi:10.3390/s21238103 46

Karolis Kiela, Marijan Jurgo, Vytautas Macaitis and Romualdas Navickas
5G Standalone and 4G Multi-Carrier Network-in-a-Box Using a Software Defined Radio Framework [†]
Reprinted from: *Sensors* 2021, 21, 5653, doi:10.3390/s21165653 66

Wagner de Oliveira, José Olimpio Rodrigues Batista, Tiago Novais, Silvio Toshiyuki Takashima, Leonardo Roccon Stange and Moacyr Martucci et al.
OpenCare5G: O-RAN in Private Network for Digital Health Applications
Reprinted from: *Sensors* 2023, 23, 1047, doi:10.3390/s23021047 84

Yunke Tian, Yong Bai and Dake Liu
Low-Latency QC-LDPC Encoder Design for 5G NR
Reprinted from: *Sensors* 2021, 21, 6266, doi:10.3390/s21186266 114

Hisham A. Kholidy
Multi-Layer Attack Graph Analysis in the 5G Edge Network Using a Dynamic Hexagonal Fuzzy Method
Reprinted from: *Sensors* 2021, 22, 9, doi:10.3390/s22010009 132

Yared Zerihun Bekele and Young-June Choi
Random Access Using Deep Reinforcement Learning in Dense Mobile Networks
Reprinted from: *Sensors* 2021, 21, 3210, doi:10.3390/s21093210 159

Daniel Gaetano Riviello, Riccardo Tuninato, Elisa Zimaglia, Roberto Fantini and Roberto Garello
Implementation of Deep-Learning-Based CSI Feedback Reporting on 5G NR-Compliant Link-Level Simulator [†]
Reprinted from: *Sensors* 2023, 23, 910, doi:10.3390/s23020910 180

Lefteris Tsipi, Michail Karavolos, Petros S. Bithas and Demosthenes Vouyioukas
Machine Learning-Based Methods for Enhancement of UAV-NOMA and D2D Cooperative Networks
Reprinted from: *Sensors* **2023**, *23*, 3014, doi:10.3390/s23063014 . . . . **201**

About the Editors

Giuseppe Caso

Giuseppe Caso is a Senior Lecturer with the Department of Mathematics and Computer Science at Karlstad University. He was previously with Ericsson Research (Kista, Sweden), Simula Metropolitan (Oslo, Norway), and Sapienza University of Rome (Rome, Italy). He received his B.Sc. degree in Information and Communication Engineering from the Federico II University of Naples (Naples, Italy) and M.Sc. and Ph.D. degrees in Communication Engineering from the Sapienza University of Rome. Dr. Caso held various visiting positions at the Leibniz University of Hannover (Hannover, Germany), King's College London (London, UK), and the Technical University of Berlin (Berlin, Germany). His research interests include wireless communications, cognitive radio networks, mobile and distributed intelligent systems, IoT technologies, and location-based services.

Özgü Alay

Ozgu Alay is a Full Professor at the University of Oslo. She received her B.Sc. and M.Sc. degrees in Electrical and Electronic Engineering from the Middle East Technical University, Turkey, and a Ph.D. degree in Electrical and Computer engineering from the Tandon School of Engineering at the New York University. She is the author of more than 70 peer-reviewed IEEE and ACM publications. Professor Alay actively serves on technical boards of major conferences and journals, and has participated as principal investigator in numerous EU-funded research projects in the area of mobile cellular systems. Her research interests include mobile networks, low-latency networking, multipath protocols, and multimedia transmission over wireless networks.

Anna Brunstrom

Anna Brunstrom is a Full Professor and Research Manager for the Distributed Intelligent Systems and COmmunications (DISCO) research group at the Karlstad University and a part-time Distinguished Researcher in the Institute of Software Engineering and Technologies (ITIS) at the University of Malaga, Spain. She received her B.Sc. degree in Computer Science and Mathematics from the Pepperdine University, Malibu, CA, USA, in 1991, and herM.Sc. and Ph.D. degrees in Computer Science from the College of William and Mary, Williamsburg, VA, USA, in 1993 and 1996, respectively. In 1996, she joined the Department of Computer Science, Karlstad University, Sweden. She has authored/coauthored 10 book chapters and over 200 international journals and conference papers. Professor Brunstrom has served as a principal investigator and a coordinator at Karlstad University in several national and international projects. She served as the co-chair of the RTP Media Congestion Avoidance Techniques (RMCAT) Working Group within the IETF from 2015 to 2023. Her research interests include transport protocol design, techniques for low-latency internet communication, multi-path communication, and performance evaluation of mobile systems including 5G/6G.

Harilaos Koumaras

Harilaos Koumaras is a Research Associate Professor at the Institute of Informatics and Telecommunications of NCSR "Demokritos" and head of the Future Communication Networks (FRONT) research group. He received his B.Sc. degree in Physics in 2002, M.Sc. degree in Electronic Automation and Information Systems in 2004, and Ph.D. degree in 2007 from the University of Athens. Dr. Koumaras has published more than 100 articles in peer-reviewed journals, international conferences and book chapters, and is an editorial board member of the Telecommunications Systems Journal, a regular TPC member of renowned international conferences, and a reviewer of various journals and magazines. He is also a founding member of the ETSI OpenCAPIF Software Development Group, and has participated as principal investigator in numerous EU-funded research projects in the area of 5G, 6G and cloud-edge computing. His research interests include 5G, B5G, 6G networks, network programmability, distributed and edge-cloud computing continuum, Network Function Virtualization (NFV), Software-defined Networking (SDN) and objective/subjective evaluation of the perceived quality of services.

Almudena Díaz Zayas

Almudena Díaz Zayas has been a Researcher at the Universidad de Málaga since 2004 and an Associate Professor since 2021. Dr. Díaz Zayas has a Ph.D. in Telecommunication Engineering from the Universidad de Málaga (2009). She participated in national and European research projects related to 5G and Beyond-5G (B5G) networks and experimentation facilities and trials such as FED4FIRE+, TRIANGLE, 5GENESIS, 5G-EPICENTRE, 5G-TACTILE, and FIDAL. She has co-authored papers in relevant journals in the field of mobile networking and computing, like IEEE Pervasive Computing, Computer Networks, IEEE Internet Computing, and Pervasive and mobile computing, and participated in relevant conferences like IEEE AINA, IEEE GLOBECOM, IEEE CCNC, IEEE NOMS and IEEE IM. Her research interests are 5G and B5G networks and experimentation platforms.

Valerio Frascolla

Valerio Frascolla is the Director of Research and Innovation with Intel. He received his Ph.D. degree in Electronic Engineering from Marche Polytechnic University, Ancona, Italy, in 2004. He is the author of over 70 peer-reviewed publications. He actively serves as a reviewer for several magazines and journals and as consortium lead for business, standardization, innovation, and exploitation matters in international research projects. Dr. Frascolla has a track record as an organizer of special sessions, workshops, and panels at flagship IEEE conferences. His main research interests include 5G and 6G system design, with focus on machine learning algorithms, spectrum management, mmWaves, and edge technologies.

Preface

Special Issue "Experimentation in 5G and beyond Networks: State of the Art and the Way Forward" collected original contributions on experimental aspects related to 5th Generation (5G) and Beyond-5G (B5G) networks and systems.

The call for papers for this Special Issue included topics such as the design, implementation, and usage of 5G/B5G experimental testbeds and platforms, open-source tools for system monitoring and management, end-to-end measurement and validation of 5G/B5G Key Performance Indicators (KPIs), and solutions based on Machine Learning (ML) and Artificial Intelligence (AI) for the enhancement of different 5G/B5G system aspects, including New Radio (NR), Core Network (CN), Software-Defined Networking (SDN) and Network Function Virtualization (NFV), cloud/edge computing and network slicing, and vertical-specific solutions in the context of enhanced Mobile Broadband (eMBB), Ultra-Reliable Low Latency Communication (URLLC) and massive Machine-Type Communication (mMTC).

Ten high-quality papers were accepted to appear in this Special Issue, covering three main research areas: 5G testing and validation, 5G enhancements, and the use of AI/ML for B5G systems. We believe that the papers provide key updates and insights into these research areas, and thus may inspire future work aimed towards the further improvement and optimization of next-generation mobile systems.

We thank all the authors who contributed their work to this Special Issue, as well as the reviewers of the submitted papers who dedicated their time and expertise to providing high-quality reviews that allowed us to finalize a successful Special Issue.

Giuseppe Caso, Özgü Alay, Anna Brunstrom, Harilaos Koumaras, Almudena Díaz Zayas, and Valerio Frascolla
Editors

Editorial

Experimentation in 5G and beyond Networks: State of the Art and the Way Forward

Giuseppe Caso [1,*], Özgü Alay [1,2], Anna Brunstrom [1], Harilaos Koumaras [3], Almudena Díaz Zayas [4] and Valerio Frascolla [5]

1. Department of Mathematics and Computer Science, Karlstad University, 65188 Karlstad, Sweden; ozgua@ifi.uio.no (Ö.A.); anna.brunstrom@kau.se (A.B.)
2. Department of Informatics, University of Oslo, 0373 Oslo, Norway
3. NCSR "Demokritos", Institute of Informatics and Telecommunications, 15341 Agia Paraskevi, Greece; koumaras@iit.demokritos.gr
4. Department of Electronics Technology, University of Malaga, 29016 Malaga, Spain; adz@uma.es
5. Intel Deutschland GmbH, Lilienthalstraße 4, 85579 Neubiberg, Germany; valerio.frascolla@intel.com
* Correspondence: giuseppe.caso@kau.se

1. Introduction

After first being standardized by the 3rd Generation Partnership Project (3GPP) in Release 15, 5th Generation (5G) mobile systems have been rapidly deployed worldwide [1]. This initial phase is being complemented by the release of enhanced versions of the standards, which are expected to enable the evolution of current 5G deployments towards Beyond-5G (B5G) and 6th Generation (6G) systems [2]. Therefore, the need for testing and validating current and planned 5G/B5G technologies and features via data-driven and measurement-based analyses has significantly increased in the last few years, ultimately resulting in key experimental research activities that bring benefit to the entire telecommunications ecosystem, including research institutions, standardization bodies, network operators, technology and equipment providers, enterprises, and verticals [3–7].

On the one hand, experimental studies make it possible to identify how network deployment, configurations, and features affect achievable performance, while guiding the derivation of solutions for system enhancement and optimization. On the other hand, they also bring complex challenges to address, including (but not limited to) the definition of Key Performance Indicators (KPIs) and of proper measurement and testing methodologies. Furthermore, the popular approach of using Artificial Intelligence (AI) and Machine Learning (ML) to address several network aspects clearly requires system experimentation activities in order to be able to properly design AI/ML solutions on top of trustable data-driven analyses [8,9].

Within the above context, the Special Issue "Experimentation in 5G and beyond Networks: State of the Art and the Way Forward" collected original contributions on experimental aspects related to 5G/B5G networks and systems. The call for papers for this Special Issue included topics such as the design, implementation, and usage of 5G/B5G experimental testbeds and platforms, open-source tools for system monitoring and management, end-to-end measurement and validation of 5G/B5G KPIs, and ML/AI-based solutions for the enhancement of different 5G/B5G system aspects, including (but not limited to) New Radio (NR) [10,11], Core Network (CN) [12], Software-Defined Networking (SDN) and Network Function Virtualization (NFV) [13], cloud/edge computing and network slicing [14], and vertical-specific solutions in the context of enhanced Mobile Broadband (eMBB), Ultra-Reliable Low Latency Communication (URLLC) and massive Machine-Type Communication (mMTC) [15].

2. Overview of Published Papers

All submissions were judged by their technical merit and relevance, and ten high-quality papers were finally accepted to appear in this Special Issue.

In the following, we provide the list of accepted contributions, followed by a short overview of each contribution after grouping them into three main research areas, i.e., (a) 5G testing and validation, (b) 5G enhancements, and (c) the use of AI/ML for B5G Systems. We believe that such papers will provide key updates and insights into these research areas, and thus may inspire future work aimed towards the further improvement and optimization of next-generation mobile systems.

List of Contributions

1. A. Díaz Zayas, G. Caso, Ö. Alay, P. Merino, A. Brunstrom, D. Tsolkas, and H. Koumaras. A Modular Experimentation Methodology for 5G Deployments: The 5GENESIS Approach. Sensors, 20(22):6652, 2020.
2. V. Sanchez-Aguero, I. Vidal, F. Valera, B. Nogales, L. L. Mendes, W. Damascena Dias, and A. Carvalho Ferreira. Deploying an NFV-based Experimentation Scenario for 5G Solutions in Underserved Areas. Sensors, 21(5):1897, 2021.
3. A. Fernández-Fernández, C. Colman-Meixner, L. Ochoa-Aday, A. Betzler, H. Khalili, M. S. Siddiqui, G. Carrozzo, S. Figuerola, R. Nejabati, and D. Simeonidou. Validating a 5G-Enabled Neutral Host Framework in City-Wide Deployments. Sensors, 21(23):8103, 2021.
4. K. Kiela, M. Jurgo, V. Macaitis, and R. Navickas. 5G Standalone and 4G Multi-Carrier Network-in-a-Box Using a Software Defined Radio Framework. Sensors, 21(16):5653, 2021.
5. W. de Oliveira, J. O. R. Batista Jr, T. Novais, S. T. Takashima, L. R. Stange, M. Martucci Jr, C. E. Cugnasca, and G. Bressan. OpenCare5G: O-RAN in Private Network for Digital Health Applications. Sensors, 23(2):1047, 2023.
6. Y. Tian, Y. Bai, and D. Liu. Low-Latency QC-LDPC Encoder Design for 5G NR. Sensors, 21(18):6266, 2021.
7. H. A. Kholidy. Multi-layer Attack Graph Analysis in the 5G Edge Network Using a Dynamic Hexagonal Fuzzy Method. Sensors, 22(1):9, 2021.
8. Y. Z. Bekele and Y.-J. Choi. Random Access Using Deep Reinforcement Learning in Dense Mobile Networks. Sensors, 21(9):3210, 2021.
9. D. G. Riviello, R. Tuninato, E. Zimaglia, R. Fantini, and R. Garello. Implementation of Deep-Learning-based CSI Feedback Reporting on 5G NR-Compliant Link-Level Simulator. Sensors, 23(2):910, 2023.
10. L. Tsipi, M. Karavolos, P. S. Bithas, and D. Vouyioukas. Machine Learning-based Methods for Enhancement of UAV-NOMA and D2D Cooperative Networks. Sensors, 23(6):3014, 2023.

2.1. 5G Testing and Validation

Five papers belong to this research area, with the main goal of experimentally analyzing 5G systems and technologies, often in the context of collaborative international projects.

In Contribution 1, Díaz et al. introduce the experimentation methodology defined by the EU H2020 project 5GENESIS, which aims to enable the testing of 5G network components as well as the validation of end-to-end KPIs, e.g., throughput, latency, and service reliability. The proposed methodology is modular, flexible, and open-source, thus enabling its adoption in any 5G testbed. The work also demonstrates the use of the methodology via real-world experiments executed in the 5G Non-Standalone (NSA) [16] network at the University of Malaga.

Arguing about the low effort of researchers and companies in providing Internet access in remote areas, Contribution 2 by Sanchez-Aguero et al. presents the results of 5G-RANGE, an EU H2020 collaborative project between Brazil and the EU. The developed experimentation platform includes a fixed Radio Access Network (RAN) and a network of

Unmanned Aerial Vehicles (UAVs). This latter can be dynamically instantiated thanks to the NFV paradigm [13], which supports sporadic communication beyond the boundaries of the fixed RAN. This work presents a preliminary deployment validation by testing voice and data services.

In Contribution 3, Fernández-Fernández at al. present the main goals and achievements of the EU H2020 project 5GCity. This project targets the design and implementation of neutral host solutions, which mobile network operators can use to accommodate the requirements of emerging services by dynamically sharing the same physical infrastructure via network slicing [14]. The proposed 5G-enabled neutral host framework is validated in the cities of Barcelona, Bristol, and Lucca.

In Contribution 4, Kiela et al. present the design and implementation of a Software Defined Radio (SDR)-based Remote Radio Head (RRH) framework. This framework enables researchers to access non-simulated cellular networks more easily, thus reducing system development time and providing test and measurement capabilities for various wireless technologies. The performance of the proposed framework is tested by creating both 4G and 5G Standalone (SA) [16] network-in-a-box, capable of operating in multi-band multi-carrier configurations. Measurement results with a single user show the achievable performance of both networks in terms of downlink/uplink throughput and latency. Moreover, a lower CPU load of the 5G RAN compared to the 4G RAN, and, conversely, a higher CPU load of the 5G Core compared to the 4G Core are observed.

Finally, Contribution 5 by de Oliveira et al. focuses on digital health verticals and presents the efforts of the Brazilian OpenCare5G project to test how 5G technologies can enable timely and efficient digital health services in remote areas. This project uses a 5G private network deployed at the Faculty of Medicine of the University of São Paulo, embedded with an Open RAN (O-RAN) infrastructure [17]. In particular, the work describes the results obtained during the first phase of the project, i.e., the execution of health examinations with portable equipment at different locations within the Faculty of Medicine of the University of São Paulo. A second phase of the project is also expected, with the execution of health exams in remote areas, where onsite personnel is supported by personnel at the University of São Paulo thanks to 5G-enabled efficient communications.

2.2. 5G Enhancements

Two papers belong to this research area, with the primary goal of proposing enhancements for current 5G systems.

Contribution 6 by Tian et al. focuses on channel coding for 5G [18]. Considering that Low-Density Parity-Check (LPDC) codes are the 3GPP-standardized coding scheme for 5G NR data channels, this work discusses the design of a Quasi-Cyclic low-latency LPDC (QC-LPDC) scheme, which significantly reduces encoding complexity and resource utilization. By leveraging existing studies, the work showcases a new power-efficient QC-LPDC design, compatible with 5G NR standards and achieving significantly lower encoding latency thanks to a multi-channel parallel coding structure.

Contribution 7 by Kholidy analyzes 5G cybersecurity and discusses security concerns for both 5G networks and connected devices [19]. A method aimed at accurately analyzing 5G vulnerabilities is proposed, which combines the Technique for Order of Preference by Similarity to Ideal Solution (TOPSIS) and hexagonal fuzzy numbers theory. Such a method finds the network graph where attacks might propagate and quantifies both attack costs and network security levels. This work validates the method on a 5G testbed, using a classical TOPSIS-based approach and a vulnerability scanner tool called Nessus as benchmarks [20].

2.3. Use of AI/ML for B5G Systems

Three papers belong to this research area, with the main goal of proposing the use of AI/ML to address different aspects of B5G systems.

In Contribution 8 by Bekele et al., the focus is on the random access procedure [21], which end devices execute to connect to the Transmission and Reception Points (TRxPs) forming the cellular RAN. Considering that 5G and B5G systems will increasingly operate in high-frequency spectrum bands, a dense RAN comprising numerous TRxPs is needed to overcome coverage shrinking. This, in turn, increases the challenge for end devices to efficiently select a TRxP in a given time during the random access. To solve this problem, the work casts the random access procedure into an optimization problem and solves it via reinforcement learning. The proposed scheme estimates the congestion of TRxPs and selects an optimal TRxP for each end device during the random access. Through simulation, it is demonstrated that the proposed algorithm improves random access performance by decreasing the average access delay compared to the standard procedure, while also increasing the probability of successful access for end devices.

Contribution 9 by Riviello et al. proposes applying deep learning for the reporting of Channel State Information (CSI) feedback, which is a key aspect in the Frequency Division Duplexing (FDD) 5G and B5G systems [22], where the knowledge of channel characteristics is key to exploiting the full potential of Multiple Input Multiple Output (MIMO) schemes [23]. Therefore, the work designs a framework adopting a convolutional neural network, called NR-CsiNet, aimed at compressing the channel matrix experienced by the user at the receiver side and then reconstructing it at the transmitter side. NR-CsiNet is based on a 5G NR fully compliant simulator that implements a channel generator based on the latest 3GPP channel model. Simulations carried under realistic scenarios, including multi-receiving antenna schemes and noisy downlink channel estimation, show promising results compared to current 5G feedback reporting schemes, in terms of both block error rate and achievable data rate.

Finally, Contribution 10 by Tsipi et al. analyzes a cooperative network including UAVs and device-to-device (D2D) communications, which are expected to play an important role in B5G/6G scenarios [24,25]. In particular, a UAV placement scheme combining supervised and unsupervised ML techniques is proposed to enhance the performance of such a network, where Non-Orthogonal Multiple Access (NOMA) is used as the underlying access scheme. Comparisons against a conventional Orthogonal Multiple Access (OMA) scheme and an alternative scheme using unsupervised ML only show that the proposed approach leads to significant gains in terms of sum rate and spectral efficiency under a varying bandwidth allocation.

3. Conclusions

In this Special Issue, we selected ten papers that address different topics related to 5G/B5G experimentation in order to delineate the state of the art and the way forward for further activities in this broad, growing, and important research topic. We hope that the selected articles may provide useful insights into the research areas of 5G testing and validation, 5G enhancements, and use of AI/ML for B5G systems, inspiring future work in the context of these interesting research fields.

We would like to thank all the authors who contributed their work to this Special Issue, as well as the reviewers of the submitted papers who dedicated their time and expertise to providing high-quality reviews that allowed us to finalize a successful Special Issue.

Author Contributions: Conceptualization, all authors; writing—original draft preparation, G.C.; writing—review and editing, all authors; All authors have read and agreed to the published version of the manuscript.

Conflicts of Interest: Author Valerio Frascolla was employed by the company Intel Deutschland GmbH. The remaining authors declare that the research was conducted in the absence of any commercial or financial relationships that could be construed as a potential conflict of interest.

References

1. Shafi, M.; Molisch, A.F.; Smith, P.J.; Haustein, T.; Zhu, P.; De Silva, P.; Tufvesson, F.; Benjebbour, A.; Wunder, G. 5G: A Tutorial Overview of Standards, Trials, Challenges, Deployment, and Practice. *IEEE J. Sel. Areas Commun.* **2017**, *35*, 1201–1221. [CrossRef]
2. Wang, C.X.; You, X.; Gao, X.; Zhu, X.; Li, Z.; Zhang, C.; Wang, H.; Huang, Y.; Chen, Y.; Haas, H.; et al. On the road to 6G: Visions, Requirements, Key Technologies and Testbeds. *IEEE Commun. Surv. Tutor.* **2023**, *25*, 905–974. [CrossRef]

3. Narayanan, A.; Ramadan, E.; Carpenter, J.; Liu, Q.; Liu, Y.; Qian, F.; Zhang, Z.L. A First Look at Commercial 5G Performance on Smartphones. In Proceedings of the Web Conference 2020, Taipei, Taiwan, 20–24 April 2020; pp. 894–905.
4. Narayanan, A.; Zhang, X.; Zhu, R.; Hassan, A.; Jin, S.; Zhu, X.; Zhang, X.; Rybkin, D.; Yang, Z.; Mao, Z.M.; et al. A Variegated Look at 5G in the Wild: Performance, Power, and QoE Implications. In Proceedings of the ACM SIGCOMM 2021 Conference, Virtual Event, 23–27 August 2021; pp. 610–625.
5. Xu, D.; Zhou, A.; Zhang, X.; Wang, G.; Liu, X.; An, C.; Shi, Y.; Liu, L.; Ma, H. Understanding Operational 5G: A First Measurement Study on its Coverage, Performance and Energy Consumption. In Proceedings of the ACM SIGCOMM 2020 Conference, Virtual Event, 10–14 August 2020; pp. 479–494.
6. Kousias, K.; Rajiullah, M.; Caso, G.; Alay, O.; Brunstorm, A.; De Nardis, L.; Neri, M.; Ali, U.; Di Benedetto, M.G. Coverage and Performance Analysis of 5G Non-Standalone Deployments. In Proceedings of the ACM Workshop on Wireless Network Testbeds, Experimental evaluation & CHaracterization (WiNTECH'22), Sydney, NSW, Australia, 17 October 2022; pp. 61–68.
7. Fiandrino, C.; Juárez Martínez-Villanueva, D.; Widmer, J. Uncovering 5G Performance on Public Transit Systems with an App-based Measurement Study. In Proceedings of the ACM Conference on Modeling Analysis and Simulation of Wireless and Mobile Systems (MSWiM'22), Montreal, QC, Canada, 24–28 October 2022; pp. 65–73.
8. Wang, C.X.; Di Renzo, M.; Stanczak, S.; Wang, S.; Larsson, E.G. Artificial Intelligence Enabled Wireless Networking for 5G and Beyond: Recent Advances and Future Challenges. *IEEE Wirel. Commun.* **2020**, *27*, 16–23. [CrossRef]
9. Kousias, K.; Rajiullah, M.; Caso, G.; Ali, U.; Alay, O.; Brunstrom, A.; De Nardis, L.; Neri, M.; Di Benedetto, M.G. A Large-Scale Dataset of 4G, NB-IoT, and 5G Non-Standalone Network Measurements. *IEEE Commun. Mag.* **2023**. [CrossRef]
10. Lin, X.; Li, J.; Baldemair, R.; Cheng, J.F.T.; Parkvall, S.; Larsson, D.C.; Koorapaty, H.; Frenne, M.; Falahati, S.; Grovlen, A.; et al. 5G New Radio: Unveiling the Essentials of the Next Generation Wireless Access Technology. *IEEE Commun. Stand. Mag.* **2019**, *3*, 30–37. [CrossRef]
11. Dahlman, E.; Parkvall, S.; Skold, J. *5G NR: The Next Generation Wireless Access Technology*; Academic Press: Cambridge, MA, USA, 2020.
12. Rommer, S.; Hedman, P.; Olsson, M.; Frid, L.; Sultana, S.; Mulligan, C. *5G Core Networks: Powering Digitalization*; Academic Press: Cambridge, MA, USA, 2019.
13. Yousaf, F.Z.; Bredel, M.; Schaller, S.; Schneider, F. NFV and SDN—Key Technology Enablers for 5G Networks. *IEEE J. Sel. Areas Commun.* **2017**, *35*, 2468–2478. [CrossRef]
14. Ordonez-Lucena, J.; Ameigeiras, P.; Lopez, D.; Ramos-Munoz, J.J.; Lorca, J.; Folgueira, J. Network Slicing for 5G with SDN/NFV: Concepts, Architectures, and Challenges. *IEEE Commun. Mag.* **2017**, *55*, 80–87. [CrossRef]
15. Navarro-Ortiz, J.; Romero-Diaz, P.; Sendra, S.; Ameigeiras, P.; Ramos-Munoz, J.J.; Lopez-Soler, J.M. A Survey on 5G Usage Scenarios and Traffic Models. *IEEE Commun. Surv. Tutor.* **2020**, *22*, 905–929. [CrossRef]
16. Liu, G.; Huang, Y.; Chen, Z.; Liu, L.; Wang, Q.; Li, N. 5G Deployment: Standalone vs. Non-Standalone from the Operator Perspective. *IEEE Commun. Mag.* **2020**, *58*, 83–89. [CrossRef]
17. Polese, M.; Bonati, L.; D'oro, S.; Basagni, S.; Melodia, T. Understanding O-RAN: Architecture, Interfaces, Algorithms, Security, and Research Challenges. *IEEE Commun. Surv. Tutor.* **2023**, *25*, 1376–1411. [CrossRef]
18. Bioglio, V.; Condo, C.; Land, I. Design of Polar Codes in 5G New Radio. *IEEE Commun. Surv. Tutor.* **2020**, *23*, 29–40. [CrossRef]
19. Ahmad, I.; Kumar, T.; Liyanage, M.; Okwuibe, J.; Ylianttila, M.; Gurtov, A. Overview of 5G Security Challenges and Solutions. *IEEE Commun. Stand. Mag.* **2018**, *2*, 36–43. [CrossRef]
20. Anderson, H. Introduction to Nessus. *Retrieved Symantec* **2003**.
21. Toor, W.T.; Basit, A.; Maroof, N.; Khan, S.A.; Saadi, M. Evolution of Random Access Process: From Legacy Networks to 5G and Beyond. *Trans. Emerg. Telecommun. Technol.* **2022**, *33*, e3776. [CrossRef]
22. Guo, J.; Wen, C.K.; Jin, S.; Li, X. AI for CSI Feedback Enhancement in 5G-Advanced. *IEEE Wirel. Commun.* **2022**. [CrossRef]
23. Papadopoulos, H.; Wang, C.; Bursalioglu, O.; Hou, X.; Kishiyama, Y. Massive MIMO Technologies and Challenges Towards 5G. *IEICE Trans. Commun.* **2016**, *99*, 602–621. [CrossRef]
24. Tran, Q.N.; Vo, N.S.; Nguyen, Q.A.; Bui, M.P.; Phan, T.M.; Lam, V.V.; Masaracchia, A. D2D Multi-Hop Multi-Path Communications in B5G Networks: A Survey on Models, Techniques, and Applications. *EAI Endorsed Trans. Ind. Netw. Intell. Syst.* **2021**, *7*, e3. [CrossRef]
25. Zhang, J.; Cui, J.; Zhong, H.; Bolodurina, I.; Liu, L. Intelligent Drone-Assisted Anonymous Authentication and Key Agreement for 5G/B5G Vehicular Ad-Hoc Networks. *IEEE Trans. Netw. Sci. Eng.* **2020**, *8*, 2982–2994. [CrossRef]

Disclaimer/Publisher's Note: The statements, opinions and data contained in all publications are solely those of the individual author(s) and contributor(s) and not of MDPI and/or the editor(s). MDPI and/or the editor(s) disclaim responsibility for any injury to people or property resulting from any ideas, methods, instructions or products referred to in the content.

Article

A Modular Experimentation Methodology for 5G Deployments: The 5GENESIS Approach

Almudena Díaz Zayas [1],*, Giuseppe Caso [2], Özgü Alay [2,3], Pedro Merino [1], Anna Brunstrom [4], Dimitris Tsolkas [5] and Harilaos Koumaras [6]

1. ITIS Software, Universidad de Málaga, Andalucía Tech, 29071 Málaga, Spain; pmerino@uma.es
2. Simula Metropolitan Center for Digital Engineering, Pilestredet 52, 0167 Oslo, Norway; giuseppe@simula.no (G.C.); ozgu@simula.no (Ö.A.)
3. Deparment of Informatics, University of Oslo, 0315 Oslo, Norway
4. Deparment of Mathematics and Computer Science, Karlstad University, 651 88 Karlstad, Sweden; anna.brunstrom@kau.se
5. Fogus Innovations & Services, 161 21 Kesariani, Greece; dtsolkas@fogus.gr
6. NCSR Demokritos, Institute of Informatics and Telecommunications, 153 41 Paraskevi, Greece; koumaras@iit.demokritos.gr
* Correspondence: adz@uma.es

Received: 3 October 2020; Accepted: 17 November 2020 ; Published: 20 November 2020

Abstract: The high heterogeneity of 5G use cases requires the extension of the traditional per-component testing procedures provided by certification organizations, in order to devise and incorporate methodologies that cover the testing requirements from vertical applications and services. In this paper, we introduce an experimentation methodology that is defined in the context of the 5GENESIS project, which aims at enabling both the testing of network components and validation of E2E KPIs. The most important contributions of this methodology are its modularity and flexibility, as well as the open-source software that was developed for its application, which enable lightweight adoption of the methodology in any 5G testbed. We also demonstrate how the methodology can be used, by executing and analyzing different experiments in a 5G Non-Standalone (NSA) deployment at the University of Malaga. The key findings of the paper are an initial 5G performance assessment and KPI analysis and the detection of under-performance issues at the application level. Those findings highlight the need for reliable testing and validation procedures towards a fair benchmarking of generic 5G services and applications.

Keywords: 5G; testbeds; experimentation; methodology

1. Introduction

The 5th Generation of mobile networks (5G) enables innovative use cases and services that provide the over the top service providers (a.k.a, verticals) with unprecedented performance capabilities. Indeed, it is expected that the 5G performance will span over the three extremes of bandwidth, latency, and capacity requirements, which enable enhanced Mobile Broadband (eMBB), Ultra Reliable and Low Latency Communication (URLLC), and massive Machine Type Communication (mMTC), respectively [1]. This potential is supported by a variety of technologies, including the Software-Defined Networking (SDN), the Network Function Virtualization (NFV), the Network Slicing, and the Multi-access Edge Computing (MEC). However, the quantification of 5G performance in an end-to-end (E2E) level is still ongoing, since the high heterogeneity of the enabled use cases requires various Key Performance Indicators (KPIs) and different target values [2,3]. Irrefutable, vertical- and use case-oriented 5G testing methodologies, and experimentation processes are required, which have to incorporate E2E aspects, far beyond the conventional component-oriented testing (which, so far, is mainly focused the radio access network [4]).

In this context, huge efforts are being made worldwide by 5G standardization, research, and stakeholder communities towards the implementation of experimental testbeds, where 5G technologies and KPIs can be reliably measured and validated in heterogeneous scenarios. Such testbeds should be flexible and automatically reconfigurable, employ different technologies (from early stage standardization to commercial components), and be able to reproduce several network conditions. This would enable common procedures for a fully automated experimentation, following a Testing as a Service (TaaS) paradigm [3]. To this end, EU and US programs, such as 5G Public Private Partnership (5G-PPP) (https://5g-ppp.eu (accessed on 30 August 2020).) and Platforms for Advanced Wireless Research (PAWR) (https://advancedwireless.org (accessed on 30 August 2020).), are specifically focusing on the realization of 5G testing platforms, aiming at providing trustworthy environments, where eMBB, URLLC, and mMTC verticals can quantify the expected performance of their services and the corresponding KPIs.

As part of the 5G-PPP initiative, the EU-funded 5GENESIS project (https://5genesis.eu (accessed on 30 August 2020)) is realizing a 5G facility composed of five different testbeds in Europe, accessible for both per-component and E2E experimentation purposes [5]. A reference architecture for common and lightweight access to the 5GENESIS testbeds has been already defined [6], along with an E2E methodology for testing and validation of 5G technologies and KPIs. More precisely, the 5GENESIS testing methodology follows a modular approach and it includes three logical components, referring to three configuration/input information classes required for running an experiment, namely, the test cases, the scenarios, and the slices. Altogether, they identify an experiment, the definition of which is also formalized in a global template, referred to as Experiment Descriptor (ED). From the architectural point of view, the information enclosed in the ED feeds a core functional block of the 5GENESIS reference architecture, the Experiment Life-cycle Manager (ELCM). ELCM manages the testing procedure and allows for automatic execution of experiments. Subsequently, a further architectural block, i.e., the Monitoring and Analytics (M&A) framework [7], is in charge of collecting KPI samples and complementary measurements during the experiment (Monitoring), and process them for a statistical validation of the KPI under test (Analytics).

In this paper, we present the 5GENESIS methodology for KPI validation, which aims to cope with the increased complexity and heterogeneity of testing in the 5G era. The main contributions are:

- we detail the methodology components and corresponding templates, i.e., test cases, scenarios, slices, and ED. The analysis reveals that the methodology can be used by any 5G testbed, even outside the 5GENESIS facility, due to its modular and open-source nature [8];
- we analyze the use of the methodology under the 5GENESIS reference architecture, describing all of the steps leading to a fully automated experiment execution, from the instantiation of needed resources to the collection and analysis of results;
- we showcase the use of the methodology for testing components and configurations in the 5G infrastructure at the University of Málaga (UMA), i.e., one of the 5GENESIS testbeds; and,
- by means of our tests in a real 5G deployment, we provide initial 5G performance assessment and empirical KPI analysis. The results are provided, together with details on adopted scenarios and network configurations, making it possible to reproduce the tests in other testbeds (under the same or different settings) for comparison and benchmarking purposes.

The rest of the article is organized, as follows. Section 2 introduces the background and related work. Section 3 provides an overview of the 5GENESIS reference architecture, with focus on key components that are related to the testing methodology. The details of the testing methodology are described in Section 4. Section 5 describes the realization of the testing methodology in the UMA testbed, including the set up procedures performed and the definition of the related ED. The experimentation results are presented in Section 6. Finally, Section 7 provides the final remarks.

2. Background and Related Work

In the following, we provide an overview of background and related work, in order to frame the context and highlight the contribution of this paper. In particular, in Section 2.1, we review the standardization efforts towards the definition of 5G KPIs and corresponding testing and validation methodologies and procedures. In Section 2.2, we summarize recent research activity on 5G testing and field trials, referring to the most relevant 5G experimentation testbeds.

2.1. Standardization on 5G KPI Testing and Validation

Playing a key role in the standardization of mobile communications, the 3rd Generation Partnership Project (3GPP) also defines the corresponding tests aiming at verifying that mobile technologies conform to standards. Over the years, 3GPP has defined the testing procedures for Universal Mobile Telecommunications System (UMTS, i.e., 3G), Long Term Evolution (LTE, i.e., 4G) and more recently 5G New Radio (NR).

Focusing on the user-end device, i.e., User Equipment (UE), 3GPP TS 38.521-X series details how a 5G NR UE must be verified at radio level, characterizing both transmit and receive parameters in terms of maximum transmit power, receiver sensitivity, and spurious emissions, among others. Conformance to Non-Standalone (NSA) scenarios, which combine NR and LTE cells for the Radio Access Network (RAN), is covered in [9], while NR-only Standalone (SA) is analyzed in [10,11], which address sub-6 GHz and mmWave frequency bands, respectively. Performance aspects that are related to demodulation under different propagation and Signal-to-Noise Ratio (SNR) conditions are defined in [12]. Additional specifications cover the testing of several 5G NR signaling protocols [13–15], while [16] focuses on Radio Resource Management (RRM) testing, including the reporting of power and quality measurements, handover latency, timing accuracy, and other functional metrics. Another relevant aspect at the UE side is the battery consumption, for which the Global Certification Forum (GCF) and CTIA-The Wireless Association have proposed a testing methodology in [17], among others.

Moving at the network side, 3GPP TS 28.552 [18] provides specifications for performance measurements of Next-Generation Radio Access Network (NG-RAN), 5G Core (5GC), and network slicing. Moreover, Radio Resource Control (RRC)-related KPIs are measured according to [19,20], while using the measurement template given in [21].

As regards NFV, the European Telecommunication Standard Institute (ETSI) Group Specification (GS) NFV-TST [22] covers the testing of functional blocks of the architecture.

The above activities and documents focus on testing of 5G components separately, and they do not address a fully E2E KPI validation. As analyzed later, our proposed testing methodology allows for both per-component testing and E2E KPIs validation.

On this latter aspect, an initial recommendation is given in 3GPP TR 37.901 [23], which addresses the testing of LTE UE at the application layer. In particular, it specifies the procedure to run throughput tests in a wide set of network scenarios and conditions. When also considering the need for running similar tests for 5G, 3GPP has recently initiated a study on 5G NR UE throughput performance at the application layer, which is progressing as TR 37.901-5 [24], as an evolution of TR 37.901. Our work in 5GENESIS aims at generalizing these recommendations, in order to cover not only throughput, but also other E2E KPIs from specific verticals, e.g., the Mission Critical Push to Talk (MCPTT) access time, for which a test case has been already defined and used [25].

Following the E2E approach, 3GPP TS 28.554 [26] uses a network slicing perspective and currently covers KPIs related to accessibility, integrity, utilization, retainability, mobility, and energy efficiency. These KPIs are based on internal counters of the network, which are only accessible to the network operators; in our methodology, in order to provide direct information on the achievable performance under different 5G use cases, the definitions of KPI privilege instead the end-user perspective, in terms of Quality of Service (QoS) and Quality of Experience (QoE).

TS 28.554 also specifies a template that allows for the categorization of KPIs along with methods, tools, and calculation steps needed for measuring and validating them. However, it lacks specifications for the test sequence and the definition of E2E scenarios. We observe that these aspects are key in order to completely define and take into account the network setup during a test, which includes the relationships between infrastructure, management and orchestration system, measurement probes, user traffic, and so on. As a matter of fact, it is hard to contextualize and compare the obtained results without a proper scenario definition; also, a clear definition of test preconditions is key for running reproducible tests and obtaining reliable results. For this reason, we have defined our testing methodology by taking [26] as a reference, and then extrapolating the provided guidelines towards covering a full list of 5G E2E KPIs. We also aim at a more general and flexible testing approach, tailored on open experimental testbeds. Hence, we propose a test case template that reuses and expands the one in [26] in terms of considered fields, while also addressing clear definitions for test sequence, preconditions, and E2E scenarios.

When considering these aspects, a document by Next Generation Mobile Networks (NGMN) [27] introduces test case sequence and scenarios, with the latter based on the definitions provided in [28]. The goal is the evaluation of 5G NR performance, and the focus is on 3GPP Release 15 (Rel-15), the first step of 5G NR standardization, which primarily considers eMBB and some aspects of URLLC use cases. For both, several KPIs are considered, e.g., latency, user throughput, and mobility, but also capacity, coverage, energy efficiency, and user experience, among others.

The NGMN approach fuses together, in a monolithic definition of test cases, the testing procedures (e.g., test sequence), network configurations (e.g., number of exploited network resources), network conditions (e.g., number of users), and traffic profiles (e.g., used protocol and packet size). As detailed in the next sections, our testing approach is instead modular, i.e., the logical components forming an experiment (test cases, scenarios, and slices) are kept separated, ultimately enabling higher flexibility and adaptability, as well as lightweight extension towards more advanced testing.

Table 1 summarizes the standards and documentation reviewed above.

Table 1. Summary of standards for 5G testing and Key Performance Indicator (KPI) validation.

Main Component	Reference	Focus
	3GPP TS 38.521-3 [9]	5GNR UE RF conformance. NSA
	3GPP TS 38.521-1/2 [10,11]	5GNR UE RF conformance. SA FR1/FR2
UE	3GPP TS 38.521-4 [12]	5GNR UE RF conformance. Performance
	3GPP TS 38.523-1/2/3 [13–15]	5GNR UE protocol conformance
	3GPP TS 38.533 [16]	5GNR UE RRM conformance
	GCF/CTIA [17]	Battery consumption
RAN/Core	3GPP TS 28.552 [18]	RAN, 5GC, and network slicing performance
RAN	3GPP TS 32.425 [19], TS 32.451 [20]	RRC aspects
NFV	ETSI GS NFV-TST 010 [22]	Testing of ETSI NFV blocks
	3GPP TR 37.901 [23], TR 37.901-5 [24]	4G/5G throughput testing at application layer
E2E	3GPP TR 28.554 [26]	Slicing performance at network side
	NGMN [27]	eMBB and uRLLC (partial) KPI testing
Network elements	3GPP TS 32.404 [21]	Measurement templates

2.2. Research on 5G KPI Testing and Validation

Rigorous testing of 5G E2E solutions is still an emerging research topic, where we find a relevant gap. There are only a few papers that are devoted to this area.

In the context of the TRIANGLE project, the work in [29] proposes a methodology in order to automate the control of all the elements in the E2E 5G network path, while [30] focuses on automating 5G apps. Both of the papers aim to test service level KPIs in a 5G E2E lab setup, while the 5GENESIS methodology described in this paper is tailored for testing and validation in real 5G deployments.

In the context of 5G field trials, several works provide ad-hoc solutions for specific use cases, scenarios, and KPIs. The authors in [31] study throughput for using 15 GHz band.

In [32], the authors test throughput and latency in vehicular communications. The work presented in [33] analyses throughput, network energy efficiency, and device connection density. The work in [34] focuses on different methods for generating and evaluating the effect of interference. Moreover, large scale performance measurements on 5G operational networks and off-the-shelf UEs have been recently presented in [35,36]. On the one hand, [35] covers a sub-6 GHz NSA deployment in a dense urban environment, revealing several insights on network coverage, handover mechanisms, UE energy consumption, and E2E throughput, latency, and application performance. On the other hand, [36] discusses throughput, latency, and application performance, along with handover operations, under four different US operators' networks, with three of them employing NSA deployment with mmWave 5G cells. The above papers provide valuable preliminary insights on 5G achievable performance; however, technology and KPI validation requires dedicated and fully controllable testing environments [3], in order to pinpoint specific causes for the observed performance levels, and ultimately guide towards focused optimized configurations. Our work contributes to these aspects by providing the definitions of E2E KPIs and of testing procedures for reliable performance assessment in dedicated environments.

Several testbeds are being developed for supporting reliable experimentation, testing, and validation of 5G technologies, paradigms, and KPIs, as anticipated in Section 1. Among others, the 5G Test Network (5GTN) presented in [37] integrates cellular access and core networks with SDN/NFV, cloud/edge computing, and Internet of Things (IoT) technologies. Targeting more specific use cases, [38] showcases NFV integration with Unmanned Aerial Vehicles (UAVs), while [39] presents a SDN-based cloud/edge computing platform for IoT management. IoT experimental testbeds for mMTC and low-power devices are also presented in [40,41], while an open solution for E2E network slicing experimentation is given in [42]. Altogether, these testbeds focus on specific 5G/IoT capabilities and use cases, while 5GENESIS aims at combining several technologies and implementing an E2E open facility for the experimentation and testing of heterogeneous verticals. Moreover, the above works do not address the design of procedures for executing properly defined experiments and test cases, which is instead a key 5GENESIS contribution, as detailed in this paper.

5GENESIS works under the 5G-PPP umbrella with other two EU-funded infrastructure projects, i.e., 5G-VINNI (https://www.5g-vinni.eu (accessed on 30 August 2020)) and 5G-EVE (https://www.5g-eve.eu (accessed on 30 August 2020).) Similar goals are also pursued by PAWR testbeds, i.e., POWDER (https://powderwireless.net (accessed on 30 August 2020).), COSMOS (https://cosmos-lab.org (accessed on 30 August 2020)) and AERPAW (https://aerpaw.org (accessed on 30 August 2020)). Altogether, these projects aim at the implementation of distributed 5G facilities in Europe (5G-PPP) and US (PAWR), where researchers, technology providers, stakeholders, and verticals can test their solutions in a reliable and reproducible manner. As analyzed later, the testing methodology that is presented in this paper is currently adopted in the 5GENESIS facility, but it can be easily reused in other 5G testbeds, also thanks to the open-source nature of the software components enabling its application [8].

3. Overview of 5GENESIS Approach to KPI Testing and Validation

Before the formalization of the proposed testing methodology, in this section we summarize the 5GENESIS reference architecture and M&A framework, with the latter being a component that is particularly important when the methodology is applied in 5GENESIS testbeds. The methodology has been adopted for experimentation in the 5GENESIS UMA testbed, which is fully compliant with the reference architecture discussed in this section, as detailed in Sections 5 and 6.

3.1. 5GENESIS Reference Architecture

The 5GENESIS approach to the analysis of KPIs for new 5G services developed by vertical industries relies on the construction of experimental platforms with a common architecture, as represented in Figure 1.

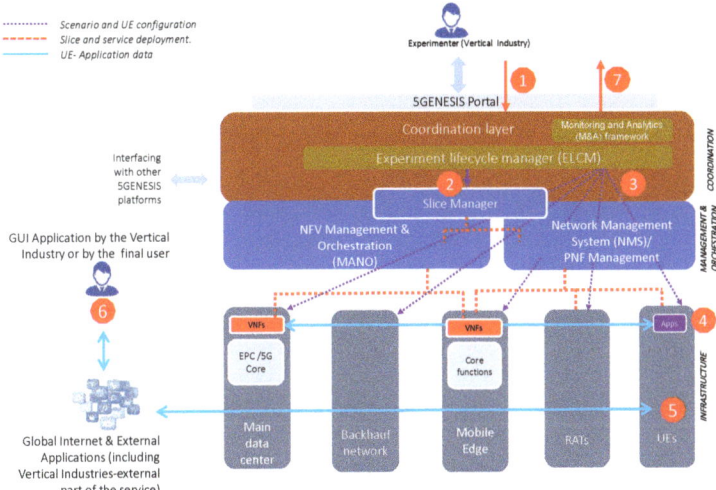

Figure 1. 5GENESIS Reference Architecture and Experimentation Flow.

The 5GENESIS architecture is structured in three main layers: Coordination, Management and Orchestration (MANO), and Infrastructure Layers. It is an abstraction of the 5G network architecture proposed by 5G-PPP Architecture Working Group in [43], focusing on the experimentation for demonstrating 5G KPIs. Hence, additional components and interactions have been included to introduce an experimentation control plane in the architecture. The 5GENESIS architecture includes the common components for Management and Orchestration (MANO) of services, network slicing, and infrastructure layer. On top of them, the Coordination Layer has been added in order to introduce the experimentation control plane and expose testing and automation features towards the verticals.

Thus, the Coordination Layer includes all of the components related to the control of the experiment execution. Moreover, it also provides the Northbound Interfaces (NBI) towards the 5GENESIS Portal, for sending the description of an experiment and retrieving the results after the execution. More details are provided in [44]. During the experimentation, the ELCM is responsible for the sequencing of experiment lifecycle stages, while maintaining the experiment status and providing feedback on the experiment execution. M&A-related components sitting in the Coordination Layer are responsible for the complete collection and analysis of the heterogeneous monitoring data that are produced during the use of the testbed. In particular, in order to collect the monitoring information from all of the elements of the testbed, the Analytics component retrieves the measurements from a unified database, in which the various measurement probes ingest, either in real-time or at the end of each experiment session, the measurements for long-term storage and data post-processing.

In the MANO Layer, the Slice Manager is in charge of the configuration and deployment of the slices. For doing this, it relies on the Network Function Virtualization Management and Orchestration (NFV MANO), which is responsible for the orchestration and lifecycle management of Network Services and Virtual Network Functions (VNFs), and on the Network Management System (NMS), which is in charge of the management of Physical Network Functions (PNFs).

The Infrastructure Layer implements the E2E 5G network, including UEs, RAN, core network, main data center, and mobile edge. The main data center and mobile edge refer to the Network Function Virtualization Infrastructure (NFVI) located at the core and at the edge of the network, respectively. Section 4 provides more details on how to relate this architecture with the experimentation methodology and how a sample experiment is run.

3.2. 5GENESIS M&A Framework

The KPI validation is managed by the M&A framework [7], which targets the collection of KPIs and complementary measurements, aiming at reliably validating the former while exploiting the latter in order to verify the infrastructure status during the experiment. Integrated onto the 5GENESIS architecture, the M&A framework currently includes several Monitoring tools and both statistical and Machine Learning (ML) Analytics functionalities. It is formed by three functional blocks:

- Infrastructure Monitoring (IM), which collects data on the status of architectural components, e.g., UE, RAN, core, and transport systems, as well as computing and storage distributed units;
- Performance Monitoring (PM), which executes measurements via dedicated probes for collecting E2E QoS/QoE indicators, e.g., throughput, latency, and vertical-specific KPIs;
- Storage and Analytics, which enable efficient data storage and perform KPI statistical validation and ML analyses.

The KPI statistical validation plays a key role in the 5GENESIS methodology. As detailed in Section 4, 5GENESIS adopts a per-iteration validation approach. Hence, an experiment, as described in the corresponding ED, consists of executing a given number of measurement iterations. The validation is first performed on each iteration, and then on the entire experiment. The procedures for calculating the statistical indicators that validate the KPIs are specified in the test case template, which is part of the ED along with scenario and slice configurations.

4. Formalization of the Experimentation Methodology

The proposed methodology has been composed in order to specify the actions that are needed for the execution of an experiment on 5G infrastructures; and, also, to structure the information flow required from the design and set of an experiment to the collection of the results. When considering the intense interest from vertical industries to use and assess the benefits of 5G, the proposed methodology could be used as a basis for any experimentation process in 5G infrastructures and, as such, it moves beyond its specific application in the infrastructure used in this paper. The open source notion of the major components that realise the methodology (referring mainly to the Open5GENESIS suite [8]) contributes a lot towards that direction.This section provides the specifications for each of the key concepts of the 5GENESIS experimentation methodology. More precisely, we focus on the formalization of the experimentation methodology. i.e., the process of i) specifying templates for the three key entities that are mentioned above, namely, the test cases, the scenarios, and the slices, and ii) identifying all of the additional to those templates information needed to run the experiment. The test cases, the scenarios, and the slices, as well as the complementary information, are needed in order to fully self-define an experiment.

4.1. Test Case

A test case describes the targeted KPI and the instructions for configuring the network and performing the measurement(s) to compute it.

Table 2 reports an example of a test case that is devoted to measure the maximum downlink (DL) throughput at the application level. User Datagram Protocol (UDP) traffic has been used because it is more appropriate for this assessment, in comparison to Transmission Control Protocol (TCP), where the measurements could be affected by flow and congestion control mechanisms. Additional test cases can be found at [25].

Table 2. Test case for assessing the maximum throughput available at the application level.

Test Case: TC_THR_UDP		Metric: Throughput	
Target KPI: UDP Throughput The UDP Throughput test case aims at assessing the maximum throughput achievable between a source and a destination. • Source of packets: Measurement probe acting as traffic generator. • Destination of packets: Measurement probe acting as recipient. • Underlying SUT: Network components between the source and destination. • Measurement conducted at layer: Application. Complementary measurement are collected at lower layers.			
Methodology: For measuring UDP Throughput, a packet stream is emitted from a source and received by a data sink (destination). The amount of data (bits) successfully transmitted per unit of time (seconds), as measured by the traffic generator, shall be recorded. A UDP-based traffic stream is created between the source and destination while using the iPerf2 tool. The test case shall include the consecutive execution of several iterations, according to the following properties: • Duration of a single iteration: at least three minutes. • Records throughput over one-second intervals within an iteration. • Number of iterations (I): at least 25.			
iPerf2 configuration:			
Parameter		iPerf option	Suggested value
Throughput measurement interval		–interval	1
Number of simultaneously transmitting probes/processes/threads		–parallel	−4 (in order to generate high data rate in the source)
Bandwidth limitation set to above the maximum bandwidth available		–b	Depends on the maximum theoretical throughput available in the network
Format to report iPerf results		–format	m [Mbps]
Calculation process and output: Once the KPI samples are collected, time-stamped (divided by iteration), and stored, evaluate relevant statistical indicators, e.g., average, median, standard deviation, percentiles, minimum, and maximum values, as follows: • Evaluate the statistical indicators separately for each iteration. • Evaluate the average of each indicator over the iterations, thus obtaining that same indicator for the test case. • Evaluate and add a Confidence Interval (CI) * to the obtained indicator, which denotes the precision of the provided outcome. * A 95% CI is suggested and it should be evaluated while assuming a Student T-distribution for the data sample, with $I − 1$ degrees of freedom. This accounts for non-Gaussian distributions of values collected at each iteration.			
Complementary measurements (if available): Throughput at Packet Data Convergence Protocol (PDCP) and Medium Access Control (MAC) layers, Reference Signal Received Power (RSRP), Reference Signal Received Quality (RSRQ), Channel Quality Indicator (CQI), Adopted Modulation, Rank Indicator (RI), Number of MIMO layers, MAC, and Radio Link Control (RLC) Downlink Block Error Rate (BLER). For each measurement (or selected ones), provide the average per iteration and for the entire test case, following the procedure in "Calculation process and output". **Note**: packet loss rate is not recorded because constant traffic in excess of the available capacity will be injected and the excess will be marked as lost packets, as could be expected.			
Preconditions: The scenario has been configured. In case of network slicing, the slice must be activated. The traffic generator should support the generation of the traffic pattern defined in "Methodology". Connect a reachable UE (end point) in the standard 3GPP interface SGi or N6 (depending on whether the UE is connected to EPC or 5GC, respectively). Deploy the monitoring probes to collect throughput and complementary measurements. Ensure that, unless specifically requested in the scenario, no unintended traffic is present in the network.			
Applicability: The measurement probes should be capable of injecting traffic into the system as well as determining the throughput of the transmission.			
Test case sequence: 1. Start monitoring probes. 2. Start the traffic generator for transmitting from the client to the server probe, as described in "Methodology". 3. Record the throughput for each time interval within a trial. 4. Stop the traffic generator. 5. Stop monitoring probes. 6. Calculate and record the KPIs as needed per iteration as defined in "Calculation process and output". 7. Repeat steps 1 to 6 for each one of the 25 iterations. 8. Compute the KPIs as defined in "Calculation process and output".			

The test case specifies the end points where the measurements are collected, the measurement tools and corresponding configurations, how to calculate the throughput, the sequence of actions for executing the test case, and the complementary measurements that can be used for troubleshooting and understanding the obtained values. More precisely, the following information is provided in the test case template:

Target KPI: this field includes the definition of the target KPI. Each test case targets only one KPI (main KPI). However, secondary measurements from complementary KPIs can also be added (see "Complementary measurements" field of this template). The definition of the main KPI specifies the related target metric, the ID of which is declared in the first row of the template. More precisely, the definition of the main KPI declares at least the reference points from which the measurement(s) are performed, the underlying system, the reference protocol stack level, and so on. Within the 5GENESIS experimentation methodology, the term "metric" refers to a generic high-level definition of a target quality factor (attribute) to be evaluated, i.e., a definition that is independent of the underlying system, the reference protocol layer, or the tool used for the measurement. The initial set of identified metrics is specified in [25], based on an abstraction of the set of 5G KPIs defined by 5G-PPP in [45].

Methodology: this field declares the procedure and configurations relevant for defining the experiment execution, including the acceptable values for the experiment duration, the iterations required to obtain statistically significant results, and the measurement interval, to mention a few.

Calculation process and output: this field describes the processing performed on the KPI samples that allows to derive the statistical indicators for the executed test case, ultimately enabling the KPI validation. As reported in the "Methodology" field, the experiment should be executed for a statistically significant number of iterations, e.g., I, in order to obtain an accurate picture of the KPI. An example of calculation process and corresponding output is given in the test case template that is presented in Table 2.

Complementary measurements: this field defines a list of secondary parameters useful to interpret the values of the target KPI. On the one hand, getting these measurements is not mandatory for the test case itself; on the other hand, the M&A framework can exploit them in order to provide more insights on the experiment execution. As a first step, an overview of the complementary measurements (e.g., in terms of per-iteration and test case statistical indicators) can be provided to the experimenter along with the results that are related to the target KPI. Moreover, such measurements can help to pinpoint anomalous and unexpected behaviors, provide correlation and predictive analyses via ML tools, and trigger architectural improvements for next experiment executions.

Preconditions: a list of test-specific information about equipment configuration and traffic description is provided in this field. Additionally, the description of the initial state of the System Under Test (SUT), required to start executing a test case sequence, is provided.

Applicability: this field reports a list of features and capabilities which are required by the system in order to guarantee the feasibility of the test.

Test case sequence: this field specifies the sequence of actions to be performed during the execution of the test case.

Besides the test case reported in Table 2 above, the 5GENESIS Consortium has already defined several test cases, including the ones for assessing latency KPIs (see Sections 5 and 6). Test cases covering further 5G KPIs are also available in [25].

4.2. Scenario

The scenario template includes information that is related to network and environment configurations, and is related to the technologies supported in the experimentation platform. From the performance perspective, the scenario quantifies the parameters that affect the values of the KPIs to be measured.

The parameters that are part of the scenario definition are different from those that are specified for the slice. The scenario parameters establish the working point of the network, including UE location and mobility conditions, and they provide a guideline for the definition of network conditions, in order to reproduce realistic situations where to perform the experiments. Hence, the scenario definition is dependent on the infrastructure. Table 3 provides an example of the description of a 5G NR NSA scenario. The accessible parameters in each testbed may differ, depending on the type of equipment available in each of them. Hence, the scenario template aims to be a guideline for the key parameters that must be known to gain a clear understanding of the results that were obtained during the testing and identify the context in which the validation is performed.

Table 3. Scenario template applied to a 5G NR NSA deployment with Line of Sight (LoS) between gNB and UE. The scenario (SC) is denoted SC_LoS_PS, where PS stands for Proactive Scheduling, a vendor-specific configuration available in the gNB (cf. Section 5.3 for more details).

Scenario ID	SC_LoS_PS
Radio Access Technology	5G NR
Standalone/Non-Standalone	Non-Standalone
LTE to NR frame shift	3 ms
Cell Power	40 dBm
Band	n78
Maximum bandwidth per component carrier	40 MHz
Subcarrier spacing	30 kHz
Number of component carriers	1
Cyclic Prefix	Normal
Number of antennas on NodeB	2
MIMO schemes (codeword and number of layers)	1 CW, 2 layers
DL MIMO mode	2×2 Close Loop Spatial Multiplexing
Modulation schemes	256-QAM
Duplex Mode	TDD
Power per subcarrier	8.94 dBm/30 kHz
TDD uplink/downlink pattern	2/8
Random access mode	Contention-based
Scheduler configuration	Proactive scheduling
User location and speed	Close to the base station, direct line of sight, static
Background traffic	No
Computational resources available in the virtualized infrastructure	N/A

4.3. Slice

Network slicing support is part of the new Service-Based Architecture (SBA) specified by 3GPP in TS 23.501 [46]. A network slice is defined as "a complete logical network (providing Telecommunication Services and Network Capabilities) including Access Network (AN) and Core Network (CN)". The management and orchestration of network slices is specified in 3GPP TR 28.801 [47]. The list of Standard Slice Types (SST) specified in [46] includes three slices: *eMBB slice*, suitable for 5G eMBB services; *URLLC slice*, oriented towards 5G URLLC use cases; and, *MIoT slice*, for massive IoT and mMTC applications. However, the standard also contemplates the use of non-standard slices.

In the 5GENESIS methodology, the slice specifies the E2E resources specifically allocated in the network in order to fulfill the performance requirements of the solution under test. A full description of the slicing mechanisms supported in 5GENESIS can be found in [48] and in the corresponding GitHub repository [49]. The template that is used to define the specific slice configuration is based on the Generic Network Slice Template (GST) defined by the Global System for Mobile Communications Association (GSMA) in [50], and Listing 1 shows a GST example. Hence, a testbed defines different instances of the slice template, one per supported slice. Subsequently, the slice is configured, depending on the capabilities of the infrastructure layer, which is, the mapping between the parameters defined in the template and the values configured in each network component depends on the available equipment, which can range from commercial base stations to emulators or software-defined solutions. However, the mapping is transparent to experimenters and vertical use case owners, which just need to choose among the list of slices offered by the testbed. The selection that is made by the experimenter is finally used to fill in the slice ID field in the ED.

Listing 1. Instantiation of the Generic Network Slice Template. Throughput and Maximum Transfer Unit (MTU) values are given in kbps and bytes, respectively.

```
{
    "base_slice_descriptor": {
        "base_slice_des_id": "AthonetEPC",
        "coverage": ["Campus"],
        "delay_tolerance": true,
        "network_DL_throughput": {
            "guaranteed": 100.000
        },
        "ue_DL_throughput": {
            "guaranteed": 100.000
        },
        "network_UL_throughput": {
            "guaranteed":10.000
        },
        "ue_UL_throughput": {
            "guaranteed": 10.000
        },
        "mtu": 1500
    },
}
```

4.4. Experiment Descriptor

The ED is a data structure that includes all of the values that are required for completely defining an experiment execution, as shown in Listing 2. It includes the following fields:

Listing 2. ED Template.

```
{
    ExperimentType: Standard/Custom/MONROE
    Automated: <bool>
    TestCases: <List[str]>
    UEs: <List[str]>   UEs IDs

    Slices: <List[str]>
    NSs: <List[Tuple[str, str]]> (NSD Id, Location)
    Scenarios: <List[str]>

    ExclusiveExecution: <bool>
    ReservationTime: <int> (Minutes)

    Application: <str>
    Parameters: <Dict[str,obj]>

    Remote: <str> Remote platform Id
    RemoteDescriptor: <Experiment Descriptor>

    Version: <str>
    Extra: <Dict[str,obj]>
}
```

Experiment type: it is part of the definition of the experiment. The 5GENESIS experimentation methodology currently supports three types of experiments. However, the methodology is sustainable and can be easily extended with new types of experiments. The standard experiments are based on the test cases specified by the 5GENESIS Consortium, and enable the comparison and benchmarking of different variants of a same solution (devices, services, applications, etc.). The custom experiments are those that are defined based on specific requirements of the solution under test. For example, in a custom test case, the measurements could be specific with respect to a product being tested. Finally, MONROE experiments are containerized experiments initially designed in the MONROE project [51,52]. Within 5GENESIS, a virtual MONROE node has been developed that decouples the MONROE software from the MONROE hardware infrastructure. The MONROE virtual node can be used at the UE, providing a generalized mechanism for running arbitrary containerized experiments without any need to update the experimentation framework.

Automated: it indicates if the experiment is fully automated, i.e., no human intervention is required for the execution. Automated experiments target the execution of exhaustive testing looking for the benchmarking of the solutions under test. Human intervention is expected when the network can be configured automatically but the applications and UEs are operated by the vertical use case owners.

Test Cases: it includes the IDs of the test cases selected to be executed in the experiment.

UEs: it includes the ID(s) of the UE(s) used during the experiment.

Slices: it contains the ID(s) of the slice(s) to be used during the experiment. The full slice definition is available in a separate data structure, as described in Section 4.3.

NSs: it refers to the Network Services (NSs) that are used during the experiment. Depending on the target of the experiment, the NSs could be deployed at different stages of the experiment. This stage is specified in the test case.

Scenarios: the ID(s) of the scenario(s) to be used during the experiment are listed in this field. The full scenario definition is available in a separate data structure, as described in Section 4.2.

Exclusive Execution: it controls the scheduling of different experiments in the testbed. An Exclusive experiment is not executed at the same time with other experiments.

Reservation Time: it defines the duration of the experiment when automation is not enabled.

Application: this field depends on the type of experiment and test case. It may be used for standard and custom experiments to specify the application to run (e.g., in the second case, the application may be directly defined by the experimenter). In the case of MONROE experiments, the field defines the container to deploy in the MONROE virtual node.

Parameters: this field depends on the type of experiment. In particular, it is used for specifying customized parameters in custom experiments, but it could be also used to include tool-specific settings not explicitly reported in the test case of a standard experiment. For MONROE experiments, the field provides the configuration for the containers involved in the experiment.

Remote: this field is necessary to support the execution of distributed experiments, possibly involving two testbeds. It is used to identify the secondary testbed that is part of the experiment.

Remote Descriptor: it contains a secondary ED with the values that are required to configure the experiment execution in the remote testbed.

Version: it specifies the ED version in use, so that the testbed can customize the handling of the ED according to any future modification, while keeping compatibility with older EDs.

Extra: this field can be used to add further information. For example, it can be useful for adding debugging or tracing information, or to support extra functionalities without changing the ED format.

Each testbed needs to create a registry detailing the type of experiments, and the list of supported test cases, scenarios, slices, NSs, and UEs, since this information is required to fill in the ED. As part of the implementation open-sourced in [8], 5GENESIS makes available a Web Portal, where this information can be easily configured and the verticals just need to select between the options available in the testbed to define an experiment.

4.5. Experiment Execution

The experiment workflow is depicted in Figure 1, on top of the 5GENESIS reference architecture. In terms of execution flow, labels 1 to 7 represent the steps for describing an experiment (1), to execute it (2 to 6) and to report results (7). Next, we illustrate the execution of an experiment with an example.

Assume that a service provider would like to assess the delay perceived at the application level in a certain device. First, the experiment is configured via the Portal. The chosen parameters will be used in order to fill in the fields of the ED. In the example, the experiment requests the execution of a Round Trip Time (RTT) test in a static scenario with LoS and good coverage, and the usage of an URLLC slice. Subsequently, the ED is delivered to the Coordination Layer first and MANO Layer then, where the Slice Manager deploys and configures the entire slice indicated by the experimenter in the ED. In the third step, the scenario is configured via the configurations that are specified in the corresponding scenario template selected by the experimenter. Among other, in this specific example, a ping application is installed in the device under test. The scenario can potentially affect the radio access technology (e.g., the signal strength of the base station), as well as the backhaul and core networks (e.g., the amount of background traffic in the backhaul). In the fourth step, the ELCM initiates the ping client, as well as the monitoring probes collecting all of the complementary measurements specified in the test case (or at least the ones available). The activation of the ping client triggers the 3GPP signaling in order to establish the data connection. In this example, the experiment test case defines a ping between the UE and the Packet Gateway (P-GW) located at the core network, so we can skip steps five and six in the execution flow, devoted to the testing of services deployed outside of the testbed (e.g., at the vertical facility). Finally, M&A post-processes the measurements and reports the obtained KPI statistical indicators to the experimenter.

The source code for the components described in this section (Portal, ELCM, Slice Manager, etc) is available under Apache license 2.0 in [8]. The license allows modifying and using the software without restrictions. The main purpose of this open initiative is to provide a general testing framework for 5G infrastructures. The framework is flexible enough to cover the testing requirements of 5G verticals; moreover, it enables the comparability and reproducibility of experiments and results across 5G infrastructures having similar features.

The repository in [8] also includes the probes that were used in Android devices to collect the radio information, the iPerf and ping agents for Windows PCs and Android devices, and a streaming agent for video streaming tests. A manual for installing and using all of the components is also available [44].

5. Experimental Setup

This section and the following one present a practical application of the testing methodology in the 5G deployment located at the UMA campus, which is described in Section 5.1. The methodology is applied in order to quantify throughput and latency KPIs in different networks scenarios. We define the test cases in Section 5.2, while presenting the scenarios and used slice in Sections 5.3 and 5.4, respectively. Finally, we report the EDs for three experiments executed for our validation purposes in Section 5.5.

5.1. 5G Deployment at UMA Campus

This section describes the 5G deployment at UMA campus, where the experiments have been executed. 3GPP TS 37.340 [53] considers different options for the deployment of 5G networks. The options range from purely 5G solutions, deployed independently from the existing network, to hybrid solutions, which combine part of the existing infrastructure with 5G NR.

Becasue of the high costs of building native 5G solutions, most operators currently prefer to lean on and evolve from the existing LTE infrastructure [35,36]. In particular, the combination of 4G and 5G radio access connected to an LTE EPC is known as NSA operation Option 3x architecture. This option is also called eUTRA New Radio-Dual Connectivity (EN-DC). Dual Connectivity (DC) was introduced in 3GPP in order to allow a UE to simultaneously transmit and receive data on multiple component carriers from/to two cell groups via a master eNB (MeNB) and a secondary eNB (SeNB). In Option 3x, DC is used in order to allow a device to connect to both 4G and 5G NR.

For this reason, the initial UMA pilot also follows the NSA Option 3x architecture. In Option 3x, the UE is connected to an eNB that acts as MeNB, and to a gNB that acts as SeNB, as shown in Figure 2. As said, there is no 5GC in this option and the gNB does not connect to the Mobility Management Entity (MME) in the EPC. The gNB connects to the eNB to receive requests to activate 5G bearers via X2 interface. Data bearers can be handled by the MeNB or SeNB, or split between these two. For the measurements that are discussed in this paper, the data are handled by the SeNB only (the gNB), which is the most popular Option 3x variant.

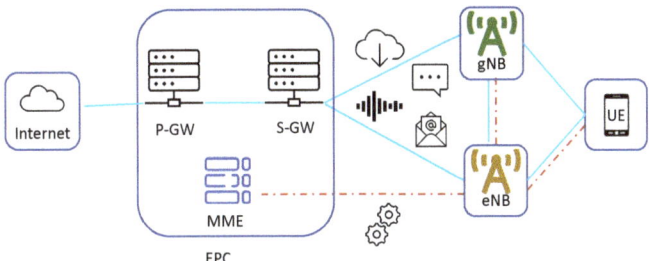

Figure 2. Core and Radio Access Network (RAN) configurations as per 5G NR NSA Option 3x.

Figure 3 shows the four paired gNBs/eNBs currently deployed in the UMA campus, along with other infrastructure components, i.e., the server rack hosting the EPC from Athonet, the Baseband Unit (BBU) from Nokia, and the main data center, in which OpenStack has been adopted as the Virtual Infrastructure Manager (VIM) and Open Source MANO (OSM) as the solution for NFV management and orchestration. Moreover, the mobile edge solution provided by Telefonica is based on OpenNebula and OSM. More details regarding the testbed components can be also found at [54].

Figure 3. 5G NR NSA deployment at UMA campus. The operation band is also reported for the Radio Remote Heads (RRHs) forming gNBs/eNBs, numbered from (1) to (4).

5.2. Test Case Definition

We have defined two test cases for throughput and latency KPI validation, referred to as TC_THR_UDP and TC_RTT, respectively.

The details of the TC_THR_UDP test case are provided in Table 2, while TC_RTT is a ping-based latency test. Similarly to TC_THR_UDP, TC_RTT also specifies 25 iterations; each iteration lasts two minutes, during which Internet Control Message Protocol (ICMP) ping is performed with ICMP ECHO REQUEST packets of 56 bytes, sent at a rate of 2 Hz. The ping source is an application running in the UE and the destination is the P-GW of the core network. The calculation process and output is the same as defined for TC_THR_UDP in Table 2.

5.3. Scenario Definition

Three different scenarios have been defined. Table 3 shows the SC_LoS_PS scenario, which refers to a LoS situation, where Proactive Scheduling (PS)—a vendor-specific feature in the gNB—is activated. The other two scenarios, which are denoted SC_LoS and SC_NLoS_PS, are similar to SC_LoS_PS, but differ in PS deactivation (SC_LoS) or UE location, which is non LoS (NLoS) in SC_NLoS_PS. (For simplicity, in the following we will also refer to SC_LoS_PS (and SC_LoS) and SC_NLoS_PS as LoS and NLoS scenarios, respectively, with clear mapping between the two notations.) Next, we discuss, with more detail, the configurations in Table 3.

After identifying the technology (5G NR) and the deployment mode (NSA), the next scenario parameter is the LTE to NR frame shift. This setting governs the relative time difference between the start of the frame timing for both technologies. With a shift of 3 ms, subframe 0 in one technology will start together with subframe 3 in the other.

Regarding the cell power, the 5G NR cell transmits at 10 W (40 dBm), with an average power density of 0.25 W/MHz in the full channel, which is located in n78 band, i.e., 3300 to 3800 MHz.

A 5G NR channel of 40 MHz is nominally adopted, with 5G NR numerology 1 and SubCarrier Spacing (SCS) of 30 kHz. In this case, the maximum number of Physical Resource Blocks (PRB) that can be used is 106, as per 3GPP TS 38.101-3 ([55] Section 5.3.2). Moreover, the 5G carrier is currently configured to use two antennas. Hence, we can enable a maximum of two layers to increase the throughput, taking advantage of the Multiple Input Multiple Output (MIMO) diversity using close loop spatial multiplexing. We also use a single beam and a maximum modulation of 256-Quadrature Amplitude Modulation (256-QAM). As per 5G NR Modulation and Coding Scheme (MCS) mapping in TS 38.214 ([56] Table 5.1.3.1), 256-QAM modulation is enabled with the maximum MCS of 27, 8 bits encoded per OFDM symbol, and a coding rate of 948/1024. In this setup, the L1 payload spectral efficiency results of 7.4063 bits per symbol.

The use of Time Division Duplex (TDD) mode, together with 30 kHz SCS, results in a time resolution of 500 μs for each individual transmission. Within such a time slot, there are 14 OFDM symbols. Of those, 11 symbols are effectively used for data transmission, as the other three are used for control information and demodulation of reference signals. At frame level, a 2/8 pattern translates to DDDDDDDSUU, i.e., a 5 ms pattern of seven DL slots (two patterns per 10 ms frame), one special slot, and two uplink (UL) slots is used. When considering that our test cases focus on DL throughput, only the DL slots are effectively used for user data transmission.

With the above setup, the maximum theoretical DL throughput is of approximately 290 Mbps, derived from multiplying the number of layers (2), PRBs (106), OFDM data symbols (11), and bits per symbol (8 bits), with the coding rate (0.926), the number of slots in DL used for data transmission (7), the patterns per frame (2), and the number of frames in one second (100).

As anticipated above, we use PS in SC_LoS_PS and SC_NLoS_PS scenarios, which is a feature that is available in the gNBs of the UMA deployment. On the one hand, in a generic scheduling configuration, when a UE needs to transmit data after being inactive for a long interval, it has to request an UL grant via scheduling requests or even a dedicated connection through Random Access Channel (RACH). Once the RACH contention is resolved or a scheduling request is successfully received, the UE will be able to transmit data. This process takes non negligible time and it may not be optimal for delay-critical use cases. On the other hand, when PS is used, the transmission latency is minimized, since the gNB pre-assigns resources to the UE, even if the latter has not explicitly requested them yet. This may clearly bring some overhead, but it could be an optimal solution for scenarios employing limited amount of mobile devices, where the delay is the critical aspect, e.g., a private 5G network dedicated to time-sensitive communications. Specifically, in our test, we adopt a PS configuration that allocates UL grants to the UE in every UL suitable opportunity, which, in this specific configuration, was 10% of the total TDD slots.

Finally, we further comment on the difference between LoS and NLoS scenarios, which clearly resides on the higher propagation losses in the latter case. In NLoS, the used gNB is not directly oriented towards the device under test, and the signal is obstructed by external and internal building walls. We executed preliminary measurements in order to characterize the additional attenuation of NLoS as compared to LoS, which resulted in about 60 dB lower received signal level and 11 dB worse signal to noise ratio when compared to the LoS case. In both cases, the UE was static and there was no background traffic in the system.

5.4. Slice Definition

The configurations for the slice used in our experiments are reported in Listing 1. The template defines the achievable DL/UL throughput for the whole slice, the guaranteed DL/UL throughput supported by the slice per UE, and the Maximum Transfer Unit (MTU). This is a default slice, in which all of the radio resources are available for the UE.

5.5. ED Definition

In this section, we show the EDs for three experiments, which have been executed in the UMA 5G deployment while using the methodology presented above. Section 6 analyzes the obtained results.

We have defined a first experiment, named Experiment 1, aiming at quantifying throughput and latency KPIs in our deployment under LoS and NLoS scenarios. Listing 3 shows the ED for this experiment. In 5GENESIS terms, Experiment 1 is a standard experiment, which sequentially executes two standard test cases, i.e., TC_THR_UDP and TC_RTT, in SC_LoS_PS and SC_NLoS_PS scenarios, by using the default available slice and a single 5G NR device, denoted UE_1. Because the applications are already defined in the test cases and no NSs are used, the Application and NSs fields of the ED can be omitted.

Listing 3. ED for Experiment 1 (evaluation of throughput and latency KPIs in LoS vs. NLoS scenarios).

```
{
    ExperimentType: Standard
    Automated: Yes
    TestCases: TC_THR_UDP, TC_RTT
    UEs: UE_1
    Slice: Default
    Scenario: SC_LoS_PS, SC_NLoS_PS
    ExclusiveExecution: yes
    Version: 2.0
}
```

Because Experiment 1 is executed with PS activated, we have designed Experiment 2 aiming at quantifying the impact of such a scheduling configuration on the observed latency. Along with the difference between LoS and NLoS (Experiment 1), Experiment 2 represents another example highlighting the possible impact of changing a scenario configuration on the validation of a KPI.

Experiment 2 is also a 5GENESIS standard experiment based on a standard test case, as shown in Listing 4. In particular, we focus on TC_RTT test case, and run it in a single device (UE_1), in both SC_LoS_PS and SC_LoS scenarios. This ultimately allows for isolating the effect of PS.

Listing 4. ED for Experiment 2 (evaluation of latency KPI with vs. without PS activated).

```
{
    ExperimentType: Standard
    Automated: Yes
    TestCases: TC_RTT
    UEs: UE_1
    Slice: Default
    Scenario: SC_LoS, SC_LoS_PS
    ExclusiveExecution: yes
    Version: 2.0
}
```

Finally, we define a third experiment, i.e., Experiment 3, to showcase the flexibility of the proposed methodology. In particular, Experiment 3 highlights how the methodology can be used for benchmarking purposes, and for underlining peculiar behaviors in off-the-shelf devices, requiring further inspection; hence, as reported in Listing 5, we execute the TC_THR_UDP test case in the SC_LoS_PS scenario, while using UE_1 and a second 5G NR device from a different vendor, denoted UE_2.

Listing 5. ED for Experiment 3 (evaluation of throughput KPI in two 5G NR devices, UE_1 and UE_2).

```
{
  ExperimentType: Standard
  Automated: Yes
  TestCases: TC_THR_UDP
  UEs: UE_1, UE_2
  Slice: Default
  Scenario: SC_LoS_PS
  ExclusiveExecution: yes
  Version: 2.0
}
```

6. Experimental Results

In this section, we discuss the results that were obtained by executing the experiments defined in Section 5.

6.1. KPI Nalidation across Different Scenarios

We start with Experiment 1, which quantifies throughput and latency KPIs in LoS vs. NLoS scenarios (and PS activated), and it provides an overview of the full usage of the proposed methodology.

Tables 4 and 5 report several statistical indicators (and corresponding 95% confidence intervals) for TC_THR_UDP and TC_RTT test cases in both scenarios, respectively. Along with the main KPIs, i.e., UDP throughput for TC_THR_UDP and RTT for TC_RTT, both tables also report an overview of selected complementary measurements, in terms of the average values measured over the entire test case duration.

As regards TC_THR_UDP, we observe that the UDP throughput in the LoS scenario is stable at around 180 Mbps, and significantly drops in NLoS, where it achieves an average value of 15 Mbps. Focusing on LoS scenario, we see that such a throughput is rather far from the theoretical maximum calculated in Section 5.3. Because our monitoring probes also allow for the collection of throughput samples at different protocol stack layers and, in particular, at Packet Data Convergence Protocol (PDCP), we investigate this aspect more in detail and report the results in Experiment 3, where we also compare the UE_1 and UE_2 performance (cf. Section 6.3).

When considering TC_RTT, we observe an average RTT of about 12 ms in the LoS scenario, which doubles to 26 ms in the NLoS scenario. In the second scenario, we also see larger variance in the KPI samples compared to the first scenario, which instead appears extremely stable. In particular, an extremely high value for the maximum RTT is registered (about 555 ms); this is followed by a large confidence interval and it significantly differs from the 95% percentile indicator (about 48 ms), leading to the conclusion that such a value may be a unique deviation not completely representative of the performance achievable in the scenario under analysis.

Table 4. Experiment 1: Statistical results of TC_THR_UDP test case in SC_LoS_PS and SC_NLoS_PS scenarios (Acronyms, as per Table 2; PDSCH MCS CW0 stands for Physical Downlink Shared Channel MCS for Codeword 0).

Parameter	Indicator	Scenario	
		LoS	NLoS
UDP Throughput [Mbps]	Average	179.45 ± 0.34	14.95 ± 0.45
	Median	179.14 ± 0.37	15.25 ± 0.09
	Min	162.86 ± 6.56	5.78 ± 1.65
	Max	195.80 ± 2.19	19.45 ± 3.34
	5% Percentile	171.22 ± 0.58	11.71 ± 1.00
	95% Percentile	188.64 ± 1.21	17.64 ± 2.53
	Standard deviation	5.47 ± 0.54	2.09 ± 0.78
SINR [dB]	Average	21.73 ± 0.07	7.27 ± 0.26
PDSCH MCS CW0	Average	27.00 ± 0.00	2.96 ± 0.02
RSRP [dBm]	Average	−52.42 ± 1.52	−115.41 ± 0.29
RSRQ [dB]	Average	−10.80 ± 0.00	−11.61 ± 0.04
PDSCH Rank	Average	2.00 ± 0.00	1.001 ± 0.001
MAC DL BLER [%]	Average	0.23 ± 0.05	8.77 ± 0.13

Table 5. Experiment 1: Statistical results for TC_RTT test case in SC_LoS_PS and SC_NLoS_PS scenarios (Acronyms as per Table 2; ReTx in MAC UL ReTx Rate stands for Retransmission).

Parameter	Indicator	Scenario	
		LoS	NLoS
RTT [ms]	Average	11.83 ± 0.05	26.15 ± 3.87
	Median	11.77 ± 0.07	19.33 ± 0.39
	Min	10.00 ± 0.00	13.19 ± 0.13
	Max	16.65 ± 0.60	555.16 ± 620.11
	5% Percentile	10.13 ± 0.02	14.39 ± 0.14
	95% Percentile	13.70 ± 0.09	42.74 ± 8.27
	Standard deviation	1.20 ± 0.04	48.33 ± 8.27
SINR [dB]	Average	21.58 ± 0.02	10.68 ± 0.14
MAC UL ReTx Rate [%]	Average	0.01 ± 0.001	14.83 ± 1.12
RSRP [dBm]	Average	−53.53 ± 0.05	−110.38 ± 0.18
RSRQ [dB]	Average	−10.80 ± 0.00	−11.15 ± 0.01
MAC DL BLER [%]	Average	0.01 ± 0.01	0.04 ± 0.02

The proposed methodology defines such indicators as a final statistical agglomeration of the measurements collected over several iterations (25 in our test cases), as defined in the "Calculation process and output" field of Table 2. As such, the methodology also allows for a more detailed, per-iteration overview of the same measurements. To showcase this aspect, we report, in Figure 4, the KPI statistics per iteration (in a boxplot format), for LoS/NLoS scenarios and TC_THR_UDP (Figure 4a) and TC_RTT (Figure 4b) test cases. Selected complementary measurements are also depicted for both test cases.

One the one hand, Figure 4a depicts the average SINR and the MCS index, which help to understand the context in which the measurements were taken. Among others, in the NLoS scenario, low SINR values directly map to low MCS index and, thus, the resulting low throughput. Given the poor signal level in NLoS, the scheduler reduces the amount of transmitted data to increase the redundancy and maintain the error rate at a reasonable level. As a matter of fact, the BLER observed in the NLoS scenario is lower than 10%, which is a typical target value when the propagation conditions are not favourable enough, so that the Hybrid Automatic Repeat reQuest (HARQ) mechanism can operate optimally. However, given that the MCS index is reduced to 3, the obtained throughput is about 15 Mbps, extremely lower than the throughput of about 180 Mbps obtained in the LoS case, where MCS index is the maximum (27) across all iterations, leading to the use of a high modulation order (256-QAM).

On the other hand, Figure4b shows that the RTT increase in the NLoS scenario directly maps with degraded radio conditions, particularly in terms of SINR, which, indeed, require a higher retransmission rate when compared to nearly-zero retransmissions observed in LoS conditions.

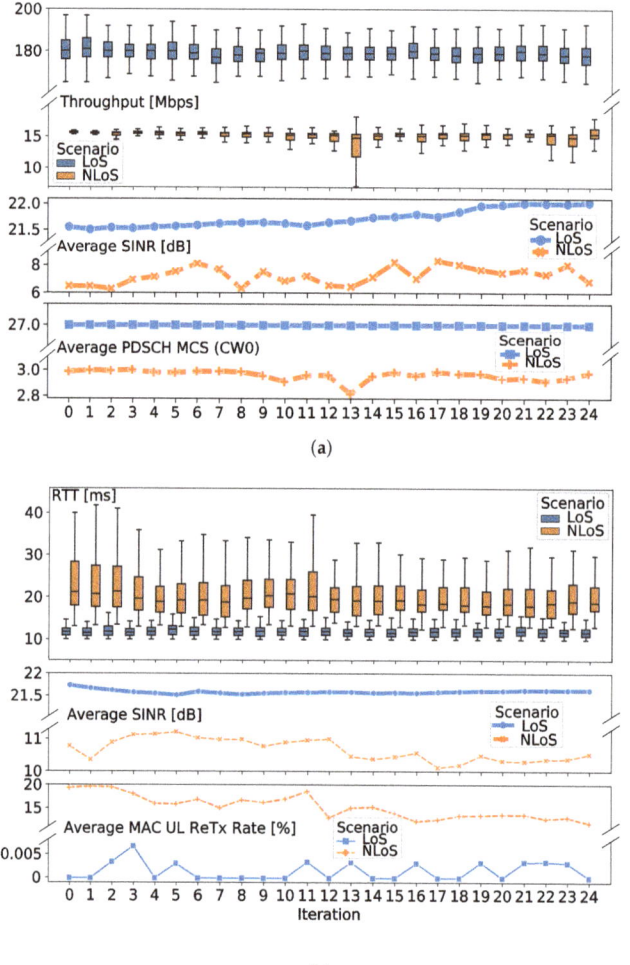

Figure 4. Experiment 1: Per-iteration statistics in SC_LoS_PS and SC_NLoS_PS scenarios and UE_1. UDP Throughput (**top**), average SINR (**middle**) and average PDSCH MCS CW0 (**bottom**) are reported for TC_THR_UDP test case (**a**). RTT (**top**), average SINR (**middle**), and average MAC UL ReTx Rate (**bottom**) are reported for TC_RTT test case (**b**).

6.2. KPI Validation across Different Configurations

We now move on to Experiment 2, which aims at highlighting the sole impact of PS on the achievable RTT. Hence, as compared to Experiment 1, this experiment focuses on the TC_RTT test case and runs it in LoS scenarios with vs. without PS activation.

Figure 5 shows the per-iteration statistics of RTT, for TC_RTT test case in SC_LoS_PS and SC_LoS scenarios when using UE_1. The comparison shows a significant impact of PS on the average RTT as well as on its variance. When PS is not active, the observed RTT ranges between 20 and 40 ms, with most of the results being concentrated between 25 and 30 ms. When PS is active, there is a smaller variance, with most of the values concentrated around 11 and 13 ms, and the remaining values in the interval from 10 to 15 ms. The result ultimately validates the impact of PS and its potential suitability for time-critical low-dense use cases, possibly delivered via a dedicated 5G network.

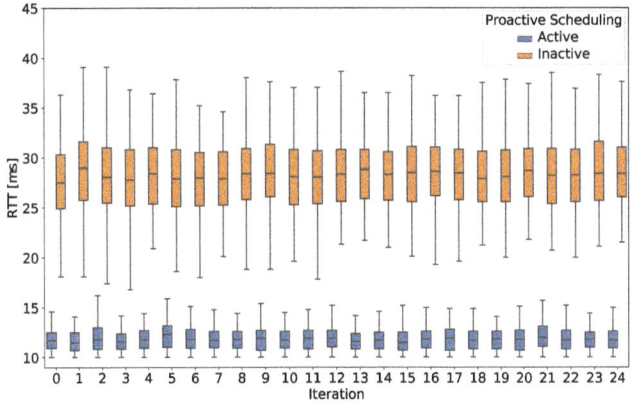

Figure 5. Experiment 2: RTT per-iteration statistics for TC_RTT test case, in SC_LoS_PS (PS active) and SC_LoS (PS inactive) scenarios and using UE_1.

6.3. KPI Validation across Different Technologies

The goal of Experiment 3 is to benchmark different UEs by means of their nominal achievable throughput, while also deepening the inspection of the mechanisms across layers of the 5G NR protocol stack. To this aim, it embeds the TC_THR_UDP test case and LoS scenario, and it is alternatively executed on UE_1 and UE_2, two 5G NR devices that are provided by different vendors. Finally, its focus is on comparing UDP and PDCP throughput statistics.

Figure 6a reports per-iteration statistics of UDP and PDCP throughput for both devices. As already analyzed in Experiment 1, we observe a UDP throughput of about 180 Mbps for UE_1 (Figure 6a). Interestingly, we see instead a PDCP throughput of around 271 Mbps, close to the theoretical maximum calculated in Section 5.3. Hence, under higher data rates possibly sustained by good coverage (i.e., LoS), UE_1 shows a quite constant and rather significant throughput drop, while moving at the application level. When considering UE_2 (Figure 6a), we see that the PDCP throughput stabilizes at a slightly lower value compared to UE_1 (around 267 Mbps). In parallel, the UDP throughput is close to its PDCP counterpart at the experiment kick-off, and then it shows a decreasing trend over the experiment duration, resulting in a difference up to 10 Mbps for the extreme values in the final iterations. These are both unexpected behaviors, repeatedly detected on the devices under test, which call for further inspection and analysis. As highlighted by these results, the statistical analysis that is currently supported in the methodology enables quantifying KPI trends, validating nominal values, and detecting possible malfunctions and anomalies leading to performance issues. We are currently working on embedding further ML-based analytical functionalities in the methodology, which could provide more insights while potentially pinpointing the root cause of the observed performance. This would ultimately lead to the introduction of enhanced schemes for improving cross-layer configurations and performance across the 5G system.

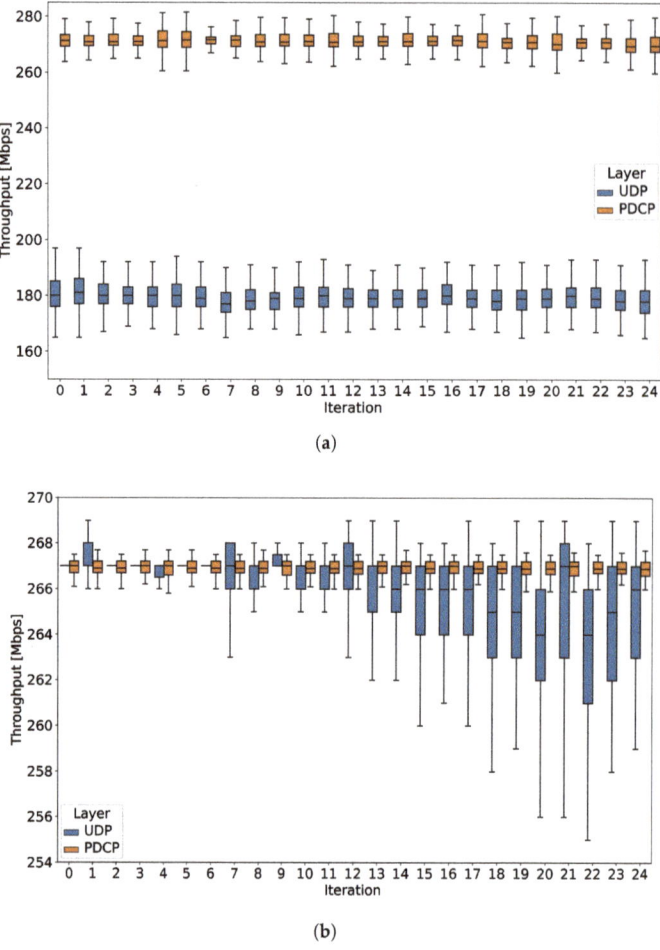

Figure 6. Experiment 3: UDP and PDCP Throughput per-iteration statistics for TC_THR_UDP test case and SC_LoS_PS scenario. Results for UE_1 and UE_2 are reported in (**a**,**b**), respectively.

Figure 6a reports per-iteration statistics of UDP and PDCP throughput for both devices. As already analyzed in Experiment 1, we observe a UDP throughput of about 180 Mbps for UE_1 (Figure 6a). Interestingly, we see instead a PDCP throughput of around 271 Mbps, close to the theoretical maximum calculated in Section 5.3. Hence, under higher data rates possibly sustained by good coverage (i.e., LoS), UE_1 shows a quite constant and rather significant throughput drop while moving at application level. When considering UE_2 (Figure 6a), we see that the PDCP throughput stabilizes at a slightly lower value when compared to UE_1 (around 267 Mbps). In parallel, the UDP throughput is close to its PDCP counterpart at the experiment kick-off, and then it shows a decreasing trend over the experiment duration, which results in a difference up to 10 Mbps for the extreme values in the final iterations. These are both unexpected behaviors, repeatedly detected on the devices under test, which call for further inspection and analysis. The statistical analysis currently supported in the methodology enables quantifying KPI trends, validating nominal values, and detecting possible malfunctions and anomalies leading to performance issues, as highlighted by these results. We are currently working on embedding further ML-based analytical functionalities in the methodology, which could provide more insights while potentially pinpointing the root cause of the observed performance. This would ultimately lead to the introduction of enhanced schemes for improving cross-layer configurations and performance across the 5G system.

7. Conclusions

In this paper, an open and flexible experimentation methodology for 5G KPI validation is introduced. This methodology overcomes the need for an end-to-end systematic experimentation methodology that allows properly defined and repeatable experiments. Such a methodology brings a key step towards a reliable and fair benchmarking of 5G services and applications.

The methodology has been applied in order to calculate the maximum achievable throughput and the latency in 5G NR scenarios. In particular, three different scenarios have been designed and the ability of the methodology has been demonstrated to (a) validate different KPIs under heterogeneous network scenarios, (b) quantify the impact of specific network configurations on the performance, and (c) pinpoint issues in off-the-shelf 5G devices.

Additionally, one of the designed scenarios has enabled to reach a minimum latency of 10 ms via activation of proactive scheduling mechanisms. This gives key insights on how to reach low latency in 5G deployments based on Release 15, which is focused on eMBB use cases. For URLLC applications, such as mission critical communications or edge computing scenarios, proactive scheduling can be a key parameter.

In future work, we will investigate testing requirements of 5G verticals such as industrial use case. We will focus on identifying specific KPIs and formalize their measurement and calculation procedures, while providing the means for executing the corresponding experiments. Moreover, we are also upgrading the 5G infrastructure to support 5G NR SA. The methodology will then be applied to check the relative performance with respect to NSA.

Author Contributions: Conceptualization and methodology, A.D.Z., G.C., Ö.A., P.M., A.B., D.T. and H.K.; Execution of experiments, A.D.Z.; Data analysis and investigation, A.D.Z., G.C., Ö.A., P.M., and A.B.; Writing—review and editing, A.D.Z., G.C., Ö.A., P.M., A.B., D.T. and H.K.; All authors have read and agreed to the published version of the manuscript.

Funding: This work has been conducted under the auspices of the 5GENESIS project. This project has received funding from the European Union's Horizon 2020 research and innovation programme under grant agreement No 815178.

Acknowledgments: The authors wish to thank the 5GENESIS Consortium as a whole for the insightful discussions during the plenary meetings that have led to the definition and refinement of the testing methodology described in this paper.

Conflicts of Interest: The authors declare no conflict of interest. The funders had no role in the design of the study; in the collection, analyses, or interpretation of data; in the writing of the manuscript, or in the decision to publish the results.

References

1. ITU-R M.2083-0. *IMT Vision-Framework and Overall Objectives of the Future Development of IMT for 2020 and Beyond*; ITU: Geneva, Switzerland, 2015.
2. Shafi, M.; Molisch, A.F. Smith, P.J.; Haustein, T.; Zhu, P.; Silva, P.D.; Tufvesson, F.; Benjebbour, A.; Wunder, G. 5G: A Tutorial Overview of Standards, Trials, Challenges, Deployment, and Practice. *IEEE J. Sel. Areas Commun.* **2017**, *35*, 1201–1221. [CrossRef]
3. 5G-PPP Test, Measurement and KPIs Validation Working Group, Validating 5G Technology Performance—Assessing 5G Architecture and Application Scenarios, 5G-PPP White Paper. Available online: https://5g-ppp.eu/wp-content/uploads/2019/06/TMV-White-Paper-V1.1-25062019.pdf (accessed on 30 September 2020).
4. Foegelle, M.D. Testing the 5G New Radio. In Proceedings of the 2019 13th European Conference on Antennas and Propagation (EuCAP'19), Krakow, Poland, 31 March–5 April 2019.

5. Koumaras, H.; Tsolkas, D.; Gardikis, G.; Gomez, P.M.; Frascolla, V.; Triantafyllopoulou, D.; Emmelmann, M.; Koumaras, V.; Osma, M.L.G.; Munaretto, D.; et al. 5GENESIS: The Genesis of a flexible 5G Facility. In Proceedings of the 2018 23rd International Workshop on Computer Aided Modeling and Design of Communication Links and Networks (CAMAD'19), Barcelona, Spain, 17–19 September 2019.
6. 5GENESIS Project. Deliverable D2.4 Final Report on Facility Design and Experimentation Planning. 2020. Available online: https://5genesis.eu/wp-content/uploads/2020/07/5GENESIS_D2.4_v1.0.pdf (accessed on 30 September 2020).
7. 5GENESIS Project. Deliverable D3.5 Monitoring and Analytics (Release A). 2019. Available online: https://5genesis.eu/wp-content/uploads/2019/10/5GENESIS_D3.5_v1.0.pdf (accessed on 30 September 2020).
8. Open 5GENESIS Suite. 2020. Available online: https://github.com/5genesis (accessed on 30 September 2020).
9. *3GPP TS 38.521-3; 3rd Generation Partnership Project; Technical Specification Group Radio Access Network; NR; User Equipment (UE) Conformance Specification; Radio Transmission and Reception; Part 3: Range 1 and Range 2 Interworking Operation with Other Radios (Release 16), v16.4*; 3GPP: Sophia Antipolis, France, May 2020.
10. *3GPP TS 38.521-1; 3rd Generation Partnership Project; Technical Specification Group Radio Access Network; NR; User Equipment (UE) Conformance Specification; Radio Transmission and Reception; Part 1: Range 1 Standalone (Release 16), v16.4*; 3GPP: Sophia Antipolis, France, July 2020.
11. *3GPP TS 38.521-2; 3rd Generation Partnership Project; Technical Specification Group Radio Access Network; NR; User Equipment (UE) Conformance Specification; Radio Transmission and Reception; Part 2: Range 2 Standalone (Release 16), v16.4*; 3GPP: Sophia Antipolis, France, July 2020.
12. *3GPP TS 38.521-4; 3rd Generation Partnership Project; Technical Specification Group Radio Access Network; NR; User Equipment (UE) Conformance Specification; Radio Transmission and Reception; Part 4: Performance (Release 16), v16.4*; 3GPP: Sophia Antipolis, France, July 2020.
13. *3GPP TS 38.523-1; 3rd Generation Partnership Project; Technical Specification Group Radio Access Network; 5GS; User Equipment (UE) Conformance Specification; Part 1: Protocol (Release 16), v16.4*; 3GPP: Sophia Antipolis, France, May 2020.
14. *3GPP TS 38.523-2; 3rd Generation Partnership Project; Technical Specification Group Radio Access Network; 5GS; User Equipment (UE) Conformance Specification; Part 2: Applicability of Protocol Test Cases (Release 16), v16.4*; 3GPP: Sophia Antipolis, France, June 2020.
15. *3GPP TS 38.523-3; 3rd Generation Partnership Project; Technical Specification Group Radio Access Network; 5GS; User Equipment (UE) Conformance Specification; Part 3: Protocol Test Suites (Release 15), v15.8*; 3GPP: Sophia Antipolis, France, June 2020.
16. *3GPP TS 38.533; 3rd Generation Partnership Project; Technical Specification Group Radio Access Network; NR; User Equipment (UE) Conformance Specification; Radio Resource Management (RRM) (Release 16)*; 3GPP: Sophia Antipolis, France, July 2020.
17. *CTIA Battery Life Programm Management Document*; CTIA: Washisgton, DC, USA, 2018.
18. *3GPP TS 28.552; 3rd Generation Partnership Project; Technical Specification Group Services and System Aspects; Management and Orchestration; Management and Orchestration; 5G Performance Measurements (Release 16), v16.6*; 3GPP: Sophia Antipolis, France, July 2020.
19. *3GPP TS 32.425; 3rd Generation Partnership Project; Telecommunication Management; Performance Management (PM); Performance Measurements Evolved Universal Terrestrial Radio Access Network (E-UTRAN) (Release 16), v16.5*; 3GPP: Sophia Antipolis, France, January 2020.
20. *3GPP TS 32.451; 3rd Generation Partnership Project; Technical Specification Group Services and System Aspects; Telecommunication Management; Key Performance Indicators (KPI) for Evolved Universal Terrestrial Radio Access Network (E-UTRAN); Requirements (Release 16), v16.0*; 3GPP: Sophia Antipolis, France, September 2019.
21. *3GPP TS 32.404; 3rd Generation Partnership Project; Technical Specification Group Services and System Aspects; Telecommunication Management; Performance Management (PM); Performance Measurements; Definitions and Template (Release 16), v16.0*; 3GPP: Sophia Antipolis, France, July 2020.
22. *ETSI GS NFV-TST 010; Network Functions Virtualisation (NFV) Release 2; Testing; API Conformance Testing Specification, v2.6.1*; ETSI: Sophia Antipolis, France, September 2020.
23. *3GPP TS 37.901; 3rd Generation Partnership Project; Technical Specification Group Radio Access Network; User Equipment (UE) Application Layer Data throughput Performance (Release 15)*; 3GPP: Sophia Antipolis, France, May 2018.

24. 3GPP TR 37.901-5; 3rd Generation Partnership Project; Technical Specification Group Radio Access Network; Study on 5G NR User Equipment (UE) Application Layer Data throughput Performance (Release 16), v16.0; 3GPP: Sophia Antipolis, France, May 2020.
25. 5GENESIS Project Deliverable D6.1 "Trials and Experimentation (Cycle 1). 2019. Available online: https://5genesis.eu/wp-content/uploads/2019/12/5GENESIS_D6.1_v2.00.pdf (accessed on 30 September 2020).
26. 3GPP TS 28.554; 3rd Generation Partnership Project; Technical Specification Group Services and System Aspects; Management and Orchestration; 5G End to End Key Performance Indicators (KPI) (Release 16), v16.5; 3GPP: Sophia Antipolis, France, July 2020.
27. NGMN Alliance. Definition of the Testing Framework for the NGMN 5G Pre-Commercial Networks Trials; NGMN: Frankfurt, Germany, 2019.
28. 3GPP TR 38.913; 3rd Generation Partnership Project; Technical Specification Group Radio Access Network; Study on Scenarios and Requirements for Next Generation Access Technologies (Release 16), v16.5; 3GPP: Sophia Antipolis, France, July 2020.
29. Díaz-Zayas, A.; García, B.; Merino, P. An End-to-End Automation Framework for Mobile Network Testbeds. *Mob. Inf. Syst.* **2019**, *2019*, 2563917. [CrossRef]
30. Espada, A.R.; Gallardo, M.D.; Salmerón, A.; Panizo, L.; Merino, P. A formal approach to automatically analyse extra-functional properties in mobile applications. *Softw. Test. Verif. Reliab.* **2019**, *29*, e1699.
31. Tateishi, T.K.; Kunta, D.; Harada, A.; Kishryama, Y.; Parkvall, S.; Dahlman, E.; Furuskog, J. Field experiments on 5G radio access using 15-GHz band in outdoor small cell environment. In Proceedings of the 2015 IEEE 26th Annual International Symposium on Personal, Indoor, and Mobile Radio Communications (PIMRC'15), Hong Kong, China, 30 August–2 September 2015; pp. 851–855.
32. Moto, K.; Mikami, M.; Serizawa, K.; Yoshino, H. Field Experimental Evaluation on 5G V2N Low Latency Communication for Application to Truck Platooning. In Proceedings of the 2019 IEEE 90th Vehicular Technology Conference (VTC2019-Fall), Honolulu, HI, USA, 22–25 September 2019; pp. 1–5.
33. Meng, X.; Li, J.; Zhou, D.; Yang, D. 5G technology requirements and related test environments for evaluation. *China Commun.* **2016**, *13*, 42–51. [CrossRef]
34. Li, X.; Deng, W.; Liu, L.; Tian, Y.; Tong, H.; Liu, J.; Ma, Y.; Wang, J.; Horsmanh, S.; Gavras, A. Novel Test Methods for 5G Network Performance Field Trial. In Proceedings of the 2020 IEEE International Conference on Communications Workshops (ICC'20 Workshops), Dublin, Ireland, 7–11 June 2020; pp. 1–6.
35. Xu, D.; Zhou, A.; Zhang, X.; Wang, G.; Liu, X.; An, C.; Shi, Y.; Liu, L.; Ma, H. Understanding Operational 5G: A First Measurement Study on Its Coverage, Performance and Energy Consumption. In Proceedings of the Annual conference of the ACM Special Interest Group on Data Communication on the Applications, Technologies, Architectures, and Protocols for Computer Communication (SIGCOMM'20), Virtual Event, NY, USA, 10–14 August 2020; pp. 479–494.
36. Narayanan, A.; Ramadan, E. A First Look at Commercial 5G Performance on Smartphones. In Proceedings of the Web Conference 2020 (WWW'20), Taipei Taiwan, 20–24 April 2020; pp. 894–905.
37. Piri, E.; Ruuska, P.; Kanstrén, T.; Mäkelä, J.; Korva, J.; Hekkala, A.; Pouttu, A.; Liinamaa, O.; Latva-aho, M.; Vierimaa, K.; et al. 5GTN: A test network for 5G application development and testing. In Proceedings of the 2016 European Conference on Networks and Communications (EuCNC), Athens, Greece, 27–30 June 2016.
38. Vidal, I.; Nogales, B.; Valera, F.; Gonzalez, L.F.; Sanchez-Aguero, V. A Multi-Site NFV Testbed for Experimentation With SUAV-Based 5G Vertical Services. *IEEE Access* **2020**, *8*, 111522–111535. [CrossRef]
39. Mavromatis, A.; Colman-Meixner, C.; Silva, A.P.; Vasilakos, X.; Nejabati, R. A Software-Defined IoT Device Management Framework for Edge and Cloud Computing. *IEEE Internet Things J.* **2020**, *7*, 1718–1735. [CrossRef]
40. Vucinic, M.; Chang, T.; Škrbić, B.; Kočan, E.; Pejanović-Djurišić, M. Key Performance Indicators of the Reference 6TiSCH Implementation in Internet-of-Things Scenarios. *IEEE Access* **2020**, *8*, 79147–79157. [CrossRef]
41. Muñoz, J.; Rincon, F.; Chang, T.; Vilajosana, X.; Vermeulen, B.; Walcariu, T. OpenTestBed: Poor Man's IoT Testbed. In Proceedings of the 2019 IEEE Conference on Computer Communications Workshops (INFOCOM'19 WKSHPS), Paris, France, 29 April–2 May 2019.
42. Garcia-Aviles, G.; Gramaglia, M.; Serrano, P.; Banchs, A. POSENS: A Practical Open Source Solution for End-to-End Network Slicing. *IEEE Wirel. Commun.* **2018**, *25*, 30–37. [CrossRef]

43. 5G PPP Architecture Working Group. View on 5G Architecture, Version 3.0. 2020. Available online: https://5g-ppp.eu/wp-content/uploads/2020/02/5G-PPP-5G-Architecture-White-Paper_final.pdf (accessed on 25 October 2020).
44. 5GENESIS Project. Deliverable D5.3 Documentation and Supporting Material for 5G Stakeholders (Release A). 2020. Available online: https://5genesis.eu/wp-content/uploads/2020/07/5GENESIS-D5.3_v1.0.pdf (accessed on 30 September 2020).
45. EURO-5G Project. Deliverable D2.6 Final Report on Programme Progress and KPIs. 2017. Available online: https://5g-ppp.eu/wp-content/uploads/2017/10/Euro-5G-D2.6_Final-report-on-programme-progress-and-KPIs.pdf (accessed on 30 September 2020).
46. *3GPP TS 23.501; 3rd Generation Partnership Project; Technical Specification Group Services and System Aspects; System Architecture for the 5G System (5GS); Stage 2; (Release 16), v16.5.1*; 3GPP: Sophia Antipolis, France, August 2020.
47. *3GPP TR 28.801; 3rd Generation Partnership Project; Technical Specification Group Services and System Aspects; Telecommunication Management; Study on Management and Orchestration of Network Slicing for Next Generation Network (Release 15), v15.1.0*; 3GPP: Sophia Antipolis, France, January 2018.
48. 5GENESIS Project. Deliverable D3.3 Slice Management (Release A). 2019. Available online: https://5genesis.eu/wp-content/uploads/2019/10/5GENESIS_D3.3_v1.0.pdf (accessed on 30 September 2020).
49. Katana Slice Manager. Available online: https://github.com/medianetlab/katana-slice_manager (accessed on 30 September 2020).
50. GSM Association. *Official Document NG.116—Generic Network Slice Template*; GSM Association: London, UK, 2020.
51. Monroe Experiments. Available online: https://github.com/MONROE-PROJECT/Experiments (accessed on 30 September 2020).
52. Mancuso, V.; Quirós, M.P.; Midoglu, C.; Moulay, M.; Comite, V.; Lutu, A.; Alay, Ö.; Alfredsson, S.; Rajiullah, M.; Brunström, A.; et al. Results from running an experiment as a service platform for mobile broadband networks in Europe. *Comput. Commun.* **2019**, *133*, 89–101. [CrossRef]
53. *3GPP TS 37.340; 3rd Generation Partnership Project; Technical Specification Group Radio Access Network; Evolved Universal Terrestrial Radio Access (E-UTRA) and NR; Multi-Connectivity; Stage 2 (Release 16), v16.2.0*; 3GPP: Sophia Antipolis, France, June 2020.
54. 5GENESIS Project. Deliverable D4.5 The Malaga Platform (Release B). 2020. Available online: https://5genesis.eu/wp-content/uploads/2020/02/5GENESIS_D4.5_v1.0.pdf (accessed on 25 October 2020).
55. *3GPP TS 38.101-3; Technical Specification 3rd Generation Partnership Project; Technical Specification Group Radio Access Network; NR; User Equipment (UE) Radio Transmission and Reception; Part 3: Range 1 and Range 2 Interworking Operation with Other Radios (Release 16), v16.4.0*; 3GPP: Sophia Antipolis, France, May 2020.
56. *3GPP TS 38.214; Technical Specification 3rd Generation Partnership Project; Technical Specification Group Radio Access Network; NR; Physical Layer Procedures for Data (Release 15), v15.10.0*; 3GPP: Sophia Antipolis, France, May 2020.

Publisher's Note: MDPI stays neutral with regard to jurisdictional claims in published maps and institutional affiliations.

© 2020 by the authors. Licensee MDPI, Basel, Switzerland. This article is an open access article distributed under the terms and conditions of the Creative Commons Attribution (CC BY) license (http://creativecommons.org/licenses/by/4.0/).

Article

Deploying an NFV-Based Experimentation Scenario for 5G Solutions in Underserved Areas

Victor Sanchez-Aguero [1,2,*], Ivan Vidal [2], Francisco Valera [2], Borja Nogales [2], Luciano Leonel Mendes [3], Wheberth Damascena Dias [3] and Alexandre Carvalho Ferreira [3]

1. IMDEA Networks Institute, Avda. del Mar Mediterráneo, 22, 28918 Madrid, Spain
2. Department of Telematic Engineering, Universidad Carlos III de Madrid, 28911 Leganes, Spain; ividal@it.uc3m.es (I.V.); fvalera@it.uc3m.es (F.V.); bdorado@pa.uc3m.es (B.N.)
3. Instituto Nacional de Telecomunicações, Santa Rita do Sapucaí 37540-000, Brazil; lucianol@inatel.br (L.L.M.); wheberth@gmail.com (W.D.D.); alexandrecf@inatel.br (A.C.F.)
* Correspondence: victor.sanchez@imdea.org

Citation: Sanchez-Aguero, V.; Vidal, I.; Valera, F.; Nogales, B.; Mendes, L.L.; Damascena Dias, W.; Carvalho Ferreira, A. Deploying an NFV-Based Experimentation Scenario for 5G Solutions in Underserved Areas. *Sensors* **2021**, *21*, 1897. https://doi.org/10.3390/s21051897

Academic Editor: Giuseppe Caso

Received: 9 February 2021
Accepted: 3 March 2021
Published: 8 March 2021

Publisher's Note: MDPI stays neutral with regard to jurisdictional claims in published maps and institutional affiliations.

Copyright: © 2021 by the authors. Licensee MDPI, Basel, Switzerland. This article is an open access article distributed under the terms and conditions of the Creative Commons Attribution (CC BY) license (https://creativecommons.org/licenses/by/4.0/).

Abstract: Presently, a significant part of the world population does not have Internet access. The fifth-generation cellular network technology evolution (5G) is focused on reducing latency, increasing the available bandwidth, and enhancing network performance. However, researchers and companies have not invested enough effort into the deployment of the Internet in remote/rural/undeveloped areas for different techno-economic reasons. This article presents the result of a collaboration between Brazil and the European Union, introducing the steps designed to create a fully operational experimentation scenario with the main purpose of integrating the different achievements of the H2020 5G-RANGE project so that they can be trialed together into a 5G networking use case. The scenario encompasses (i) a novel radio access network that targets a bandwidth of 100 Mb/s in a cell radius of 50 km, and (ii) a network of Small Unmanned Aerial Vehicles (SUAV). This set of SUAVs is NFV-enabled, on top of which Virtual Network Functions (VNF) can be automatically deployed to support occasional network communications beyond the boundaries of the 5G-RANGE radio cells. The whole deployment implies the use of a virtual private overlay network enabling the preliminary validation of the scenario components from their respective remote locations, and simplifying their subsequent integration into a single local demonstrator, the configuration of the required GRE/IPSec tunnels, the integration of the new 5G-RANGE physical, MAC and network layer components and the overall validation with voice and data services.

Keywords: 5th generation cellular networks (5G); remote area network; Small Unmanned Aerial Vehicles (SUAVs); Network Functions Virtualization (NFV); 3rd Generation Partnership Project (3GPP)

1. Introduction and Motivation

The fifth generation of cellular network technology (5G) is becoming a reality. Researchers and industry are working conscientiously to build ground-breaking solutions that increase transmission speeds, reduce latency, decrease energy consumption, or improve connectivity. The 3rd Generation Partnership Project (3GPP) [1] is working on a series of releases to compose the 5G network scenarios that are being developed to fulfil the requirements imposed by enhanced Mobile Broadband (eMBB) [2], Ultra-Reliable Low Latency Communications (URLLC) [3], and massive Machine Type Communications (mMTC) [4]. Release 15 [5] of 3GPP specifications focused on high data rates for eMBB, with a peak downlink rate of 20 Gb/s and 10 Gb/s uplink rate. Release 16 [6] is focusing on reducing the end-to-end latency and increasing robustness for URLLC, and Release 17 [7] is under specification to reduce power consumption on power-limited devices and increase the number of connections for mMTC.

Besides these promising improvements, presently the International Telecommunication Union estimates that 46.4% of the world population cannot properly access the Internet, and connectivity in remote/low populated areas is normally considered to require considerable effort and investments [8]. However, one of the key performance indicators [9] to be achieved at an operational level of the 5G ecosystem, is to provide ubiquitous access including rural and remote areas. In continental-size countries, such as Brazil, one major application scenario is the remote and rural area coverage, where a large parcel of the population is living without connectivity and where informatization of the fields is required to increase farms productivity. Since costs are the major hurdle for mobile network operators, 5G must also present an operation mode that allows for extensive coverage, reducing the number of base stations and spectrum costs. In addition, this solution will have substantial social benefits, such as guaranteeing universal access to education and healthcare, or the digital integration of different isolated communities and countries.

Over the past few years, there has been considerable proliferation of experimentation projects in 5G technologies. In general, there is no commercial deployment of the 5G technology (most of the deployments are still based on legacy infrastructure and standalone 5G solutions have not been deployed yet in many places). Accordingly, most of the experimentation is done under consortium projects involving relevant entities, including end users, technology developers, and operators. In Europe, many projects have been funded by the European Union to provide 5G experimentation facilities and foster the adoption of 5G technologies by vertical sectors. These projects include 5G-VINNI [10], the 5GINFIRE [11], the 5Growth [12], the 5G-DIVE [13], or the 5G-EVE [14].

This article presents an experience report after building a use case scenario with 5G technologies (Figure 1) within the Horizon 2020 5G-RANGE (Remote area Access Network for 5th GEneration) project [15], a 3-year European and Brazilian cooperation effort, whose main objective is the design and implementation of a remote area access network solution under 3GPP specifications and the 5G standard technologies. The contribution presented in this paper has been deployed at the Instituto Nacional de Telecomunicações (Inatel), in Santa Rita do Sapucaí, Brazil, and the 5G Telefonica Open Network Innovation Centre laboratory (5TONIC) [16] in Madrid, Spain. 5TONIC is one of the leading laboratories for 5G experimentation based in Madrid, Spain. The 5TONIC laboratory is established to provide an open ecosystem where members from business, industry, and academia collaborate with the telecoms research projects.

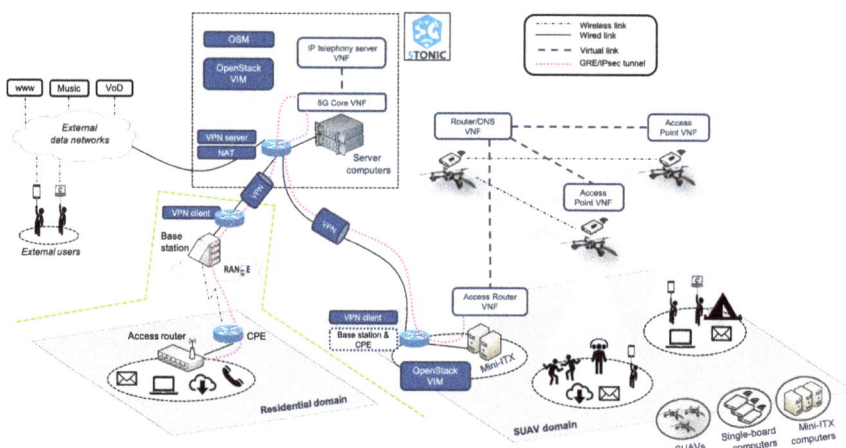

Figure 1. Overview of the testbed components and the experimentation scenario.

Previous works by the authors present two of the main achievements of 5G-RANGE such as a multi-site Network Function Virtualization (NFV) testbed designed for experimentation with Small Unmanned Aerial Vehicles (SUAV) [17], or the new physical (radio) and MAC (Medium Access Control) layers developed to overcome the long-range link under 5G key performance indicators, targeting a cell radius of 50 Km with 100 Mb/s at the edge and closing the connectivity gap in remote and rural areas [18].

However, this article shows the whole experimentation scenario that has been built integrating both solutions and presents them in two different domains that can interact with each other. One of the domains includes the physical and MAC layers that allow for Dynamic Spectrum Allocation [19] by exploiting vacant TV channels using Cognitive Radio techniques [20]. Spectrum sensing, low out-of-band emissions, fragmented spectrum access [21] and cognitive cycle are some of the features that must be incorporated in the physical and MAC layers to allow 5G networks to be used to close the connectivity gap in remote and rural areas. The other domain includes the SUAV scenario where network functions can be automatically deployed to support casual network communications beyond the boundaries of the 5G-RANGE radio cells, or to cover shadow areas within the radio cells themselves (e.g., fire extinction, search and rescue operations, festive events, field inspections).

The article is also showing the methodology to perform this type of complex integrations with different domains located in remote locations. The domains are connected using a VPN-based overlay network (so that they can transparently be deployed anywhere) and through a baseline 5G core software.

In addition, it is shown how all the network layer components in both domains (as suggested by the 3GPP) are virtualized and executed as Virtualized Network Functions (VNFs), using a Management and Orchestration (MANO) platform defined by the ETSI in the context of NFV paradigm. Wireless APs that offer network access connectivity to end users within their vicinity may be deployed as VNFs in several SUAVs, some other SUAVs or Ground Units could deploy virtualized network routers, supporting the exchange of data between users in the geographic area, or a gateway function can be available at specific locations, enabling for data communications between users and external data networks through a 5G Core (which would also be provided in the form of one or several VNFs in the operator domain). The article shows how this approach enables an easier and more flexible incorporation of additional domains to the scenario, aiding the development of proof-of-concept activities involving Internet, third-party, and operator-specific services, such as web browsing, email, video on demand, and IP telephony. Finally, the article provides different measurements performed over the infrastructure.

2. Background on 5G-RANGE Technologies

To support effective network communications over remote areas, 5G-RANGE has followed a practical approach: (i) the development of novel physical and MAC layer mechanisms, able to efficiently handle data communications over long distances; (ii) the adoption of well-known and widely used technologies, as well as recognized standards under development in the context of 5G networking, to provide end-user terminals with end-to-end network connectivity, and support the provision of an operator, third-party, and Internet services. In addition, the design of mechanisms to enable cost-effective network services over delimited geographic areas (e.g., to support network communications beyond the boundaries of the 5G-RANGE radio cells) is also considered.

This section identifies and provides a brief overview of these technologies, outlining the technological background that has driven the design and the development of the experimental testbed described in the following section.

2.1. Physical and MAC Layers

The 5G-RANGE project has developed an innovative new radio physical layer using a powerful channel code scheme to enable a robust long-range link. A polar code [22] with a variable coding rate is used to protect the data received from the upper layers, increasing the system performance in terms of bit and block error rates. The encoded data are mapped into Quadrature Amplitude Modulation (QAM) symbols, where modulation order can be selected according to the channel conditions (from 4-QAM up to 256-QAM).

After the QAM mapping, the data symbols are applied to the Multiple-Input Multiple-Output (MIMO) block, which can operate in two different modes. In the first mode, a space-time block coding [23] is used to enhance the system robustness for users located far from the base station. This mode allows the receiver to combine the data transmitted by the two antennas, resulting in a maximum diversity gain that is twice the number of receive antennas. The second operation relies on space multiplexing [24], where the two transmit antennas are used to send different data blocks, doubling the overall data rate of the system. Typically, space-time block coding is used to enhance the system robustness for users located far from the base station, while space multiplexing is used to increase the data rate for those users close to it.

This physical layer is controlled and configured by the MAC layer, according to the channel conditions. The main novelty introduced at this layer is the cognitive cycle, exploiting vacant TV channels using cognitive radio techniques [20]. The User Equipment (UE) can be instructed by the base station to perform a spectrum measurement at its location infers whether the channel is available or occupied. The Collaborative Spectrum Sensing Optimized for Remote Areas [25] block acquires samples collected from the channel and each requested UE performs a Primary User detection algorithm. The outcome of this measurement is one of two hypotheses: H0, stating that the channel is available or H1, stating that the channel is occupied. The measurements are sent to the base station, where a dynamic spectrum allocation [19] function is responsible to fuse all the measurements into a single decision variable. Data from a geolocation database can also be used to aid the decision process, i.e., allowing the selection of the channels that shall be investigated as potential idle channels. Once a set of channels is identified as vacant, a resource scheduler allocates the user data to protocol data units, which will be delivered to the physical layer. These protocol data units also carry the configuration of the physical layer to be employed by each user (e.g., code rate, QAM mapper and MIMO scheme). Data recovered by the physical layer are also delivered to the MAC layer using the same protocol data unit structure.

2.2. Network Layer

The network layer has a fundamental role to support end-user communications. It complements the physical and MAC layers of the radio access network with the required features to provide the UE with secure end-to-end network connectivity towards other UE and external networks. Figure 2 outlines the role of the network layer within the 5G-RANGE architecture.

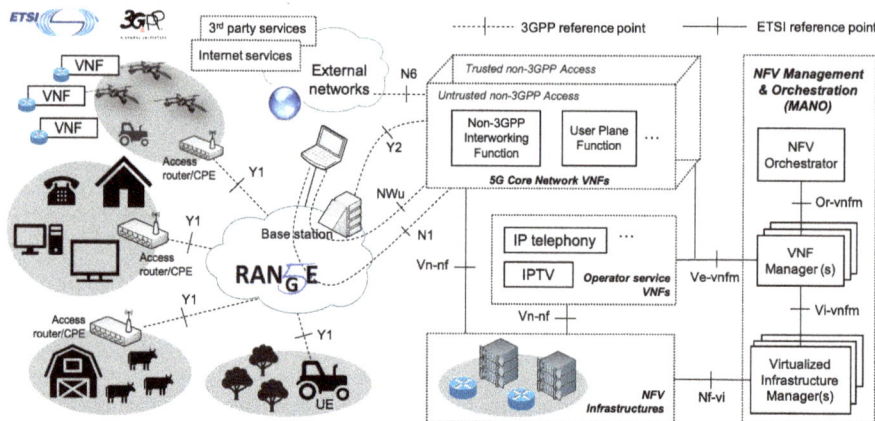

Figure 2. High-level overview of the 5G-RANGE architecture.

The connectivity service offered by the network layer is realized with the use of a 5G core network, as defined by the 3GPP [1]. The 5G core network identifies a set of well-defined protocols and interfaces allowing the interconnection of non-3GPP access networks (e.g., the 5G-RANGE access network), which may support trusted or untrusted connectivity to a 5G core network or, more generally, to a public mobile network infrastructure. Moreover, it enables the establishment of protected communications towards the UE, using standard tunneling protocols over the access network (for non-3GPP accesses, these are GRE (Generic Routing Encapsulation) [26] and IPsec (Internet Protocol security) [27]).

From an architectural perspective, the 5G-RANGE network layer relies on ETSI Network Functions Virtualization (NFV). This way, the different elements of the 5G core network, as well as the constituent functions of operator and third-party services, can be executed as Virtual Network Functions (VNFs). The lifecycle management of all the VNFs framed at the network layer follows the procedures indicated by the ETSI Management and Orchestration (MANO) framework. Figure 2 outlines the 5G-RANGE architecture.

In 5G-RANGE, ETSI NFV is also considered to support the cost-effective deployment of lightweight network functions on localized remote geographic areas. In this respect, the approach taken by the project leverages resource-constrained platforms that can be embedded in vehicles that may exist or be deployed in the remote area (e.g., SUAVs, harvesters, tractors, etc.). These vehicles are consequently transformed into functional mobile compute nodes, offering computing, storage and network resources that can be under the control of a MANO platform to support the execution of VNFs. They have the potential to be placed around specific locations and be interconnected, allowing the on-demand creation of functional NFV infrastructures over localized geographic areas. This NFV infrastructure can be used to complement the access network resources, and provide cost-effective telecommunication services controlled by a MANO platform. This way, the proposed approach allows the on-demand creation of a functional NFV infrastructure over a localized geographic area. This infrastructure can be used to complement the access network resources and provision cost-effective telecommunication services under the control of a MANO platform. In addition, the NFV infrastructure facilitates the dissemination of data across the deployment area, through the multi-hop ad hoc network built by the mobile compute nodes.

In 5G-RANGE, this approach has been explored in different use cases, including service provisioning beyond the boundary of radio cells [28], supporting emergency communication services in remote areas [29], and disseminating vertical-specific data, particularly in smart farming scenarios [17].

2.3. NFV Testbed Description and VNF Repository

As previously commented, the goal of this work is to build the scenario shown in Figure 1. For this purpose, we have used an NFV testbed that is available at the 5TONIC laboratory [16] based in Madrid, Spain. A detailed description of the NFV testbed can be found in [17]. For the sake of completeness, in the following we present a summary of its main features and components. The testbed includes a functional MANO platform based on Open-Source MANO (OSM), an ETSI-hosted project providing an NFV orchestration software stack. A well-known and widely adopted cloud computing solution, OpenStack, was selected to provide the Virtual Infrastructure Manager (VIM) functionalities. Both the OSM stack and the OpenStack controller run in independent virtual machines, easing the management of the MANO components and their vertical scaling to satisfy operational needs. The MANO platform supports the automated deployment of VNFs over an NFV infrastructure composed by three server computers, accounting for a total of 24 vCPUs, 96 GB of RAM, and 6 TB of storage. These VNFs may also access Internet services, through a Network Address Translation (NAT) function provided at 5TONIC edge router.

To increase the potential for experimentation with 5G-RANGE technologies, the baseline testbed supports the flexible incorporation of network domains, by means of an overlay network architecture based on a Virtual Private Network (VPN) service hosted at 5TONIC.

Each of these domains may include hardware and software components prototyped by 5G-RANGE partners. It may also host an NFV infrastructure that can be attached to the 5TONIC MANO platform. This way, the addition of new domains allows configuring moderately complex experimentation scenarios, enabling the validation of 5G-RANGE developments along with other assets produced or adopted by the project. Each network domain can be independently managed and evolved, for instance, with the introduction of new functionalities implemented in the context of the project.

Following the aforementioned approach, the testbed integrates a SUAV domain with a portable NFV infrastructure, enabling the creation of experimentation scenarios with mobile compute nodes. The portable NFV infrastructure encompasses six single-board computers, Raspberry Pi 3 Model B+, each with two Wi-Fi interfaces. Given their size and weight, these adequately represent the type of resource-constrained platforms that could be onboarded onto SUAVs. The infrastructure also includes five mini-ITX computers, which may serve as ground equipment to deploy more resource-demanding VNFs. To enable flight experiments, the portable NFV infrastructure is completed with four Parrot Bebop 2 SUAVs, each transporting a Raspberry Pi 3 Model B+. An additional mini-ITX computer hosts a VPN client and an OpenStack VIM, each running in a virtual machine. The former behaves as a network router with a virtual link to 5TONIC. The OpenStack VIM exposes the resources of the portable NFV infrastructure to the 5TONIC OSM stack.

On the other hand, the testbed includes the prototypes of a 3GPP UE and a 5G core network. The UE can also behave as an access router, supporting the connectivity of additional end-user devices. Both prototypes implement the data-plane protocol stack defined by 3GPP for an untrusted non-3GPP access [1]. The access router can be provisioned as a VNF at each network domain, in case an NFV infrastructure is available at the domain. Alternatively, it can be deployed as a hardware device, because an implementation of the access router has been made available on a single-board computer, Raspberry Pi model 3B+. Every access router function is connected to the 5G core network function through a GRE over IPsec tunnel, as dictated by 3GPP specifications for non-3GPP accesses. The 5G core network component has been provisioned as a VNF. Hence, different experiments can use independent instances of this network function, which can be deployed by the MANO platform on the 5TONIC NFV infrastructure. In addition, the 5G core network prototype implements a GRE/IPsec tunnel endpoint and provides connectivity to external networks. From that perspective, it can be seen as a baseline implementation of the data-plane protocol stack of a Non-3GPP InterWorking Function and a User Plane Function, as defined by 3GPP. The access router and the core network functions have been implemented using the Linux *ip-gre* module, and the *ipsec-tools* and *racoon* Linux packages. Additionally, a VNF has been implemented providing the functionalities of an IP telephony server based on the open-source SIP server *Kamailio*. It can be deployed over the 5TONIC NFV infrastructure, supporting the registration of end-user SIP phones and the establishment of voice and video calls in experimentation scenarios.

To enable experimentation activities with resource-constrained compute nodes (e.g., single-board computers onboarded on SUAVs), the testbed offers two additional VNFs: an Access Point VNF, providing the functions of a Wi-Fi access point and a DHCP server, and a Router/DNS VNF. Both VNFs have been prototyped as lightweight software functions using Linux and virtualization containers, so that they can be executed on the single-board computers of the SUAVs domain. All these components are available under an open-source license in the 5G-RANGE network layer repository [30].

3. Experimentation Scenario: Methodology from Design to Validation

Figure 1 shows the scenario that has been created with the goal of validating 5G-RANGE technologies in the context of a specific use case. The subsequent subsections detail the followed methodology from the design to validation. To facilitate the presentation of Sections 3 and 4, and the understanding of the applied methodology, Figure 3 provides the overall flowchart illustrating the definition, deployment, integration and validation of the experimentation scenario.

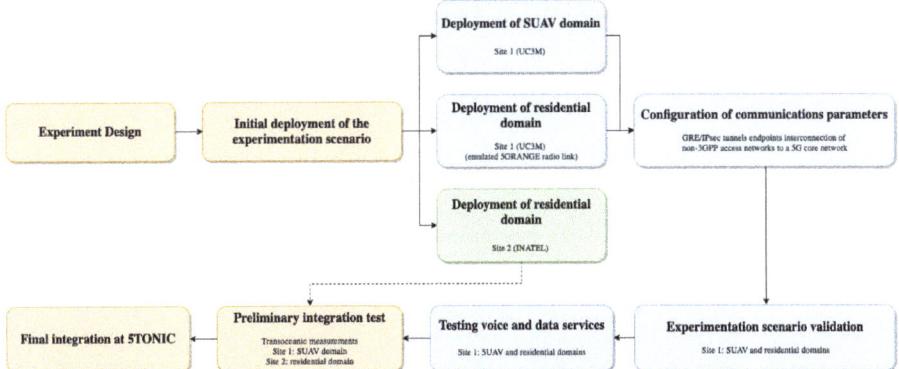

Figure 3. Methodology to define, deploy, integrate and validate the experimentation scenario.

3.1. Description of the Experimentation Scenario

In the experimentation scenario, an access router is physically available at a residential environment in a remote area, serving as a wireless access point. The access router enables data exchange between residential users and external networks, through the GRE/IPsec tunnel established with the 5G core network. Hence, users within the remote area may access Internet and operator-specific services, such as web browsing, email, audio/video live streaming, or IP telephony. The radio access network is supported by a base station and a customer premises equipment (CPE), which implement the physical and MAC layer protocols of 5G-RANGE. Figure 4 shows the protocol stack involved at the different network functions of the residential domain, the access network, and the 5G core network to support data exchange.

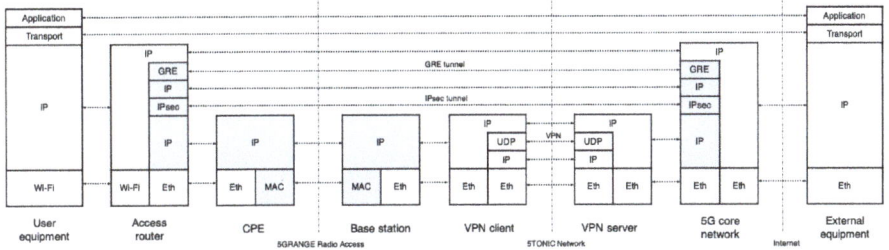

Figure 4. Data-plane protocol stack of the residential environment.

The experimentation scenario also reproduces a situation where similar Internet and operator-specific services are to be provided to users beyond the limits of a 5G-RANGE radio cell (e.g., users in a festive event, or emergency response teams in a fire extinction or search and rescue operation). For this purpose, several SUAVs are deployed over the area, hosting a set of network functions that enable the provision of those services. In this case, the SUAVs are hovering in a static position, providing their intended services on a defined geographical area. These network functions include two wireless access points embedded as VNFs on two SUAVs, which serve as wireless hotspots to end users within their vicinity. A network router and a DNS server are jointly deployed as a VNF on a third SUAV. This VNF presents a virtual link towards an access router, which is virtualized on a ground equipment within the radio coverage of a 5G-RANGE radio cell (in a realistic scenario, this wireless link could rely on a multi-hop network path conformed by several wireless routers and SUAVs). The access router behaves as a GRE/IPsec tunnel endpoint towards the 5G core network, supporting data communications between end users and external networks. Communications among users in the residential and SUAV domains are supported through their radio access networks and the 5G core network.

3.2. Initial Deployment of the Experimentation Scenario

The experimentation scenario has been created as a composition of two network domains: one hosting the components of the residential environment (the residential domain); and a second one with the SUAV infrastructure (the SUAV domain). As a first step to build the experimentation scenario, we used our testbed resources to build the residential domain at 5TONIC. This domain includes two single-board computers (Raspberry Pi 3 Model B+), representing a 5G-RANGE base station and a CPE. This initial deployment of the experimentation scenario obviates the physical and MAC layer components of the 5G-RANGE access network (these will be integrated in the experimentation scenario at a later stage). Instead, the base station and the CPE are interconnected through a 100 Mb/s switch, providing the equivalent maximum throughput of the 5G-RANGE access network. The base station is connected to a mini-ITX computer, which deploys a VPN client. This implements a virtual link towards 5TONIC, making each device at the domain accessible from the laboratory. The CPE is connected to an access router function, supported by another single-board computer (Raspberry Pi 3 model B+). The access router provides the functions of a wireless access point, offering network access connectivity to an end-user device (a laptop), and implements a GRE/IPsec tunnel endpoint towards the 5G core network.

The 5G core network component is part of a network service that has automatically been deployed through the MANO platform of the 5TONIC NFV testbed. The network service includes a set of VNFs that are instantiated on the SUAV domain, offering the functionalities of wireless access points, routers, and other supporting functions on SUAV units. An access router VNF is deployed on a ground compute node (a mini-ITX computer), supporting the exchange of information with external networks. For this purpose, the access router behaves as a GRE/IPsec tunnel endpoint towards the 5G core network VNF. The latter is deployed at 5TONIC premises along with an IP telephony server VNF, which supports the establishment of calls among end users in our experimentation scenario. The deployment of the whole network service was accomplished at 5TONIC premises, where a specific location for indoor flights is available. Finally, an additional mini-ITX computer deploys the VPN client that handles the communication of the SUAV domain with other testbed components.

3.3. Configuration of GRE/IPsec Tunnel Endpoints

The use of GRE, IPsec, and the VPN service, may cause excessive fragmentation on data packets. When packets arrive to the access router or the 5G core network, they are fragmented by GRE before being processed by IPsec. This is because the default MTU of the GRE interface is 1476 bytes, a lower value than the typical size of regular data packets (1500 bytes). The GRE tunnel interface splits each data packet into two fragments, encapsulating them into new IP packets with a GRE and an outer IP header. With a size of 1500 bytes, the first of these packets is also required to be fragmented after being processed by IPsec (after appending the IPsec protocol overhead, the packet exceeds the MTU of the outgoing link). A similar situation occurs at the VPN endpoint, which processes three data packets and performs an additional fragmentation of the first packet (after appending the VPN protocol overhead, the first packet exceeds the MTU of the outgoing link). These fragmentation processes lead to increased overhead in terms of protocol headers and encryption of smaller packets, which necessarily impacts the achievable throughput.

As suggested in [31], this situation can be mitigated with an appropriate configuration of the MTU at the GRE tunnel interfaces. With a suitable value lower than 1500 bytes, data packets would only be fragmented at the GRE tunnel once, producing fragments with a size such that subsequent IPsec and VPN protocol overheads could be accommodated without additional fragmentation processes. Considering the reference MTU values indicated in [31], along with the protocol overhead of the VPN service, we have set the MTU on the GRE tunnel interface to 1360 bytes in our experimentation scenario.

For this purpose, we performed a set of experiments to verify their functional behavior and their performance in the provision of network communications. These experiments have also granted a better understanding on the impact of protocol overheads introduced by the GRE and IPsec processes needed to establish the proper connectivity towards the 5G core network, as well as of the VPN service that interconnects each network domain to the 5TONIC infrastructure. To evaluate the effect of this setting, we have done a performance evaluation, deploying all the elements of Figure 4 as virtual machines at the 5TONIC NFV infrastructure (except the CPE and the base station components). The deployment served to reproduce the communication scheme shown in the figure, including a virtual UE and a virtual external equipment, and excluding the components that are specific to the physical/MAC layers of 5G-RANGE (i.e., the physical/MAC and BS functions of Figure 4).

Figure 5 presents a synoptic overview of the results of our evaluation. Our tests with the *iPerf* tool show a maximum average throughput of 443.97 Mb/s between the user and the external equipment (*GRE'/IPsec/VPN* case in the figure), with an observable increase of approximately 6.7% with respect to the case where the MTU on the GRE tunnel interface is set to its default value of 1500 bytes (*GRE/IPsec/VPN*). These performance figures suggest the capacity of the access router and the 5G core network prototypes to accommodate the requirements for all the experimentation scenarios considered in 5G-RANGE, given that the maximum throughput required in a 5G-RANGE access network segment is 100 Mb/s. The optimized MTU value of 1360 bytes was used at the GRE tunnel interfaces in all our subsequent experiments. The errors bars correspond to the standard deviation.

To gain a better understanding of the performance overhead introduced by GRE/IPsec tunneling processes, the figure also presents the maximum average throughput for the cases where: GRE is disabled and the tunnel endpoints are only supported by IPsec (*IPsec/VPN* in Figure 5); and GRE/IPsec are disabled, and the access router and the 5G core network behave as network routers (*VPN* case).

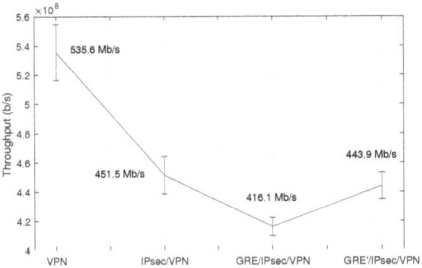

Figure 5. Performance evaluation of GRE/IPsec tunnel endpoints.

3.4. Validation of the Experimentation Scenario

After the deployment of the experimentation scenario, we evaluated the throughput that could be achieved between a network domain and the 5G core network component. Our measurements with the *iPerf* tool reveal an available throughput of 248 Mb/s between a VPN client and the 5G core network VNF (these measurements are similar in both the SUAV and residential domains). This value is obviously lower than the already commented 443.97 Mb/s (see Figure 5) and this is because this new value corresponds to a measurement in a real network. In any case, it is still considerably above the data rate considered in the design of the 5G-RANGE radio access, i.e., 100 Mb/s.

As expected, the available throughput on the UAVs is lower than the available throughput in the VPN client as they communicate over a multi-hop ad hoc Wi-Fi network. The tests from the Access Point VNF SUAV result in average throughput of 22.7 Mbps, while the tests from the Router/DNS VNF SUAV have come out with 53.6 Mbps providing suitable values for subsequent experimentation activities.

On the other hand, tests with the Linux *Ping* command between the VPN client of the SUAV domain and the 5G core network VNF result in an average RTT of 1.59 ms, providing a low value that is suitable for subsequent experimentation activities. We want to highlight that in scenarios spanning remote domains, the network path between a domain and the 5G core network would be established across the Internet, being subject to network congestion and potential bandwidth limitations and high end-to-end network delays. Although this is not necessarily a limiting factor to build distributed experimentation scenarios, it should be considered when designing the tests that will be performed on top of them.

4. Multimedia Tests and Final Integration

4.1. Testing Voice and Data Services

Once the viability and suitable operation of both the access network and the extension of the network formed by the SUAVs have been confirmed, different multimedia services have been trialed. These tests have been also replicated with the real radio equipment, once it was integrated in the laboratory for a project review demonstration. The experimentation scenario has been used to test a representative set of voice and data services that might be demanded by end users in remote areas. This has served to verify the appropriateness of our testbed to develop proof-of-concept activities in the context of a specific use case.

First, we established a voice call between a user in the residential domain and a user in the SUAV domain using a softphone based on the SIP protocol (Session Initiation Protocol) [32], *Bria*, which was installed on one laptop in each domain. The softphones were configured to use the IP telephony service VNF of Figure 1. Figure 6 represents the transmission rate (*SIP TX*) and the received throughput (*SIP RX*) of the voice traffic, measured at the laptop in the residential domain. Around second 75, the video was turned on in both softphones, resulting in a traffic increment (from a few Kb/s up to approximately 2 Mb/s). The average *jitter* in both directions was 0.5 ms, resulting in appropriate interactive real-time communications. The user experience during the call has been satisfactory, with no audio glitches nor skipped video frames.

In a second experiment, a group call was set up using Skype. The call involved the same users as in the previous experiment, with an additional third user connected to Skype through an external network (a commercial fixed access). Figure 6 shows the transmission rate and the received throughput of the voice traffic observed by the residential domain user. The video was activated approximately within 70 s, causing a consequent increase of the traffic. The received traffic nearly doubles the transmitted traffic because, in a Skype video conference, the video stream of each participant is routed to an external server cluster, which in turns forwards it to every other participant. That way, the received throughput corresponds to the video transmitted by the other two participants in the call.

Finally, the laptop at the residential domain was used to access a 4 K video from YouTube. Figure 7 shows the throughput of the received video at the laptop (labelled as *video throughput*). The video was continuously played out with no freezing nor skipped video frames.

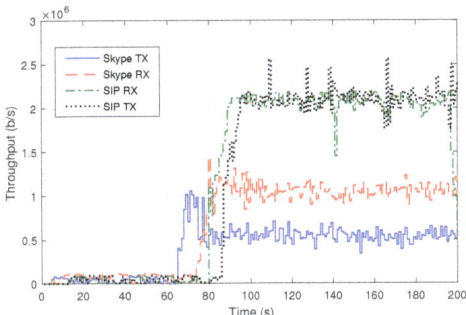

Figure 6. Data rates of SIP and Skype calls.

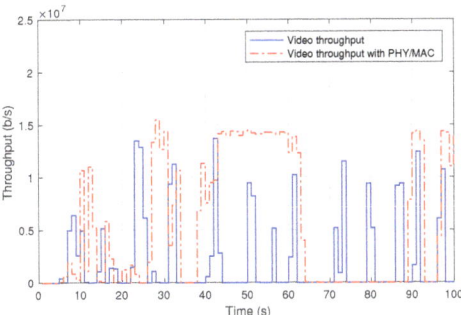

Figure 7. Data rates of video-on-demand service.

4.2. Final Integration and Validation

In the previous section, we verified the appropriateness of our testbed to develop proof-of-concept activities in the context of a specific use case. In this section, we present the methodology followed to integrate the prototypes of a 5G-RANGE base station and a CPE into the experimentation scenario. These prototypes are available at Inatel in Brazil, and were temporarily brought to 5TONIC for a demonstration.

The transceiver prototype [15] has been developed using the software-defined radio strategy, where the entire base band processing is implemented using C language over GNU Radio platform. This approach leads to the maximum flexibility, since the radio behavior can easily be adapted to the different channel conditions. In this prototype, data from the network layer is delivered to the MAC layer through an Ethernet connection. The MAC layer shares the physical resources for the different users according to their individual throughput demands and channel responses. Adaptive modulation and coding is used to guarantee a desired quality-of-service in terms of bit error rate. Modulation order and coding rate for each user is automatically defined based on the channel quality report provided by the mobile terminals. Once the data is mapped to the physical resources, the information is processed by the channel encoder and modulated using generalized frequency division multiplexing, an innovative waveform capable of providing robustness against doubly dispersive channels. In this prototype, a 2×2 MIMO system has been implemented, providing spatial multiplexing gain for users that are nearby the base station and diversity gain for those located far away from it. Once the data is processed by the base band unit, it is delivered to the digital-analog converter, coupled with the radio frequency head. In our implementation, universal software radio peripheral are used to receive the digital samples from the computer running the transceiver's MAC and physical cores, converting them to the radio frequency signal to be delivered to the transmit antennas. A power amplifier provides 6 watts per antenna, allowing the signal to be received up to 50 km from the base station, with data rates up to 100 Mb/s over a 24 MHz channel.

Spectrum sensing is also implemented using the software-defined radio approach. It is performed by the mobile terminals and the collected measurements are periodically sent to the base station using the control channel. The MAC layer uses this information to decide which channels are available to be allocated to the users.

To facilitate integration activities, we leveraged the capacity of our NFV testbed to incorporate remote network domains. In particular, the residential domain of Figure 1 was initially replicated at Inatel, replacing the single-board, back-to-back connected computers by the base station and the customer premises equipment prototypes. The VPN client at Inatel was configured with the same security credentials as the VPN client of the 5TONIC residential domain. All the equipment and networks at the Inatel domain were configured with the same IP addresses as their correspondent equipment and networks at the 5TONIC residential domain. An access router function was also deployed. To ease the deployment of this function, the memory card of the device providing the access router at 5TONIC was cloned, being installed on a Raspberry Pi 3 model B+ at Inatel.

We want to highlight that this methodology allowed addressing most of the integration aspects in advance, before the physical/MAC layer prototypes were brought to 5TONIC. Following this method, we have performed a straightforward final integration. Otherwise, following a traditional methodology, several configurations must be made after the integration into a single local demonstrator, such as (i) configure the addressing space, (ii) configure the GRE/IPsec tunnel, (iii) the integration of physical, MAC, and network layer components, or (iv) the overall validation with voices and data services. This work would be even more time-consuming in this case since the institutions are located on different continents. Thanks to the proposed methodology, all these assignments have been configured prior to the final integration. In addition, it enabled the realization of preliminary configuration and tests, verifying the proper interaction among the components at the Inatel residential domain and those available at 5TONIC. Taking advantage of the VPN service, these tests were conducted as if the Inatel residential environment was locally available at 5TONIC. Of course, the aforementioned tests were limited by the performance of the transoceanic network path between 5TONIC and Inatel, which supports an average throughput of 15.07 Mb/s in the 5TONIC to Brazil direction, 6.62 Mb/s in the reverse direction, and an average RTT of 232.46 ms (these values were obtained during a period of 20 days, taking measurements every hour). This information can be appreciated in Figure 8. The data is plotted following the standard boxplot shape, which represents the obtained measurements of the available throughput grouped in quartiles.

When the physical/MAC layer equipment was brought to 5TONIC, their integration into the experimental scenario only required the decommission of the two single-board, back-to-back connected computers of the 5TONIC residential environment, which were simply replaced by the physical/MAC layer prototypes. The whole process could be realized in a reduced time frame (less than half working day), making the whole experimentation scenario rapidly ready for the practical demonstration. As an example, Figure 7 also shows the throughput of a 4K video received from YouTube at the 5TONIC residential domain. The video was delivered through the base station and the customer premises equipment prototypes, being uninterruptedly played out and with an appropriate user experience. The traffic pattern is similar to the one shown in the previous section, although not identical, since both experiments were conducted at distant moments in time, using different videos.

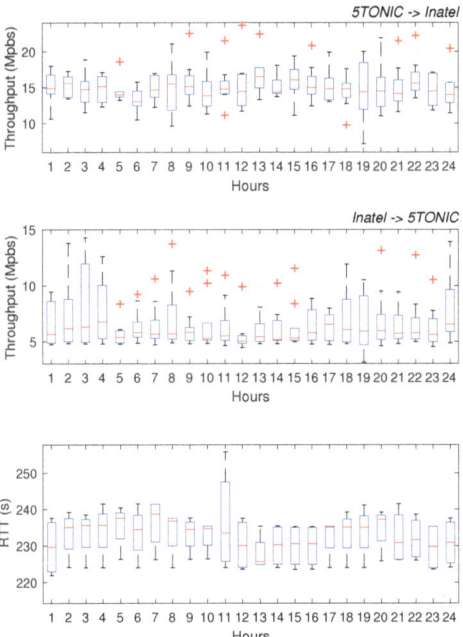

Figure 8. Transoceanic network path performance between 5TONIC and Inatel.

5. Conclusions and Future Work

This article presents an experience report after building a use case practical scenario to trial 5G network technologies for remote areas. The scenario was created using an existing NFV testbed that supports the flexible incorporation of network domains, this way easing integrating activities. Our experience suggests that the use of distributed network domains has the potential to reduce implementation and test cycles, providing realistic and moderately complex scenarios to stakeholders, who may test new developments along with other assets available at the different domains. In addition, it facilitates joint demonstration activities, as any remote domain can easily be redeployed at a central location (i.e., 5TONIC in case of the 5G-RANGE project) using the same security credentials. The design and development of the different parts of the experiment have been done remotely and later integrated together. This is possible thanks to the use of a VPN established from each site towards the 5TONIC laboratory, which holds the 5Gcore functionality, allowing the integration of the different network domains. This procedure facilitates the preliminary validation analyses to enable a fast and straightforward real integration procedure. Also, in this article, we have proved with commodity equipment that both (i) to comply with 3GPP/5G standards, and (ii) to use the VPN as an integration and deployment tool, does not limit the system performance.

Our future work will explore the potential of the 5G-RANGE testbed to develop experimentation scenarios for other innovative use cases in remote areas. In addition, we will work on the evolution of the testbed, considering new releases of its software base (i.e., OSM and OpenStack), as well as emergent open-source virtualization technologies for resource-constrained mobile nodes (e.g., Kubernetes and fog05).

Author Contributions: Conceptualization, V.S.-A., I.V., F.V., B.N., L.L.M., W.D.D. and A.C.F.; methodology, V.S.-A., I.V., F.V., B.N., L.L.M., W.D.D. and A.C.F.; software, V.S.-A., B.N., W.D.D. and A.C.F.; validation, V.S.-A., I.V., F.V., B.N., L.L.M., W.D.D. and A.C.F.; formal analysis, V.S.-A., I.V., F.V., B.N., L.L.M., W.D.D. and A.C.F.; investigation, V.S.-A., I.V., F.V., B.N., L.L.M., W.D.D. and A.C.F.;

resources, I.V., F.V. and L.L.M.; writing—original draft preparation, V.S.-A., I.V., F.V., L.L.M. and W.D.D.; writing—review and editing, V.S.-A., I.V. and F.V.; visualization, V.S.-A., I.V. and F.V.; supervision, I.V., F.V., L.L.M.; project administration, F.V. and L.L.M.; funding acquisition, F.V. and L.L.M.; All authors have read and agreed to the published version of the manuscript.

Funding: This article has been partially supported by the H2020 5G-RANGE project (grant agreement 777137), the TRUE5G project funded by the Spanish National Research Agency (PID2019-108713RB-C52/AEI/10.13039/501100011033), and CNPq Brazil (grant 305085/2018-2).

Data Availability Statement: Not applicable.

Acknowledgments: The authors wish to thank Luis F. Gonzalez for his assistance and support during the integration process at 5TONIC.

Conflicts of Interest: The authors declare no conflict of interest.

Abbreviations

The following abbreviations are used in this manuscript:

5G	Fifth generation of cellular network technology
3GPP	3rd Generation Partnership Project
eMMBB	enhanced Mobile Broadband
URLLC	Ultra-Reliable Low Latency Communications
mMTC	massive Machine Type Communications
MAC	Medium Access Control
5TONIC	5G Telefonica Open Network Innovation Centre laboratory
SUAV	Small Unmanned Aerial Vehicle
QAM	Quadrature Amplitude Modulation
MIMO	Multiple-Input Multiple-Output
NFV	Network Functions Virtualization
VNF	Virtual Network Function
MANO	Management and Orchestration
OSM	Open-Source MANO
VPN	Virtual Private Network
CPE	Customer Premises Equipment
SIP	Session Initiation Protocol
IPsec	Internet Protocol security
GRE	Generic Routing Encapsulation

References

1. 3rd Generation Partnership Project. System Architecture for the 5G System; Stage 2. Technical Specification Group Services and System Aspects, 3GPP Technical Specification 23.501, Version 16.2.0. 2019. Available online: https://www.etsi.org/deliver/etsi_ts/123500_123599/123501/15.03.00_60/ts_123501v150300p.pdf (accessed on 5 March 2021).
2. Ghosh, A.; Maeder, A.; Baker, M.; Chandramouli, D. 5G evolution: A view on 5G cellular technology beyond 3GPP release 15. *IEEE Access* **2019**, *7*, 127639–127651. [CrossRef]
3. Soldani, D.; Guo, Y.J.; Barani, B.; Mogensen, P.; Chih-Lin, I.; Das, S.K. 5G for ultra-reliable low-latency communications. *IEEE Netw.* **2018**, *32*, 6–7. [CrossRef]
4. Pan, Q.; Wen, X.; Lu, Z.; Jing, W.; Li, L. Cluster-Based Group Paging for Massive Machine Type Communications Under 5G Networks. *IEEE Access* **2018**, *6*, 64891–64904. [CrossRef]
5. Hoglund, A.; Van, D.P.; Tirronen, T.; Liberg, O.; Sui, Y.; Yavuz, E.A. 3GPP release 15 early data transmission. *IEEE Commun. Stand. Mag.* **2018**, *2*, 90–96. [CrossRef]
6. Inoue, T. 5G NR Release 16 and Millimeter Wave Integrated Access and Backhaul. In Proceedings of the 2020 IEEE Radio and Wireless Symposium (RWS), San Antonio, TX, USA, 26–29 January 2020; pp. 56–59.
7. Flynn, K. A Global Partnership, Release 17. 2020. Available online: https://www.3gpp.org/release-17 (accessed on 5 March 2021).
8. Union, I.T. UN Broadband Commission Sets Global Broadband Targets to Bring Online the World's 3.8 Billion not Connected to the Internet. 2020. Available online: https://www.itu.int/en/mediacentre/Pages/2018-PR01.aspx (accessed on 5 March 2021).
9. 5GPPP. KPIs. 2020. Available online: https://5g-ppp.eu/kpis/ (accessed on 5 March 2021).
10. Kalogiros, C.; Zois, G.; Darzanos, G.; Hallingby, H.K.; Lønsethagen, H.; Weiss, M.B.; Gavras, A. The potential of 5G experimentation-as-a-service paradigm for operators and vertical industries: The case of 5G-VINNI facility. In Proceedings of the 2019 IEEE 2nd 5G World Forum (5GWF), Dresden, Germany, 30 September–2 October 2019; pp. 347–352.

11. Silva, A.P.; Tranoris, C.; Denazis, S.; Sargento, S.; Pereira, J.; Luís, M.; Moreira, R.; Silva, F.; Vidal, I.; Nogales, B.; et al. 5GinFIRE: An end-to-end open5G vertical network function ecosystem. *Ad Hoc Netw.* **2019**, *93*, 101895. [CrossRef]
12. Li, X.; Garcia-Saavedra, A.; Perez, X.C.; Bernardos, C.J.; Guimaraes, C.; Antevski, K.; Mangues, J.; Baranda, J.; Zeydan, E.; Corujo, D.; et al. 5Growth: An End-to-End Service Platform for Automated Deployment and Management of Vertical Services over 5G Networks. *IEEE Commun. Mag.* **2021**, *1*, 1–2.
13. Guimarães, C.; Oliva Delgado, A.D.L.; Azcorra Saloña, A. 5G-DIVE: Edge Intelligence for Vertical Experimentation 2019. In Proceedings of the Global Experimentation for Future Internet (GEFI) 2019 Workshop, Coimbra, Portugal, 7–8 November 2019.
14. Moggio, F.; Boldi, M.; Canale, S.; Suraci, V.; Casetti, C.; Bernini, G.; Landi, G.; Giaccone, P. 5G EVE a European platform for 5G Application deployment. In Proceedings of the 14th International Workshop on Wireless Network Testbeds, Experimental Evaluation & Characterization, London, UK, 21 September 2020.
15. Ferreira, A.; Mendes, L.; Dias, W.; Marins, T.; Gaspar, D.; Matos, A.; Silva, C.; Sokal, B. 5G-RANGE Project Field Trial. In Proceedings of the 2019 European Conference on Networks and Communications (EuCNC), Valencia, Spain, 18–21 June 2019; pp. 490–494.
16. 5TONIC. The 5TONIC Laboratory. 2020. Available online: https://www.5tonic.org (accessed on 5 March 2021).
17. Vidal, I.; Nogales, B.; Valera, F.; Gonzalez, L.F.; Sanchez-Aguero, V.; Jacob, E.; Cervelló-Pastor, C. A Multi-Site NFV Testbed for Experimentation with SUAV-Based 5G Vertical Services. *IEEE Access* **2020**, *8*, 111522–111535. [CrossRef]
18. Dias, W.; Ferreira, A.; Kagami, R.; Ferreira, J.S.; Silva, D.; Mendes, L. 5G-RANGE: A transceiver for remote areas based on software-defined radio. In Proceedings of the 2020 European Conference on Networks and Communications (EuCNC), Dubrovnik, Croatia, 15–18 June 2020; pp. 100–104.
19. Yan, X.; Qijun, S.; Hongshun, Z.; Lulu, S. Dynamic spectrum allocation based on cognitive radio. In Proceedings of the 2009 5th Asia-Pacific Conference on Environmental Electromagnetics, Xi'an, China, 16–20 September 2009; pp. 254–257.
20. Deepak, G.; Navaie, K.; Ni, Q. Radio resource allocation in collaborative cognitive radio networks based on primary sensing profile. *IEEE Access* **2018**, *6*, 50344–50357. [CrossRef]
21. Akhoundi, F.; Sharifi-Malvajerdi, S.; Poursaeed, O.; Salehi, J.A. Analytical studies of fragmented-spectrum multi-level OFDM-CDMA technique in cognitive radio networks. In Proceedings of the 2016 IEEE 7th Annual Ubiquitous Computing, Electronics & Mobile Communication Conference (UEMCON), New York, NY, USA, 20–22 October 2016; pp. 1–6.
22. Hu, M.; Li, J.; Lv, Y. A comparative study of polar code decoding algorithms. In Proceedings of the 2017 IEEE 3rd Information Technology and Mechatronics Engineering Conference (ITOEC), Chongqing, China, 3–5 October 2017; pp. 1221–1225.
23. Tu, H.H.; Lee, C.W.; Lai, I.W. Low-Complexity Maximum Likelihood (ML) Decoder for Space-Time Block Coded Spatial Permutation Modulation (STBC-SPM). In Proceedings of the 2019 International Symposium on Intelligent Signal Processing and Communication Systems (ISPACS), Taipei, Taiwan, 3–6 December 2019; pp. 1–2.
24. Kalachikov, A.A.; Shelkunov, N.S. Performance evaluation of the detection algorithms for MIMO spatial multiplexing based on analytical wireless MIMO channel models. In Proceedings of the 2018 XIV International Scientific-Technical Conference on Actual Problems of Electronics Instrument Engineering (APEIE), Novosibirsk, Russia, 2–6 October 2018; pp. 180–183.
25. Vartiainen, J.; Karvonen, H.; Matinmikko-Blue, M.; Mendes, L.; Saarnisaari, H.; Matos, A. Energy Detection Based Spectrum Sensing for Rural Area Networks. *EAI Endorsed Trans. Wirel. Spectr.* **2020**, *4*. [CrossRef]
26. Farinacci, D.; Li, T.; Hanks, S.; Meyer, D.; Traina, P. RFC2784: Generic Routing Encapsulation (GRE). 2000. Available online: https://tools.ietf.org/html/rfc2784 (accessed on 5 March 2021).
27. Hoffman, P. Cryptographic suites for IPsec. *RFC 4308 (Propos. Stand.)* **2005**. Available online: https://tools.ietf.org/html/rfc4308 (accessed on 5 March 2021).
28. Nogales, B.; Vidal, I.; Sanchez-Aguero, V.; Valera, F.; Gonzalez, L.F.; Azcorra, A. Automated Deployment of an Internet Protocol Telephony Service on Unmanned Aerial Vehicles Using Network Functions Virtualization. *JoVE (J. Vis. Exp.)* **2019**, e60425. [CrossRef] [PubMed]
29. Sanchez-Aguero, V.; Valera, F.; Vidal, I.; Tipantuña, C.; Hesselbach, X. Energy-Aware Management in Multi-UAV Deployments: Modelling and Strategies. *Sensors* **2020**, *20*, 2791. [CrossRef] [PubMed]
30. 5G-RANGE Repository: Open Source NFV Packages and Descriptors. 2020. Available online: http://vm-images.netcom.it.uc3m.es/5GRANGE/ (accessed on 5 March 2021).
31. Wu, C.; Vyncke, E. Resolve IPv4 Fragmentation, MTU, MSS, and PMTUD Issues with GRE and IPsec. 2019. Available online: https://www.cisco.com/c/en/us/support/docs/ip/generic-routing-encapsulation-gre/25885-pmtud-ipfrag.html (accessed on 5 March 2021).
32. Rosenberg, J.; Schulzrinne, H.; Camarillo, G.; Johnston, A.; Peterson, J.; Sparks, R.; Handley, M.; Schooler, E. RFC3261: SIP: Session Initiation Protocol. 2002. Available online: https://tools.ietf.org/html/rfc3261 (accessed on 5 March 2021).

Article

Validating a 5G-Enabled Neutral Host Framework in City-Wide Deployments

Adriana Fernández-Fernández [1,*], Carlos Colman-Meixner [2], Leonardo Ochoa-Aday [1,†], August Betzler [1], Hamzeh Khalili [1,‡], Muhammad Shuaib Siddiqui [1], Gino Carrozzo [3], Sergi Figuerola [1] and Reza Nejabati [2] and Dimitra Simeonidou [2]

[1] i2CAT Foundation, 08034 Barcelona, Spain; lochoa@redhat.com (L.O.-A.); august.betzler@i2cat.net (A.B.); khalili.hamzeh@gmail.com (H.K.); shuaib.siddiqui@i2cat.net (M.S.S.); sergi.figuerola@i2cat.net (S.F.)
[2] High Performance Networks Group, Smart Internet Laboratory, Faculty of Engineering, University of Bristol, Bristol BS8 1QU, UK; carlos.colmanmeixner@bristol.ac.uk (C.C.-M.); Reza.Nejabati@bristol.ac.uk (R.N.); dimitra.simeonidou@bristol.ac.uk (D.S.)
[3] Nextworks s.r.l., 56122 Pisa, Italy; g.carrozzo@nextworks.it
* Correspondence: adriana.fernandez@i2cat.net
† Current affiliation: Red Hat Inc., 08021 Barcelona, Spain.
‡ Current affiliation: NORMIQ, 08906 Barcelona, Spain.

Citation: Fernández-Fernández, A.; Colman-Meixner, C.; Ochoa-Aday, L.; Betzler, A.; Khalili, H.; Siddiqui, M.S.; Carrozzo, G.; Figuerola, S.; Nejabati, R.; Simeonidou, D. Validating a 5G-Enabled Neutral Host Framework in City-Wide Deployments. *Sensors* **2021**, *21*, 8103. https://doi.org/10.3390/s21238103

Academic Editors: Giuseppe Caso, Özgü Alay, Anna Brunstrom, Harilaos Koumaras, Almudena Díaz Zayas and Valerio Frascolla

Received: 20 October 2021
Accepted: 1 December 2021
Published: 3 December 2021

Publisher's Note: MDPI stays neutral with regard to jurisdictional claims in published maps and institutional affiliations.

Copyright: © 2021 by the authors. Licensee MDPI, Basel, Switzerland. This article is an open access article distributed under the terms and conditions of the Creative Commons Attribution (CC BY) license (https://creativecommons.org/licenses/by/4.0/).

Abstract: Along with the adoption of 5G, the development of neutral host solutions provides a unique opportunity for mobile networks operators to accommodate the needs of emerging use-cases and in the consolidation of new business models. By exploiting the concept of network slicing, as one key enabler in the transition to 5G, infrastructure and service providers can logically split a shared physical network into multiple isolated and customized networks to flexibly address the specific demands of those tenant slices. Motivated by this reality, the H2020 5GCity project proposed a novel 5G-enabled neutral host framework for three European cities: Barcelona (ESP), Bristol (UK), and Lucca (IT). This article revises the main achievements and contributions of the 5GCity project, focusing on the deployment and validation of the proposed framework. The developed neutral host framework encompasses two main parts: the infrastructure and the software platform. A detailed description of the framework implementation, in terms of functional capabilities and practical implications of city-wide deployments, is provided in this article. This work also presents the performance evaluation of the proposed solution during the implementation of real vertical use cases. Obtained results validate the feasibility of the neutral host model and the proposed framework to be deployed in city-wide 5G infrastructures.

Keywords: 5G; NFV; neutral host; network slicing; city-wide deployments; testbed design

1. Introduction

In the apogee of a new digital era, communication technologies and businesses evolved towards 11 billion interconnected devices worldwide, triggering a rapid adoption of online and mobile digital services [1,2]. This reality of continuously increasing traffic poses new challenges in terms of performance and business sustainability. In this context, the fifth-generation (5G) of mobile networks is a promising solution for the needs of an extremely mobile and hyper-connected society [3].

The 5G architecture combines emerging Radio Access Network (RAN) technologies with advances in Software-Defined Networks (SDN) and Network Function Virtualization (NFV) [4]. Such enabling technologies unleash the potential of 5G in terms of service orchestration, infrastructure virtualization, cloud and edge computing, end-to-end network slicing, and mobile communication with higher throughput and lower latency. In this way, 5G copes with performance challenges by supporting a much larger and diverse number of services, including data-intensive and delay-sensitive applications (e.g., immersive reality, industry 4.0, smart city) [5]. However, 5G still faces challenges in the integration and deployment of such enablers, as well as in the evaluation of business feasibility and sustainability.

Enabled by the introduction of network slicing in 5G [6], the neutral host model is changing the whole telecommunication business ecosystem by transforming the traditional market to be more pervasive and open to new opportunities for infrastructure and service providers [7]. Under the neutral host model, infrastructure and service providers can find new ways to monetize their services and share the cost of infrastructure upgrade (capital expenditure (CAPEX)) and ensure a quick return of investments (ROI) and business sustainability [8].

Several private and public initiatives are supporting research and innovation projects to deal with challenges for 5G technology realization (5G Public Private Partnership (5G PPP) in Europe [9] and the International Mobile Telecommunication 2020 (IMT2020) at International Telecommunication Union (ITU) [10]. However, few projects in the ecosystem are focused on infrastructure sharing and business changes to improve, integrate, and demonstrate 5G neutral hosting capabilities in a hyper-connected city infrastructure with real use cases. Hence, as part of 5GPPP and European Commission (EC) Horizon 2020 (H2020) initiatives, the 5GCity project [11] focused on the design, development, deployment, and validation of a novel 5G-enabled neutral host framework for real-world deployments in three European cities: Barcelona (ESP), Bristol (UK), and Lucca (IT).

In this article, we refer to the term 5G-enabled neutral host framework to define a system capable of dynamically managing and orchestrating a virtualized network infrastructure to allocate 5G services with disparate requirements for multiple relevant stakeholders. The 5G-enabled neutral host framework provides multitenancy to a city-wide deployment by realizing and combining enhancements of 5G enabling technologies required by the neutral host model. This article revises the main achievements and contributions of the 5GCity project, focusing on the deployment and validation of the proposed 5G-enabled neutral host framework in the three aforementioned cities. The developed neutral host framework consists of a software platform for slicing and orchestrating computing and network resources from a 5G-enabled cloud, edge, and radio infrastructure. A detailed description of the framework implementation, in terms of functional capabilities and practical implications in city-wide deployments, is described in this work. In addition, this paper presents the validation of the proposed neutral host framework in city-wide deployments and provides the obtained results of measuring several Key Performance Indicators (KPIs) with real smart-city and media use cases.

The remainder of this article is organized as follows. Section 2 provides some background related to the neutral host model and enabling technologies for network slicing such as cloud/edge orchestration and RAN virtualization. Section 3 details the overall framework design of the proposed neutral host platform and architecture. Then, in Section 4, we describe the city-wide deployment of the proposed framework for each one of three considered city pilots (Barcelona, Bristol, and Lucca). Section 5 outlines the envisioned workflow for use case deployments using the developed neutral host platform. Following that, the framework validation and obtained results in terms of several KPIs are discussed in Section 6. Finally, Section 7 concludes this article.

2. Background on Neutral Host Concept and Enabling Technologies

The 5G technology is increasing network convergence, flexibility, and mobile broadband capacity in response to the growth in number and diversity of consumers, industries, and service demands in society [2,12]. However, without network infrastructure sharing [13,14], deployments of 5G networks in dense environments will not be feasible and sustainable because it will require hundreds of isolated access networks, which is unrealistic.

A neutral and sliceable 5G infrastructure is a promising solution for network infrastructure sharing challenges [10,15]. From a user's point of view, the system behavior and services using the resources of a neutral host should be available without user intervention and, ideally, these should be seamless and identical to those provided by their hosted clients' dedicated resources. This concept was around for some time, but within 5G ecosystems it cannot exploit its full potential due to:

- An increasing need for enhanced and ubiquitous connectivity in urban context coupled with more demanding requirements of radio coverage and bandwidth.
- The pivotal role within 5G of smart cities, in which municipalities may act as potential 5G neutral host providers.
- A neutral host framework is a perfect candidate to fully satisfy the 5G requirements for different use cases (e.g., eMBB, URLLC, mMTC) concurrently deployed over a shared infrastructure.

The neutral host model has an important business dimension focused on the creation of new Service Level Agreements (SLAs) categories to rule the interactions between the host and content/service providers [16,17]. A key enabler of the neutral host model is a flexible and automated network slice allocation allowing programmability of policies according to the created SLAs, while enforcing dynamic up/down scaling decisions of infrastructure resources, assigned to service providers. As such, a tenant uses the neutral host framework to establish end-to-end segmented slices, representing partitions of the network, storage, and computing resources. In turn, those slices are leased to service providers to operate allocated resources for the mapping of their services.

Indeed, a neutral host framework provides automated or dynamic multi-tenancy by combining a wide range of well-known technical enablers via end-to-end network slicing. While network slicing is not new in the academia and industry community, the 5G technology and the neutral host model are revitalizing the interest from the community by extending it to the next level [18].

The Next Generation Mobile Networks (NGMN) [15] redefines the classical network slicing of a single virtual network (e.g., Layer 2 (L2) Virtual Local Area Networks (VLANs) [19], Layer 2 and Layer 3 (L2–L3) Virtual Private Networks (VPNs) [20]) to an end-to-end network slicing formed by several virtual networks mapped across cloud, edge, and RAN infrastructures. Later, the 3rd Generation Partnership Project (3GPP) with its standard [21] and the European Telecommunications Standards Institute (ETSI) NFV division with its standard [16] extended the NGMN definition of network slicing as a set of Network Services (NSs) interconnected by VLANs representing slices (or resource segments) from multiple infrastructures.

Overall, end-to-end network slicing in 5G requires an NFV Management and Orchestration (MANO) solution to deploy Virtual Network Functions (VNFs) on cloud/edge resources and a virtualized RAN solution to slice and control the radio resources [22].

2.1. Cloud/Edge Computing and Orchestration

A Multi-Access Edge Computing (MEC) network architecture uses edge resources to enable cloud computing capabilities and IT service environments at the edge of the cellular network [23]. As a result, this environment is characterized by applications running close to the User Equipment (UE).

The neutral host model leverages multiple MEC deployments to fully cope with 5G requirements in terms of bandwidth, coverage, and latency. Indeed, distributed edge resources allow neutral host frameworks to deploy end-to-end services across distributed pools of edge resources, enforcing ultra-low latency and high bandwidth, while real-time access to radio network information can be leveraged by applications.

A MEC architecture poses some real challenges for the design of end-to-end services, mainly since the resources locally offered can be limited, thus highlighting the need for tightly centralized orchestration, which can dynamically operate the life-cycle of edge computing applications [17,24].

End-to-end network slicing, over the distributed cloud and edge resources for enhanced computing and processing capabilities, requires extensions or a new NFV MANO framework to support multitier orchestration, covering also different edges (e.g., extended edge). As such, multitier orchestration in network slicing is getting attention from industry and academia [23].

Among well-known NFV MANO solutions only Open Source MANO (OSM) [25], an ETSI-compliant and hosted project, and SONATA [26] are capable of network slicing lifecycle management. As a result, our platform leverages ETSI OSM as the NFV MANO solution [27]. Moreover, to provide pervasive neutral host services our framework goes beyond the edge to the extended edge by deploying a multitier NFV Orchestrator (NFVO) module [28,29] (cf. Section 3).

2.2. Virtualized Multiradio Access Network

The Cloud Radio Access Network (C-RAN) concept [30] defines the splitting and virtualization of cellular building blocks by placing Layer 1 (L1) functions close to the antennas and virtualized functions from upper layers integrated with NFV and SDN (i.e., Software Defined Radio (SDR)) architectures. In this context, projects such as Open-RAN [31], O-RAN Alliance [32], and NG-RAN architecture [33] are focusing on the splitting and virtualization of radio functions to integrate with SDN and NFV platforms for slicing.

Targeted for 5G framework and strictly coupled with edge architectures, the virtualized RAN (vRAN) approach empowers the neutral host scenario with the capability of sharing the radio access part, by slicing its resources in multiple tenants, each one operated by a different Mobile Virtual Network Operator (MVNO). Moreover, given the high flexibility of the neutral host framework, different sharing and architecture models (i.e., Multioperator Radio Access Network (MORAN) and Multioperator Core Network (MOCN)) can be realized, thus providing a wide range of deployment solutions.

For neutral host and 5G deployments, network slicing between Multiradio Access Technologies (Multi-RAT) will be essential. Hence, efforts from industry and academia are focusing on the integration of Long Term Evolution (LTE) and 5G New Radio (5GNR) technologies with various slicing approaches [34] (e.g., assigning shares of the available airtime to different clients) from different wireless technologies (e.g., Li-Fi, Wi-Fi 6).

To integrate multiple RAN technologies in the envisioned network slicing, a RAN controller is essential to slice, allocate, and monitor radio resources (in similar ways that the Virtual Infrastructure Manager (VIM) does with computing resources). A recently proposed SODALITE framework integrates back-haul traffic from Wi-Fi and 4G/5G in dense small cell networks [35]. Then, two well-known RAN controller platforms are the flexRAN [36] built on open-source LTE stack with OpenAirInterface [37] and EmPOWER [38] which adds Wi-Fi and Long Range (LoRa) radio technologies to LTE. Our neutral host framework goes beyond a novel RAN controller supporting LTE and Wi-Fi by adding capabilities to multiple RAN controllers from multiple vendors and radio technologies [39] (cf. Section 3).

2.3. Our Contribution

Some other relevant 5GPPP projects that also deal with expanding network slicing functionalities are 5G SESAME [40], 5G ESSENCE [41], and SLICENET [42]. In particular, 5G SESAME and 5G ESSENCE focused more on the integration of RAN virtualization and slicing with SDN and NFVO architectures, while SLICENET focused on a platform for E2E network slicing beyond 5G technology. Compared to the aforementioned approaches, our neutral host framework innovates in the integration and extension of 5G enablers developed by academia and industry to demonstrate network slicing in real city-wide deployments. This materializes with the introduction of novel functional entities to the proposed architecture (cf. Section 3) (e.g., Multitier Orchestrator; Multi-RAT RAN Controller) that enhance the system capabilities to better handle multiple technologies for neutral host deployments that meet 5G services requirements.

In addition to the complexity associated with the integration and demonstration of all the technologies mentioned above, implementing a neutral host solution becomes even more challenging when considering real-world city scenarios. In this regard, the infrastructure planning and deployment phases play a fundamental role in achieving the potential added values of the system in operational conditions. While the feasibility of city-driven neutral host deployments was acknowledged from the study of business model perspective in previous works [43–45], there is a lack of literature validating the practical implementation of such deployments. The main contributions of this work are precisely oriented to close this gap regarding the deployment and validation of 5G-enabled neutral host frameworks in the real world. To the best of our knowledge, this paper is the first to describe a comprehensive deployment and validation of a 5G-enabled neutral host framework in three different city-wide deployments.

3. Overview of Neutral Host Framework

In short, the 5G-enabled neutral host framework allows tenants to create and consume slices using a set of virtualized resources over a common infrastructure. The conceived framework, presented in Figure 1, is split vertically across three layers: Service/Application layer; Orchestration & Control layer; and Infrastructure layer.

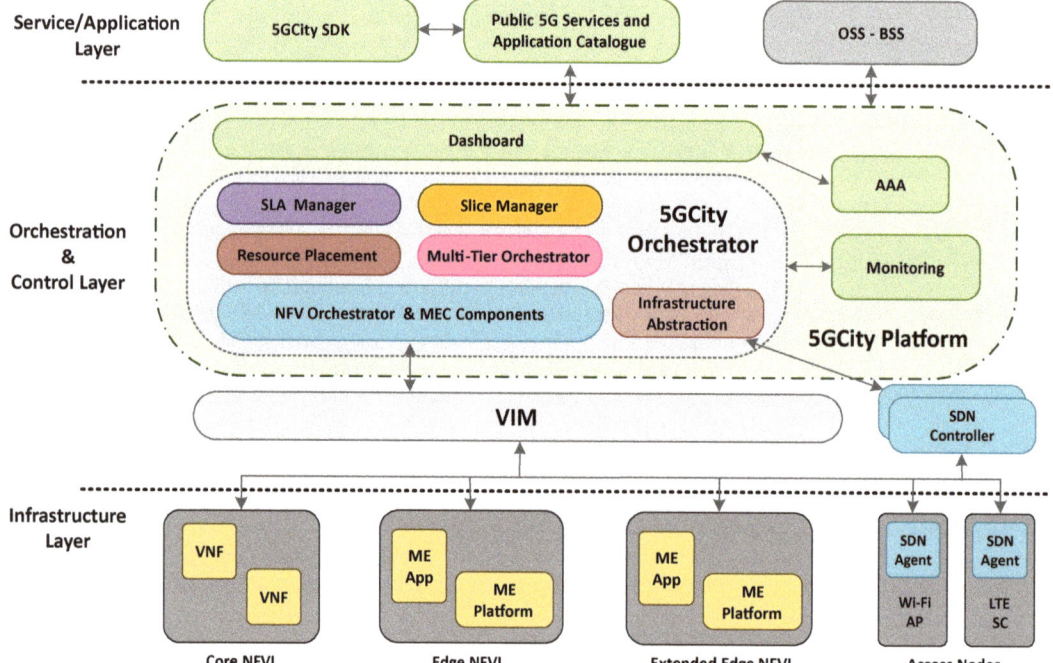

Figure 1. Neutral host framework.

3.1. Service/Application Layer

In the Application layer, a set of tools oriented to facilitate service design and composition is available for service providers, tenants, and any related third party. In particular, the innovative nature of the neutral host framework is further enhanced at the service layer with a *Software Development Kit* (*SDK*) for network functions developers and service providers to combine new and pre-existing functions for new service deployments. Likewise, a *5G Service & Apps Catalogue* is also provided to store network services previously created and published. This component is also responsible for the onboarding of functions and services into the NFVO.

3.2. Orchestration & Control Layer

The Orchestration & Control layer is the logical core of our neutral host framework [27] composed of multiple functional blocks for control, management, and orchestration across its 3-tier architecture. A *Dashboard* with a Graphical User Interface (GUI) and a component for *Authentication, Authorization, and Accounting (AAA)* are placed at the northbound side, to facilitate the interaction between infrastructure owners and tenants and to enforce the required security and billing. Network slices of different tenants are properly separated for security reasons, and the full isolation of information and data is preserved.

The *Slice Manager* has a central role in the platform, especially in the provision of the required logic for dynamic creation and management of slices. Each slice is defined as a collection of logical network partitions or chunks, combined with the network services deployed on top of them [46]. Apart from managing the registration of infrastructure resources and the creation and removal of chunks and slices, the *Slice Manager* performs several automated tasks seamlessly, to:

- Activate deployed slices by launching required servers (i.e., mobile core for serving cellular network slices and DHCP servers for IP assignment of Wi-Fi slices), together with the corresponding configuration of radio access chunks.
- Perform required postinstantiation configurations to deploy VNFs, in terms of enabling external connectivity, registering tasks and alerts for monitoring purposes (in the *Monitoring* component), and DNS deployments.
- React to triggered alerts to conduct the corresponding actions (as established by the *SLA Manager* [47]), such as horizontal scaling of specific VNFs.

To compute the optimal allocation of VNFs to be deployed over a given slice, a *Resource Placement* component is also provided. In essence, this component determines the most suitable VNF-to-compute-chunk mapping by taking into consideration the service requirements and the resources usage.

The orchestration capabilities of the presented platform are extended to support NFV/MEC integration following the ETSI MEC specification [24] by complementing the NFVO with MEC components that handle Mobile Edge (ME) applications [28]. In particular, the MEC Application Orchestrator (MEAO) enables the definition and management of ME platforms, applications, and services running on different mobile edge hosts. Likewise, the ME Platform components not only manage the MEC services but also handle the notifications when there are changes in the management of a given ME application or service. Hence, the *Multitier Orchestrator* component [29] is included to provide an abstracted view in front of multiple underlying orchestrators.

Additionally, this platform also enables virtual RAN slicing and RAN function virtualization for 5GNR, LTE, and Wi-Fi. To do so, *SDN-based RAN controllers* are placed beneath the aforementioned components to manage the radio components and enforce many of the required actions. To support multiple underlying RAN controllers and technologies, the *Infrastructure Abstraction* module is located as an intermediate component between the *Slice Manager* and the underlying SDN controllers.

3.3. Infrastructure Layer

The Infrastructure layer contains the resources in terms of computing, network, and radio components managed by the neutral host. This layer is graphically divided into several Network Functions Virtualization Infrastructure (NFVI) sections and access nodes to identify the distributed compute and radio architecture conceived for municipalities and infrastructure owners acting as 5G neutral host providers. Moreover, this framework is also aligned with 5G performance requirements by providing edge computing capabilities. This will result in real-time access to radio network information, thereby unlocking the potential of advanced future applications.

4. City-Wide Deployments

Following the architecture presented in Section 3, the proposed neutral host framework was deployed in the cities of Barcelona, Bristol, and Lucca. In this section, we describe the deployment of the proposed framework in each one of three considered city pilots. A logical view of the three infrastructure deployments is depicted in Figure 2.

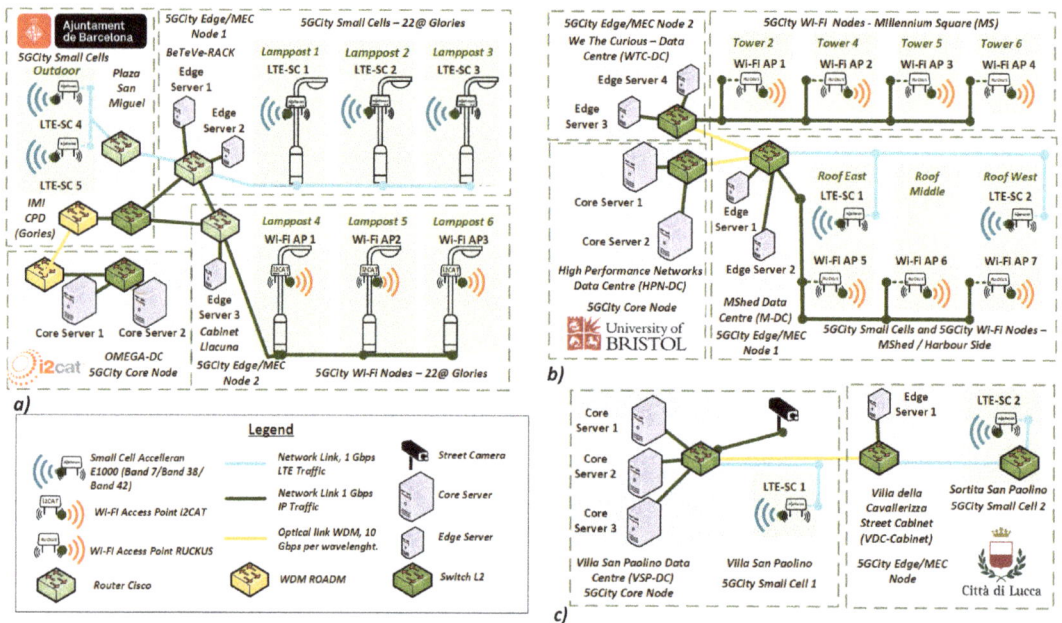

Figure 2. Infrastructure design for (**a**) Barcelona, (**b**) Bristol and (**c**) Lucca.

The general methodology followed for deploying the proposed neutral host framework consisted of the following sequential phases in every city pilot:

(i) Infrastructure Deployment: the conceived three-tier architecture, including a RAN tier, an edge tier, which can be further extended to be closer to end-users, and a core Data Center (DC) tier, is mapped into physical infrastructure resources consisting of radio components, edge/MEC servers, and DC servers;

(ii) Infrastructure Setup Validation: to verify the correct installation and performance of the deployed infrastructure in the three cities, a similar set of validation tests was conducted. The main objective of these tests was to verify performance and better profile configurations in the three pilot environments;

(iii) Platform Installation: deployed servers at edge and DC sites in every city provide computing resources to host the different components of the software platform of the neutral host framework. In general, each software module of the platform is installed as a Virtual Machine (VM) in the virtualized computing infrastructure and interconnected to allow the required interaction among them;

(iv) Platform Setup Validation: the validation of the deployed platform consisted of a set of functional tests aimed at verifying the correct integration of the various orchestration elements, as well as the execution of lifecycle management operations for infrastructure resources, slices, and network services.

Next, we first detail the infrastructure components deployed per testbed. Then, we describe the platform implementation, which is a common factor for the three city pilots.

4.1. Infrastructure Deployment in the City of Barcelona

The neutral host infrastructure deployed in Barcelona comprises three city areas: (i) the core node hosted in *OMEGA-DC* at i2CAT Foundation; (ii) the edge computing nodes and on-street RAN deployed in the super square *22@ area (Glòries)*; (iii) an additional RAN deployed within the city hall (*Plaza Sant Miquel*), located in the *Barrio Gòtico* district. This third location added value to the media use cases by providing connectivity in the most central and lively area of the city with the potential to cover major public events. The resulting physical deployment of the neutral host infrastructure interconnecting the three city areas of Barcelona is presented in Figure 3a.

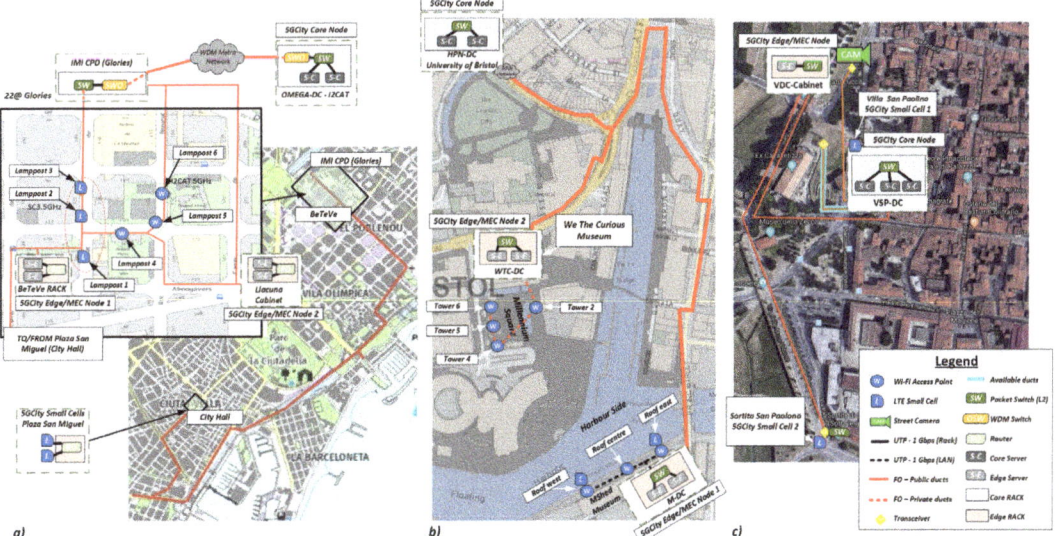

Figure 3. Infrastructure deployed in (**a**) Barcelona, (**b**) Bristol and (**c**) Lucca.

4.1.1. Core Tier

The core DC in Barcelona infrastructure is deployed in the *OMEGA-DC* at i2CAT. This DC hosts two compute servers providing the core NFVI. The fiber infrastructure connects this location to the on-street components deployed in the *22@ area* and the city hall using L2/L3 network devices. To add resilience, two end-to-end fiber connections of 10 Gbps were deployed. Each fiber provides end-to-end redundancy in case of interruptions.

4.1.2. Edge/MEC Tier

The edge/MEC nodes in Barcelona are installed in two locations within the *22@ area*. The primary location is in BeTeVé premises, hosting two edge servers, which act as edge NFVI. The second edge/MEC node is deployed in a street cabinet at the crossing of the *Llacuna* and *Pere IV* streets, where an edge server provides the extended edge NFVI. These two edge locations are equipped with dedicated L2/L3 routers (Cisco ASR920) to connect the edge computing nodes with the core DC located at i2CAT. Likewise, as shown in Figure 3a, the edge/MEC locations are connected to the RAN elements in *22@ area* and the city hall using a dedicated fiber.

4.1.3. RAN Tier

The RAN equipment in the *22@ area* is mounted on six lampposts with their own energy supply and 1 Gbps fiber connection. Three of them are equipped with LTE small cells (Accelleran E1010), whereas the other three lampposts are equipped with Wi-Fi nodes (i2CAT custom hardware). The RAN equipment in the city hall consists of two LTE small cells installed next to the *Salo de Cent* room covering city council meetings and public events. The small cells deployed in Barcelona use Band 42 and follow the TDD config mode 2 on 20 MHz, providing a maximum of 90 Mbps Down-Link (DL) and 10 Mbps Up-Link (UL).

4.2. Infrastructure Deployment in the City of Bristol

The neutral host infrastructure deployed in Bristol extends the 5GUK test network [48] by implementing a larger radio coverage and including a new site at the *MShed Museum*. This new location enables a wider experimentation area covering the harbour part on the other side of the *Avon* river. The overall connectivity and main infrastructure locations of the Bristol pilot deployment are depicted in Figure 3b.

4.2.1. Core Tier

The core DC of Bristol infrastructure is deployed at the University of Bristol High-Performance Network Group Data Centre (HPN-DC). More in detail, this DC hosts two compute servers configured as core NFVI, which are interconnected via fiber to the other two pilot locations in *We-The-Curious* (WTC-DC) and *MShed Museum* (M-DC).

4.2.2. Edge/MEC Tier

In Bristol, the edge/MEC nodes are deployed in two locations: the *We-The-Curious* (WTC-DC) and the *MShed Museum* (M-DC). In both locations, standard rack servers and edge-format servers are installed, which are configured to act as edge NFVI. Both locations are interconnected with the core DC and corresponding RAN devices.

4.2.3. RAN Tier

For the RAN in Bristol, a total of four towers in the *Millennium Square* are used, each one equipped with a dedicated Wi-Fi node (Ruckus T710) to provide coverage to the square and the close surrounding areas, down to the harbourside area. Additionally, the *MShed Museum* location hosts two small cells (Accelleran E1000 series) and three Wi-Fi nodes (Ruckus T710) at East Roof, Middle Roof, and West Roof, respectively. The location of each node can be corroborated in Figure 3b. Similar to Barcelona, the small cells deployed in Bristol use Band 42 and follow the TDD config mode 2 on 20 MHz with a maximum throughput of 90 Mbps in DL and 10 Mbps in UL.

4.3. Infrastructure Deployment in the City of Lucca

The deployment of the neutral host infrastructure in Lucca was conceived to take into account the very specific historical characteristics of the city (historic walls and pathways on top) and the most appropriate target areas for demonstrations and validations of the use cases planned for Lucca. For this reason, the infrastructure deployment in Lucca has privileged green areas and squares close to the historical wall with pathways, since public events typically occur there. An overview of the physical deployment of the neutral host infrastructure in the Lucca pilot is presented in Figure 3c.

4.3.1. Core Tier

The core DC in Lucca is deployed in *Villa San Paolino* (VSP-DC) hosting three compute servers, one for orchestration and interconnection services (VPN concentrator), whereas the two others act as core NFVI to host the workload from the various use cases. The three servers are interconnected with the edge cabinet and an outdoor CCTV IP camera (required for one of the use cases deployed in this city pilot) via a fiber network. One of the compute servers includes a GPU for video analytic.

4.3.2. Edge/MEC Tier

The edge/MEC node deployed at *Villa della Cavallerizza* is hosted in a street cabinet, which is connected via a fiber link to the core DC in VSP-DC. One compute node is installed in the cabinet, which is used as edge NFVI. In the same cabinet, one L2 switching device interconnects the edge server with the small cell in *Sortita San Paolino* and the core DC.

4.3.3. RAN Tier

In Lucca, the RAN infrastructure is composed of two small cells (Accelleran E1013), which are deployed in two different locations around the city (i.e., *Villa San Paolino* and *Sortita San Paolino*). In this case, the deployed small cells use Band 38 and are configured to follow the TDD config mode 1 on 15 MHz, providing a maximum of 55 Mbps DL and 13 Mbps UL.

4.4. Deployment of the Neutral Host Platform

A meticulous planning of computing resources and network connectivity design was required to properly instantiate all the components of the neutral host platform in the three city pilots, following its latest release [49]. For the sake of illustration, Figure 4 represents the mapping of the platform components with respect to the infrastructure deployed in each city. In general, each software module of the platform is deployed as a VM placed in the compute nodes of the core and edge NFVI.

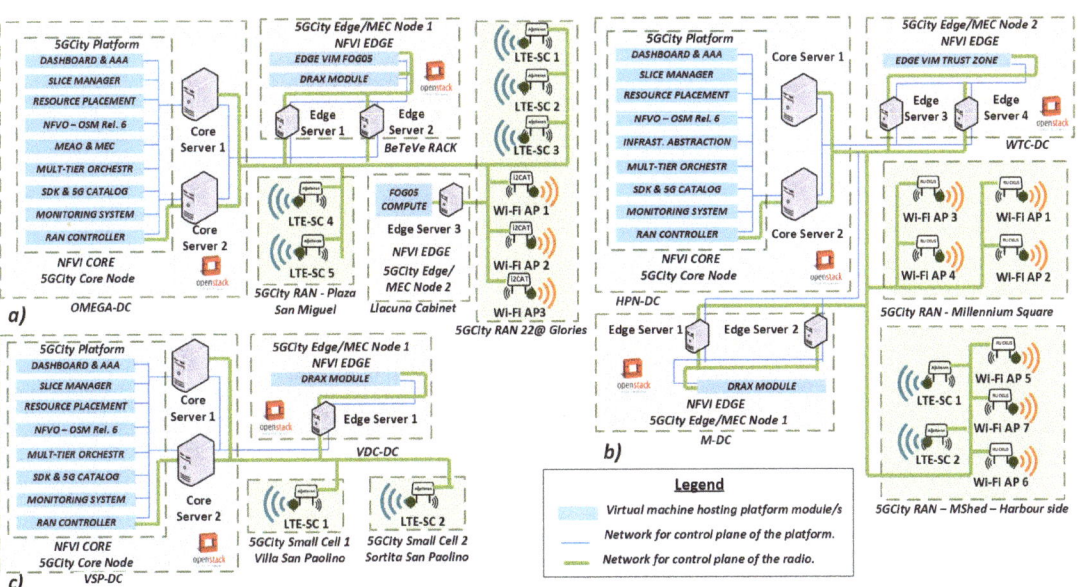

Figure 4. Platform deployed in (**a**) Barcelona, (**b**) Bristol and (**c**) Lucca.

Below, we provide a brief description of the main technologies that enable the deployment of the neutral host platform:

- The VIM was implemented in the core and edge DCs using OpenStack (release Queens). This cloud platform is currently the most widely deployed open-source cloud infrastructure software in the industry.
- Additionally, to support the deployment of NSs based on containers, we also installed Fog05 [50] as the extended edge VIM of the platform. This open-source project enables the deployment of services in resource-constrained devices, which are close to end-users, thus minimizing the service latency.
- To orchestrate the lifecycle of NSs within the 5G-enabled slices, we deployed OSM as the NFVO of the platform.

- Finally, as part of the vRAN capabilities offered by the neutral host framework, we also deployed the dRAX Open Interface RAN Intelligence [51] solution. This cloud-native component runs virtualized in the edge/MEC infrastructure to manage the associated small cells as radio units, which effectively unlocks the potential of 5G network slices for multitenant operators. All this while ensuring low latency and processing at the edge for deployed radio services.

The rest of the components that integrate the neutral host platform (as described in Section 3), were developed as open-source software and released in the GitHub space of the 5GCity project [52].

4.4.1. Automated Deployment

An automated approach was followed to efficiently deploy the platform components in the city-wide pilots. Deployment tasks were divided into two categories, namely Day 0 and Day 1 configurations.

- *Day 0 Configurations:* The tasks automated in this group were related to the creation of VMs for each of the platform components. To this end, we used Terraform [53], a cloud-agnostic management tool that provides a flexible way to define the computing and networking requirements of platform components as a blueprint that can be deployed at any moment.
- *Day 1 Configurations:* Once the VMs are instantiated on the cloud infrastructure, the following task to address is related to the code installation and configuration. This was accomplished using Ansible [54], which has proven to be very efficient to configure, deploy, and orchestrate the code of each platform component.

The aforementioned automated deployment approach allows us to properly replicate the deployment across multiple instances of the platform. In this way, the platform deployment was efficiently conducted saving efforts and time by significantly reducing the probability of error-prone operations.

4.4.2. Platform Deployment Validation

Given the importance of ensuring the proper deployment and functionality of the conceived platform, multiple validation tests were executed. In general, tests were designed taking into account the components involved, the defined interactions, as well as the expected results. Therefore, two groups of tests were conducted:

- *Individual tests:* All elements of the platform were individually tested after accomplishing the deployment of each component to corroborate their functionality. These tests validated the attainment of the expected behavior of every developed module and feature.
- *Integration tests:* To verify the proper interaction between components of the platform, specific integration tests were performed. Particularly, the performance of these tests validated the entire workflow involved in the lifecycle automation of a neutral host framework, in terms of infrastructure (registration, configuration, and removal), slices (creation, activation, and removal), and services (onboarding, instantiation, and removal).

5. Use Cases Deployment

The deployment of use cases over the proposed neutral host framework follows a common workflow. In general, tenants access and interact with the framework via the platform Dashboard. The following subsections describe the operations performed by tenants using the platform to deploy different vertical use cases, as described in [55]. For illustrative purposes in this section, we refer to the deployment of a media vertical use case for real-time video acquisition and production at the edge.

5.1. VNF and NS Composition and On-Boarding

At first, users create the virtualized functions and services to be instantiated, through the following steps:

- The platform administrator acting as neutral host provider creates a dedicated repository and user account for the media vertical tenant. The referred user is granted the role of Designer, which allows tenants to design functions as well as compose them into services.
- In turn, the media vertical tenant, using the platform SDK, conducts the creation of the required functions and composes an NS for the application.
- Once the service creation is completed, the resulting function and service descriptors are published into the 5G Apps & Services Catalogue of the platform.

5.2. Slice Creation and Activation

Next, a customized and dedicated slice is created. In particular, each slice is conceived as a collection of compute, network and radio chunks, as logical and isolated partitions over the common infrastructure. To perform this step, the media vertical tenant composes an end-to-end slice by selecting the desired compute, network and radio infrastructure resources and specifying the requirements to be allocated into the slice. The slice creation request is then processed by the Slice Manager, which interacts with other platform components (i.e., OpenStack, as VIM; OSM, as NFVO; and the RAN Controller, as radio devices manager) to create the required chunks at each network segment.

Following the slice creation, the next step is its activation. Essentially, as the considered media vertical use case requires cellular access for the final users to consume the media application via smartphones attached to the slice, the activation step consists of the instantiation of an open-source mobile core server [56] together with the required configurations of the radio access nodes included in the slice. These configurations include setting the Public Land Mobile Network ID (PLMNID) that is assigned to that slice. Similarly, when Wi-Fi nodes are part of the wireless chunk of the slice, a DHCP server is automatically deployed by the platform as well, to support the service operation in terms of IP addresses allocation.

5.3. Network Service Instantiation

Once the function and services descriptors, as well as the slice, are available, the last step is the instantiation of the virtualized service over the given slice. In this step, the application is deployed in the form of VMs or containers. More in detail, the virtualized functions are placed over the compute chunk of the slice and connected to the network chunk, providing end-to-end connectivity with the access chunk of the slice. The successful instantiation of the network services related to the considered media vertical over the neutral host framework are reported by the platform Dashboard and can be also corroborated by checking underlying systems (such as OSM and OpenStack).

Additionally, to complement the programmability principles of the proposed framework, a DNS server is automatically deployed by the platform to support the service operation in terms of IP addresses and domain names resolution.

6. Validation of Use Cases

In this section, we focus our attention on the performance validation of the proposed neutral host framework. In particular, several slices are created to demonstrate the multi-tenancy as an intrinsic feature of the neutral host model.

6.1. KPIs and Measurement Methodology

The conducted experimental trials enable the measurement of relevant KPIs, which reflect the service requirements and contribute to validating the benefits of the proposed framework. The definition and measurement methodology are described next for each one of the considered KPIs.

6.1.1. User Experienced Data Rate

The minimum data rate required to ensure a sufficient quality experience (without considering broadcast services) [5]. In this evaluation, the measurement of this KPI is done at the application server, by monitoring the throughput achieved by a single UE that generates traffic towards the server.

6.1.2. Data Plane Delay

The time required to transfer a given piece of information between two nodes, measured from the moment it is transmitted by the source to the moment it is successfully received at the destination. This metric was evaluated by computing half of the round trip time experienced between a UE and a remote server.

In particular, in the scope of the proposed framework, this performance was improved by enabling a more suitable allocation of remote servers closer to the end-user, i.e., at the edge to reduce network latency.

6.1.3. Slice Deployment Time (SDT)

The overall time required to deliver an active slice over the neutral host infrastructure. In essence, the SDT refers to the time required for the creation and activation of an end-to-end network slice, including the creation and configuration of all the virtual components that are entailed in the slice. This metric takes into account the execution of two main steps in the neutral host platform workflow: the slice creation and activation (see Section 5.2).

- Slice Creation Time (SCT): refers to the amount of time it takes the Slice Manager to return the results of a submitted slice creation request to an end-user. This operation includes the sequential creation of all the chunks belonging to the slice and the grouping of those chunks. This time is measured from the moment when the creation request of a slice is sent to the Slice Manager, until receiving the confirmation that the slice was created.
- Slice Activation Time (SAT): refers to the amount of time it takes the Slice Manager to return the results of a submitted slice activation request to an end-user. This operation includes the instantiation of the mobile core and the configuration of the corresponding PLMNID in the RAN nodes included in the slice. This time is measured from the moment that the request is sent to the Slice Manager, until receiving the confirmation that the slice is ready to be used. Such confirmation is provided after receiving the acknowledgement from OpenStack about the mobile core instantiation and from the RAN Controller regarding the radio nodes configuration. Note that still additional seconds might be required to complete both operations as well as to finalize the Day1 configurations on the mobile core (based on cloud-init).

Henceforth, in the scope of the proposed framework, the SDT can be computed according to the following equation:

$$SDT = SCT + SAT \qquad (1)$$

To compute this KPI, a custom Python script was developed to automate the slice deployment, time measurement and slice removal by sending the required REST API calls to the platform Slice Manager. This script measures and stores the times involved in each operation in a database, simulating user requests (like the ones done via the Dashboard).

6.1.4. Service Instantiation Time (SIT)

The time required for the provisioning and deployment of an NS over a given slice. This operation includes three main actions, namely:

- Set up of the networking in OpenStack required to connect each VNF included in the NS with the Monitoring component;
- Computation of the VNFs allocation (i.e., VNF-to-compute-chunk mapping) according to the algorithm employed by the Resource Placement component;

- Deployment and configuration of the NS instance through OSM as NFVO.

In essence, the SIT is measured from the instant when the instantiation request of an NS is sent to the Slice Manager, until the moment when the service instantiation is completed, i.e., when all the virtual components that are entailed in the service descriptor are active and running. Since in the proposed framework OSM is used as NFVO, the indication of a successful deployment is triggered when the service instance in OSM appears as running (operational status) and configured (configuration status).

As with the SDT, to compute this KPI, a custom Python script was used to automate the service instantiation over a given slice by sending the required REST API calls to the Slice Manager. For this test, all the required descriptors are available in the platform Catalogue and onboarded to OSM. Likewise, all the required images are already available in OpenStack, therefore only the instantiation time is considered without including the descriptors creation and onboarding processes.

6.1.5. Service Scaling Time (SST)

The time required to launch an additional instance of a specific VNF contained in a given NS. This operation is requested via the platform Dashboard as a particular case of reaction in the face of an alarm triggering event. Once a reaction request for a given NS is launched, the rule associated with that event for horizontal scaling (i.e., scale-out/in) is retrieved and the corresponding scaling request is consequently delegated to OSM (manually triggered approach).

In particular, the SST is measured from the instant when the reaction request of an NS is sent to the Slice Manager, until the moment when the new instance is running. As with the SIT, a scaling request is successfully completed upon the appearance of the running indicator as operational status in OSM. The time required by the Monitoring component for anomaly detection and alarm triggering is not contemplated by this metric.

As with the previous two metrics, this KPI is measured via a custom Python script that automates the service scaling operation by sending the required REST API calls to the Slice Manager. After completing this action, the script also performs the service and slice removal to leave the system in the original state before repeating the entire sequence (i.e., slice deployment; service instantiation; service scaling; service removal; slice removal). Multiple iterations of this deployment lifecycle are conducted to obtain meaningful results.

6.2. Results Analysis

To demonstrate the benefits of the proposed framework, we deploy three slices over the neutral host infrastructure and measure the required SDT as expressed in Equation (1). The composition of such slices consists of one compute chunk, one network chunk and one radio chunk with radio nodes to provide cellular access to the end-users. Additionally, we deploy an NS with a "moderate" level of complexity (composed of four VNFs and two VLs) over such slices and, afterwards, we scale out one of the involved VNFs. The corresponding time performance results, averaged over 30 iterations, appear in Figure 5 considering each one of the involved operations over the three city pilots.

In Figure 5, we can appreciate that, in the considered scenarios, the slice deployment takes on average less than 37 s. For the sake of completeness, the associated SCT and SAT values are also included in the figure to better illustrate the impact of both operations on the resulting SDT. Meanwhile, the instantiation of the four VNFs composing the considered service is completed in around 84, 96, and 123 s over the Barcelona, Bristol and Lucca pilots, respectively. In terms of scaling, average SSTs of less than 45 s are also observed.

Although obtained results in most of the cases are very well aligned with the expected KPI outcomes, some differences in performance are observed when comparing the three city testbeds. In particular, higher SDT, SIT, and SST are experienced in the Lucca pilot, which is mainly due to the smaller capabilities of the servers deployed in that city. Nevertheless, observed differences between the three pilots are not significant, and in overall, this analysis demonstrates the good performance, in terms of deployment times, of the proposed neutral host solution to be deployed in city-wide 5G infrastructures.

To evaluate the impact of using the proposed framework for service orchestration, we compare the obtained results for SIT and SST considering as baseline the standalone use of OSM to perform the instantiation and scaling operations. Figures 6 and 7 illustrate the performed comparison at a more granular level by depicting each one of the 30 iterations considered in this evaluation, over the Barcelona testbed. The motivation behind this analysis is to quantify the time overhead incurred by the proposed platform during the instantiation (Figure 6) and scaling (Figure 7) actions that are not directly introduced by the underlying NFVO.

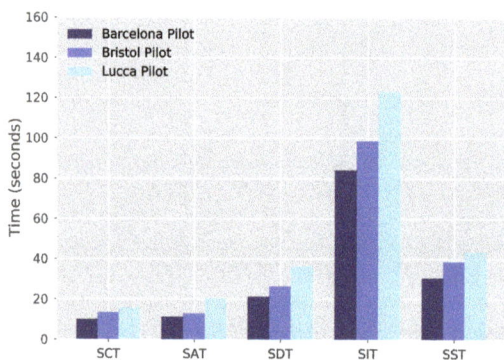

Figure 5. Deployment times of neutral host platform.

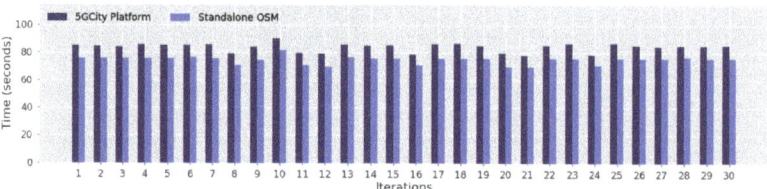

Figure 6. Time overhead against standalone OSM for Service Instantiation Time.

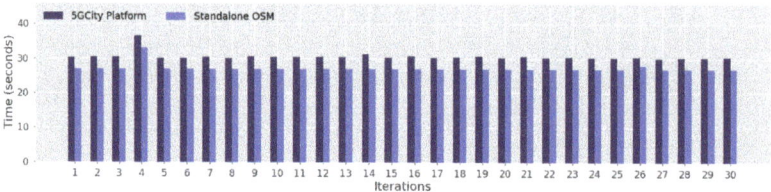

Figure 7. Time overhead against standalone OSM for Service Scaling Time.

Figure 6 shows that the overhead in terms of SIT remains acceptable, with values around 10 s in the performed evaluation. This overhead is due to the time required by the two first tasks listed before during the definition of the SIT KPI (i.e., networking setup and placement computation, see Section 6.1.4), which are performed by the proposed platform before conducting the third task, which directly corresponds to the service instantiation executed through OSM.

Likewise, Figure 7 evidences low overhead values in terms of SST, which are around 3 additional seconds. In this case, the observed overhead is a result of the automated reaction management that is done by the Slice Manager to retrieve the associated information (such as scaling type and identifier of the involved VNF) that is needed to handle this request, before actually conducting the service scaling via OSM.

Summing up, Table 1 compiles the average results obtained for each one of the five KPIs considered in this evaluation during the trials conducted in the three city pilots.

Table 1. KPI measurements.

KPI	Barcelona	Bristol	Lucca
User Experienced Data Rate	44.7 Mbps	45.5 Mbps	44.7 Mbps
Data Plane Delay	9.85 ms	8.5 ms	8 ms
Slice Deployment Time	21.35 s	26.53 s	36.72 s
Service Instantiation Time	84.04 s	98.63 s	123.09 s
Service Scaling Time	30.59 s	38.74 s	43.68 s

In addition to the previously discussed results in terms of SDT, SIT, and SST, the User Experienced Data Rate and Data Plane Delay measurements are also outlined in this table.

Regarding the User Experienced Data Rate, measured values report the cumulative DL throughput achieved by end-users in the considered multitenant scenario with three concurrent active slices, sampled every second during a period of 60 s. As for the Data Plane Delay, values included in Table 1 were measured against a remote server located in the edge computing hosts of each testbed. Therefore, obtained results show the network latency incurred between user equipment and edge computing instances, without including the processing time of network functions. These measurements may be impacted by several factors, such as the existing traffic load, distance from radio nodes, and propagation conditions.

Overall, the conducted trials and performed evaluations validate the feasibility of the proposed neutral host framework by demonstrating the correct operation and benefits of its technology components. Furthermore, regarding the slicing and orchestration (main research focus of our solution), related results demonstrate that the developed platform performs well, achieving the 5G PPP programmatic KPI for *Service Creation Times in minutes instead of hours*.

7. Conclusions

Turning a city into a distributed, multitenant and neutral host model-compliant infrastructure demands a comprehensive framework able to support and integrate end-to-end 5G services upon different network technologies. Towards such a goal, this article provides insights into the design and deployment of a three-tier infrastructure and an orchestration platform that enables municipalities and infrastructure providers to create dynamic end-to-end slices composed of both virtualized cloud/edge and network resources and to lease such slices to third party operators/verticals. The developed solution also provides lifecycle management and orchestration of 5G-based edge services, together with the control of the available underlying city-wide infrastructure. Through the execution of use case trials, the benefits of using the neutral host model for deploying, provisioning, and managing vertical services over a virtualized and shared infrastructure was demonstrated. Moreover, obtained results confirm the feasibility of the proposed framework to be deployed as a neutral host solution in city-wide 5G infrastructures.

Our future work will further exploit, in the context of the 5GVictori project, the potential of the 5GUK testbed to develop media vertical demos and experimentation scenarios over common large-scale field trials. In addition, we will work on the evolution of neutral host platform components, such as the Slice Manager and the RAN Controller, to support 5G Non-Standalone (NSA) and SA technologies together with the deployment of slices with distributed mobile core architectures based on the separation of user and control plane functions.

Author Contributions: Conceptualization, A.F.-F., C.C.-M., L.O.-A., A.B., H.K., M.S.S., G.C., S.F., R.N. and D.S.; methodology, A.F.-F., C.C.-M., L.O.-A., A.B., H.K. and M.S.S.; software, A.F.-F. and L.O.-A.; validation, A.F.-F., C.C.-M., L.O.-A. and A.B.; formal analysis, A.F.-F., C.C.-M., L.O.-A., A.B. and H.K.; investigation, A.F.-F., C.C.-M., L.O.-A., A.B. and H.K.; resources, M.S.S., G.C., S.F., R.N. and D.S.; writing—original draft preparation, A.F.-F., C.C.-M., L.O.-A., A.B. and H.K.; writing—review and editing, A.F.-F., C.C.-M., M.S.S., G.C., S.F., R.N. and D.S.; visualization, A.F.-F., C.C.-M. and L.O.-A.; supervision, A.F.-F., C.C.-M., M.S.S. and G.C.; project administration, A.F.-F., C.C.-M., M.S.S., G.C., S.F., R.N. and D.S.; funding acquisition M.S.S., G.C., S.F., R.N. and D.S. All authors have read and agreed to the published version of the manuscript.

Funding: This work was funded by the European Commission through H2020 projects 5GCity (grant agreement No. 761508) and 5G-VICTORI (grant agreement No. 857201), and from the CERCA Programme, Generalitat de Catalunya. The paper solely reflects the views of the authors.

Institutional Review Board Statement: Not applicable.

Informed Consent Statement: Not applicable.

Data Availability Statement: Not applicable.

Acknowledgments: Authors thank the 5GCity Consortium for useful insights to this work.

Conflicts of Interest: The authors declare no conflict of interest. The funders had no role in the design of the study; in the collection, analyses, or interpretation of data; in the writing of the manuscript, or in the decision to publish the results.

Abbreviations

The following abbreviations are used in this manuscript:

3GPP	3rd Generation Partnership Project
5G PPP	5G Public Private Partnership
5GNR	5G New Radio
AAA	Authentication, Authorization, and Accounting
C-RAN	Cloud Radio Access Network
CAPEX	Capital Expenditure
DC	Data Center
DHCP	Dynamic Host Configuration Protocol
DL	Down-Link
DNS	Domain Name System
eMBB	enhanced Mobile Broadband
ETSI	European Telecommunications Standards Institute
EU	European Union
GUI	Graphical User Interface
IMT	International Mobile Telecommunication
ITU	International Telecommunication Union
KPI	Key Performance Indicator
LoRa	Long Range
LTE	Long Term Evolution
MANO	Management and Orchestration
MEAO	MEC Application Orchestrator
MEC	Multi-Access Edge Computing
mMTC	massive Machine Type Communications
MOCN	Multi-Operator Core Network
MORAN	Multi-Operator Radio Access Network
MVNO	Mobile Virtual Network Operator
NFV	Network Function Virtualization
NFVI	Network Functions Virtualization Infrastructure
NFVO	NFV Orchestrator
NGMN	Next GenerationMobile Networks
NS	Network Service
NSA	Non-Standalone

OSM	Open Source MANO
PLMNID	Public Land Mobile Network ID
RAN	Radio Access Network
RAT	Radio Access Technologies
ROI	Return of Investments
SDK	Software Development Kit
SDN	Software-Defined Networks
SDR	Software Defined Radio
SLA	Service Level Agreement
UE	User Equipment
UL	Up-Link
URLLC	Ultra-Reliable Low Latency Communications
vEPC	virtual Evolved Packet Core
VIM	Virtual Infrastructure Manager
VLAN	Virtual Local Area Network
VM	Virtual Machine
VNF	Virtual Network Function
VPN	Virtual Private Network

References

1. Cisco Systems. Cisco Visual Networking Index: Global Mobile Data Traffic Forecast Update, 2016–2021. Available online: https://www.cisco.com/c/en/us/solutions/collateral/service-provider/visual-networking-index-vni/mobile-white-paper-c11-520862.html (accessed on 5 October 2021).
2. Alliance, N. 5G White Paper. Next Generation Mobile Networks 2015. Version 1.0. Available online: https://ngmn.org/wp-content/uploads/NGMN_5G_White_Paper_V1_0.pdf (accessed on 5 October 2021).
3. Gupta, A.; Jha, R.K. A Survey of 5G Network: Architecture and Emerging Technologies. *IEEE Access* **2015**, *3*, 1206–1232. [CrossRef]
4. 5GPP. View on 5G Architecture. 5G Public Private Partnership (5GPPP) Architecture Working Group 2019. Version 3.0. Available online: https://5g-ppp.eu/wp-content/uploads/2019/07/5G-PPP-5G-Architecture-White-Paper_v3.0_PublicConsultation.pdf (accessed on 5 October 2021).
5. 3GPP. *Service Requirements for the 5G System*; Technical Specification (TS) 22.261 Version 17.2.0; 3rd Generation Partnership Project (3GPP): Sophia Antipolis, France, 2020.
6. Ordonez-Lucena, J.; Ameigeiras, P.; Lopez, D.; Ramos-Munoz, J.J.; Lorca, J.; Folgueira, J. Network Slicing for 5G with SDN/NFV: Concepts, Architectures, and Challenges. *IEEE Commun. Mag.* **2017**, *55*, 80–87. [CrossRef]
7. ATIS. *Neutral Host Solutions for Multi-Operator Wireless Coverage in Managed Spaces*; Alliance for Telecommunications Industry Solutions (ATIS): Washington, DC, USA, 2016.
8. Paglierani, P.; Neokosmidis, I.; Rokkas, T.; Meani, C.; Nasr, K.M.; Moessner, K.; Sayyad Khodashenas, P. Techno-economic analysis of 5G immersive media services in cloud-enabled small cell networks: The neutral host business model. *Trans. Emerg. Telecommun. Technol.* **2020**, *31*, e3746. [CrossRef]
9. EU 5G PPP. 5G Vision. The 5G Infrastructure Public Private Partnership: The Next Generation of Communication Networks and Services. Available online: https://5g-ppp.eu/wp-content/uploads/2015/02/5G-Vision-Brochure-v1.pdf (accessed on 5 October 2021).
10. ITU. *IMT Vision—Framework and Overall Objectives of the Future Development of IMT for 2020 and Beyond*; Recommendation ITU-R M.2083-0; International Telecommunication Unit (ITU): Geneva, Switzerland, 2015.
11. H2020 5GCity Project. A Distributed Cloud & Radio Platform for 5G Neutral Hosts. Available online: https://www.5gcity.eu/ (accessed on 5 October 2021).
12. Samdanis, K.; Costa-Perez, X.; Sciancalepore, V. From Network Sharing to Multi-Tenancy: The 5G Network Slice Broker. *IEEE Commun. Mag.* **2016**, *54*, 32–39. [CrossRef]
13. Fernández-Fernández, A.; De Angelis, M.; Giardina, P.G.; Taylor, J.; Chainho, P.; Valero, J.M.J.; Ochoa-Aday, L.; López, D.R.; Carrozzo, G.; Siddiqui, M.S. Multi-Party Collaboration in 5G Networks via DLT-Enabled Marketplaces: A Pragmatic Approach. In Proceedings of the 2021 Joint European Conference on Networks and Communications, 6G Summit (EuCNC/6G Summit), Porto, Portugal, 8–11 June 2021; pp. 550–555. [CrossRef]
14. Theodorou, V.; Lekidis, A.; Bozios, T.; Meth, K.; Fernández-Fernández, A.; Taylor, J.; Diogo, P.; Martins, P.; Behravesh, R. Blockchain-based Zero Touch Service Assurance in Cross-domain Network Slicing. In Proceedings of the 2021 Joint European Conference on Networks and Communications, 6G Summit (EuCNC/6G Summit), Porto, Portugal, 8–11 June 2021; pp. 395–400. [CrossRef]
15. NGMN. *Description of Network Slicing Concept*; Next Generation Mobile Networks (NGMN) Alliance: Frankfurt am Main, Germany, 2016.
16. ETSI. *Network Functions Virtualisation (NFV)—Report on Network Slicing Support with ETSI NFV Architecture Framework, GR NFV-EVE*; Group Report (GR) 012 v3.1.1; European Telecommunications Standards Institute (ETSI): Sophia Antipolis, France, 2017.

17. Taleb, T.; Dutta, S.; Ksentini, A.; Iqbal, M.; Flinck, H. Mobile Edge Computing Potential in Making Cities Smarter. *IEEE Commun. Mag.* **2017**, *55*, 38–43. [CrossRef]
18. Fischer, A.; Botero, J.F.; Beck, M.T.; de Meer, H.; Hesselbach, X. Virtual Network Embedding: A Survey. *IEEE Commun. Surv. Tutor.* **2013**, *15*, 1888–1906. [CrossRef]
19. Rajaravivarma, V. Virtual local area network technology and applications. In Proceedings of the Twenty-Ninth Southeastern Symposium on System Theory, Cookeville, TN, USA, 9–11 March 1997; pp. 49–52.
20. Mazhin, G.A.; Bag-Mohammadi, M.; Ghasemi, M.; Feizi, S. Multi-layer architecture for realization of network virtualization using MPLS technology. *ICT Express* **2017**, *3*, 43–47. [CrossRef]
21. 3GPP. *Study on Management and Orchestration of Network Slicing for Next Generation Network*; Technical Report (TR) 28.80; 3rd Generation Partnership Project (3GPP): Sophia Antipolis, France, 2018.
22. Costa-Perez, X.; Swetina, J.; Guo, T.; Mahindra, R.; Rangarajan, S. Radio access network virtualization for future mobile carrier networks. *IEEE Commun. Mag.* **2013**, *51*, 27–35. [CrossRef]
23. Taleb, T.; Samdanis, K.; Mada, B.; Flinck, H.; Dutta, S.; Sabella, D. On Multi-Access Edge Computing: A Survey of the Emerging 5G Network Edge Cloud Architecture and Orchestration. *IEEE Commun. Surv. Tutor.* **2017**, *19*, 1657–1681. [CrossRef]
24. ETSI. *Mobile Edge Computing (MEC)—Deployment of Mobile Edge Computing in an NFV Environment*; Group Report (GR) 017 V1.1.1; European Telecommunications Standards Institute (ETSI): Sophia Antipolis, France, 2018.
25. OSM. Open Source Mano. Available online: https://osm.etsi.org/ (accessed on 5 October 2021).
26. SONATA Project. SONATA NFV: Agile Service Development and Orchestration in 5G Virtualized Networks. Available online: http://www.sonata-nfv.eu/ (accessed on 5 October 2021).
27. Khalili, H.; Papageorgiou, A.; Siddiqui, S.; Colman-Meixner, C.; Carrozzo, G.; Nejabati, R.; Simeonidou, D. Network Slicing-aware NFV Orchestration for 5G Service Platforms. In Proceedings of the 2019 European Conference on Networks and Communications (EuCNC), Valencia, Spain, 18–21 June 2019; pp. 25–30.
28. Baldoni, G.; Cruschelli, P.; Paolino, M.; Colman-Meixner, C.; Albanese, A.; Papageorgiou, A.; Khalili, H.; Siddiqui, S.; Simeonidou, D. Edge Computing Enhancements in an NFV-based Ecosystem for 5G Neutral Hosts. In Proceedings of the 2018 IEEE Conference on Network Function Virtualization and Software Defined Networks (NFV-SDN), Verona, Italy, 27–29 November 2018; pp. 1–5.
29. Mena, M.P.; Papageorgiou, A.; Ochoa-Aday, L.; Siddiqui, S. Enhancing the Performance of 5G Slicing Operations via Multi-Tier Orchestration. In Proceedings of the 23rd Conference on Innovations in Clouds, Internet and Networks (ICIN 2020), Paris, France, 24–27 February 2020; pp. 1–8.
30. China Mobile. *C-RAN: The Road towards Green RAN*; White Paper; version 2.5; China Mobile Research Institute: Beijing, China, 2011.
31. Yang, M.; Li, Y.; Jin, D.; Su, L.; Ma, S.; Zeng, L. OpenRAN: A Software-Defined Ran Architecture via Virtualization. *SIGCOMM Comput. Commun. Rev.* **2013**, *43*, 549–550. [CrossRef]
32. O-RAN Alliance. O-RAN: Use Cases and Deployment Scenarios. O-RAN Alliance, White Paper 2020. Available online: https://www.o-ran.org/s/O-RAN-Use-Cases-and-Deployment-Scenarios-Whitepaper-February-2020.pdf (accessed on 5 October 2021).
33. Ferrus, R.; Sallent, O.; Perez-Romero, J.; Agusti, R. On 5G Radio Access Network Slicing: Radio Interface Protocol Features and Configuration. *IEEE Commun. Mag.* **2018**, *56*, 184–192. [CrossRef]
34. Dezfouli, B.; Esmaeelzadeh, V.; Sheth, J.; Radi, M. A Review of Software-Defined WLANs: Architectures and Central Control Mechanisms. *IEEE Commun. Surv. Tutor.* **2019**, *21*, 431–463. [CrossRef]
35. Betzler, A.; Camps-Mur, D.; Garcia-Villegas, E.; Demirkol, I.; Aleixendri, J.J. SODALITE: SDN Wireless Backhauling for Dense 4G/5G Small Cell Networks. *IEEE Trans. Netw. Serv. Manag.* **2019**, *16*, 1709–1723. [CrossRef]
36. Foukas, X.; Nikaein, N.; Kassem, M.M.; Marina, M.K.; Kontovasilis, K. FlexRAN: A Flexible and Programmable Platform for Software-Defined Radio Access Networks. In *CoNEXT '16: Proceedings of the 12th International on Conference on Emerging Networking EXperiments and Technologies*; Association for Computing Machinery: New York, NY, USA, 2016; pp. 427–441.
37. Nikaein, N.; Marina, M.K.; Manickam, S.; Dawson, A.; Knopp, R.; Bonnet, C. OpenAirInterface: A Flexible Platform for 5G Research. *SIGCOMM Comput. Commun. Rev.* **2014**, *44*, 33–38. [CrossRef]
38. Coronado, E.; Khan, S.N.; Riggio, R. 5G-EmPOWER: A Software-Defined Networking Platform for 5G Radio Access Networks. *IEEE Trans. Netw. Serv. Manag.* **2019**, *16*, 715–728. [CrossRef]
39. Paolino, M.; Carrozzo, G.; Betzler, A.; Colman-Meixner, C.; Khalili, H.; Siddiqui, S.; Sechkova, T.; Simeonidou, D. Compute and network virtualization at the edge for 5G smart cities neutral host infrastructures. In Proceedings of the 2019 IEEE 2nd 5G World Forum (5GWF), Dresden, Germany, 30 September–2 October 2019; pp. 560–565.
40. Sallent, O.; Perez-Romero, J.; Ferrus, R.; Agusti, R. On Radio Access Network Slicing from a Radio Resource Management Perspective. *IEEE Wirel. Commun.* **2017**, *24*, 166–174. [CrossRef]
41. H2020 5G ESSENCE Project. 5G ESSENCE—Embedded Network Services for 5G Experiences. Available online: https://www.5g-essence-h2020.eu/ (accessed on 5 October 2021).
42. H2020 5G SLICENET Project. 5G SLICENET—End-to-End Cognitive Network Slicing and Slice Management Framework in Virtualised Multi-Domain, Multi-Tenant 5G Networks. Available online: https://slicenet.eu/ (accessed on 5 October 2021).
43. Benseny, J.; Walia, J.; Finley, B.; Hämmäinen, H. Feasibility of the City-driven Neutral Host Operator: The case of Helsinki. In Proceedings of the 30th European Conference of the International Telecommunications Society (ITS): "Towards a Connected and Automated Societ", Helsinki, Finland, 16–19 June 2019.

44. Kibria, M.G.; Villardi, G.P.; Nguyen, K.; Liao, W.; Ishizu, K.; Kojima, F. Shared Spectrum Access Communications: A Neutral Host Micro Operator Approach. *IEEE J. Sel. Areas Commun.* **2017**, *35*, 1741–1753. [CrossRef]
45. Benseny, J.; Walia, J.; Hämmäinen, H.; Salmelin, J. City strategies for a 5G small cell network on light poles. In Proceedings of the 2019 CTTE-FITCE: Smart Cities Information and Communication Technology (CTTE-FITCE), Ghent, Belgium, 25–27 September 2019; pp. 1–6.
46. Papageorgiou, A.; Fernández-Fernández, A.; Siddiqui, S.; Carrozzo, G. On 5G Network Slice Modelling: Service-, Resource-, or Deployment-driven? *Comput. Commun.* **2020**, *149*, 232–240. [CrossRef]
47. Papageorgiou, A.; Fernández-Fernández, A.; Ochoa-Aday, L.; Peláez, M.S.; Siddiqui, M.S. SLA Management Procedures in 5G Slicing-based Systems. In Proceedings of the 2020 European Conference on Networks and Communications (EuCNC), Dubrovnik, Croatia, 15–18 June 2020; pp. 7–11.
48. Smart Internet Lab—University of Bristol, UK. 5GUK Test Network—Bristol. Available online: http://www.bristol.ac.uk/engineering/research/smart/5guk/ (accessed on 5 October 2021).
49. 5GCity Project. D4.4 Final 5GCity Orchestrator Release. 2019. Available online: https://www.5gcity.eu/deliverables/ (accessed on 5 October 2021).
50. Corsaro, A.; Baldoni, G. fogØ5: Unifying the Computing, Networking and Storage Fabrics End-to-End. In Proceedings of the 2018 3rd Cloudification of the Internet of Things (CIoT), Paris, France, 2–4 July 2018; pp. 1–8.
51. Accelleran. DRAX™ Open Interface RAN Intelligence. 2020. Available online: https://www.accelleran.com/5gcitydrax/ (accessed on 5 October 2021).
52. i2CAT Foundation. H2020 5GCity Project. 2020. Available online: https://github.com/5GCity (accessed on 5 October 2021).
53. HashiCorp. Terraform OpenStack Provider. Version 0.12.24. Available online: https://www.terraform.io/docs/providers/openstack/index.htm (accessed on 5 October 2021).
54. Red Hat. Ansible Playbooks. Version 2.9.7. Available online: https://docs.ansible.com/ansible/latest/user_guide/playbooks_intro.html (accessed on 5 October 2021).
55. Colman-Meixner, C.; Khalili, H.; Antoniou, K.; Siddiqui, M.S.; Papageorgiou, A.; Albanese, A.; Cruschelli, P.; Carrozzo, G.; Vignaroli, L.; Ulisses, A.; et al. Deploying a Novel 5G-Enabled Architecture on City Infrastructure for Ultra-High Definition and Immersive Media Production and Broadcasting. *IEEE Trans. Broadcast.* **2019**, *65*, 392–403. [CrossRef]
56. Open5GS. Open Source Project of 5GC and EPC (Release-16). Available online: https://open5gs.org/ (accessed on 5 October 2021).

Article

5G Standalone and 4G Multi-Carrier Network-in-a-Box Using a Software Defined Radio Framework †

Karolis Kiela [1,2], Marijan Jurgo [1,2], Vytautas Macaitis [1,2] and Romualdas Navickas [2,*]

[1] Lime Microsystems, Surrey Tech Centre, Occam Road, The Surrey Research Park, Guildford GU2 7YG, Surrey, UK; k.kiela@limemicro.com (K.K.); m.jurgo@limemicro.com (M.J.); v.macaitis@limemicro.com (V.M.)

[2] Micro and Nanoelectronics Systems Design and Research Laboratory, Vilnius Gediminas Technical University, 10257 Vilnius, Lithuania

* Correspondence: mikronanolab@vgtu.lt or romualdas.navickas@vilniustech.lt; Tel.: +370-699-38963

† This paper is an extension version of the conference paper: Kiela, K.; Jurgo, M.; Navickas, R. Structure of V2X-IoT framework for ITS applications. In Proceedings of the 2020 43rd International Conference on Telecommunications and Signal Processing (TSP), Milan, Italy, 7–9 July 2020.

Citation: Kiela, K.; Jurgo, M.; Macaitis, V.; Navickas, R. 5G Standalone and 4G Multi-Carrier Network-in-a-Box Using a Software Defined Radio Framework. *Sensors* **2021**, *21*, 5653. https://doi.org/10.3390/s21165653

Academic Editors: Giuseppe Caso, Özgü Alay, Anna Brunstrom, Harilaos Koumaras, Almudena Díaz Zayas and Valerio Frascolla

Received: 19 July 2021
Accepted: 21 August 2021
Published: 22 August 2021

Publisher's Note: MDPI stays neutral with regard to jurisdictional claims in published maps and institutional affiliations.

Copyright: © 2021 by the authors. Licensee MDPI, Basel, Switzerland. This article is an open access article distributed under the terms and conditions of the Creative Commons Attribution (CC BY) license (https://creativecommons.org/licenses/by/4.0/).

Abstract: In this work, an open Radio Access Network (RAN), compatible, scalable and highly flexible Software Defined Radio (SDR)-based Remote Radio Head (RRH) framework is proposed and designed. Such framework can be used to implement flexible wideband radio solutions, which can be deployed in any region, have common radio management features, and support various channel bandwidths. Moreover, it enables easier access for researchers to nonsimulated cellular networks, reduce system development time, provide test and measurement capabilities, and support existing and emerging wireless communication technologies. The performance of the proposed SDR framework is validated by creating a Network-in-a-Box (NIB) that can operate in multiband multicarrier 4G or 5G standalone (SA) configurations, with an output power of up to 33 dBm. Measurement results show, that the 4G and 5G NIB can achieve, respectively, up to 883 Mbps and 765 Mbps downlink data transfer speeds for a 100 MHz aggregated bandwidth. However, if six carriers are used in the 4G NIB, 1062 Mbps downlink data transfer speed can be achieved. When single user equipment (UE) is used, maximum uplink data transfer speed is 65.8 Mbps and 92.6 Mbps in case of 4G and 5G, respectively. The average packet latency in case of 5G is up to 45.1% lower than 4G. CPU load by the eNodeB and gNodeB is proportional to occupied bandwidth, but under the same aggregated DL bandwidth conditions, gNodeB load on the CPU is lower. Moreover, if only 1 UE is active, under same aggregated bandwidth conditions, the EPC CPU load is up to four times lower than the 5GC.

Keywords: RAN; RRH; SDR; NIB; 5G; 4G; framework; standalone; multicarrier; aggregation

1. Introduction

1.1. Background

The mobile communication industry has seen a dramatic growth in the last two decades since various social communication and entertainment services shifted to mobile technology-oriented user equipment (UE). While earlier generations of cellular technology (such as 4G) focused on connectivity, 5G expands on this by delivering connected experiences from the cloud to customers [1]. Because 4G is well in the commercial deployment stage, 5G and the future mobile technologies (such as 6G) have become a global research and development topic [2], where low power consumption, massive equipment connectivity, ultra-low latency, security, services, deployment and management cost are key challenges [1,2].

Compared to 4G technology, 5G networks are more software-driven and can utilise new networking principles such as Software-Defined Networking (SDN) architectures, virtualisation, Multi-access Edge Computing (MEC) to achieve dynamic network management and enhanced Mobile Broadband (eMBB) [1–3]. MEC enables SDN and virtualisation technology to flexibly and quickly manage resources, which can be brought from the remote cloud to the wireless edge in the proximity of the UE [4]. MEC in 5G moves the data plane from the cloud as close to the UE as possible, and, as a result, latency, data security, reliability, and stability are improved, and control level of provided services becomes higher [4,5].

As opposed to mobile broadband, current low power, low bandwidth scenarios, namely Internet of Things (IoT), usually use 4G technology-based LTE-M and NB-IoT Low Power Wide Area Network (LPWAN) radio standards. Other common wireless standards used in IoT technologies are Zigbee, LoRaWAN, IEEE 802.11ah (HaLow) and 802.11af (White-Fi) [6]. On the other hand, 5G will be at the core of the emerging IoT revolution, with support for Ultra-Reliable Low Latency Communications (URLLC), massive Machine-Type Communications (mMTC), Device-to-Device (D2D), Machine-to-Machine (M2M) communication [1,2,7]. 5G is also expected to play a major role in Intelligent Transport Systems (ITS), smart city applications, smart industrial software, smart homes, and implementation of many high-end, mission-critical IoT initiatives [1].

Another advantage of 5G is the utilisation of network slicing and open Radio Access Network (RAN) technologies, which can reduce deployment costs of new generation cellular technology due to reuse of the infrastructure, what in turn can also open up new market opportunities [3,8,9]. Open RAN allows to decouple the radio hardware from the radio functionality. The Baseband Unit (BBU) can run in the cloud (cloud RAN or C-RAN) or in a commercial off-the-shelf (COTS) local server (virtual RAN or vRAN), while having a stable, high-speed connection with the Remote Radio Head (RRH). By shifting BBU to the cloud or COTS server, C-RAN and vRAN allow to split the functions of a Radio Access Technology (RAT) between dedicated hardware and software instances [10]. If implementation level of the software communication stack is highest—that is, physical layer 1 (L1) is implemented in BBU—it is possible to have direct access to samples from RRH, which now acts as the radio front-end only. While implementing L1 related functions in RRH could reduce transmission bandwidth between RRH and BBU, this would decrease flexibility in network upgrades and would be less convenient for multicell collaborative signal processing [11].

1.2. Motivation

To achieve the desired flexibility, scalability, and resource reusability inherent in the open RAN technology, RRH hardware must also meet the same criteria. One of the widely developed and promising technologies is a Software Defined Radio (SDR). SDR-based transceivers can be used to implement a flexible wideband radio solutions, which can be deployed in any region, have common radio management features, support various channel bandwidths and can be used as O-RAN compliant white-box hardware [12]. O-RAN, not to be confused with open RAN, refers to the O-RAN Alliance, which is a name for a specification group defining next generation RAN infrastructures. SDR-based RRH usually utilises SDR Radio Frequency (RF) transceivers to transmit and receive data in a wide frequency range, usually implemented as a single integrated circuit (IC) [13]. In addition to the RF transceiver, SDR-based RRHs usually use Field-Programmable Gate Array (FPGA) ICs to implement functionalities of the physical layer using digital signal processing algorithms implemented in an embedded system with the aid of a specific software [14,15].

Just a few years ago, the majority of researchers had no access to actual cellular networks, and even when they did, it was limited to individual network components or functionalities [3]. Now, an ever-increasing number of frameworks and projects of the RAN-oriented software stack are becoming available. On the other hand, availability of the SDR-based RRH frameworks is still limited. In survey [3], the reviewed RAN-oriented software stack to SDR RRH hardware provider ratio was 3.25:1. In another survey [16], the available software versus hardware framework ratio was 2.75:1.

To meet open RAN goals of reducing vendor dependency for RAN hardware, it is necessary not only to develop open RAN and 5G Core (5GC) software, but also to develop SDR-based frameworks, and, on their basis, complete Network-in-a-box (NIB) solutions that reduce system development time, provide test and measurement capabilities, and support existing and emerging wireless communication technologies [6,17].

1.3. Related Work

Related work to our research can be broken into three categories:
1. RAN and NIB related surveys.
2. RAN simulation-based performance evaluation.
3. Performance evaluations of networks using NIB testbeds.

In this subsection, an overview of most prominent works from each category will be presented.

An extensive survey on RAN architectures for 5G mobile networks regarding energy consumption, operations expenditure, resource allocation, spectrum efficiency, system architecture, and network performance is presented in [11]. The paper also investigates key technologies of the 5G systems, such as MEC, SDN, and network slicing; and major 5G RATs such as millimetre wave (mmWave), massive multiple-input and multiple-output (MIMO), D2D, mMTC; and it provides insight into some major research challenges in these fields.

In [3], a survey on open source 5G RAN and 5GC is presented, in which RAN and core network software, virtualisation and management frameworks are analysed. In addition, this survey analyses SDR support for open-source radio units and 5G testbed that can be used to instantiate software-based 5G networks.

Software and hardware tools used in NIB solutions are surveyed in [16]. The paper analyses NIB related works regarding to radio access and backhaul technology, use cases, ease of deployment, edge services, network self-organising features, capacity, and Quality of Service (QoS), hardware implementation approach.

5G RAN performance evaluation can be done in two ways: by using simulators [18,19], or by using testbeds containing all the required hardware and software. In [9], 5G deployment scenarios for Standalone (SA) and Nonstandalone (NSA) are evaluated through coverage, power consumption and handover simulation results. The evaluation is done in the 900–3500 MHz RF frequency range, based on a UE using 100 MHz bandwidth. Based on simulation and analysis results, it is summarised that SA outperforms NSA in terms of UE power consumption, network deployment complexity, and cost.

5G network MEC service simulation for downlink (DL) resource-block occupancy, frame latency at different frame sizes and UE count is presented in [20]. 4G, 5G NSA and 5G SA scenarios are analysed working at 2000 MHz RF frequency range, with a varying number of UEs (up to 40) using 20 MHz bandwidth. The results show, that deploying 5G NSA and especially 5G SA should remove the 4G bottleneck from Quality of Experience (QoE) perspective and add considerable user capacity.

In [21], simulation of vehicle platooning using Cellular Vehicle-to-Everything (C-V2X) and D2D communication is analysed. The results show that D2D allows one to save 73% of DL frequency resources, which results in less energy consumed by the gNodeBs (gNBs).

While 5G performance evaluation using a simulation-based approach is a convenient way to evaluate performance of different services or communications, simulation based results should always be properly validated to ensure that the results obtained with it are credible and match real world deployment scenarios [21]. This requirement cannot always be met, and in certain scenarios it is even not viable. Simulations also do not necessarily consider open RAN solution based on dynamic behaviour of a general-purpose processor (GPP), for example Central Processing Unit's (CPU) resource allocation. Hence, whenever possible, RAN performance evaluation using NIB-based testbeds should be the preferred choice if this option is available.

A GPP-based software defined 4G NIB testbed is presented in [22]. Here, the authors compare different full 4G stack solutions, including OpenAirInterface (OAI), Amarisoft and srsLTE. The testbed uses a 6 core, 3.2 GHz processor to implement a 20 MHz bandwidth, frequency division duplex (FDD), single-input and single-output (SISO) transmission mode (TM). Performance evaluation was done with a DL carrier frequency of 2.660 GHz (Band 7) and achieved a maximum data rate of 70, 70, 30 Mbps in DL and 28, 45, 28 Mbps in uplink (UL) when using respectively OAI, Amarisoft and srsLTE RAN and core software. Ettus B210 SDR and Amarisoft proprietary PCIe SDR was used for eNodeB (eNB) radio front-end. In the presented testbed, Amarisoft software performed best in respect to CPU utilisation, maximum radio link throughput and stability over time, and delay. It should be noted that both RAN and core software used separate GPPs.

A 5G NSA and 4G NIB solution using an open-source software stack based on OpenAirInterface (OAI) is presented in [8]. eNB/gNB and Evolved Packet Core (EPC) software is executed on two separate GPPs, while eNB and gNB front ends are based on Ettus B210 (SDR). 5G NSA implementation uses 40 MHz bandwidth and achieves a maximum DL data rate of 30.7 Mbps when operating at Band 78. In 4G mode operating at Band 3 and Band 40 with a bandwidth of 5 and 10 MHz, data speeds of 5.31 and 8.73 Mbps are achieved respectively in DL.

Another 5G NSA and 4G testbed is reported in [23]. It uses Option 3X architecture in a COTS infrastructure with 64 CPUs and 128 GigaByte (GB) Random Access Memory (RAM), where 16 CPUs are actively used for the core network. 5G NSA implementation uses 100 MHz bandwidth and achieves a maximum DL and UL data rate of 885 and 92 Mbps, respectively, when operating at Band 78. In 4G mode operating at Band 3 with a bandwidth of 80 MHz, data speeds of 420 Mbps and 87 Mbps are achieved in DL and UL, respectively.

It should be noted that none of the reviewed NIBs use high-power radio Front End Modules (FEM), so they cannot be used in larger scale testbed evaluation scenarios, for example, network rollouts. Moreover, the reviewed 5G NSA NIB solutions do not specify 5G radio link time division duplex (TDD) and TM configurations, which hinders performance comparison.

Due to limited flexibility of available SDR-based RRH frameworks, available NIB solutions are limited to single band operation in both 4G and 5G. Hence, solutions for expansion of the existing system capacity in existing infrastructure, for example usage of higher-level Carrier aggregation (CA), are not sufficiently explored and compared with 5G technology.

In our previous work [6], we have presented structure of V2X–IoT framework for ITS applications. However, it was mostly theoretical work based on findings from our previous reports. In this work, our previously proposed structure is adapted and an open RAN compatible, scalable and highly flexible SDR-based RRH framework is proposed and designed. The performance of the proposed SDR framework is validated by creating an NIB that can operate in multiband multicarrier 4G or 5G SA configurations. To the best of the authors' knowledge, none of the previous NIB related works provide a bandwidth-to-bandwidth 4G to 5G SA performance evaluation. This article consists of four chapters. In the second chapter, structure of SDR framework is presented. In the third chapter, structure of NIB is presented. In the fourth chapter, NIB performance evaluation results are reported. The final chapter concludes the presentation.

2. Structure of Software Defined Radio Framework

2.1. Structure of the Software Defined Radio Framework Hardware

As was shown in our previous works [6,17], frameworks and/or development kits that are currently available on the market are most suited for applications with a small selection of pre-defined standards. Such frameworks are not flexible enough in situations where there is a need to implement a solution which is based on a new or emerging application/standard. There is a need for a sufficiently flexible framework that can be used to evaluate current and to develop new communication networks or their architectures and concurrently verify them at hardware and software level. Therefore, SDR-based framework hardware structure is proposed whose simplified block diagram is shown in Figure 1.

This structure is described in detail in [6]. The main feature of such framework is the capability to reconfigure software and hardware, what enables the framework to be used in many deployment and verification scenarios. The software flexibility is provided by the FPGA, which can be configured in such a way to accelerate solution verification; i.e., it has reconfigurable hardware solutions for specific functions, such as image processing or filtering.

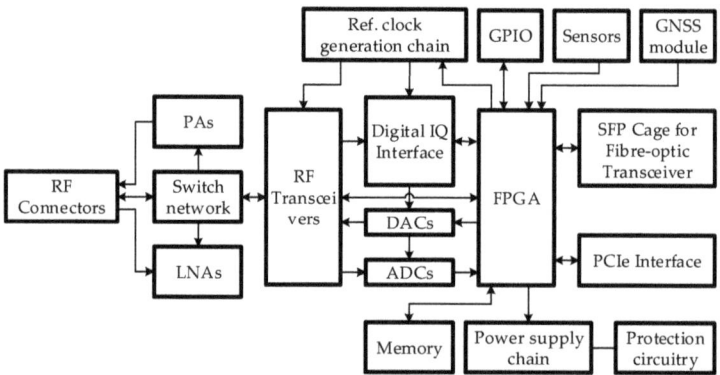

Figure 1. A structure of the proposed SDR framework hardware [6].

The most important function of the FPGA is the transmission and pre-processing of the digital signal to and from the RF transceivers. Analog-to-digital converter (ADC) and the digital-to-analog converter (DAC) are used to convert analog signals to digital and vice-versa. Clock signal generator is used to generate clock frequency for the ADC and DAC. This generator uses a reference clock frequency generation module with a temperature stabilised, voltage-controlled quartz crystal oscillator, all of which are also controlled by the FPGA. The quartz oscillator can be tuned by varying its control voltage. This allows implementing frequency synchronization by using an external or Global Navigation Satellite System (GNSS) module reference signal.

The FPGA is connected using several input/output (I/O) interfaces that are used for firmware programming, control and sending/receiving data: general-purpose I/O (GPIO); SFP cage for fibre-optic transceiver, PCIe interface. Moreover, memory modules, various sensors (temperature, acceleration, humidity, etc.) are connected to the FPGA, which can be employed if SDR framework is used not only in mobile communication equipment, but also for other purposes, such as application in intelligent transport systems (ITS).

GNSS module is used for positioning and tracking. Moreover, it is used for time or frequency synchronisation.

FPGA is also used to manage power supply, which is needed to implement flexible extension of the framework by connecting additional modules with different power supply requirements.

The flexibility of the radio components is implemented through a set of SDR RF transceivers. These transceivers should be broadband and support at least two wireless standards operating in frequency-division duplex simultaneously. The RF transceivers are connected to the reference clock signal generation module, which provides the reference signals needed for the internal high frequency synthesisers. The RF transceivers are coupled with an external band filter module, which allows implementation of specific, or stringent, filtering requirements. High frequency input/output ports of the RF transceivers can be connected to additional transmitter power amplifier (PA) and/or receiver low noise amplifier (LNA). The switching of the high frequency I/O is accomplished by utilising RF switches.

2.2. Structure of the Software Defined Radio Based Framework Software

Software of our proposed framework is also described in [6]. At the highest level of abstraction, a software of the framework is divided into two interconnected blocks as shown in Figure 2a. Processing device software is designed to simplify the management of the framework and can be used to process, visualise (render), send and receive data from the hardware. This part of the program has a graphical user interface, is used to load or update firmware and may be integrated with other software.

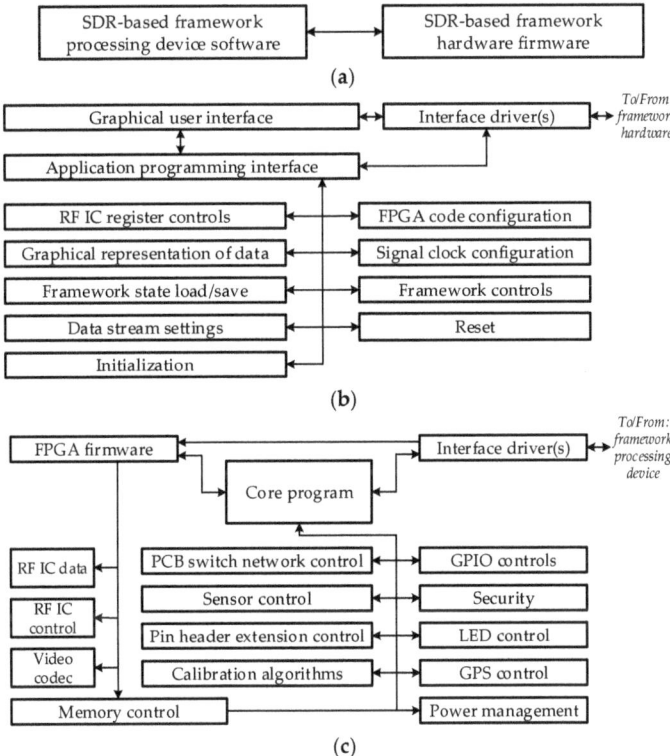

Figure 2. Structure of the software for the software defined radio-based framework [6]: (**a**) highest level of abstraction; (**b**) structure of the processing device software; (**c**) structure of the firmware.

Hardware firmware implements low level of abstraction functions and functions such as digital filtering, interpolation and decimation, signal framing, timestamping, creating, and managing communication settings between the processing device and hardware, and other functions.

Because the hardware of the proposed framework is very versatile, software also has to be platform-independent for simplified integration with other existing systems or systems which are in development, including mobile devices. Structure of the framework processing device software is shown in Figure 2b.

The interface driver(s) are used to establish and maintain a connection between the processing device and hardware. A graphical user interface is used to simplify the control of the framework functions and to display relevant information on the display unit of the processing device. An application programming interface is a part of the lower-level programming code that describes the functions or procedures used in the software of the framework processing device. It is used for integration with other programs or operating systems.

RF IC register controls are used to configure the registers of the RF transceivers and set wanted parameters. Graphical representation of data is used to visualise results of digital processing (measurement) of sent or received signals (data). State load/save function of the framework provides the possibility to boot or save a known configuration and could be used for quick verification, configuration loading, error checking. Data stream settings are used to set parameters of the communication between processing device unit and hardware, while FPGA code configuration is responsible for loading or updating firmware code. Signal clock configuration is used to set and control clock generator for the ADC/DAC and the parameters of the reference clock generation path. The framework controls part is used for general purpose hardware controls (switches, DAC values, etc.), Initialisation—to set the hardware of the framework to default settings and adjust the interface parameters, while Reset block is used to reset the hardware logic.

Firmware is loaded and updated using framework's processing device software. Functionality depends on specific hardware configuration of the framework and can be easily upgraded (introduction of new features) or optimised (cost optimisation).

Structure of the framework's firmware is shown in Figure 2c. As in the case of the processing device software, the interface driver(s) are used to establish and maintain a connection between the processing device and hardware. Core program contains implementation of functions that process digital signals, execute calibration algorithms, and control external hardware devices or extension boards. This piece of code uses a processor (for example, ARM family processor). The segment of the core program can be further subdivided into the smaller code blocks. GPIO controls are used to control general purpose I/O module (direction, data type). The security segment is used for data encryption and secure authentication between different devices. GNSS control is used to configure the global navigation satellite system module, send positioning, time synchronisation, reference pulse signals from it to the processing device or any other hardware. PCB switch network and pin header extension respectively control the analog signal (RF and IF) signal switches and configuration of the extension ports, while sensor control is used to receive sensor information and generate control signals for them. The calibration algorithm of the radio module's transmitter and receiver (DC offset, quadrature imbalance, filter bandwidth, etc.) is implemented in the calibration algorithm's block. Power management code implements management of power circuits and can be used for configuration of various power modes, voltage/current control/limitation, and power-down sequencing of individual systems. Memory control manages memory resources, while LED control provides visual indication of the hardware status.

FPGA firmware code defines its hardware functions (digital interfaces, codecs, etc.). It also implements RF IC data and RF IC control functions, interface configuration, and it can use video codec for data compression and processing.

3. Design of Network-in-a-Box

3.1. Design of Software Defined Radio Framework Hardware

Based on the structure of the proposed SDR framework's hardware presented in Section 2.1, a hardware of SDR-based framework (see Figure 3a) was developed based on Lime Microsystems technology in a single printed circuit board (PCB), with a length of 190 mm and a width of 107 mm. SDR framework uses three LMS7002M field programmable RF (FPRF) transceiver ICs. Two FPRFs are used to enable operation on two separate frequency bands simultaneously, with up to 100 MHz RF channels. The third FPRF IC can be used for spectrum monitoring, test signal generation and implementation of a calibration functionality. It can also be used as a dedicated receive chain to implement digital predistortion (DPD) solutions.

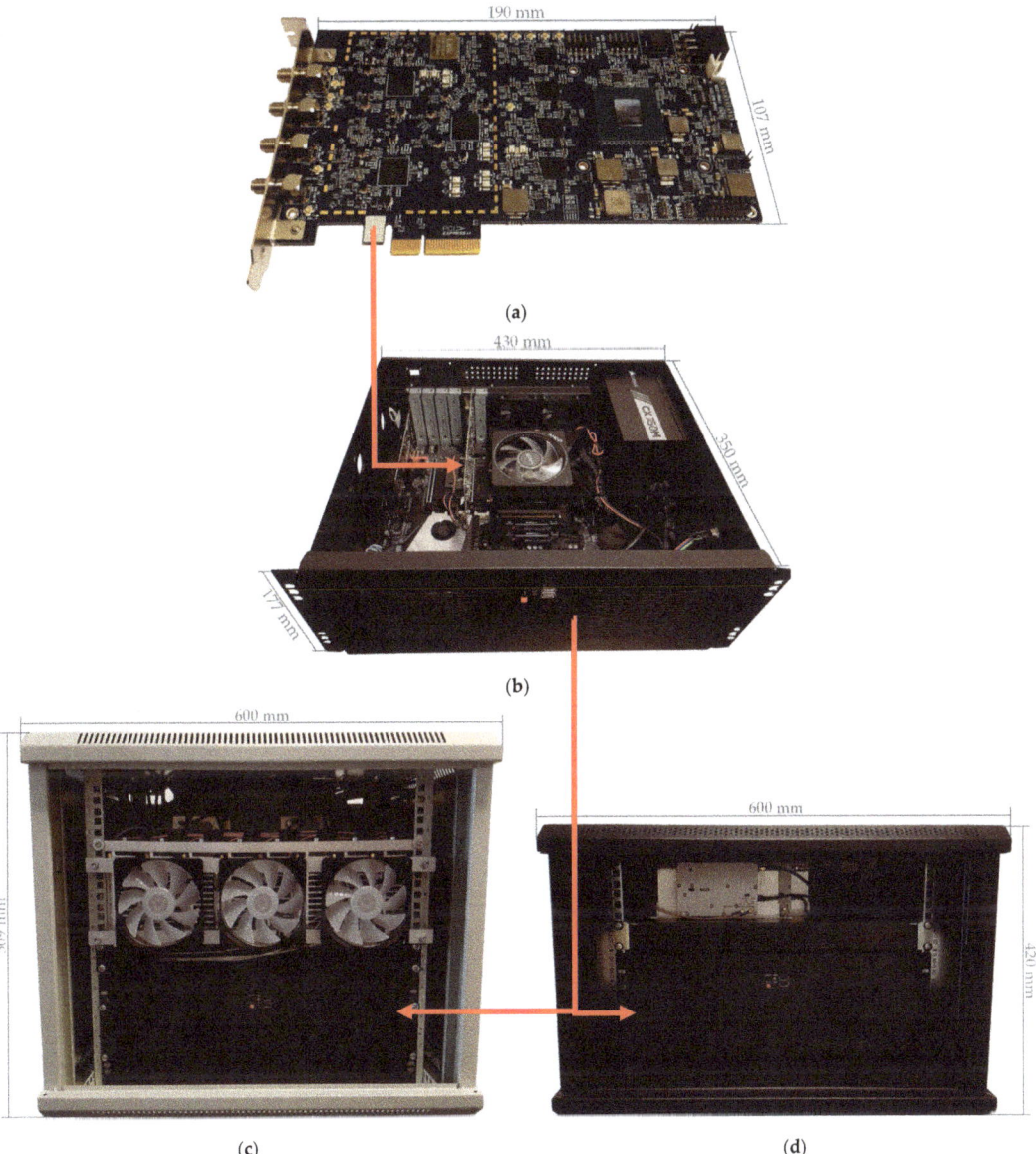

Figure 3. Network-in-a-box (NIB) structure: (**a**) software defined radio framework hardware; (**b**) general purpose processor core; (**c**) complete 4G carrier aggregation NIB (4G-CA) hardware with radio frequency front-end; (**d**) complete 5G standalone NIB (5G-SA) hardware with radio frequency front-end.

Xilinx XC7A200T-2FBG676C FPGA from the Xilinx Artix-7 Family is used in SDR-based framework. Main blocks implemented in the FPGA are as follows:

- MicroBlaze soft microprocessor, which provides periphery controls.
- PCIe IP core, which provides data transfer between external host and FPGA through PCIe Gen2 interface.
- Receive-Transmit block, which is used to transfer IQ sample packets from/to LMS7002M transceiver chip and provide IQ sample synchronisation.

- LMS7002M interface block, which is used to send and receive data to/from LMS7002M IC.
- External ADC and DAC converter blocks, which is used to capture/transmit data from/to external ADCs and DACs.
- Synthesiser block, which provides required clock signals for receive-transmit blocks.

Table 1 provides utilisation of the main FPGA resources—slice look-up tables (LUTs), slice registers, block RAM (BRAM), digital signal processors (DSP).

Table 1. Utilisation of the main FPGA resources.

Resource	Available	Used	Utilisation, %
Slice LUTs	133800	75551	56.47
LUT as Logic	133800	72875	54.47
LUT as Memory	46200	2676	5.79
Slice Registers	267600	48805	18.24
Block RAM	365	117	32.05
DSP	740	122	16.49

3.2. Design of Netowrk-in-a-Box Hardware

The designed NIB can be separated into two modular parts: GPP core and high power FEM. The designed SDR framework is a part of the GPP core in our NIB solution and is used as a highly configurable RF block in the RRH. The SDR framework is connected to the COTS x86 architecture GPP via a PCIe Gen2 interface.

GPP core is shown in Figure 3b. The main components are as follows: AMD Ryzen $3900\times$ processor with base clock equal to 3.8 GHz; 16 GB, 3600 MHz memory; 512 GB solid-state drive; case size is 350 mm $\times$ 430 mm $\times$ 177 mm. Main hardware components of the GPP core are summarized in Table 2.

For performance evaluation, two NIB testbeds with different configurations were used:
1. 4G-CA: configuration supports operation on four different 4G FDD bands (1, 3, 7, 28).
2. 5G-SA: configuration supports operation on one 5G TDD band (78).

The other part of the RRH is the high power FEMs. Both NIB configurations use commercially available off-the-shelf FEMs with same RF specifications (only their count differs) which are presented in Table 3. FEM's maximum modulated output power is 33 dBm, passband ripple—2.5 dB, noise figure ranges from 2 to 3.5 dB, error vector magnitude (EVM) ranges from 1.5 to 2 percent, and peak power consumption is 25 W.

Table 2. Hardware summary of general-purpose processor core of the network-in-a-box.

Computer	Processor	AMD Ryzen $3900\times$, 3.8 GHz
	Memory	2×8 GB, 3600 MHz
	Storage	512 GB SSD
Software Defined Radio Framework	RF transceiver	LMS7002M
	FPGA	XC7A200T-2FBG676C
	MIMO	2×2 per FPRF IC, 4×4 total
	Connectivity	PCIe $\times 4$ (Gen2)

Table 3. Specification of the Front-End Module.

Parameter	Value
Modulated output power, dBm	33
Passband ripple, dB	2.5
Noise figure, dB	2–3.5
Error vector magnitude,%	1.5–2
Peak power consumption, W	25

The 4G-CA NIB is housed in a standard 19-inch, 9U (509 mm × 600 mm × 450 mm) communication rack cabinet with a size of (see Figure 3c). Similarly, the 5G-SA NIB is housed in a lower, standard 19-inch, 7U (420 mm × 600 mm × 450 mm) rack cabinet because of its lower count of FEMs (see Figure 3d). As mentioned earlier, both GPP core and FEMs are modular and can be swapped in and out, upgraded to meet various NIB testbed use case scenarios.

4. Performance Evaluation of the Network-in-a-Box

4.1. Performance Evaluation Environment

Both 4G-CA and 5G-SA NIB configurations use Amarisoft software to implement functionality of the local RAN (eNB and gNB) and network core (EPC and 5GC). For control of the SDR framework, Lime Suite was used, which is an open-source collection of software supporting different hardware platforms and drivers for the FPRF.

4G-CA was configured for FDD operation, using a 20 MHz bandwidth for each carrier for all CA configuration test cases. Six different CA configurations used for 4G-CA NIB performance evaluation are presented in Table 4.

Table 4. Carrier aggregation configurations used during 4G-CA performance evaluation.

Carrier Aggregation Configuration	Number of Carriers	Frequency Band	DL Center Frequency, MHz	Bandwidth, MHz	Total Bandwidth, MHz
3A	1	3	1846	20	20
3C	2	3	1856	20 + 20	40
3C + 7A	3	3	1856	20 + 20	60
		7	2660	20	
3C + 7C	4	3	1856	20 + 20	80
		7	2670	20 + 20	
3C + 7C + 1A	5	3	1856	20 + 20	100
		7	2670	20 + 20	
		1	2160	20	
3C + 7C + 1A + 28A	6	3	1856	20 + 20	120
		7	2670	20 + 20	
		1	2160	20	
		28	775	20	

In all test cases of the performance evaluation, the following common parameters apply for both NIB configurations:

- MIMO channel output power at antenna port is set to 33 dBm.
- The same MIMO omni directional antennas, mounted at a 2 m height, that work from 700 MHz to 3800 MHz with an average gain of 2 dBi were used at all ports.
- UEs were connected over-air, 5 m from the antennas and placed at a height of 1 m.
- 2 transmit (TX) and 1 receive (RX) antennas per band was used for DL and UL, respectively.

Results of the 4G-CA NIB single channel power measurement for CA configuration. 3C + 7C + 1A + 28A are shown in Figure 4. Measured channel power across all bands show a ±1 dBm variation from wanted levels.

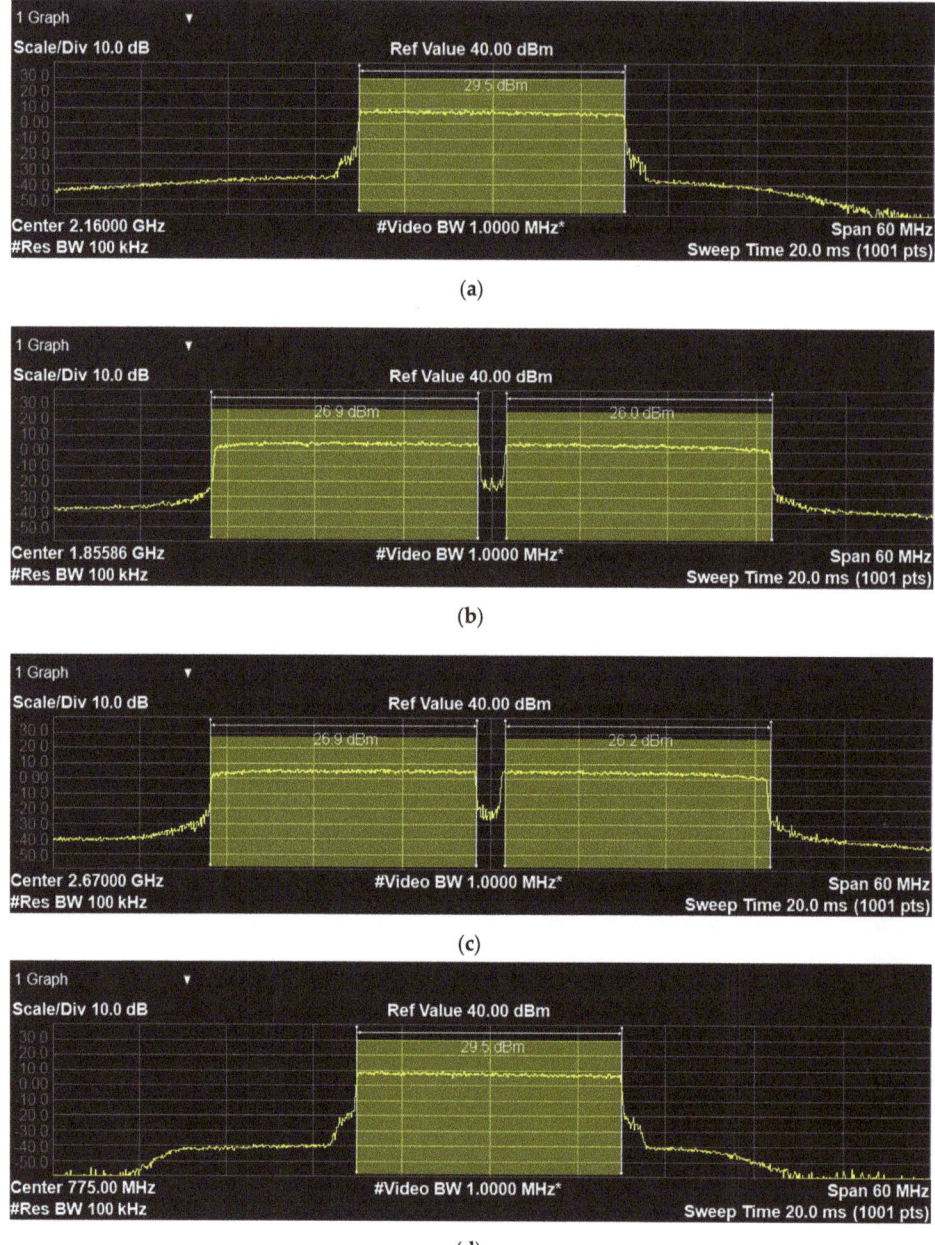

Figure 4. Results of the single channel power measurement for 4G carrier aggregation: (**a**) band 1, 20 MHz bandwidth, single carrier; (**b**) band 3, 40 MHz aggregated bandwidth, two contiguous carriers; (**c**) band 7, 40 MHz aggregated bandwidth, two contiguous carriers; (**d**) band 28, 20 MHz bandwidth, single carrier.

5G-SA was configured for TDD operation, using a 30 kHz subcarrier spacing. For all test cases of the bandwidth configuration, TDD pattern 1 with a 5 ms periodicity was used, having 7 DL and 2 UL slots, and 2 DL/UL symbols. Five bandwidth settings, ranging from 20 MHz to 100 MHz in 20 MHz intervals, were used for 5G-SA NIB performance evaluation.

Result of the 5G-SA NIB single channel power measurement, when configured for 100 MHz bandwidth operation, is shown in Figure 5.

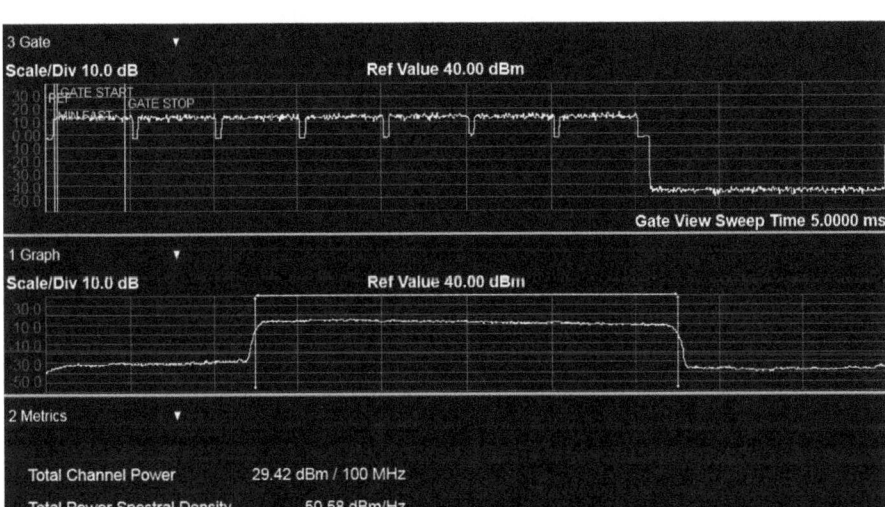

Figure 5. Time-gated spectrum analysis for a time division duplex with a 5 ms transmission periodicity and single-channel power measurement results for 5G standalone operation, band 78, 100 MHz bandwidth.

Two Telit LM960A18 UEs and single Huawei P40 Pro UE were used for 4G-CA and 5G-SA NIB performance evaluation, respectively. A second Telit UE was used for 5 and 6 CA test cases to utilise the full bandwidth of the 4G-CA NIB.

4.2. Data Transfer Speed

Iperf program was used to generate data traffic in both UL and DL directions during measurements of the data transfer speed. Measured 4G-CA transfer speeds are presented in Table 5. Average downlink speed ranges from 189 Mbps to 1023.8 Mbps when number of carriers is changed from 1 to 6. Average uplink speed ranges from 65.8 Mbps to 131.2 Mbps, when number of carriers is changed from 1 to 6. Maximum downlink and uplink speed is 1062 Mbps and 131.6 Mbps, respectively, when six carriers are used. Maximum uplink speed increases twice for 5 and 6 CA test cases due to the usage of a second Telit UE.

Table 5. 4G carrier aggregation transfer speed.

Number of Carriers	Total Bandwidth, MHz	Maximum DL Speed, Mbps	Average DL Speed, Mbps	Maximum UL Speed, Mbps	Average UL Speed, Mbps
1	20	189.0	189.0	65.8	65.8
2	40	373.0	367.3	65.8	65.7
3	60	549.0	543.2	65.8	65.6
4	80	719.0	700.2	65.8	65.1
5	100	883.0	856.6	131.6	131.2
6	120	1062.0	1023.8	131.6	131.2

Measured 5G-SA transfer speeds are presented in Table 6. Average downlink speed ranges from 145.3 Mbps to 755.6 Mbps when bandwidth is changed from 20 MHz to 100 MHz. Average uplink speed ranges from 15 Mbps to 91.5 Mbps, when bandwidth is changed from 20 MHz to 100 MHz. Maximum downlink and uplink speed is respectively 765 Mbps and 92.6 Mbps, when 100 MHz bandwidth is set.

Table 6. 5G standalone transfer speed.

Bandwidth, MHz	Maximum DL Speed, Mbps	Average DL Speed, Mbps	Maximum UL Speed, Mbps	Average UL Speed, Mbps
20	146.0	145.3	15.3	15.0
40	310.0	306.6	34.3	34.1
60	476.0	472.2	53.5	53.1
80	636.0	633.0	69.3	68.7
100	762.0	755.6	92.6	91.5

Figure 6 shows the uplink constellation diagram with a 0% packet error rate for the both 4G-CA and 5G-SA, when both NIBs are operating at a total aggregated bandwidth of 100 MHz.

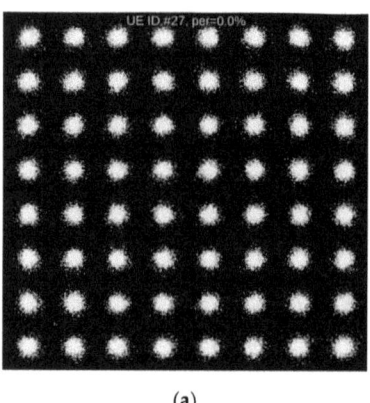 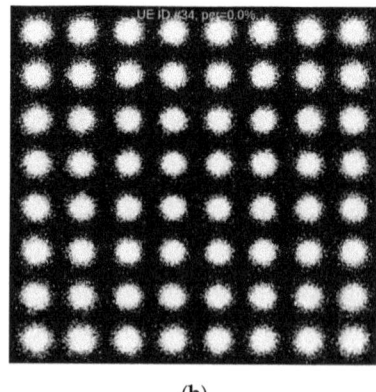

(a)   (b)

Figure 6. Uplink constellation diagram: (a) 4G carrier aggregation test case (5 carriers); (b) 5G standalone test case (100 MHz).

4.3. Latency

Data of the round-trip packet latency over 4G and 5G links are respectively presented in Tables 7 and 8. It should be noted that both eNodeB and gNodeB used a scheduling request period of 40 ms. Average ratio was measured from transfer of 100 packets. Relative change of the average packet latency over 4G link to the average packet latency over 5G link is presented in Table 9. It is seen from the data that average packet latency is lower over 5G link; it is up to −40.5% and −45.1% lower when the transmission of the packets is initiated from BTS and UE side, respectively.

Table 7. Round-trip packet latency over 4G.

Ping Source		BTS to UE				UE to BTS			
	Ping Period, ms	1	10	100	1000	1	10	100	1000
Packet size = 100 bytes	Minimum latency, ms	16.0	21.8	17.9	18.7	14.0	13.0	19.0	21.0
	Average latency, ms	34.0	31.1	38.1	39.5	32.0	44.0	37.0	47.0
	Maximum latency, ms	48.9	55.3	58.1	57.1	59.0	65.0	58.0	60.0
	Standard deviation, ms	9.4	8.3	11.7	11.2	13.7	11.0	7.8	11.1
Packet size = 1000 bytes	Minimum latency, ms	22.1	23.9	26.8	26.2	22.0	25.0	28.0	22.0
	Average latency, ms	31.4	41.2	45.8	46.0	51.0	48.0	42.0	49.0
	Maximum latency, ms	52.1	68.1	65.9	66.1	67.0	67.0	68.0	65.0
	Standard deviation, ms	7.2	13.9	11.3	11.4	10.8	9.4	9.5	11.7

Table 8. Round-trip packet latency over 5G.

Ping Source		BTS to UE				UE to BTS			
	Ping Period, ms	1	10	100	1000	1	10	100	1000
Packet size = 100 bytes	Minimum latency. ms	9.6	11.9	12.0	12.0	13.0	15.0	14.0	16.0
	Average latency. ms	23.4	22.7	26.4	30.1	27.0	27.0	27.0	27.0
	Maximum latency. ms	44.2	40.0	40.3	43.7	42.0	44.0	46.0	49.0
	Standard deviation. ms	8.5	6.3	7.4	7.8	6.9	7.8	6.7	6.9
Packet size = 1000 bytes	Minimum latency. ms	9.8	13.8	20.7	21.9	24.0	25.0	24.0	23.0
	Average latency. ms	23.4	24.5	30.2	33.1	28.0	29.0	31.0	31.0
	Maximum latency. ms	40.3	40.5	49.0	48.5	43.0	45.0	46.0	47.0
	Standard deviation. ms	7.8	7.9	6.1	6.2	4.1	4.3	4.9	6.0

Table 9. Relative change of the average packet latency over 4G to 5G.

Ping Source	BTS to UE				UE to BTS			
Ping Period, ms	1	10	100	1000	1	10	100	1000
Relative change for 100 bytes,%	−31.2	−27.0	−30.7	−23.8	−15.6	−38.6	−27.0	−42.6
Relative change for 1000 bytes,%	−25.5	−40.5	−34.1	−28.0	−45.1	−39.6	−26.2	−36.7

4.4. Central Processor Load

Load of the CPU for 4G and 5G links is shown respectively in Tables 10 and 11. It is seen that in both 4G and 5G cases, CPU load by the eNodeB and gNodeB is proportional to occupied bandwidth. This is expected because sample rate and loading of the CPU increases with bandwidth due to the need of additional signal processing. In both test cases, gNodeB loads CPU less than eNodeB, so it is more effective from a processing perspective.

Table 10. Load of the CPU running 4G carrier aggregation.

Number of Carriers	Total Bandwidth, MHz	eNodeB CPU Load, Test Case 1 [1],%	eNodeB CPU Load, Test Case 3 [2],%	EPC CPU Load, Test Case 3 [2],%	Total CPU Load, Test Case 3 [2],%
1	20	5.3	9.0	3.3	12.3
2	40	12.7	19.0	3.3	22.3
3	60	17.8	27.3	3.3	30.7
4	80	23.6	35.8	4.2	40.0
5	100	30.5	49.2	7.8 [3]	57.0
6	120	36.7	63.3	7.8 [3]	71.2

[1] eNodeB and EPC active, FEM disabled. [2] eNodeB and EPC active, FEM enabled, full DL and UL traffic. [3] CPU load doubles due to second Telit UE.

Table 11. Load of the CPU running 5G standalone.

Bandwidth, MHz	gNodeB CPU Load, Test Case 1 [1],%	gNodeB CPU Load, Test Case 3 [2],%	5GC CPU Load, Test Case 3 [2],%	Total CPU load, Test Case 3 [2],%
20	4.5	6.9	16.7	23.6
40	8.8	13.9	16.7	30.6
60	14.4	21.7	17.5	39.2
80	18.6	30.0	17.5	47.5
100 [3]	20.0	30.8	18.1	48.9

[1] gNodeB and 5GC active, FEM disabled. [2] gNodeB and 5GC active, FEM enabled, full DL and UL traffic. [3] Sample rate is same as in 80 MHz bandwidth case.

It can be seen that EPC CPU load depends on UE count only and is independent of CA configuration when UE count is constant. This is understandable because UEs only use a single band for UL traffic. It can also be observed that 5GC CPU load in Test Case 3 is also fairly constant and bandwidth-independent.

It can be concluded that in most NIB use case scenarios and under normal operating conditions (no simulated heavy traffic), EPC and 5GC software can be used locally without the need to move them on separate GPP systems, a practice often found in related works.

4.5. Power Consumption

Power consumption of the 4G-CA and 5G-SA NIBs respectively is presented in Tables 12 and 13. Results of the power consumption do not include idle system power when network stack software is not running. Power consumption of idle 4G-CA and 5G-SA NIBs is respectively equal to 96 W and 90 W. Power consumption of the 4G-CA NIB increases in Test Case 1 and 2 when number of carriers increases. In Test Case 1, it changes from 38 W to 87 W, and in Test Case 2 it changes from 71 W to 216 W, when number of carriers increases from 1 to 6. Total power consumption when full DL and UL traffic is initiated changes from 100 W to 277 W, when number of carriers is changed from 1 to 6. Large power consumption changes in both Test Case 2 and 3 can be seen when additional band is used for higher CA configuration because of additional FEM usage.

Table 12. Power consumption of the 4G-CA network-in-a-box.

Number of Carriers	Total Bandwidth, MHz	Power Consumption, Test Case 1 [1], W	Power Consumption, Test Case 2 [2], W	Power Consumption, Test Case 3 [3], W
1	20	38	71	100
2	40	50	79	107
3	60	58	138	163
4	80	66	143	168
5	100	74	179	231
6	120	84	216	277

[1] eNodeB and EPC active, FEM disabled. [2] eNodeB and EPC active, FEM enabled. [3] eNodeB and EPC active, FEM enabled, full DL and UL traffic.

Table 13. Power consumption of the 5G-SA network-in-a-box.

Bandwidth, MHz	Power Consumption, Test Case 1 [1], W	Power Consumption, Test Case 2 [2], W	Power Consumption, Test Case 3 [3], W
20	42	72	104
40	54	81	112
60	60	90	120
80	68	95	130
100 [4]	68	95	130

[1] gNodeB and 5GC active, FEM disabled. [2] gNodeB and 5GC active, FEM enabled. [3] gNodeB and 5GC active, FEM enabled, full DL and UL traffic. [4] Sample rate is same as in 80 MHz bandwidth case.

Similarly, power consumption of the 5G-SA NIB increases in all three Test Cases when bandwidth increases. In Test Case 1, it changes from 42 W to 68 W, in Test Case 2 it changes from 72 W to 95 W, and in Test Case 3 it changes from 104 W to 130 W, when bandwidth increases from 20 MHz to 100 MHz. Lower total power consumption of the 5G-SA when full DL and UL traffic is initiated is mainly due to a lower count of FEMs. From a processing perspective, if at least three carriers are used for the 4G link, 5G is more power efficient. Power consumption for 80 MHz and 100 MHz bandwidths are identical due to same sample rate used in both cases.

In both 4G-CA and 5G-SA configurations, total power consumption increase in Test Case 3, when comparing it to Test Case 2, is mainly due to increase of average channel power, hence the additional FEM power consumption under continuous DL traffic conditions.

5. Conclusions

With an ever-increasing number of frameworks and projects of the RAN-oriented software stack becoming accessible to researchers and consumers, availability of the SDR-based RRH frameworks remains limited. Due to limited flexibility of available SDR-based RRH frameworks, available NIB solutions are restricted to single band operation in both 4G and 5G. Hence, solutions for expansion of the existing system capacity in existing infrastructure, for example usage of higher-level 4G CA, are not sufficiently explored and compared with 5G technology.

In this work, an open RAN-compatible, scalable, and highly flexible SDR-based RRH framework is proposed and designed. The main feature of the proposed framework is the ability of software and hardware reconfiguration with minimum changes to the overall framework.

The performance of the proposed SDR framework is validated by creating two NIB-based testbeds that can operate in multiband multicarrier 4G or 5G SA configurations capable of RF operation from 700 MHz to 3800 MHz. The designed NIBs are separated into two modular parts—COTS-based GPP core and high-power FEM—capable of providing a maximum channel output power of 33 dBm at all bands.

For 4G-CA, when 1 UE is active, a maximum of 883 Mbps DL and 65.8 Mbps UL data transfer speed is achieved when an aggregated bandwidth of 100 MHz is used. Under the same aggregated bandwidth conditions, 5G-SA achieves a 762 Mbps DL and 92.6 Mbps UL data transfer speeds. If six carriers are used in the 4G NIB, 1062 Mbps downlink data transfer speed can be achieved.

Average packet latency is lower in the 5G-SA; it is up to 40.5% and 45.1% lower when the transmission of the packets is initiated the from BTS and UE side, respectively, when comparing with the 4G-CA.

CPU load by the eNodeB and gNodeB is proportional to occupied bandwidth, but under the same aggregated DL bandwidth conditions, gNodeB is more effective from a processing perspective and loads CPU less than eNodeB. When only 1 UE is active, the EPC CPU load is up to four times lower than the 5GC under same aggregated bandwidth conditions.

FEMs are one of the main power consumers of a high-power NIB solutions. For 5G SA, power consumption at different bandwidth configurations is determined by CPU efficiency because power consumption of the FEM module is nearly constant. For 4G-CA, usage of higher number of carriers not only increases CPU power draw but also multiplies the FEM power draw due to the need of additional modules to support operation at different bands.

As a future step, based on the validated SDR framework, a new FPRF IC is planned to be developed. The new IC will support most of the RF and digital features of current SDR framework in a single package.

Author Contributions: Conceptualization, K.K.; methodology, K.K.; software, M.J.; validation, K.K., V.M. and M.J.; formal analysis, V.M.; investigation, K.K.; resources, M.J.; data curation, M.J.; writing—original draft preparation, K.K.; writing—review and editing, M.J., V.M. and R.N.; visualization, K.K., M.J. and V.M.; supervision, R.N.; project administration, R.N.; funding acquisition, R.N. All authors have read and agreed to the published version of the manuscript.

Funding: This project has received funding from European Regional Development Fund (project No 01.2.2-LMT-K-718-01-0054) under grant agreement with the Research Council of Lithuania (LMTLT).

Institutional Review Board Statement: Not applicable.

Informed Consent Statement: Not applicable.

Acknowledgments: The team of authors wishes to express their gratitude to European Regional Development Fund and the Research Council of Lithuania for financially supporting this research as a part of "Design and Research of Internet of Things (IoT) Framework Model and Tools for Intelligent Transport Systems" project, grant number DOTSUT-235, No. 01.2.2-LMT-K-718-01-0054.

Conflicts of Interest: The authors declare no conflict of interest.

References

1. Tadros, C.N.; Rizk, M.R.M.; Mokhtar, B.M. Software Defined Network-Based Management for Enhanced 5G Network Services. *IEEE Access* **2020**, *8*, 53997–54008. [CrossRef]
2. Long, Q.; Chen, Y.; Zhang, H.; Lei, X. Software Defined 5G and 6G Networks: A Survey. *Mob. Netw. Appl.* **2019**. [CrossRef]
3. Bonati, L.; Polese, M.; D'Oro, S.; Basagni, S.; Melodia, T. Open, Programmable, and Virtualized 5G Networks: State-of-the-Art and the Road Ahead. *Comput. Netw.* **2020**, *182*, 107516. [CrossRef]
4. Kao, L.-C.; Liao, W. 5G Intelligent A+: A Pioneer Multi-Access Edge Computing Solution for 5G Private Networks. *IEEE Commun. Stand. Mag.* **2021**, *5*, 78–84. [CrossRef]
5. Franci, D.; Coltellacci, S.; Grillo, E.; Pavoncello, S.; Aureli, T.; Cintoli, R.; Migliore, M.D. Experimental Procedure for Fifth Generation (5G) Electromagnetic Field (EMF) Measurement and Maximum Power Extrapolation for Human Exposure Assessment. *Environments* **2020**, *7*, 22. [CrossRef]
6. Kiela, K.; Jurgo, M.; Navickas, R. Structure of V2X-IoT framework for ITS applications. In Proceedings of the 2020 43rd International Conference on Telecommunications and Signal Processing (TSP), Milan, Italy, 7–9 July 2020; pp. 229–234.
7. Lopes Ferreira, M.; Canas Ferreira, J. An FPGA-Oriented Baseband Modulator Architecture for 4G/5G Communication Scenarios. *Electronics* **2018**, *8*, 2. [CrossRef]
8. Aijaz, A.; Holden, B.; Meng, F. Open and Programmable 5G Network-in-a-Box: Technology Demonstration and Evaluation Results. *arXiv* **2021**, arXiv:2104.11074.
9. Liu, G.; Huang, Y.; Chen, Z.; Liu, L.; Wang, Q.; Li, N. 5G Deployment: Standalone vs. Non-Standalone from the Operator Perspective. *IEEE Commun. Mag.* **2020**, *58*, 83–89. [CrossRef]
10. Liu, W.; Santos, J.F.; van de Belt, J.; Jiao, X.; Moerman, I.; Marquez-Barja, J.; DaSilva, L.; Pollin, S. Enabling Virtual Radio Functions on Software Defined Radio for Future Wireless Networks. *Wirel. Pers. Commun.* **2020**, *113*, 1579–1595. [CrossRef]
11. Habibi, M.A.; Nasimi, M.; Han, B.; Schotten, H.D. A Comprehensive Survey of RAN Architectures Toward 5G Mobile Communication System. *IEEE Access* **2019**, *7*, 70371–70421. [CrossRef]
12. Chih-Lin, I.; Kuklinski, S.; Chen, T.; Ladid, L. A Perspective of O-RAN Integration with MEC, SON, and Network Slicing in the 5G Era. *IEEE Netw.* **2020**, *34*, 3–4. [CrossRef]
13. Kiela, K.; Jurgo, M.; Macaitis, V.; Navickas, R. Wideband Reconfigurable Integrated Low-Pass Filter for 5G Compatible Software Defined Radio Solutions. *Electronics* **2021**, *10*, 734. [CrossRef]
14. Duarte, L.; Gomes, R.; Ribeiro, C.; Caldeirinha, R.F.S. A Software-Defined Radio for Future Wireless Communication Systems at 60 GHz. *Electronics* **2019**, *8*, 1490. [CrossRef]
15. Benzin, A.; Osterland, D.; Dill, M.; Caire, G. Centralized Single FPGA Real Time Zero Forcing Massive MIMO 5G Basestation Hardware and Gateware. In Proceedings of the 2020 IEEE 21st International Workshop on Signal Processing Advances in Wireless Communications (SPAWC), Atlanta, GA, USA, 26–29 May 2020; Volume 2020, pp. 1–5.
16. Pozza, M.; Rao, A.; Flinck, H.; Tarkoma, S. Network-in-a-box: A survey about on-demand flexible networks. *IEEE Commun. Surv. Tutor.* **2018**, *20*, 2407–2428. [CrossRef]
17. Kiela, K.; Barzdenas, V.; Jurgo, M.; Macaitis, V.; Rafanavicius, J.; Vasjanov, A.; Kladovscikov, L.; Navickas, R. Review of V2X–IoT Standards and Frameworks for ITS Applications. *Appl. Sci.* **2020**, *10*, 4314. [CrossRef]
18. Nardini, G.; Stea, G.; Virdis, A. Simu5G. Available online: https://simu5g.org/ (accessed on 5 August 2021).
19. Centre Tecnològic de Telecomunicacions de Catalunya 5G-LENA. Available online: https://5g-lena.cttc.es/ (accessed on 10 July 2021).
20. Virdis, A.; Nardini, G.; Stea, G.; Sabella, D. End-to-End Performance Evaluation of MEC Deployments in 5G Scenarios. *J. Sens. Actuator Netw.* **2020**, *9*, 57. [CrossRef]

21. Nardini, G.; Sabella, D.; Stea, G.; Thakkar, P.; Virdis, A. Simu5G–An OMNeT++ Library for End-to-End Performance Evaluation of 5G Networks. *IEEE Access* **2020**, *8*, 181176–181191. [CrossRef]
22. Issa, A.; Hakem, N.; Kandil, N.; Chehri, A. Performance Analysis of Mobile Network Software Testbed. In *Human Centred Intelligent Systems*; Springer: Singapore, 30 May 2021; Volume 189, pp. 305–319, ISBN 9789811557835.
23. Soos, G.; Ficzere, D.; Varga, P.; Szalay, Z. Practical 5G KPI Measurement Results on a Non-Standalone Architecture. In Proceedings of the NOMS 2020–2020 IEEE/IFIP Network Operations and Management Symposium, Budapest, Hungary, 20–24 April 2020; pp. 1–5.

Article

OpenCare5G: O-RAN in Private Network for Digital Health Applications

Wagner de Oliveira [1,†], José Olimpio Rodrigues Batista, Jr. [1,*,†], Tiago Novais [2], Silvio Toshiyuki Takashima [3], Leonardo Roccon Stange [4], Moacyr Martucci, Jr. [1], Carlos Eduardo Cugnasca [1] and Graça Bressan [1]

1. Department of Computer Engineering and Digital Systems, Escola Politécnica, University of São Paulo, São Paulo 05508-010, Brazil
2. Department of Clients & Industries, Deloitte Touche Tohmatsu, São Paulo 04711-130, Brazil
3. NEC Latin America S.A., São Paulo 05001-100, Brazil
4. Meta, Menlo Park, CA 94025, USA
* Correspondence: olimpio.rodrigues@usp.br
† These authors contributed equally to this work.

Citation: de Oliveira, W.; Batista, J.O.R., Jr.; Novais, T.; Takashima, S.T.; Stange, L.R.; Martucci, M., Jr.; Cugnasca, C.E.; Bressan, G. OpenCare5G: O-RAN in Private Network for Digital Health Applications. *Sensors* **2023**, *23*, 1047. https://doi.org/10.3390/s23021047

Academic Editors: Giuseppe Caso, Anna Brunstrom, Özgü Alay, Harilaos Koumaras, Almudena Díaz Zayas and Valerio Frascolla

Received: 30 November 2022
Revised: 7 January 2023
Accepted: 10 January 2023
Published: 16 January 2023

Copyright: © 2023 by the authors. Licensee MDPI, Basel, Switzerland. This article is an open access article distributed under the terms and conditions of the Creative Commons Attribution (CC BY) license (https://creativecommons.org/licenses/by/4.0/).

Abstract: Digital Health is a new way for medicine to work together with computer engineering and ICT to carry out tests and obtain reliable information about the health status of citizens in the most remote places in Brazil in near-real time, applying new technologies and digital tools in the process. InovaHC is the technological innovation core of the Clinics Hospital of the Faculty of Medicine of the University of São Paulo (HCFMUSP). It is the first national medical institution to seek new opportunities offered by 5G technology and test its application in the first private network for Digital Health in the largest hospital complex in Latin America through the OpenCare5G Project. This project uses an Open RAN concept and network disaggregation with lower costs than the traditional concept used by the telecommunications industry. The technological project connected to the 5G network was divided into two phases for proof-of-concept testing: the first with an initial focus on carrying out examinations with portable ultrasound equipment in different locations at HCFMUSP, and the second focusing on carrying out remote examinations with health professionals in other states of Brazil, who will be working in remote areas in other states with little or no ICT infrastructure together with a doctor analyzing exams in real time at HCFMUSP in São Paulo. The objective of the project is to evaluate the connectivity and capacity of the 5G private network in these the proof-of-concept tests for transmitting the volume of data from remote exams with higher speed and lower latency. We are in the first phase of the proof of concept testing to achieve the expected success. This project is a catalyst for innovation in health, connecting resources and entrepreneurs to generate solutions for the innovation ecosystem of organizations. It is coordinated by Deloitte with the participation of the Escola Politécnica da USP (The School of Engineering—University of São Paulo), Airspan, Itaú Bank, Siemens Healthineers, NEC, Telecom Infra Projet, ABDI and IDB. The use of 5G Open RAN technology in public health is concluded to be of extreme social, economic, and fundamental importance for HCFMUSP, citizens, and the development of health research to promote great positive impacts ranging from attracting investment in the country to improving the quality of patient care.

Keywords: 5G; B5G; digital health; Open RAN; private network

1. Introduction

Digital Health uses information and communication technology (ICT) resources to produce, provide and make available reliable information about the health conditions of patients. It is a strategic inclusion mechanism, making specialized health assistance available to remote places in Brazil [1]. Digital Health incorporates recent advances in health innovation technology by implementing hardware (HW), software (SW), IoT devices, big data and artificial intelligence (AI) [2] to concentrate high volumes of information in databases, applications, and networks. It enables more accurate follow-up and brings greater security to patients, especially when performing tests remotely in near-real time to obtain the fastest diagnoses. Private networks are also a good tool for ensuring that communication can be safe and provide the desired network quality for health professionals and public managers in the healthcare system [3].

Doctors from InovaHC, Center for Technological Innovation at the Hospital of Clinics, Faculty of Medicine, University of São Paulo (HCFMUSP), started an evolutionary 5G technological project to improve the provision of basic services to populations living in remote areas of Brazil. The initiative, called "Aysu" in the Tupi-Guarani language, will bring medical assistance to the riverside and indigenous population of the Amazon Region. In August 2021, interventional radiologists from the Institute of Radiology at HCFMUSP (InRad) landed on the banks of the Tapajos River, Para State, 2348 km from HCFMUSP in the city of São Paulo, to perform ultrasound exams and assist in the medical care of populations in situations of vulnerability to diseases and epidemic.

The doctors at InRad are part of Zoe, a non-governmental organization (NGO) established to offer treatment and care to those without or with little access to qualified healthcare. The doctors spent a few days providing care on the boat Abare, a kind of basic floating health unit on the river that offers primary care, carrying out 200 exams with two pieces of portable ultrasound equipment of the most varied types in children, young people, men, and women.

With the COVID-19 pandemic, the role of the Abare boat in assisting riverside communities became even more important. The vessel is where people receive basic supplies and protection items, such as masks and alcohol gel [3]. HCFMUSP is a large public technological health center with equipment and devices with all the necessary resources in place, but in the remote places served, these resources are minimal. In addition to primary care, the doctors performed cancer and thyroid diagnoses, pregnancy and hernia tests, not to mention the exchange of experiences between doctors and the local population and interaction with the local communities' indigenous leaders, shamans, and chiefs. Through this exchange, the doctors were able to experience the dynamics of the village and gain access to knowledge about the forest and local wisdom based on the concept of community life.

In the third expedition of the InRad doctors in 2022, they carried out 377 clinical consultations in children, the elderly, and chronic patients, in addition to 125 ultrasound examinations in indigenous communities of Alto do Xingu. The action, carried out in partnership with "SESAI, more Indian Health" and the NGO "Xingu + Catu". The difference in this expedition was the provision of on-site service to assist the indigenous people in the villages, allowing them to remain in their homes, as shown in Figure 1.

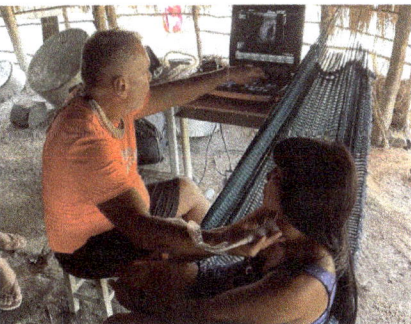

Figure 1. Indigenous patient care by InradHC doctors in the village of Alto do Xingu.

To reach the villages at the base pole in Alto Xingu, in the northeast region of the State of Mato Grosso, in the southern portion of the Brazilian Amazon, the path taken by health professionals is long and they need to travel by ferry, boat, car, and even by foot, but the effort is rewarded by being able to take the portable ultrasound equipment to these communities.

Then InovaHC professionals developed a partnership with the diverse ecosystem of different actors among technology, telecommunications, government, universities and financial institutions. Called the OpenCare5G Project [4], it is a highly innovative initiative to study and test healthcare applications in the construction of the first 5G private network. The Open Radio Access Network (O-RAN) utilizes the O-RAN 5G concept [3,5–12] to transport health data and to help in the analysis of medical exams by health professionals using local and remote hospital portable devices and equipment.

With this implementation, health professionals will be able to provide care in the middle of the rain forest using this equipment or others connected to the 5G private network safely, and carry out immediate diagnoses with their peers at HCFMUSP in São Paulo. The project has been coordinated by Deloitte and implemented by Airspan, Escola Politécnica da USP (EPUSP the School of Engineering—University of São Paulo), Itaú Bank, Siemens Healthineers, Telecom Infra Project (TIP), Brazilian Agency for Industrial Development (ABDI), Inter-American Development Bank (IDB) and NEC, responsible for the integration of the O-RAN 5G network [4].

The Itaú Bank, the first bank in Brazil to use O-RAN to provide a 5G connection to its network, will provide its expertise in technology, which will make it possible to carry out pilot projects. Bank experts will explore the possibilities of an innovative system in a joint learning process. An important point is that in the project, a 5G Core Network (5GCN) will be used at Itaú Bank (with Cisco, Dell and HP equipment), using the infrastructure of its datacenter, located in the Ipiranga neighborhood, 9 km from HCFMUSP with a LAN-to-LAN fiber optic connection provided by the local telecom company.

The use of a 5G private network aimed at the "freedom" to make the bank's indoor network, without depending, in principle, on incumbent telecom companies. Itaú Bank has 6000 datacenters, since each branch is considered one of these centers. That is, there is the potential to have 6000 agencies connected to the private O-RAN network throughout the country.

Field tests will be carried out with "real use cases" of data received and sent from exams, images, and voice to evaluate the data-transmission capacity of 5G connectivity, the response time and the feasibility of performing remote exams using the higher speed and lower latency than the 5G and Beyond 5G (B5G) private networks could offer [13]. The project proof of concept (PoC) will initially focus on the first phase to perform local and remote ultrasound scans, later extending to tests of CT images that will be sent to the cloud, in which there will be processing at the edge through machine learning and AI, collaborating to improve the patient's journey and provide more access to health services, since the analysis of diagnosis can currently take days.

The remainder of this paper is organized as follows: Section 2 contextualizes the related work; Section 3 presents the proposed solution framework; Section 4 describes the scenario, the methodology and PoCs used in the experiments, and reports and discusses the results. Finally, Section 5 concludes the work.

2. Related Work

This section contextualizes some problems that may arise with the application of O-RAN in Digital Health in heterogeneous mobile network scenarios for 5G and the use of 5G-CPE (Wi-Fi 6) to support the expected contribution of this work.

The fundamental shift in networking has resulted in three independent but dominant trends in the tech industry: virtualization, open ecosystems and cloudification [14]. These concepts are not new, but the cell phone industry has been delaying their adoption. Core network virtualization is complete, and all the focus is now on RAN virtualization.

There are no articles dealing with the use of a 5G private network employing O-RAN for Digital Health in Brazil. This is the first article aiming at that.

Table 1 summarizes the related work.

The authors of [15] propose that O-RAN takes advantage of hardware and software disaggregation [16–18] and creates a unified architecture with various advancements, such as low latency. In addition to facilitating network automation, O-RAN provides several benefits, including:

- Agility in software-enabled architecture unification makes network suitable for existing, past and future generations;
- Deployment flexibility for disaggregation and software association makes the network flexible for installation, update and extension;
- Real-time responsiveness, since vRAN is service-specific network-oriented software that behaves based on the intended service to real-time services and requires very low latency from less critical services;
- Reduction in operating costs by estimating the plug-and-play feature of O-RAN; modern learning methods can reduce the maintenance cost dramatically when compared with traditional solutions.

Table 1. Summary of related work.

Work	Contribution	Limitations	Future Work
Singh, Singh and Kumbhani (2020) [15]	The disaggregation of hardware and software creates a unified architecture through various advancements and brings many benefits such as low latency and network slicing. In addition to facilitating network automation, O-RAN offers several benefits such as agility, deployment flexibility, real-time responsiveness and operating cost reduction.	Reduction in operating cost by estimating the plug-and-play feature of O-RAN; modern learning methods can reduce maintenance cost up to 80%.	Implementing RIC policies close to real-time and non-real-time control loop meeting economic and ecological aspects; coordination, updating and training are difficult with modern ML and AI learning techniques and the challenging handling of data (between layers).
Wang et al. (2022) [19]	They modeled the RU-DU resource allocation problem in an O-RAN as a packing problem, proposing a self-play reinforcement learning strategy. They applied the combined approach of deep neural network with Monte-Carlo Tree Search (MCTS) to solve this combinatorial optimization problem.	Learning by auto-run eliminates the need for demonstrator data, which can be expensive and time-consuming to collect.	Mapping RU shift requirements to local mobile edge computing centers for future centralized processing that would significantly reduce power consumption in cellular networks. That is, we study the resource allocation problem between the RU-DU of the O-RAN system modeled as a 2D packing problem.
Lekshmi and Ponnekanti (2019) [20]	ML can play significant roles in learning from the wireless environment variations, categorizing problems, anticipating challenges, predicting outcomes, and exploring possible solutions, decisions, and actions.	Current RANs are reactive and base stations run algorithms on the centralized server to meet user demands. However, in 5G, even ms of delay can cause a great impact.	Sustaining advanced RLM requires an efficient implementation of ML-based traffic optimization that can handle large volumes of data in 5G networks.
Polese et al. (2022) [21]	O-RAN networks will dramatically change the design, deployment, and next-generation operations for cellular and other networks, allowing, among other things, transformative applications of ML for RAN optimization and control.	RAN reconfiguration with equipment whose operations cannot be adjusted to support diverse deployments and different traffic profiles; limited co-ordination between network nodes.	Real-time control loops will be included that operate in the real-time domain, i.e., below 10 ms for RRM at the RAN node level, or even below 1 ms for device management and optimization.

The result is that, by placing the software at the center of the network, it is possible to unify the connectivity gains of all generations under one umbrella. By doing so, millions of dollars may be saved [15].

O-RAN was developed for democratizing access to and reducing the cost of future mobile data networks by supporting network services with various Quality of Service (QoS) requirements, such as massive IoT or IoT devices (e.g., portable ultrasound equipment) and uRLLC [19]. In O-RAN, networking functionality is disaggregated into radio units (RUs), distributed units (DUs) and centralized units (CUs), which allows for flexible software in COTS. Furthermore, mapping RU shift requirements to local mobile edge computing centers for future centralized processing would significantly reduce power consumption in cellular networks.

That is, the study of the resource allocation problem between the RU-DU of the O-RAN system was modeled as a 2D packing problem of RU-DU resources in O-RAN, proposing a self-play reinforcement learning strategy. They apply the combined approach of deep neural networks with Monte-Carlo Tree Search (MCTS) to solve this combinatorial optimization problem.

With high throughput and function approximation capability, a deep neural network modeled resource allocation policy can generalize under dynamic network conditions. Learning by auto-run eliminates the need for demonstrator data, which can be expensive and time-consuming to collect [19].

The authors describe that the application of ML as a data analysis method allows machines to explore data and make predictive and proactive decisions in real time [20]. ML can play significant roles in learning from variations in the wireless environment, categorizing problems, anticipating challenges, predicting outcomes, and exploring possible solutions, decisions, and actions [20].

The ML framework can exploit data from different types of UEs to predict traffic volume and dynamically allocate available network resources. In 5G, the RRM (Radio Resource Management) framework in the RAN includes various control functions based on radio measurements and other observations of various user devices or network elements.

Current RANs are reactive and base stations run algorithms on CUs to meet user demands. However, in 5G, even milliseconds of delay can cause a great impact. To enable certain mission-critical applications, such as remote robotic surgery, the 5G network must be predictive and proactive, rather than just reactive. In O-RAN, computing and storage resources must be distributed among the different datacenters that can host the ML algorithm to proactively serve users.

Sustaining advanced Radio Link Monitoring (RLM) requires an efficient implementation of ML-based traffic optimization that can handle large volumes of data in 5G networks. This learning framework would be able to run algorithms autonomously to deal with latency, meeting the RRM functionality and reliability requirements of users [19].

Polese et al. [21] define the management and optimization of new network systems that require solutions that, by opening the RAN access network, expose data and analysis and allow advanced data-driven optimization, closed-loop control and automation. They describe that the challenges are not easy to overcome, as current approaches to cellular networks are the opposite of open. In RAN, network components are monolithic units, complete solutions that implement each layer of the cellular protocol stack, provided by a limited number of vendors and seen by operators as black boxes [21].

O-RAN embraces and extends the 3GPP NR 7.2 split to base stations between the RU and the DU. We can thus have the functionalities of the base station in CU, DU and RU. Furthermore, it connects them to intelligent controller systems through open interfaces that can transmit telemetry of the RAN and implement actions and policies to control it.

Note that the O-RAN architecture includes two RAN Intelligent Controllers (RICs) that perform network management and control at near-real-time (10 ms to 1 s) and non-real-time (greater than 1 s) timescales, which have not been used in the OpenCare5G project.

Future work will be focused on extensions to real-time control loops, including loops that operate in the real-time domain, i.e., below 10 ms, for managing radio resources at the RAN node level, or even below 1 ms for device management and optimization. Typical examples of real-time control include programming, beam management and feedback-free detection of physical layer parameters (e.g., modulation and coding scheme, interference recognition). These loops, which have a limited scale in terms of optimized devices, are not part of the current O-RAN architecture, but are mentioned in some specifications as for further study [21].

3. Proposed Solution

OpenCare5G has been conducted according to the efforts presented below.

3.1. OpenCare5G Project Architecture

The first step was to define a new approach using the Private Health Network Architecture with the trends in the design of a Gigabit-based packet data network, sharing the 5G Internet with the Customer Premises Equipment (CPE) in the local network via Wi-Fi 6 (802.11ax) that imposes new requirements to build, test, operate and update it.

The 5G xHaul O-RAN Operations, Administration, and Maintenance (OAM) Private Network Project Architecture via vRAN was divided into three segments of logical "nodes", also called functional blocks, that are areas/connection points for the functions. Then an Infrastructure Layer with the Network Fronthaul (gNB-RU) of the Radio unit, Midhaul (gNB-DU) of the Distribution Unit, and Backhaul (gNB-CU) of the virtual centralized unit towards the 5GCN in the Itaú datacenter was provided, forming the access network by virtualized radio (vRAN) of the End-to-End (E2E) design [22].

We have requested of Anatel, the Brazilian telecommunications regulator, the use of the radio frequency spectrum by telecommunications systems associated with the Private Limited Service (PLS) for allocating the 5G band of restricted interest for health [1,3,23]. This is meant for exploration nationwide, in the private regime with a frequency spectrum in band n77 5G 3700–3800 MHz, 100 MHz bandwidth with vRAN performing baseband functions as software [3,24].

The 5G xHaul O-RAN OAM vRAN Private Network Project Architecture will provide connectivity and interoperability through radios, hardware, software, containers, virtual machines, and cloud-native open interfaces from different manufacturers with an approach of using less hardware and achieving greater economy. The ability to increase flexibility and easily scale up and down workloads should scale to meet changing network demands for mobile bandwidth, ultra-reliable secure communication and ultra-low data latency as shown in Figure 2 [14,25–27].

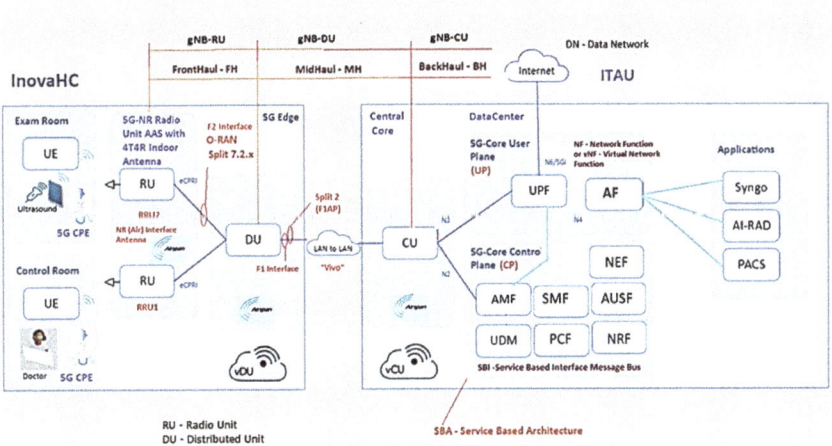

Figure 2. 5G xHaul network architecture of the Inovac OpenCare5G Project with simplified O-RAN OAM in the infrastructure layer. Based on [21].

Figure 3 shows the 5G xHaul network architecture of the Inovac OpenCare5G Project with Complete O-RAN OAM via vRAN in the infrastructure, mobile and services layers, showing the subnets connected to the User Equipment (UE)/Exam Room, UE/Control Room Doctor, Radio Units/Subnetwork, 5G CPE (Device), Fronthaul Transport Network, Subnetwork/Sync, DU/vDU, Midhaul 1 Transport Network, Midhaul 2 Transport Network, CU/vCU, Backhaul Transport Network, 5GCN in Cloud and Network Slice for 5G NR.

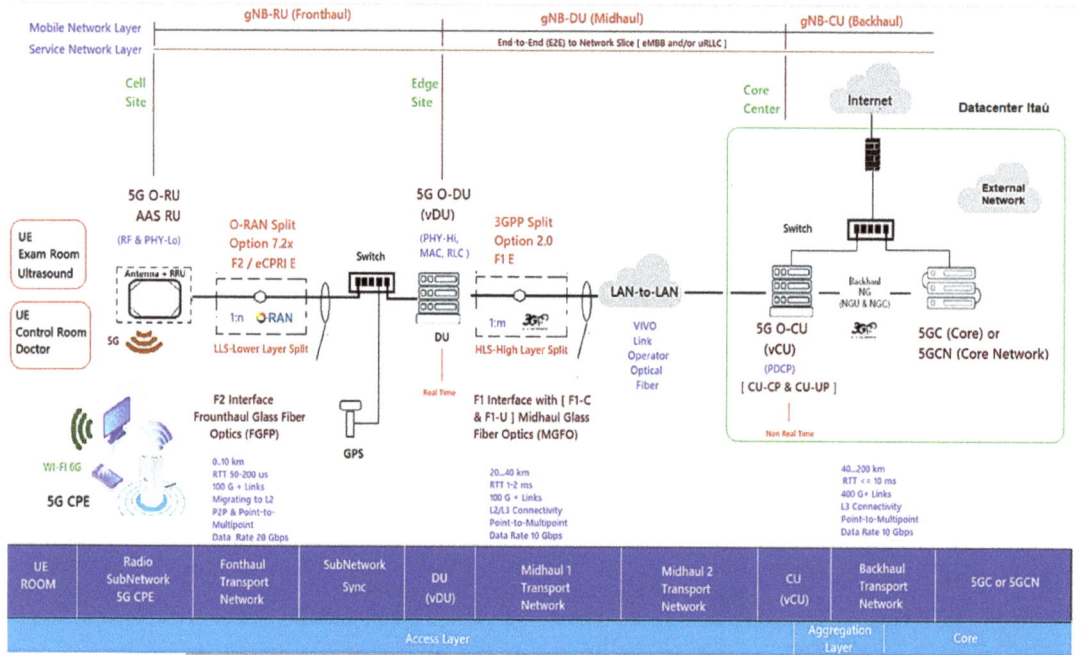

Figure 3. Architecture of the 5G xHaul network of the Inovac OpenCare5G with O-RAN OAM, complete vRAN in the infrastructure, mobile and services layers. Based on [14,26–28].

Figures 2 and 3 show the following components:

1. The Radio Subnetwork of the gNB-RU (Fronthaul) which has two radio units (RUs) formed by an active internal antenna (Advanced Antenna System - AAS RU) coupled to the Remote Radio Unit (RRU) for the 5G NR Sub-6GHz type 4T4R. The physical interface for glass fiber optics to control coverage and mitigate interference with "digital beamforming" on demand with internal connectivity is able to increase the transfer rate for speeds above 2 Gbps up to 10 Gbps for the two distinct environments (Exam and Control Room) at HCFMUSP with the following specifications [29,30]:

    - Type Airvelocity 2700 RU from Airspan company for 5G RAN;
    - 2 AAS-RU units with 4 4T4R AAS active antennas, 3.7–3.8 GHz range, n77 band, FM, DC;
    - 5G Sub-6 radiates radio frequency energy;
    - F2 Fronthaul interface between the RU and the DU for 10 GbE;
    - vRAN Split 7.2x; the RU/DU must conform to functional split RAN 7.2a, Duplex Operation Mode and 100 MHz Bandwidth [29];

2. The Indoor 5G CPE in the subnetwork of the gNB-RU (Fronthaul) with two CPEs provides connectivity, speed and latency similar to optical fiber connecting electronic devices via 5G; it distributes signal by Wi-Fi 6 (802.11ax) to the doctors' examination

room and ultrasound equipment examination room at HCFMUSP. Its implementation alleviates network congestion and efficiency in the face of high traffic demand;

3. The Fronthaul Transport Network of gNB-RU is connected by glass fiber optics to obtain broadband with synchronous ethernet interface, using wave-length division multiplexing (WDM) connected to RU to improve the efficiency/throughput of the medium with an enhanced common public radio dynamic interface (eCPRI PDU) encapsulated in ethernet for VLAN, class 2;

4. Between RU/DU, O-RAN Alliance (Open RAN) of User Plan (UP) traffic service points, time synchronization via Global Positioning System (GPS) [25,31]. At this stage we have the Fronthaul packet network carrying the eCPRI PDU traffic so that it is virtually lossless. Depending on the use case in 5G, the latency in the Fronthaul network is not more than tens of microseconds;

5. The DU/CU must combine to allow dual connectivity between the Sub-6GHz and 5G network bands, as well as coordinated transmission to eliminate interference to the minimum possible [29];

- In the "Subnetwork/Sync" we have the switch and the GPS connection with the gNB-RU (Fronthaul);
- The DU/vDU of the gNB-DU (Midhaul) of the distribution unit (DU) mounted on a COTS server with docker system for vDU containerization;
- Midhaul 1 Transport Network from gNB-DU (Midhaul) with glass fiber optics and split 2.0 interface for LAN-to-LAN connection Midhaul 2 Transport Network from gNB-DU (Midhaul) to Unit Centralized (5G-O-CU);
- The CU/vCU of the gNB-CU (Backhaul) of the Centralized Unit (5G-O-CU) mounted on a COTS Server performing the containerization and virtualization of the vCU in the native cloud connected to the 5G Core (5GC) server, which is connected to the datacenter in Itaú, 9 km from HCFMUSP.

The remote unit (RU) hosts the L1 layer and the lower PHY-Low sublayer in real time, and the vCU is responsible for non-real-time functions such as RAN resource management, encryption and retransmission. Normally, a single vCU can manage many DUs, and a single DU can connect to multiple RUs [24].

In 5GCN, the Service Based Architecture (SBA) defines the network components with a set of network functions interconnected by containers and non-containers, as shown in Figures 2 and 3.

5G NR/NGC Protocol Framework Stack

Figure 4 depicts the conceptual model of the open systems interconnection (OSI) being used in 5G, based on the functionalities of each layer and distinguished by the concepts of services, interfaces and protocols. The OSI model divides functions into seven layers that serve as a reference for developers to program networks and so that they can communicate and work independently of the manufacturer. It is a theoretical model for developers and scholars and the great secret is standardization and interoperability [32].

The TCP/IP model is a four-layer oriented model, forming the stack of the protocol structurecurrently in use, but we need to know both models to interpret the 5G Protocol Framework Stack.

With the implementation of the structure of the datacenter LAN/4G/LTE stacks for the 5G NR/NGC, the layers and sublayers of the structured stack of protocols for interconnection, communication and other functionalities of hardware and software underwent alterations and were included in the functional division options proposed by 3GPP in conjunction with disaggregated O-RAN.

Based on the simplified Radio Protocol Stacks in the comparison of UMTS/LTE/5G Air Interface or datacenter LAN with 4G/LTE/5G RAN network stacks, we will have the "5G NR/NGC SA Protocol Stack" with different technical terms and a functional division"Intra-MAC split" among RU/DU/CU, as shown in layers L1, L2 and L3 and their sublayers in Figure 4 [33].

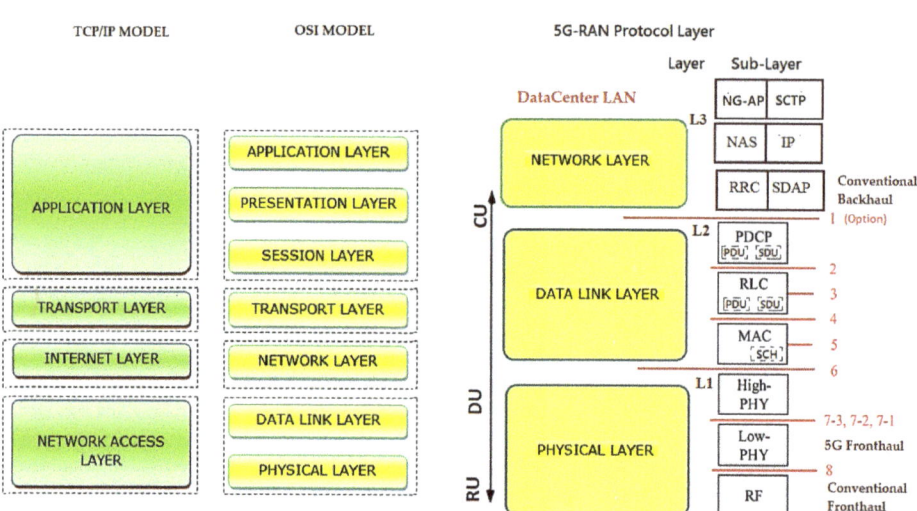

Figure 4. Radio protocol stack simplified in the UMTS/LTE/5G air interface or datacenter LAN with 4G/LTE/5G RAN Network stacks—Comparison to have the "5G NR/NGC SA Protocol Stack". Based on [32–36].

Based on the OSI model, each layer has its own structure called Protocol Data Unit for data, segments, packets, frames and bits (PDU). This division into layers brings several advantages, such as the decomposition of network communications into smaller, simpler parts and standardization of network components, enabling communication between different types of hardware and network software, preventing changes in one layer from affecting the others. Each layer of the model must provide its services exclusively to the layer immediately above and, consequently, the function of each layer depends on the services of the layer immediately below [32].

Therefore, based on the OSI/TCP-IP model, the "5G NR/NGC SA Protocol Structure Stack" was formed, in which 3GPP released the 38.300 v1 specification on NR and NG-RAN. These standards, termed Phase 2, include details about the 5G NR network and the protocol architecture shown in Figure 4 with the three layers L1, L2 and L3 and their sublayers [34,37]:

- Layer L1 on sublayer RF, PHY Low(L) and High(H);
- Layer L2 on sublayer MAC (L/H)/(SCH), RLC (L/H) and PDCP (L/H);
- Layer L3 on sublayer RRC and SDAP, only SA and not NSA, NAS and IP.

Figure 5 demonstrates the architecture of layers L1, L2 and L3 for DownLink (DL) and UpLink (UL), where the:

- PHY sublayer offers transport channels to the MAC sublayer;
- MAC sublayer offers logical channels to the RLC sublayer;
- RLC sublayer offers RLC channels to the PDCP sublayer;
- PDCP sublayer offers Radio Bearers to the SDAP sublayer;
- SDAP sublayer provides the QoS flows.

The "5G NR/NGC SA Protocol Framework Stack" is designed to support lower delays and higher data rates with QoS in the sublayers shown in Figure 6 for UE and 5G gNB base station with DL or UL directions of data packets [37].

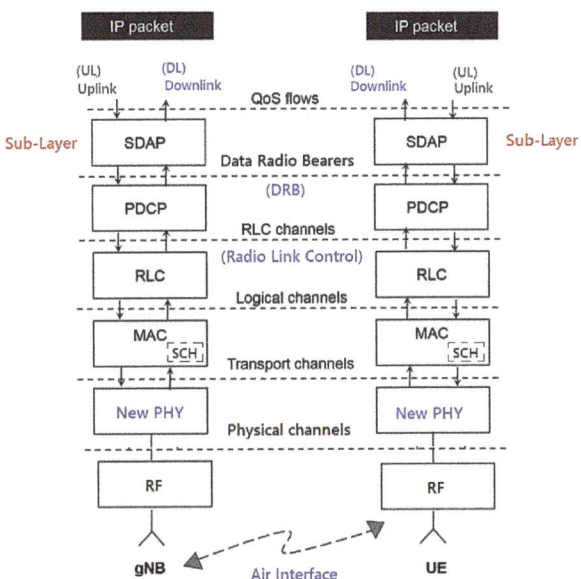

Figure 5. 5G NR/NGC SA protocol stack. Based on [38,39].

As shown in Figure 5:

- Packet Data Convergence Protocol (PDCP) is the first sublayer in the 5G NR protocol stack that receives/transmits network layer traffic (TCP/IP traffic);
- Data Radio Bearer (DRB) has the logical connection used within the 5G protocol stack to carry protocol data units (PDUs);
- The Service Data Adaptation Protocol (SDAP) functionality is to map the QoS flows for the DRB in the PDCP sublayer in the DL and UL directions [40].

The channels shown in Figure 5 help us organize and simplify the design of the stack for each sublayer. It is prioritized and optimized in different ways for the channels during the DL and the UL [41,42]. There are three types of specific channels [40]:

- Logical channels that define the type of data to be transferred with the traffic (user data), such as "paging messages", dedicated control information;
- Transport channels that define the information to be transported to the physical layer and the characteristics of the data, such as error protection, channel coding, the cyclic redundancy check (CRC) and the size of the data packet;
- Physical channels characterized by their time and access protocols, data rates as traffic channels [40].

3.2. Fronthaul Challenges and Functional Division Options

O-RAN provides the option of placing functions on the network at different locations and along the signal path; this option is called a functional RAN split and is referred to as Lower Layer Split (LLS) and Higher Layer Split (HLS), as shown in Figure 3. The project's 5G private network is allowed to improve its performance and make some compensations due to RAN disaggregation, making the decision of which node/site/unit should control certain operations of the functional division of the RAN.

3GPP defined Options 1–8 of interfaces for the functional division to interconnect them, in the F2 network interfaces of the gNB-RU (Fronthaul) to connect (RU->DU), in which we have the eCPRI traffic interface (class 2, functional split 7.2x) in Figure 6. eCPRI requires time synchronization (frequency and phase) to be achieved by the packet-in-band method through IEEE 1588v2 to operate reliably in the project [43]. The F1 interface (functional split 2.0) on the gNB-DU (Midhaul) (DU->CU) was previously discussed and is shown in Figure 6 in relation to layers L1, L2 and L3 of the RU, DU and CU [44].

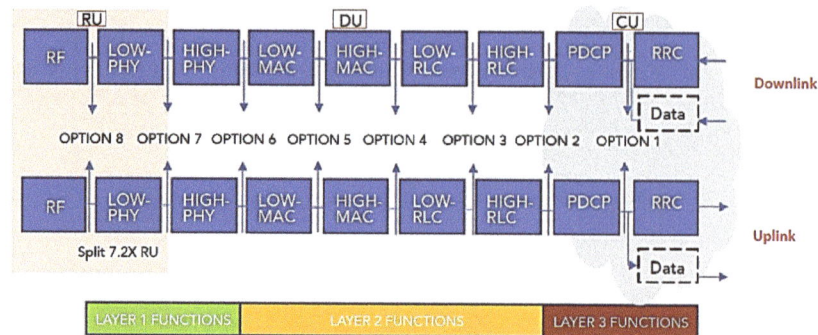

Figure 6. Eight functional split options with 5G xHaul network architecture for gNB-RU (Fronthaul) (RU->DU), gNB-DU (Midhaul) (DU->CU) and Backhaul (CU->core network). Based on [40].

The functional division options allow the Fronthaul and Midhaul network interfaces of the DU/CU to face the challenges of increased traffic and the intelligence of placing close to the RU (AAS-RU and the RRU) versus the DUs [45,46]. O-RAN can distribute the baseband processing over the logical nodes, thus defining the characteristics of these links, choosing which of the RAN's functional divisions (Split of 2-8), logical to the sublayer of the device, improves the split ratio. Fronthaul to Backhaul (Device->RU->DU->CU [5G NGC]) in relation to the sublayers of the 5G NR/NGC SA is shown in Figure 7.

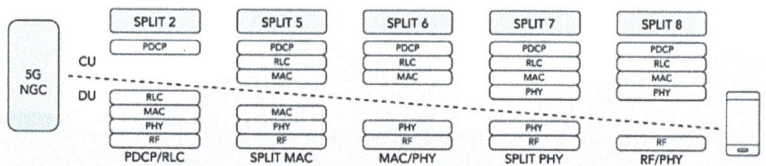

Figure 7. RAN splits—logical to sub-Layer 5G NR/NGC SA. Based on [46].

In OpenCare5Gt, the F2 option was used with the Fronthaul 7-2x functional division between the RU->DU for the 5G Sub-6 GHz spectrum, to obtain more bandwidth and speed by the RU performed in the physical sublayer " PHY-Low" and "PHY-High" (Split 7 / Split PHY) in Figure 7 [47].

3.3. Installation of the RU (AAS-RU and the RRU)

Figure 8 shows the Antenna Radiation Diagram with angular reference of 20° in relation to the horizon for frequencies of 3400–3800 MHz. The RU is installed on the ceiling of the Intervention Center of the InradHC at HCFMUSP (Exam Room–Ultrasound).

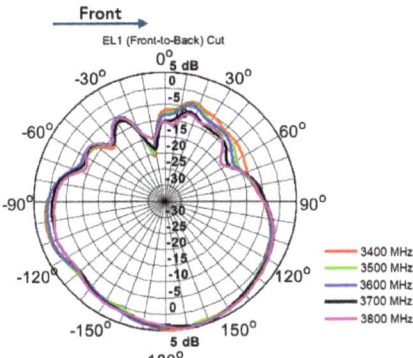

Figure 8. Antenna radiation diagram. Based on [48].

3.4. DU (Distributed Unit)

The COTs server (HWs/SWs) DU is installed in the InradHC datacenter, shown in Figures 2 and 3 to perform cDU containerization with Docker (platform as a service with operating system level containers to deliver software in container packages isolated from each other), where baseband processing is performed in real time [49].

The RU/cDU process layers from PHY-High to RLC-High are shown in Figure 6 of "Radio Protocol Stack Simplified in the UMTS/LTE/5G Air Interface" [47,49]. With cDU containerization, we will have flexibility of placing processes in different locations in the O-RAN environment, which, in our use case, is in the InradHC datacenter. This logical node includes a subset of the gNB-RU functions (Fronthaul) with the Spit 7.2x functional division and its operation controlled by the CU/vCU.

The cDU controls the L2 layer, with the MAC-Low sublayer up to the RLC-High, and in Figures 2, 3 and 9 we have the gNB-DU that hosts the upper part of the "PHY-High" sublayer, partially controlled through the CU to the RLC-High, as shown in Figure 6. Figure 9 shows the X2 terminal which is the interface between the O-RAN RU/DU node and the CU/ACP/Kubernetes (K8s) 5GCN.

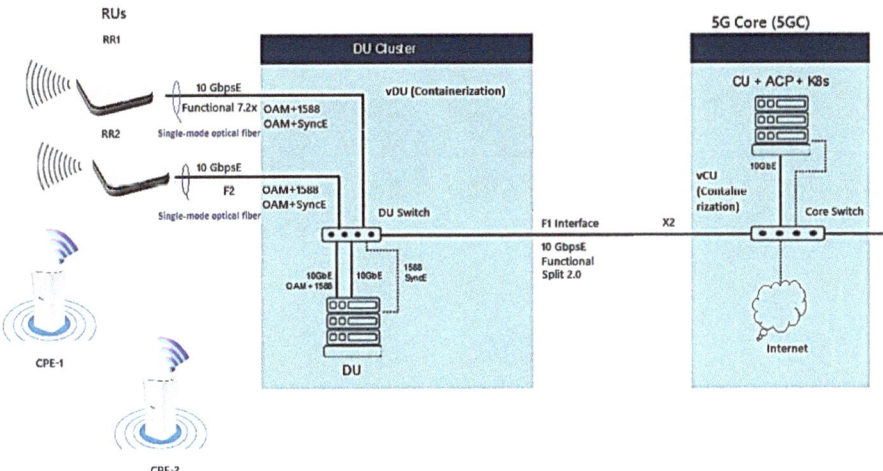

Figure 9. Simplified architecture of RUs+CPEs+DU+5GC. Based on [28,50].

3.5. 5G Core Network (5GCN)

Our 5GCN is detailed in this subsection.

3.5.1. Core Architecture Based on Services and Reference Point

The Core Architecture is SBA and PR based on the 5GC through the 5G base stations shown in the architecture of Figures 2 and 3 to perform the baseband functions using the vRAN in the project with the interfaces that carry out the interactions with the NFs.

Figure 10 illustrates the 5GCN SBA Architecture and Reference Point (PR) with the E2E CP protocol stack and its main interfaces.

In the project, new open interfaces were defined in the SBA and PR core architecture at points "F" and "E1" within the O-RAN node interface between the PHY and RU sublayers with the eCPRI protocol. One node ends in the CP in "C" of Figures 10 and 11 of the gNB-CU, called gNB-CU-CP. The other node that end the user plane "U" of the gNB-CU and is termed gNB-CU-UP. The default open interface between these nodes is specified as "E1", shown in Figures 10 and 11.

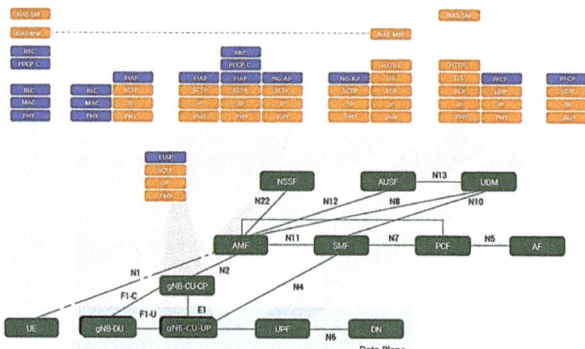

Figure 10. Architecture of the core 5G SBA and reference point with the end-to-end control plane protocol stack and its main interfaces. Based on [51].

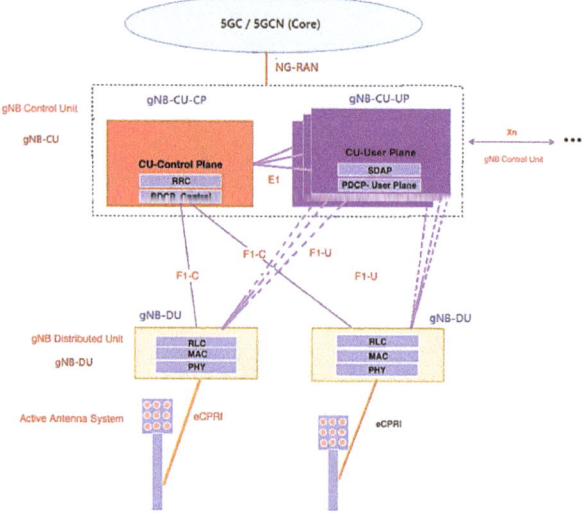

Figure 11. gNB-CU-CP and gNB-CU-UP separation architecture. Based on [50,52–54].

According to Figures 2, 3, 10 and 11, in OpenCare5G the gNB (5G NR Node) is divided into a Distributed Unit (gNB-DU), a Centralized Unit Control Plane (gNB-CU-CP) and a Centralized Unit Data Plane (gNB-CU-DP). Therefore, there is a separation of the control plane (gNB-CU-CP) and the user plane (gNB-CU-UP) that form CUPS in gNB-CU, as per 3GPP [51].

3.5.2. CUPS—Architecture for Control and User Plane Separation

The 5G/GC(Core) SA network was conceived based on the SBA and the PR of Figure 11 for the communication between the nodes with the network functions (NFs) in which the 3GPP defined an application programming interface (API) that works over the Hypertext Transfer Protocol (HTTP) and follows the Representational State Transfer (REST) model [38].

With the SBA NFs for the access and mobility management function (AMF) and the user plane function (UPF), we will have the division of the 5G NR protocol stack through the user plane (UP) and the control plane (CP) forming the 5G NR/NGC SA Protocol Structure Stack's separation of control plane and users (CUPS) architecture via F1-C, F1-U and E1, with the gNB-DU, splitting the gNB-CU in gNB-CU-CP and gNB-CU-UP [52,54].

Figures 11 and 12 depict the UP architecture that provides user data, while the CP provides connection configuration for mobility and security between the UE and the 5G(gNB) base station [23]. The 5G NR transports information over multiple physical channels. Both gNB-CU-CP and gNB-CU-DP are NF functions for virtualized networks running on the CU server in 5G vRAN with multiple instances and CUPS concept for expansion on demand, in which [52,54]:

- A gNB can consist of one gNB-CU-CP for several gNB-CU-UPs and one gNB-DU;
- At the same time, one gNB can consist of one gNB-CU-CP for several gNB-CU-UPs and several gNB-DUs;
- gNB-CU-CP is connected to gNB-DU by the F1-C interface;
- gNB-CU-UP is connected to gNB-DU by the F1-U interface;
- gNB-CU-CP is connected to gNB-CU-UP by the E1 interface;
- One gNB-DU is connected to only one gNB-CU-CP;
- One gNB-CU-UP is connected to only one gNB-CU-CP.

The gNB-CU-Control Plane (gNB-CU-CP) consists of:

- A logical node hosting the RRC;
- The CP part of the PDCP protocol of the gNB-CU for an gNB;
- The gNB-CU-CP terminates the E1 interface connected with the gNB-CU-UP and the F1-C interface connected with the gNB-DU [53].

The gNB-CU-User Plane (gNB-CU-UP) consists of:

- A logical node hosting the UP part of the PDCP protocol of the gNB-CU for an gNB, and the UP part of the PDCP protocol and the SDAP protocol of the gNB-CU;
- The gNB-CU-UP terminates the E1 interface connected with the gNB-CU-CP and the F1-U interface connected with the gNB-DU [53].

3.5.3. User Plane and Control Plane for UE/Device and gNB Protocol Stack with Network Functions AMF and UPF

The 5G NR/NGC SA protocol stack for the Access Stratum (AS) is divided into CP and UP with the interfaces shown as UE, gNB, AMF and UPF in Figure 12, based on Figures 2 and 3.

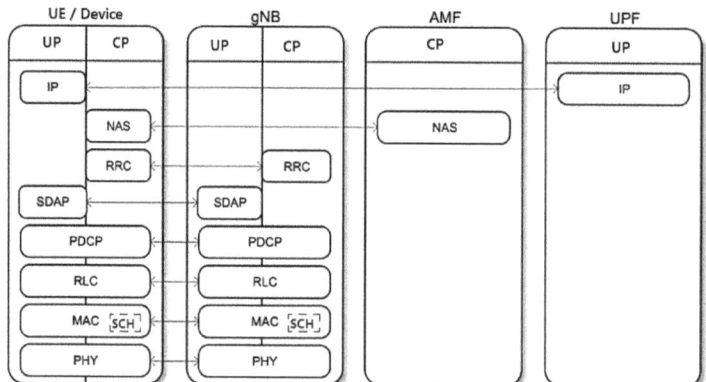

Figure 12. Access stratum for the user and control planes for UE/device and gNB protocol stack with network functions AMF and UPF. Based on [37,40,42,52].

The protocol stack has the following data:

- Device UP (Device/UE) connects to the UPF network function via IP-to-IP;
- CP is connected via NAS-to-NAS by the AMF network function;
- The NAS and RRC sublayers are unique to the PC;
- The message-based IP transport protocol known as SCTP is used between the eNB (Evolved NodeB) and the MME (Mobility Management Entity) to transport the NAS messages;
- Reliable message transfer between eNB and MME;
- RRC deals with the general configuration of a cell including the PDCP, RLC, MAC and PHY sublayers [40];
- The SDAP sublayer deals with the mapping between the QoS flow and the radio bearers;
- IP (Internet Protocol) packets are mapped to radio bearers according to their QoS requirements;
- The PDCP sublayer is primarily responsible for IP header compression/decompression, reordering and duplicate detection, encryption/decryption and integrity protection;
- The RLC sublayer performs error correction through an automatic repeat request (ARQ) mechanism, segmentation/resegmentation of IP packets (header compression) and sequential delivery of data units to upper sublayers;
- The MAC sublayer is responsible for error correction through the ARQ3 hybrid mechanism (HARQ), uplink and downlink scheduling [40];
- The PHY sublayer handles encoding/decoding, modulation/demodulation, multi-antenna processing and mapping signals to physical time-frequency resources;
- The CP is responsible for control signaling for connection configuration, mobility and security;
- Control signaling originates from a core network or from an RRC sublayer in the gNB;
- The PHY sublayer is the key component of the NR physical layer technology that undergoes modulation, waveform, multi-antenna, transmission and channel coding [38].

3.6. Network Services Based on Adaptive Network Slicing on Open RAN

Network Slicing is an important 5G 3GPP defined resource that allows PLS to support specific use cases and a dedicated set of these network resources and matched service level agreements (SLAs) for each use case. It has been considered in OpenCare5G.

OpenCare5G has not implemented the infrastructure for virtualization of network functions for orchestration (NFVI Orchestration). Support for network slicing is being improved in the reference version for the project in its first adoption of 5GC, SA Release 16. However, these features will only be implemented later.

3.7. Virtualization and Containerization for vDU and vCU

Figures 2 and 3 show the implementation of the Airspan O-RANGE Software architecture through to Figure 13 with container network functions (CNF) for vDU using Docker Engine and container and virtualized network functions (vCU) with hypervisor. These will be used in the project to serve the vRAN, to allow a modular, scalable architecture that is flexibile in its implementation.

Figure 13 shows:

- Block 1, the physical hardware infrastructure of the O-DU and O-CU servers, network and storage in COTS;
- Block 2, the Host Server for the host operating system (HOS) connected to the network, offering information, resources, services and applications needed by the user and other nodes in the network;
- Block 3 provides virtual containers with Docker Engine, which is the heart of the Docker System to realize the client–server architecture application installed on the host server [55]. The system uses Container Docker and Machine Virtualization (VM) concepts over the hypervisor. With containers, processing is performed directly on the host server, using the Docker mechanism to make it faster and lighter [55].

In Block 4, we have the container network functions CNF with implementation via POD (Passed Out Drunk) of K8s with Docker, realizing a set of one or more Linux containers in the K8s application.

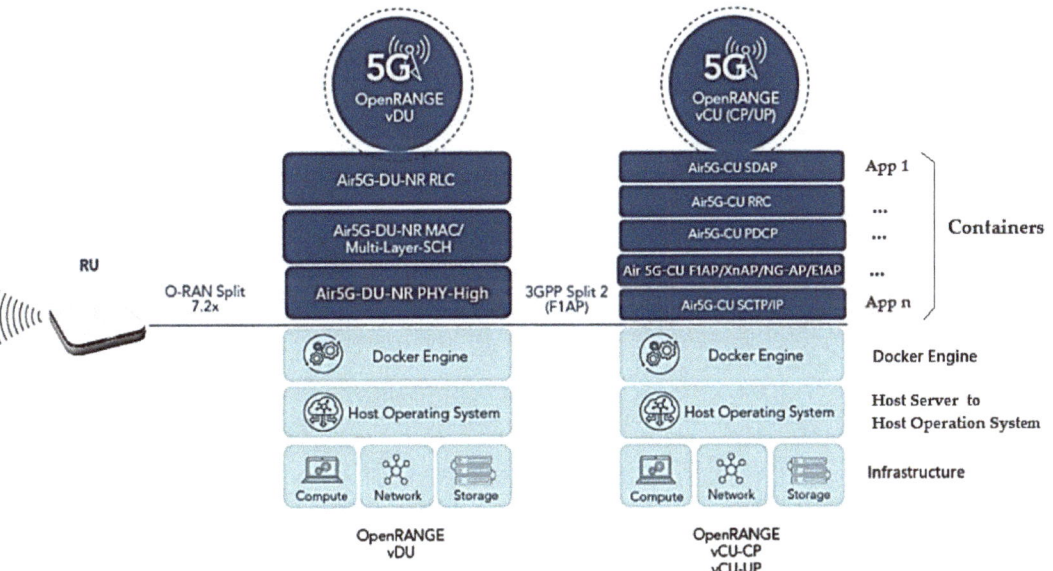

Figure 13. Architecture of Container Network Functions (CNF) with applications running on O-DU/O-CU Servers with OpenRange Software for vDU and vCU. Based on [46].

- PODs are composed of a container in the most common use cases or several tightly coupled containers. These containers are grouped into PODs so that resources are shared more efficiently. That is, we will have 1-n application containers (App) on top of the vDU, as the containers are abstractions in the 1-n application layer with Docker (Bins/Libs) packaging the application and its dependencies into the container in a single operating system (OS) with resources shared between containers [55];

- Each application in the project virtual container runs in its own isolated process controlled by the Docker Engine, as if it were a host operating system. However, it will not virtualize the entire environment on the cDU and cvCU Servers. It will work on top of the n application and its dependencies, creating virtualization only at the host operating system level and not on the entire server, making the project system light and managing to initialize the applications in seconds compared to the traditional VMs. Less RAM, CPU and storage will thus be used to offer lower latency [55].

Five new application protocols were introduced into the Airspan O-RANGE software architecture in the project using vCU-CP and vCU-UP with end-to-end control plane protocols, depicted in Figure 13:

- F1AP (F1 Application Protocol) is used to relay Packet Data Convergence Protocol (PDCP) CP messages and Radio Resource Control (RRC) messages between the gNB-DU and the gNB-CU-CP;
- E1AP (E1 Application Protocol) is used to program GTP-U tunnels for the datapath in gNB-CU-DP;
- XnAP (Xn Application Protocol) is the control protocol used between gNBs to support a variety of O-RAN-related procedures, such as establishing dual connectivity, coordinating Xn-based handovers (duplication), O-RAN data forwarding and paging. It is used in the SCTP sublayer to coordinate gNB-CU-MC functionality (MultiCast functionality within gNB-CU);
- NG-AP (NG Application Protocol) provides CP signaling between the node via NG-RAN and the access and mobility management function (AMF). The services provided by the NG-AP are divided into UE-associated and non-UE-associated;
- SCTP (Flow Control Transport Protocol) is similar to TCP in terms of fundamentals, but adds features that compensate for some weaknesses of TCP.

There is a need to implement requirements to provide a base virtual port for Single Root Input/Output Virtualization (SR-IOV) to allow isolating resources via PCI Express between different users on the server O-DU. When these hardware features enable virtual functions, they can be segmented and accessed on K8s PODs to share network resources and secure network traffic [56].

That is, SR-IOV is used when applications running on K8s clusters need high bandwidth and low latency performance, and when used with VMs, SR-IOV allows applications to bypass the vSwitch, allowing itself so that the VM directly access the device instead of going through the vSwitch to a CP port and a port for UP traffic per instance on the O-DU Server instance [56].

The Intel SR-IOV Network Device Plugin with K8s extends capabilities to address high-performance network I/O by discovering and advertising SR-IOV Network Virtual Functions (VFs) on a K8s host. Thus, SR-IOV is used for CNFs in 5G configuration. Applications can achieve high throughput, different levels of hardware QoS with low latency [56].

3.8. cvCU—5GCN Containerized/Virtualized Unit

The O-CU Server-Centralized Unit utilizes cvCU containerization and virtualization where the less-time-sensitive non-real-time packet-processing functions reside and the unit handles all upper-layer functions of the protocol stack of the PDCP [57].

The cvCU also accounts for non-real-time functions at L2 (MAC-Low) and L3 (PDCP-Low) that are performed at the RRC and PDCP layers to perform data packet convergence in conjunction with CUPS of CP and UP [14].

In Figure 14, there is an interface of the E2 nodes, in which the RIC will not be used, only the controls of procedures and functionalities of this E2 node between two CU-C-Plane endpoints and CU-U-Plane close to near-real-time between cDU and cvCU in 5G [14].

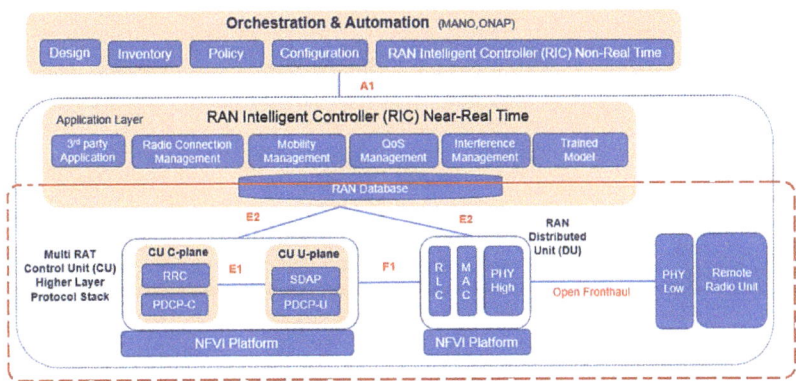

Figure 14. Architecture of CNF with applications running on O-DU/O-CU servers with OpenRange Software for vDU and vCU. Based on [58,59].

VNFs are managed by the NFVI which encompasses all the network hardware and software needed to support and connect these VNFs in a private network in which a VNF is allowed to be instantiated, managed, scaled up or down.

3.9. Platform Control with ACP

The Airspan Control Platform (ACP) is a control system architecture software element for RU, vDU and vCU in servers to manage network functions, as shown in Figure 15.

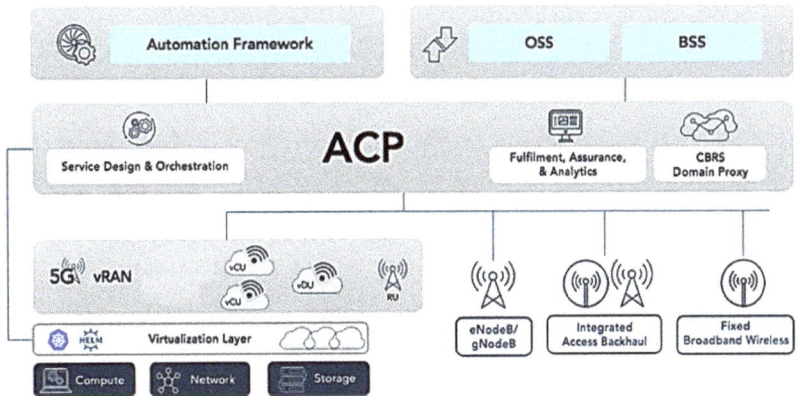

Figure 15. ACP—Airspan Control Platform. Based on [60].

The ACP software is installed and run on the O-CU server, where all containers are monitored and configured from within the ACP. The network configuration needs to reflect the management K8s so that the ACP can communicate with all nodes within the K8s cluster [60].

After installation, the ACP is installed using the SA credentials to create the database backend for the web frontend, in which we have the connectivity of the ACP via the Kubernetes Management Network (KMN) for the ACP to control all PODs contained within the worker nodes [60].

With ACP, the project has the flexibility to allow for single or multiple technologies to take control and provide end-to-end management, and to integrate into Operating System and Support (OSS) stacks to automate network management [61].

4. Experimental Evaluation

This work adopts an engineering and empirical strategy. It is based on the scientific method since it applies data analysis to the results obtained under the performed procedures.

The execution methods of OpenCare5G adopt a top-down approach, an organized way of developing network projects, with an analysis of each layer of the 5G architecture, starting with the service layer, where the demands of the applications come from, and ending with the infrastructure layer.

The tests for capturing real data for analysis were conducted according to the explanation in this section. The purpose of the project at this stage is examining the use cases in the service modality of the communication protocols of existing and new equipment that will be incorporated into the 5G network, as shown in Figures 2 and 3. We will have multiple applications, including data communication, video and audio signals, voice, text, as well as capture and transmission of telemedicine data.

4.1. Definition of the Test Plan

The test plan was divided into two main phases:

- The first phase is related to the PoC-1 involving an active 5G private network with the architecture set up at the InRad of HCFMUSP in two rooms—the Intervention Sector Room and Ultrasound Exam Room—to use the portable ultrasound (USG) on a patient lying down on a stretcher. He was accompanied by Doctor 1, who performed the USG of the abdomen, and Doctor 2, a radiologist in the central room in front of a monitoring station who analyzed the data captured from the exams, and whose rooms are covered by the 5G network;
- The second phase is related to PoC-2 involving the same 5G private network remotely connected to the Computational Tomography MRI/CT.

In these use cases, the focus is also on validating technical criteria involving latency and signal bandwidth in the 5G network of these PoCs, among other functional characteristics of the telecommunications engineering process in real time.

4.2. Proof of Concept 1

We performed the PoC-1-1 with a verification test of the latency and bandwidth of the ultrasound exam, by capturing files over the 5G network from Philips portable equipment, model Lumity, type C5-2 Transducer. Its technical specifications are as follows:

- Model Limity C5-2 transducer;
- Curved broadband;
- Operating frequency range from 2 to 5 MHz;
- Curvature radius of 50 mm;
- 2D color Doppler imaging, M-mode, advanced XRES for multivariate harmonic imaging, SonoCT;
- High-resolution diagnostic imaging for deeper applications: preconfigured enhancements for abdominal, gallbladder, gynecology/obstetrics and lung imaging;
- Central venous catheter marker;
- USB-C Transducer.

We performed PoC-1-2 with a latency verification test and ultrasound scan bandwidth, by capturing the files over the 5G network from Mobisson portable equipment, model M3. Its technical specifications are as follows:

- Transducer: Model M3;
- Convex;
- Weight: 240 g;
- Wireless;
- Operating Frequency Range from 3.5 to 5 MHz;

- Depth from 90 to 280 mm;
- 3-h autonomy in continuous use, 6-hour in standby;
- Features: Harmonics, Sector Gain, Noise Smoothing;
- Applications: Performs abdominal and cardiac ultrasound, obstetrical and prenatal exams, renal evaluations and quick identification of lesions and internal bleeding.

Performing Ultrasound Exams on PoC-1-1 and PoC-1-2

The PoC-1-1 tests were performed with the Philips portable ultrasound examination equipment. Figure 16 shows the patient lying on a stretcher, with the USG procedure in the abdomen being performed by Dr. 1, an interventional and endovascular surgery radiologist at HCFMUSP.

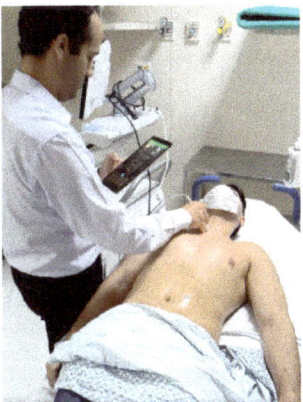

Figure 16. Doctor 1 performing ultrasound on the patient.

The other professional, Dr. 2, an interventional radiologist, handled the screens for analysis of the ultrasound of the patient lying on the stretcher at a distance, analyzing the cameras where the patient was in the process of telemedicine. He observed and analyzed the test process with Dr. 1, conducting real-time guidance on the distance ultrasound, in addition to capturing the images to store them, and later carry out the clinical report of the exam.

That is, the focus was on the medical assessment of the equipment use case by Dr. 2. He subjectively assessed whether, with the proposed new O-RAN 5G architecture, there will be an improvement or not in the results collected from the images derived from the ultrasound equipment in the PoC-1 tests.

The PoC 1 was carried out on 26 October 2022 on the second floor of the InRad building, where project antenna A is located, and in the radio intervention department where antenna B is located. The 5G signal was generated in the Airspan Core from the datacenter in Itaú located 9 km from HCFMUSP.

In the location of Antenna A (Doctor Central Room), there was a notebook connected to the dedicated CPE to receive the 5G signal dissipated by the antenna installed there. This machine had a headset and a dedicated webcam. In the locality, radiologist Dr. 2 was responsible for receiving the images and directing the other professional with guidelines for conducting the USG transducer. The portable point-of-care USG equipment used for this PoC was the Philips Lumify, which has a dedicated application for transmitting images in real-time, called Reacts.

The proposal to use the Philips-Lumify equipment was because it was the only equipment that had an accompanying streaming application that provided quality, real-time images at the time of PoC-1 so that the guiding physician could offer remote guidance within the scope from the project. Other streaming platforms tested before PoC-1 showed lower image-quality results.

At the location of antenna B, a Samsung T515 tablet was anchored to the 5G network, connected via Wi-Fi 6 to the 5G CPE that receives the signal dissipated in the environment. The Philips-Lumify product application was installed on the tablet, which, when connecting the transducer via cable to the device, enabled the application to view the USG images to be captured. In this locality, Dr. 1 was responsible for performing the exam, interacting with the radiology doctor in the orientation room.

The radiological images of the ultrasound exam were transmitted using the Reacts Platform, integrated into the Philips-Lumify device application, which required registering two accounts in the Reacts application, executor and advisor. The PoC was divided into the stage of perception of executing professionals and USG exam advisor in real-time in relation to the exam, as well as the technical verification by the application analyst in relation to data traffic in the 5G network.

When the examiner viewed the images, the product was verified to deliver the versioning of the interface and functionality expected by the project, according to the perception of the physician who performed this role.

When transmitting the images to the advisor, the exam executor again expressed that the visualization interface for the exam was satisfactory by dividing his screen into three blocks: one in the upper left corner with his image from the front camera of the tablet, another with the advisor's image in the upper right corner, and occupying the remaining 3/4 of the screen with USG images and application functionalities.

This stage therefore follows as expected for the project. When connecting to the Reacts platform, the application demonstrated good responsiveness, managing to transmit the images to the guiding medical professional located at the other end.

It was possible to clearly hear the communication between the two professionals; the images were transmitted with minor limitations, possibly related to the network connection speed and limitations of the tablet, which was still connected to the 5G CPE Wi-Fi network. The examination advisor in the report room questioned some difficulty in receiving the images on the Reacts platform, possibly due to connectivity and to the device used to run the application, the Samsung T515 tablet.

The advisor reported that it was possible to direct the information to the executor to carry out the instructions for viewing the ultrasound images on the screen, but with limitations. In general, the advisor reported that this moment was acceptable for the first version of the PoC. However, he showed that he was not satisfied with using only one solution and he hoped that the PoC would be carried out for other USG devices, such as the brand Mobissom, connected to Reacts or another similar telemedicine application.

4.3. Proof of Concept 2

We performed the PoC-2 with a set of image file exams (*DICOM) generated with MRI/CT on a patient at the Intervention Center of the InRad of HCFMUSP, as illustrated in Figure 17. The MRI/CT (Magnetic Resonance Imaging/Computed Tomography) from Siemens Healthcare Scanner Room with Softwares sVC (syngo Virtual Cockpit Modality and Steering Clients type VA16A) remote access is a multimodality reading solution built on a client–server platform. In legacy solutions, the machine technician is usually located in a room adjacent to the MRI/CT. sVC allows an operator to remotely command the CT machine from a different location. With this, hospitals can benefit from operational costs and specialized doctors can be more readily available.

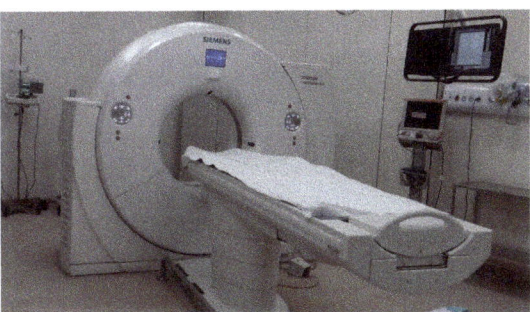

Figure 17. MRI/CT scanner room.

All MRI/CT image files were sent and obtained via PACS (Picture Archiving and Communication System) via sVC software (syngo Virtual Cockpit Modality and Steering clients) to facilitate handling and visualization via 2D and 3D in the 5G private network.

In PoC-2-1, we monitor, manipulate and visualize images from the MRI/CT unit by analyzing the latency of packet times from one point to another in the network and the bandwidth that defines the speed and capacity of the 5G private network, as shown in Figure 18.

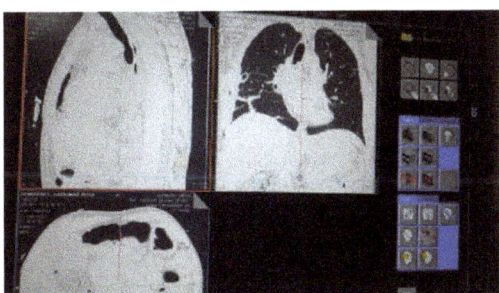

Figure 18. Manipulation and visualization of images from the tomograph via 5G network.

Figure 19 presents the architecture of the 5G network for Modality/sVC simulation.

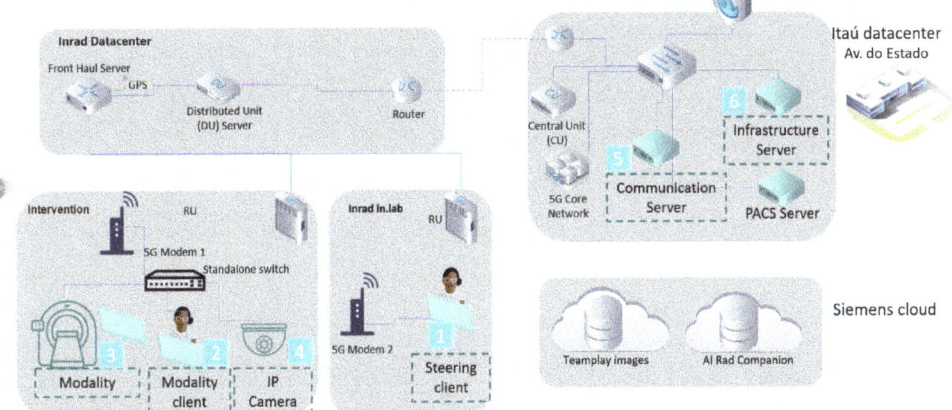

Figure 19. Architecture with the 5G network for Modality/sVC Simulation.

4.4. Results and Discussion

The tests carried out for the use cases of data received and sent from exams, images, voice and text to evaluate the data transmission capacity of 5G connectivity demonstrated the effectiveness of our methodology.

PoC-1 evaluated the connectivity of the 5G network in terms of transmitting USG images in a product already commercially available that benefits from a dedicated communication platform, Reacts. Hence, with a specific product that offers the opportunity for collaboration, the project team can have answers to questions that are still unanswered. In fact, the project aims to cover a large number of portable USG equipment to perform USG exams in remote locations. In view of the above, the scenario proposed for the examination follows the expected scope, and we collectively chose to consider the PoC satisfactory, due to the limitations found.

Figure 20 presents the results of the second phase of the 5G private network test for PoC-2-1, which are also reported and discussed in Table 2.

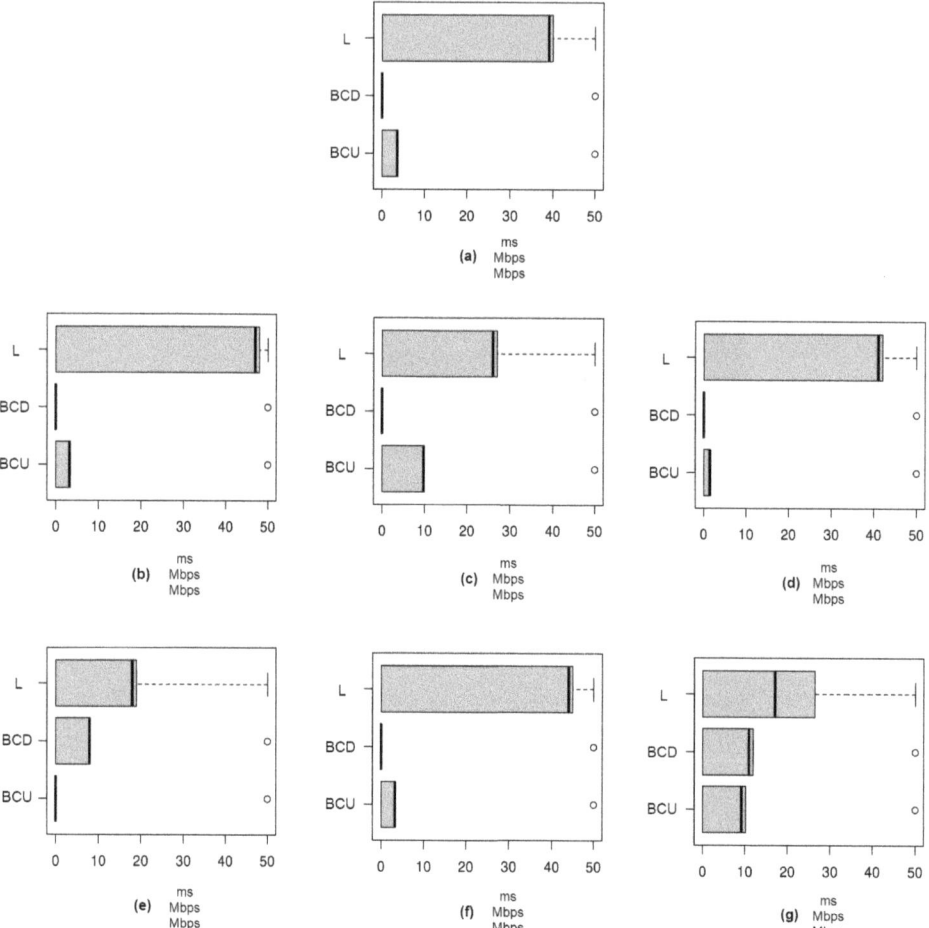

Figure 20. Boxplot of tests in the second phase of the 5G private network for PoC-2-1. (**a**) Test 1: VNC; (**b**) Test 2-1: VNC; (**c**) Test 2-2: PACS; (**d**) Test 3-1: VNC; (**e**) Test 3-2: PACS; (**f**) Test 4-1: VNC; (**g**) Test 4-2: PACS. BCD: Bandwidth Consumption in Download; BCU: Bandwidth Consumption in Upload; L: Latency.

Table 2. Tests results with sVC in PoC-2-1.

Steering [1]	Description	Results [2]	Evaluation
Test 1	Access, via VNC Client on PC1, to the VNC Server on PC2.	[PC2 (Test 1)—VNC protocol: L = 40 ms; BCU = 3.79 Mbps; BCD = NA].	Application responding normally to commands, without loss of performance.
Test 2	Access, via VNC Client on PC1, to the VNC Server on PC2, with image transfer towards PC2 -> PACS Itaú.	[PC1 (Test 2-1)—via VNC: L = 48 ms; BCU = 3.39 Mbps; BCD = NA] / [PC1 (Test 2-2)—via PACS: L = 27 ms; BCU = 9.94 Mbps; BCD = NA].	Application responding normally to commands, without loss of performance.
Test 3	Access, via VNC Client on PC1, to the VNC Server on PC2, with image transfer towards PACS Itaú -> PC2.	[PC1 (Test 3-1)—via VNC: L = 42 ms; BCU = 1.57 Mbps; BCD = NA] / [PC1 (Test 3-2)—via PACS: L = 19 ms; BCU = NA; BCD = 7.93 Mbps].	Application responding normally to commands, without loss of performance.
Test 4	Access, via VNC Client on PC1, to the VNC Server on PC2, with image transfer towards PC2 -> PACS Itaú and PACS Itaú -> PC2.	[PC1 (Test 4-1)—via VNC: L = 45 ms; BCU = 3.38 Mbps; BCD = NA] / [PC1 (Test 4-2)—via PACS: L = 17–26 ms; BCU = 10.21 Mbps; BCD = 11.95 Mbps].	Application responding normally to commands, without loss of performance.

[1] Requirements proposed for each steering: Network bandwidth $\geq$ 40 Mbps; Latency $\leq$ 30 ms. [2] BCD: Bandwidth Consumption in Download; BCU: Bandwidth Consumption in Upload; L: Latency; NA: Not Available.

5. Conclusions

OpenCare5G is a pioneering project in Brazil that is already contributing to quality healthcare through the InovaHC of HCFMUSP. In addition to the implementation of 5G this year, the OpenCare5G project innovates and aims to attract investors from various sectors of information technology, telecommunications and other industries to promote further research in different areas of medicine and engineering as well as foster a complete technology ecosystem, through medtechs, healthtechs and market partners.

The formation of an ecosystem with market partners facilitates this strategy and in this first phase, the 5G private network at HCFMUSP is active and carrying out PoC tests with portable ultrasound equipment and computational tomography via the 5G Network. InRad wants the technology to allow an operator, who can be a healthcare professional, a nurse or a paramedic, to perform the tests remotely with the help of a specialist doctor at the other end, who will also evaluate the images.

The adherence of the 5G network to the demands and tests carried out in this work is evident. We are not focusing on more complex scientific–technological issues such as remote surgeries at this time. Preliminarily, we aim to evolve the state of the art to expand and democratize 5G access to improve quality of life, causing social and economic impacts.

Any network intermittency may have occurred (e.g., some process in the DU/CU consuming too much memory or CPU) in our tests. Some process within the Siemens solution is consuming a lot of memory/processing within the personal computers involved in the tests. We are still investigating the observed latency increase.

Applications of the mobile network for exams do not have issues such as sensitivity to latency in critical missions, as in the case of robotic surgeries. The scope is connectivity that allows images to be sent for follow-up in near-real time. The analysis of a diagnosis currently takes days. This fact is thus important for society to understand that there are several cases of 5G/B5G use. Robotic surgery is a future goal, but this little investment in connectivity will already make an enormous difference in the future.

Future Work

The OpenCare5G project has a forward-looking expansion plan that includes:

- Urban PoC: Expanding the concept demonstrated in PoC-1-1-1 to an urban environment within the State of São Paulo. The ultrasound exam room will be located in a basic healthcare unit in the range of 200 km to 400 km from the central room doctor based at InRad of HCFMUSP. The remote ultrasound room will constitute an additional node to the private 5G network, deploying a local DU/Fronthaul switch infrastructure at the UBS. The medical procedure will be refined and submitted for the approval of the relevant medical committees to evaluate actual patients of the public healthcare system. We aim to deploy this phase within one year of finishing the current PoCs;

- Rural PoC: Expanding the concept demonstrated in PoC-1-1-1 to a remote environment within the Brazilian Amazon region. The ultrasound exam room will be located in an Indigenous basic healthcare unit or a similar location and a reference central room doctor will be deployed in the city of Santarém, State of Pará. Alternatives to backhaul coverage, such as low-orbit satellites, may be considered. The medical procedure will be refined and submitted for the approval of the relevant medical committees to best cater to the native population in the region. We aim to deploy this phase within one year of finishing the current PoCs;
- Geographical expansion: Expanding the urban and rural PoCs to additional regions in the country;
- Functional use cases: Increasing the usage of ultrasound diagnosis in prenatal care, heart exams and calculus detection, among others. Addition of other remote assistances to the portfolio. Implementation of further sVC (remote operation for tomography and magnetic resonance machines) in 5G-connected hospitals;
- Implementation of AI image analysis;
- Promotion of medtechs/healthtechs' engagement and knowledge diffusion;
- Evaluation of synergistic technologies in "green or ecologically correct networks to support the expansion of the intelligent connected edge with minimal network energy consumption;
- Implementations for network security to overcome challenges in patients' data privacy and confidentiality;
- Advanced testbeds for novel communication technologies, including network slicing [62–64].

Author Contributions: Conceptualization, W.d.O., J.O.R.B.J., T.N. and S.T.T.; methodology, W.d.O., T.N. and S.T.T.; software, S.T.T.; validation, W.d.O., J.O.R.B.J., T.N. and S.T.T.; formal analysis, T.N., L.R.S., M.M.J., C.E.C. and G.B.; investigation, W.d.O. and S.T.T.; resources, T.N., and S.T.T.; data curation, W.d.O., J.O.R.B.J. and S.T.T.; writing—original draft preparation, W.d.O. and J.O.R.B.J.; writing—review and editing, W.d.O., J.O.R.B.J., T.N., L.R.S., M.M.J., C.E.C. and G.B.; visualization, W.d.O., J.O.R.B.J., T.N., M.M.J., C.E.C. and G.B.; supervision, M.M.J.; project administration, T.N. All authors have read and agreed to the published version of the manuscript.

Funding: This research received no external funding.

Institutional Review Board Statement: Not applicable.

Informed Consent Statement: Not applicable.

Data Availability Statement: Not applicable.

Acknowledgments: This work is supported by the Department of Computer Engineering and Digital Systems (PCS) of Escola Politécnica da USP (EPUSP the School of Engineering—University of São Paulo), Brazil; by the Coordination for the Improvement of Higher Education Personnel (CAPES) in Brazil; by the Science and Technology Center (CCT), Research Support Foundation of the São Paulo State (FAPESP) project # 2021/11.905-0 in Brazil; by Deloitte Touche Tohmatsu, Brazil; by NEC Latin America S.A., Brazil; by the Brazilian Agency for Industrial Development (ABDI), Brazil; by Clinical Hospital (HCFMUSP), Brazil; by the Itaú Bank, Brazil; by ANATEL, Brazil; by Airspan, Brazil; by Siemens Healthineers, Brazil; and by Telecom Infra Project (TIP), United States. The authors also express their gratitude for the contributions of Antonio Valerio Netto, Márcio Meira, Marcos Menezes, Cleiton Alessandro Vieira Caldeira, Vinicius Lopes Gandara, Gleidson de Oliveira Dutra and Maria Cristina Vidal Borba.

Conflicts of Interest: The authors declare that: (i) they have no known competing financial interests or personal relationships that could have influenced the work reported in this paper; (ii) in the test performed: there was no patient. The project team performed the test in the case of ultrasound. We accessed the machine without a patient for tomography; there were no clinical diagnoses; technicians and physicians only evaluated the demo for test image quality.

Abbreviations

The following abbreviations are used in this manuscript:

3GPP	Third Generation Partnership Project
4G	Fourth Generation Mobile Networks
5G	Fifth Generation Mobile Networks
5GC	5G Core
5GCN	5G Core Network
6G	Sixth Generation Mobile Networks
AAS	Advanced Antenna System
ABDI	Brazilian Association for Industrial Development
ACP	Airspan Control Platform
AF	Application Function
AI	Artificial Intelligence
AMF	Access and Mobility Management Function
ANATEL	National Telecommunications Agency
AP	Access Point
API	Application Programming Interface
AS	Access Stratum
B5G	Beyond 5G
BAM	Bayesian Attractor Model
BCD	Bandwidth Consumption in Download
BCU	Bandwidth Consumption in Upload
BF	BeamForming
CNF	Container Network Function
COTS	Commercial-Off-The-Shelf
CP	Control Plane
CPE	Customer Premise Equipment
CRC	Cyclic Redundancy Check
CT	Computed Tomography
CU	Centralized Unit
CUPS	Control and User Plane Separation
DICOM	Digital Imaging and Communications in Medicine
DL	Downlink
DU	Distributed Unit
eCPRI	enhanced Common Public Radio Interface
E2E	End-To-End
F1AP	F1 Application Protocol
gNB	Next generation Node B – 5G Radio base station
gNB-CU	5G Radio base station for Centralized Unit
gNB-DU	5G Radio base station for Distribution Unit
gNB-RU	5G Radio base station for Remote Unit
GPS	Global Positioning System
HCFMUSP	Hospital of the Clinics, Faculty of Medicine, University of São Paulo
HLS	Higher Layer Split
HTTP	Hypertext Transfer Protocol
HW	Hardware
ICT	Information and Communication Technology
IDB	Inter-American Development Bank
InovaHC	Technological Innovation Center at HCFMUSP
InRad	Institute of Radiology at HCFMUSP
IoT	Internet of Things

IP	Internet Protocol
IT	Information Technology
K8s	Kubernetes
KMN	Kubernetes Management Network
L	Latency
LAN	Local Area Network
LLS	Lower Layer Split
LTE	Long Term Evolution
MAC	Media Access Control
MANO	Management ANd Orchestration
MCTS	Monte-Carlo Tree Search
MRI	Magnetic Resonance Imaging
NA	Not Available
NAS	Non-Access-Stratum
NEC	Nippon Electric Company
NF	Network Function
NFVI	Network Functions Visualization Infrastructure
NGC	Next Generation Core
NR	New Radio
NRF	Network Repository Function
O-RAN	Open RAN
OAM	Operations, Administration and Maintenance
ONAP	Open Network Automation Platform
Open RAN	Open Radio Access Networks
OS	Operating System
OSI	Open Systems Interconnection
OSS	Operational System Support
PACS	Picture Archiving and Communication System
PC	Personal Computer
PDCP	Packet Data Convergence Protocol
PDU	Protocol Data Unit
PHY	PHysical Layer
PoC	Proof of Concept
PLS	Private Limited Service
POD	Passed Out Drunk
PR	Reference Point
QoS	Quality of Service
RAN	Radio Access Network
REST	Representational State Transfer
RF	Radio Frequency
RIC	RAN Intelligent Controller
RLC	Radio Link Control
RLM	Radio Link Monitoring
RRC	Radio Resource Control
RRM	Radio Resource Management
RRU	Remote Radio Unit
RTT	Round Trip Time
RU	Radio Unit
SA	Standalone
SBA	Service Based Architecture
SCH	Shared CHannel
SDAP	Service Data Adaptation Protocol
SLA	Service Level Agreement
sVC	syngo Virtual Cockpit
SW	Software
TCP	Transmission Control Protocol
TIP	Telecom Infra Project

UE	User Equipment	
UP	User Plane	
UP	User Plane Function	
UMTS	Universal Mobile Telecommunications System	
URLLC	ultra-Reliable Low-Latency Communication	
USG	Ultrasound	
VLAN	Virtual Local Area Network	
VM	Virtual Machine	
VNC	Virtual Network Computing	
vRAN	virtualized Radio Access Networks	
vSwitch	virtualized Switch	
WDM	Wave-length Division Multiplexing	

References

1. Tan, C.P. Digital Healthcare Innovations and Implementation Considerations Under the COVID-19 Pandemic. In Proceedings of the 2021 International Conference on Biomedical Innovations and Applications (BIA), Varna, Bulgaria, 2–4 June 2022; Volume 1, pp. 37–40. [CrossRef]
2. Modina, N.; Ferrari, R.; Magarini, M. A machine learning-based design of PRACH receiver in 5G. *Procedia Comput. Sci.* **2019**, *151*, 1100–1107. [CrossRef]
3. Trakadas, P.; Sarakis, L.; Giannopoulos, A.; Spantideas, S.; Capsalis, N.; Gkonis, P.; Karkazis, P.; Rigazzi, G.; Antonopoulos, A.; Cambeiro, M.A.; et al. A Cost-Efficient 5G Non-Public Network Architectural Approach: Key Concepts and Enablers, Building Blocks and Potential Use Cases. *Sensors* **2021**, *21*, 5578. [CrossRef] [PubMed]
4. TIP News. Industry Collaboration to Conduct First 5G Private Network Field Trial at the Largest Hospital in Latin America, 2021. Available online: https://telecominfraproject.com/industry-collaboration-conduct-first-5g-private-network-field-trial-at-largest-hospital-in-latin-america/ (accessed on 4 January 2023).
5. D'Oro, S.; Bonati, L.; Polese, M.; Melodia, T. OrchestRAN: Network Automation through Orchestrated Intelligence in the Open RAN. In Proceedings of the IEEE INFOCOM—IEEE Conference on Computer Communications, London, UK, 2–5 May 2022; pp. 270–279. [CrossRef]
6. Klement, F.; Katzenbeisser, S.; Ulitzsch, V.; Krämer, J.; Stanczak, S.; Utkovski, Z.; Bjelakovic, I.; Wunder, G. Open or not open: Are conventional radio access networks more secure and trustworthy than Open-RAN? *arXiv* **2022**, arXiv:2204.12227.
7. Lacava, A.; Polese, M.; Sivaraj, R.; Soundrarajan, R.; Bhati, B.S.; Singh, T.; Zugno, T.; Cuomo, F.; Melodia, T. Programmable and Customized Intelligence for Traffic Steering in 5G Networks Using Open RAN Architectures. *arXiv* **2022**, arXiv:2209.14171.
8. Wypiór, D.; Klinkowski, M.; Michalski, I. Open RAN—Radio Access Network Evolution, Benefits and Market Trends. *Appl. Sci.* **2022**, *12*, 408. [CrossRef]
9. Brik, B.; Boutiba, K.; Ksentini, A. Deep Learning for B5G Open Radio Access Network: Evolution, Survey, Case Studies, and Challenges. *IEEE Open J. Commun. Soc.* **2022**, *3*, 228–250. [CrossRef]
10. Arnaz, A.; Lipman, J.; Abolhasan, M.; Hiltunen, M. Toward Integrating Intelligence and Programmability in Open Radio Access Networks: A Comprehensive Survey. *IEEE Access* **2022**, *10*, 67747–67770. [CrossRef]
11. Kazemifard, N.; Shah-Mansouri, V. Minimum delay function placement and resource allocation for Open RAN (O-RAN) 5G networks. *Comput. Netw.* **2021**, *188*, 107809. [CrossRef]
12. Abdalla, A.S.; Upadhyaya, P.S.; Shah, V.K.; Marojevic, V. Toward Next Generation Open Radio Access Networks–What O-RAN Can and Cannot Do! *IEEE Netw.* **2022**, *36*, 206–213. [CrossRef]
13. Dryjański, M.; Kułacz, Ł.; Kliks, A. Toward Modular and Flexible Open RAN Implementations in 6G Networks: Traffic Steering Use Case and O-RAN xApps. *Sensors* **2021**, *21*, 8137. [CrossRef] [PubMed]
14. RCR WIRELESS. RAN Splits—Logical View. RCR Wireles News. Intelligence on All Things Wireless. 2022. Available online: https://www.rcrwireless.com/20200708/opinion/readerforum/open-ran-101-ru-du-cu-reader-forum/ (accessed on 3 January 2023).
15. Singh, S.K.; Singh, R.; Kumbhani, B. The Evolution of Radio Access Network Towards Open-RAN: Challenges and Opportunities. In Proceedings of the 2020 IEEE Wireless Communications and Networking Conference Workshops (WCNCW), Seoul, Korea, 6–9 April 2020; pp. 1–6. [CrossRef]
16. Batista, J.O.R., Jr.; Mostaco, G.M.; Silva, R.F.D.; Bressan, G.; Martucci, M.; Cugnasca, C.E. Distributing the Cloud Towards Autonomous Resilient 5G Networking. In Proceedings of the ICTC 2019—10th International Conference on ICT Convergence: Leading the Autonomous Future, Jeju, Korea, 16–18 October 2019; pp. 854–859. [CrossRef]
17. Batista, J.O.R., Jr.; Mostaco, G.M.; Silva, R.F.D.; Bressan, G.; Cugnasca, C.E.; Martucci, M. Towards 5G Requirements: Performance Evaluation of a Simulated WSN Using SDN Technology. In Proceedings of the 12th EFITA (European Federation for Information Technology in Agriculture, Food and the Environment) HAICTA-WCCA Congress, Rhodes island, Greece, 27–29 June 2019; pp. 24–29.

18. Batista, J.O.R.; Mostaço, G.M.; Silva, R.F.; Bressan, G.; Cugnasca, C.E.; Martucci, M. Evaluating the Performance of a Simulated Softwarized Agricultural Wireless Sensor Network. In *Information and Communication Technologies for Agriculture—Theme I: Sensors*; Bochtis, D.D., Lampridi, M., Petropoulos, G.P., Ampatzidis, Y., Pardalos, P., Eds.; Springer International Publishing: Cham, Switzerland, 2022; pp. 121–137. [CrossRef]
19. Wang, X.; Thomas, J.D.; Piechocki, R.J.; Kapoor, S.; Santos-Rodríguez, R.; Parekh, A. Self-play learning strategies for resource assignment in Open-RAN networks. *Comput. Netw.* **2022**, *206*, 108682. [CrossRef]
20. Lekshmi, S.; Ponnekanti, S. Open RAN Deployment Using Advanced Radio Link Manager Framework to Support Mission Critical Services in 5G. *EAI Endorsed Trans. Cloud Syst.* **2019**, *5*, 162140. [CrossRef]
21. Polese, M.; Bonati, L.; D'Oro, S.; Basagni, S.; Melodia, T. Understanding O-RAN: Architecture, Interfaces, Algorithms, Security, and Research Challenges). *arXiv* **2022**, arXiv:2202.01032.
22. I, C.L.; Li, H.; Korhonen, J.; Huang, J.; Han, L. RAN Revolution With NGFI (xhaul) for 5G. *J. Light. Technol.* **2018**, *36*, 541–550. [CrossRef]
23. Loung, V.Y.K.; Ngah, R.; Han, C.T.; Din, J. Ensure public health safety, security, quality of service and smooth deployment of 5G infrastructure in Malaysia. In Proceedings of the 2021 IEEE Symposium on Wireless Technology & Applications (ISWTA), Shah Alam, Malaysia, 17 August 2021; pp. 32–36. [CrossRef]
24. Sangam, P. A Fresh Look at Building 5G Radio Access Networks. 2021. Available online: https://www.rcrwireless.com/20211217/analyst-angle/a-fresh-look-at-building-5g-radio-access-networks-analyst-angle (accessed on 3 January 2023).
25. VIAVI. Preparing Transport Networks for 5G. White Paper. Available online: https://images.comms.viavisolutions.com/Web/Viavi/%7Bc2e00431-255e-4c65-8e01-af0b15f78503%7D_5Gtransport-wp-maa-nse-ae.pdf?_ga=2.64855471.1030071352.1665198568-512617025.1663786640/ (accessed on 3 January 2023).
26. Brown, G. New Transport Network Architectures for 5G. pp. 1–11. Available online: https://www.fujitsu.com/us/Images/New-Transport-Network-Architectures-for-5G-RAN.pdf (accessed on 3 January 2023).
27. Red Hat. What is vRAN? 2022. Available online: https://www.redhat.com/en/topics/virtualization/what-is-vran/ (accessed on 3 January 2023).
28. 5G-Encode. Final Report. Platform Commissioning. 2022. pp. 1–45. Available online: https://irp.cdn-website.com/4984c9ba/files/uploaded/5G%20ENCODE%20Final%20Combined%20Report%20v1-2.pdf (accessed on 3 January 2023).
29. Airspan. AirVelocity 2700 5G SUB-6HZ, 4T4R Indoor Radio Unit. Airspan 5G, Installation Guide, Document Part Number DUG01251, Document Revision A3. 2021. pp. 1–27. Available online: https://fcc.report/FCC-ID/PIDAV2700CBL/5461514.pdf (accessed on 3 January 2023)
30. NEC. Radio Unit, O-RAN Compliant 5G Radio Unit. 2022. Available online: https://br.nec.com/pt_BR/global/solutions/5g/pt/O-RAN_Compliant_5G_Radio_Unit.html (accessed on 3 January 2023).
31. Google. Dynamic eCPRI header Compression. Data Provided by IFI CLAIMS Patent Services. Google Patents. 2021. Available online: https://patents.google.com/patent/US11234163B1/en (accessed on 3 January 2023).
32. Ram, V. OSI vs. TCP/IP Reference Model. 2020. Available online: https://www.tutorialspoint.com/OSI-vs-TCP-IP-Reference-Model#:~:text=OSI%20model%20is%20a%20generic,clear%20distinction%20between%20these%20three/ (accessed on 3 January 2023).
33. Larsen, L.M.P.; Checko, A.; Christiansen, H.L. A Survey of the Functional Splits Proposed for 5G Mobile Crosshaul Networks. *IEEE Commun. Surv. Tutor.* **2019**, *21*, 146–172. [CrossRef]
34. DEVOPEDIA. 5G NR MAC. DEVOPEDIA for Developers by Developers. 2021. Available online: https://devopedia.org/5g-nr-mac (accessed on 3 January 2023).
35. Kasparec, F. Telecom: Virtualizing Radio Access Networks (RAN)—Why and How? 2021. Available online: https://www.linkedin.com/pulse/telecom-virtualizing-radio-access-networks-ran-why-how-franz-kasparec/ (accessed on 3 January 2023).
36. ATOS. Virtualizing Radio Access Networks. CT-210505-AR-WP-Virtualizing-Radio-Access-Networks-en v7. Trusted partner for your Digital Journey. White Paper 2021. pp. 1–7. Available online: https://atos.net/wp-content/uploads/2021/05/CT-210505-AR-WP-Virtualizing-Radio-Access-Networks-en-v7.pdf (accessed on 3 January 2023).
37. Techplayon. 5G NR Radio Protocol Stack (Layer 2 and Layer 3). 2017. Available online: https://www.techplayon.com/5g-nr-radio-protocol-stack-layer-2-layer-3/ (accessed on 3 January 2023).
38. Liberg, O.; Sundberg, M.; Wang, Y.P.E.; Bergman, J.; Sachs, J.; Wikström, G. Chapter 2—Global cellular IoT standards. In *Cellular Internet of Things*, 2nd ed.; Liberg, O., Sundberg, M., Wang, Y.P.E., Bergman, J., Sachs, J., Wikström, G., Eds.; Academic Press: Cambridge, MA, USA, 2020; pp. 11–39. [CrossRef]
39. Carrasco, O.; Miatton, F.; Diaz, S.; Herzog, U.; Frascolla, V.; Fitch, M.; Briggs, K.; Miscopein, B.; Domenico, A.d.; Georgakopoulos, A. Centralized Radio Resource Management for 5G small cells as LSA enabler. In Proceedings of the European Conference on Networks and Communications (EUCNC), Athens, Greece, 27–30 June 2016. [CrossRef]
40. Benetel, O. Functional Splits: The Foundation of an Open 5G RAN, 2021. Available online: https://www.5gtechnologyworld.com/functional-splits-the-foundation-of-an-open-5g-ran/ (accessed on 21 November 2022).
41. DEVOPEDIA. 5G NR Channels. 2021. Available online: https://devopedia.org/5g-nr-channels (accessed on 21 November 2022).
42. Kumar, D. 5G(NR)-Fundamentals. 2020. Available online: https://www.5gfundamental.com/ (accessed on 21 November 2022).
43. Microchip. 5G / LTE Radios. 2020. Available online: https://www.microsemi.com/applications/5g-mobile-infrastructure/5g-lte-radios/ (accessed on 3 January 2023).

44. Moniem-tech. Functional Split Options for 5G Networks. 2021. Available online: https://moniem-tech.com/2021/04/05/functional-split-options-for-5g-networks/ (accessed on 3 January 2023).
45. Moniem-tech. Why 7.2x split is the Best Split Option? Moniem-Tech Communication Engineering Frontier Knowledge Base. 2022. pp. 1–39. Available online: https://moniem-tech.com/2022/03/13/why-7-2x-split-is-the-best-split-option/ (accessed on 3 January 2023).
46. Airspan. Flexible Cloud Architecture with Powerful Openrange Software. Dynamic Fronthaul. pp. 1–39. Available online: https://www.airspan.com/openrange-software/ (accessed on 3 January 2023).
47. Jordan, E. What are Radio Unit, Distributed Units and Centralised Units in Open RAN Functional Split? 2021. Available online: https://www.techchannel.news/26/02/2021/what-are-radio-unit-distributed-units-and-centralised-units-in-open-ran-functional-split/ (accessed on 3 January 2023).
48. Airspan. AirVelocity 2700 n78/n77/n48—Antenna Details; Airspan: Boca Raton, FL, USA, 2021; pp. 1–29.
49. iGR. Open RAN Integration: Run with It. 2021. pp. 1–27. Available online: https://www.parallelwireless.com/wp-content/uploads/iGR-OpenRAN-Integration-White-Paper-Feb-2021.pdf (accessed on 3 January 2023).
50. Techplayon. 5G NR Interfaces X2/Xn, S1/NG, F1 and E1 Functions, 2019. Available online: https://www.techplayon.com/5g-nr-interfaces-x2-xn-s1-ng-f1-and-e1-functions/ (accessed on 3 January 2023).
51. Bhat, R.R. Addressing Security for 5G Cloud Radio Access Networks. 2019. Available online: https://www.a10networks.com/blog/addressing-security-for-5g-cloud-radio-access-networks/ (accessed on 3 January 2023).
52. Rinaldi, F.; Raschella, A.; Pizzi, S. 5G NR System Design: A Concise Survey of Key Features and Capabilities, 2021. Available online: https://www.researchgate.net/figure/gNB-architecture-with-separation-of-gNB-CU-CP-and-gNB-CU-UP_fig2_355441113/ (accessed on 3 January 2023).
53. 3GPP. 3GPP TS 38.401. 5G; NG-RAN; Architecture Description. Version 15.2.0 (Release 15). pp. 1–40. Available online: https://standards.iteh.ai/catalog/standards/etsi/ec793328-0f0c-419b-bc66-dbb355c1eeb4/etsi-ts-138-401-v15-2-0-2018-07 (accessed on 3 January 2023).
54. Tech-invite. 3GPP Space, IETF RFCs, SIP. 2022. Available online: https://www.tech-invite.com/3m38/toc/tinv-3gpp-38-401_c.html (accessed on 3 January 2023).
55. AVI. Docker Architecture and Its Components for Beginners. 2022. Available online: https://geekflare.com/docker-architecture/ (accessed on 3 January 2023).
56. Chemitiganti, V. Part 1—Accelerating the 5G Dataplane with SR IOV and DPDK. 2021. Available online: https://www.vamsitalkstech.com/5g/accelerating-the-5g-dataplane-with-sr-iov-and-dpdk-%C2%BD/ (accessed on 3 January 2023).
57. Mavenir. Open RAN, An Alternative Way to Build Networks. Accelerating Network Transformation with Cloud-Native Open RAN. 2022. Available online: https://www.mavenir.com/portfolio/mavair/radio-access/openran/ (accessed on 3 January 2023).
58. Techplayon. What is E2 Interface in Open RAN? 2022. Available online: https://www.techplayon.com/what-is-e2-interface-in-open-ran (accessed on 3 January 2023).
59. Open5G. Why Open Is the Key to 5G. January 2021 Magazine. 2030 Project and iGR. 2021. Available online: https://issuu.com/intersectmedia/docs/open5g_ebook-v6/ (accessed on 3 January 2023).
60. Airspan. Airspan Control Platform (ACP): A Complete, Effective Network Function Controller & Manager. 2022. Available online: https://www.airspan.com/airspan-control-platform-acp/ (accessed on 2 January 2023).
61. Wang, T.H.; Chen, Y.C.; Huang, S.J.; Hsu, K.S.; Hu, C.H. Design of a Network Management System for 5G Open RAN. In Proceedings of the 2021 22nd Asia-Pacific Network Operations and Management Symposium (APNOMS), Tainan, Taiwan, 8–10 September 2021; pp. 138–141. [CrossRef]
62. da Silva, D.C.; Batista, J.O.R.; de Sousa, M.A.F.; Mostaço, G.M.; Monteiro, C.d.C.; Bressan, G.; Cugnasca, C.E.; Silveira, R.M. A Novel Approach to Multi-Provider Network Slice Selector for 5G and Future Communication Systems. Sensors 2022, 22, 6066. [CrossRef] [PubMed]
63. Batista, J.O.R., Jr.; da Silva, D.C.; Martucci, M., Jr.; Silveira, R.M.; Cugnasca, C.E. A multi-provider end-to-end dynamic orchestration architecture approach for 5g and future communication systems. Appl. Sci. 2021, 11, 11914. [CrossRef]
64. Saraiva de Sousa, N.F.; Lachos Perez, D.A.; Rosa, R.V.; Santos, M.A.; Esteve Rothenberg, C. Network Service Orchestration: A survey. Comput. Commun. 2019, 142–143, 69–94. [CrossRef]

Disclaimer/Publisher's Note: The statements, opinions and data contained in all publications are solely those of the individual author(s) and contributor(s) and not of MDPI and/or the editor(s). MDPI and/or the editor(s) disclaim responsibility for any injury to people or property resulting from any ideas, methods, instructions or products referred to in the content.

Article
Low-Latency QC-LDPC Encoder Design for 5G NR

Yunke Tian, Yong Bai and Dake Liu *

State Key Laboratory of Marine Resource Utilization in South China Sea, School of Information and Communication Engineering, Hainan University, Haikou 570228, China; tianyunke19@hainanu.edu.cn (Y.T.); bai@hainanu.edu.cn (Y.B.)
* Correspondence: liu.dake@outlook.com

Abstract: In order to meet the low latency and high throughput requirements of data transmission in 5th generation (5G) New Radio (NR), it is necessary to minimize the low power encoding hardware latency on transmitter and achieve lower base station power consumption within a fixed transmission time interval (TTI). This paper investigates parallel design and implementation of 5G quasi-cyclic low-density parity-check (QC-LDPC) codes encoder. The designed QC-LDPC encoder employs a multi-channel parallel structure to obtain multiple parity check bits and thus reduce encoding latency significantly. The proposed encoder maps high parallelism encoding algorithms to a configurable circuit architecture, achieving flexibility and support for all 5G NR code length and code rate. The experimental results show that under the 800 MHz system frequency, the achieved data throughput ranges from 62 to 257.9 Gbps, and the maximum code length encoding time under base graph 1 (BG1) is only 33.75 ns, which is the critical encoding time of our proposed encoder. Finally, our proposed encoder was synthesized on SMIC 28 nm CMOS technology; the result confirmed the effectiveness and feasibility of our design.

Keywords: 5G New Radio; QC-LDPC codes; channel encoding; encoder; low latency

1. Introduction

LDPC codes was determined as the 5G NR data channel coding scheme at the 2016 3GPP Conference [1]. After that, the research on implementation of 5G LDPC codes is gradually increasing. In [2], the base matrix of the initial code rate is split, and the smaller sub-base matrix is used to replace the whole base matrix, which improves the efficiency and throughput of encoding and decoding. In [3–5], the optimization method of LDPC codes in 5G three scenarios was proposed.

Low latency implementation of LDPC encoding has always been a focus of LDPC application research. For the implementation of the encoder, if the algorithm of multiplying the generator matrix G is directly used, the data storage and computational complexity is quadratic in the code length. To address this issue, a simplified algorithm (RU method) is proposed in [6] by transforming the sparse parity check matrix H into an approximate lower triangular form to quickly calculate the parity bits. In [7], two encoders based on the RU method have been implemented, but the amount of storage and calculations required increased significantly. After that, through the structural design of the LDPC codes, a quasi-cyclic structure was proposed to greatly reduce the complexity of encoding and the utilization of storage resources.

Some recent studies have focused on the hardware implementation of QC-LDPC codes encoding. Owing to the fact that the encoding complexity of the RU method is lower than that of the direct encoding algorithm, many encoder designs are based on the RU method for structural optimization. The most significant innovation is the parallelized encoding architecture. In [8], an area efficient parallel LDPC encoding scheme is proposed for QC-LDPC codes. This architecture uses multiple parallel cyclic shift network and bit selection algorithm to reduce the hardware complexity. In [9], a multigigabit QC-LDPC encoding architecture is proposed; this architecture leverages the inherent parallelism of QC structural by simultaneously processing multiple bits according to optimal scheduling. In [10], a high-efficiency multi-rate encoder for IEEE 802.16e QC-LDPC codes is proposed; this design uses the double diagonal structure in the parity matrix to avoid the inverse matrix operation that requires a lot of calculations. Meanwhile, a parallel matrix vector multiplication structure and storage compression are used to increase the encoding speed and significantly reduce the number of storage bits required. In [11], a fully parallel QC-LDPC encoder based on a reduced complexity XOR tree designed specifically for the IEEE 802.11n standard was proposed. In [12], a pipeline architecture for QC-LDPC encoder was proposed. The design can be easily reconstructed to support variable code rates and code lengths through parameter configuration. In [13], the encoder stores the matrix vector in random access memory (RAM). The row index of the non-zero entry in each column of the sparse check matrix is used as the write address of the RAM, which reduces the complexity of storage and calculation.

In 5G NR, the channel coding scheme also adopts QC-LDPC codes. For the compatibility of multiple scenarios, the 5G standard has developed two different base graphs, BG1 and BG2, which correspond to two different base matrices, H_{BG1} and H_{BG2}. According to the lifting sizes of 5G QC-LDPC codes, the H_{BG} matrix corresponds to a total of 16 parity check matrices (PCM) which defines the 5G LDPC coding schemes [14]. Therefore, the hardware that supports 5G NR codes must provide a high level of flexibility to satisfy different PCMs.

5G NR has three scenarios, enhance Moblie BroadBand (eMBB), Ultra Reliable Low Latency Communication (URLLC), and massive Machnice Type Communication (mMTC). Specifically, it requires a peak throughput of 10 Gbps for the uplink, 20 Gbps for the downlink, and a user-plane delay of 4 ms for eMBB and 1 ms for URLLC. After evaluation by 3GPP, it is confirmed that the LDPC encoding scheme under BG2 designed for eMBB scenarios is used in URLLC scenarios (mainly low latency) [15]. In [16], a prototype of 5G physical downlink shared channel (PDSCH) transmitter was carried out on software defined radio (SDR), with channel coding experiments including complete processing flow of data transmission in TS38.212, and the system performance of 5G NR was evaluated. In some studies, 5G LDPC encoder is designed according to the complete encoding chain of uplink and downlink channels [17,18], including cyclic redundancy check (CRC) encoding, code block segmentation, LDPC encoding, rate matching, and bit interleaving. By assembling all the processes in the encoding chain, fully functional encoding hardware products can be delivered. At the base station transmitter, channel coding is the crucial operation that affects the bit processing time in physical layer. Therefore, it is necessary to propose a higher parallel encoding algorithm and hardware architecture for 5G QC-LDPC.

There are some references regarding the hardware implementation of 5G LDPC encoder. In [19], an efficient LPDC encoding algorithm was proposed, and a high throughput and low latency encoding architecture is implemented. Synthesis results on TSMC 65-nm CMOS technology with different submatrix sizes were carried out. In [20], a flexible and high-throughput 5G LDPC encoder was implemented on the compute unified device architecture (CUDA) platform through the scheme proposed in [19], and the throughput of 38–62 Gbps from 1/2 to 8/9 rate was achieved on a single GPU. In [21], an encoder with the advantages of parallel encoding and pipeline operation is proposed; it was synthesized in a 65 nm CMOS technology and the parallelism of this scheme is higher compared with [19]. In [22], a serial-optimized QC-LDPC encoder is proposed, which uses genetic algorithm to optimize the encoding. In the case of short codes, multiple check matrix sub-blocks can be partially processed in parallel. The same degree of parallelism as the long code is achieved.

This paper focuses on low latency LDPC encoding specified in 3GPP. One purpose is achieving low power budget in a 5G NR baseband. If we design a LDPC encoder with lower latency, we can give extra computing time in a TTI to other algorithms with heavy power consumption. Thus the degree of parallelization can be relaxed for heavy power algorithms such as channel equalization and detection in uplink [23]. The total power consumption in a base station can therefore be reduced. In order to resolve the issues in the existing schemes, the main contributions of our work are as follows:

(1) The proposed encoder is optimized according to the structure of the parity matrix in 5G standard, which can achieve lower latency and higher throughput than the existing work. Compared with the clock consumption in [19], our design reduces the encoding latency by 56%.

(2) A parallel CRC is seamlessly integrated into the design enabling LDPC encoding from transport block (TB) level, which means that LDPC encoding can be started from TB input. Thus, the complete encoding calculation of PDSCH is implemented.

(3) The encoder is designed to be fully compatible with 5G NR standard and with flexibility and extendibility. Our design uses the largest lifting size as the hardware scale in the shift networks (CNs) of the encoding calculation. Meanwhile, a configurable circuit module is added to CNs to deal with different encoding scenarios. The parameter adaptation module schedules the configurable circuit to change the input and output of the CNs. Hence, the ASIC synthesis of the encoder can support full-size PCM, including all code lengths and code rates encoding for transport blocks (TBs).

Our design is verified and proven by synthesized register transfer level (RTL) design and silicon layout. The IC layout is based on CMOS technology of SMIC 28nm. The results show that at 800 MHz, the encoding time of maximum code length in BG1 is only 33.75 ns (27 clocks), which sufficiently meets the throughput requirement and offers a lower latency for the 5G NR standard.

The rest of this paper is organized as follows. Section 2 describes the coding process of 5G LDPC codes and the structure of the parity check matrix. In Section 3, a high parallel encoding method and the corresponding encoder structure are proposed. The design details and flexible configuration are discussed in Section 4. The silicon verification and comparison results are given in Section 5. Section 6 concludes our paper.

2. 5G NR QC-LDPC Encoding

2.1. LDPC Encoding Specification in 5G NR

In 5G mobile base station, PDSCH channel is used for information transmission at the base station transmitter, and its transmission data is composed of transport blocks (TBs). The information transmission process is shown in Figure 1.

In a TTI, a transmission channel delivers up to two transport blocks to the physical layer, A bits TB attaches either 24 bits CRC or 16 bits CRC according to TB length, and TB can be further partitioned to code word (CW). It needs to be divided into C code block of B bits, each code block will attach 24 bits CB-CRC, and finally it becomes the transport block size (TBS) of K bits. K_{cb} is the maximum length of the code block with CRC, K_{cb} is 8448 for BG1, and 3840 for BG2. The base graph and TB length also specifies the number of columns K_b in the kernel matrix of the parity check matrix H. So $K = K_b \times Z$, where Z is lifting size and is also the length of each CW. Each C code block after segmentation consists of K_b CW. After LDPC encoding is completed, a code length of N bits is outputted. The encoding output result N bits is composed of n Z-length CW. The encoding of each C code block is independent. After the respective LDPC encoding, rate matching and interleaving are performed respectively. The 5G QC-LDPC encoding process is shown in Figure 2.

2.2. Characteristics of 5G QC-LDPC Codes

The matrix H is uniquely defined by the matrix H_{BG}, extended permutation matrix P (also PCM), and lifting size Z. The matrix P passes through a matrix dispersion, and the elements in P are replaced by $Z \times Z$ cyclic unit matrix or zero matrix, resulting in a complete parity check matrix H. Sets of LDPC lifting size Z and its corresponding shift value table are described in the NR standard specification TS 38.212 [1].

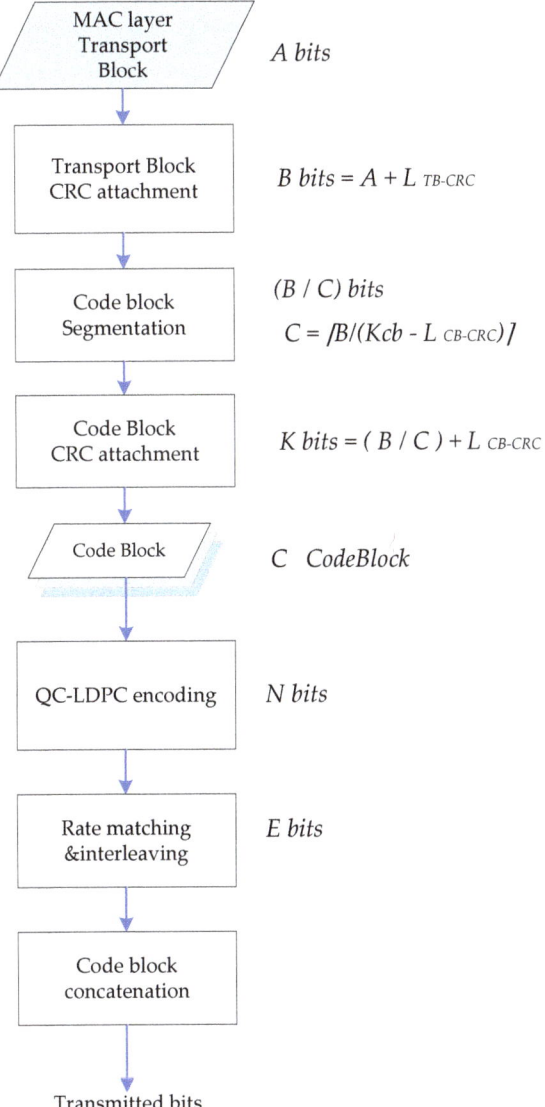

Figure 1. 5G PDSCH information transmission process.

Figure 3 shows the parameters and region division of matrix H under BG1 and BG2. Region [A B] is kernel matrix and [C D I] and the all zero matrix in the upper right corner are extended matrix. The kernel matrix can be used to encode information bits at a high bit rate. There are four kinds of B matrix corresponding to the parity bits. The B matrix adopts a dual-diagonal special structure to avoid complicated operations involved in encoding, such as matrix inversion. When the target code rate is higher than that of the kernel matrix, punching is performed on the parity bits. If the target code rate is lower than that of the kernel matrix, the parity bits with low rate are obtained using the single parity relationship of the extended matrix. Because there are many non-zero elements in the first two columns of the H matrix, in order to improve the decoding performance, the information bits corresponding to the first two columns will be punched, Figure 4 shows the matrix structure of 5G LDPC codes and the corresponding punching and shortening operations. 5G QC-LDPC can support any length of code by filling bits at the end of the message and combining with multiple lifting sizes. Through punching operation, it also can support incremental redundancy hybrid automatic repeated request (IR-HARQ) and various code rates.

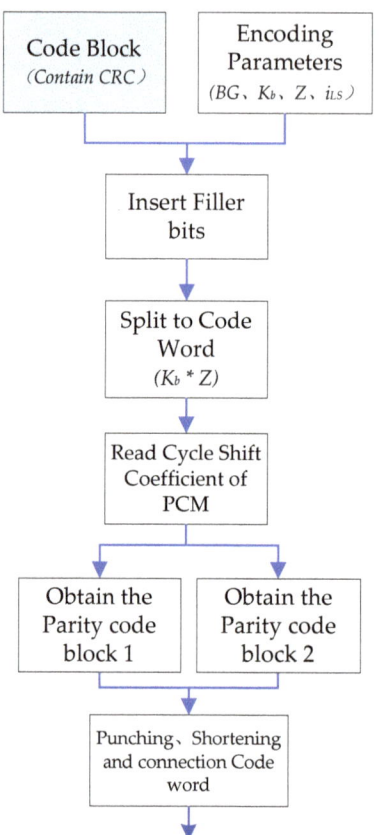

Figure 2. 5G QC-LDPC encoding process.

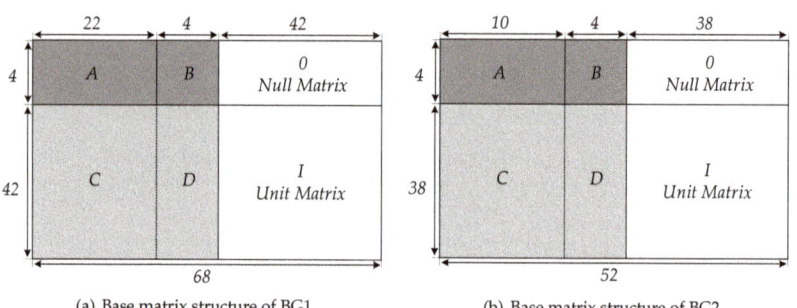

(a) Base matrix structure of BG1   (b) Base matrix structure of BG2

Figure 3. Region division and parameters of base matrix.

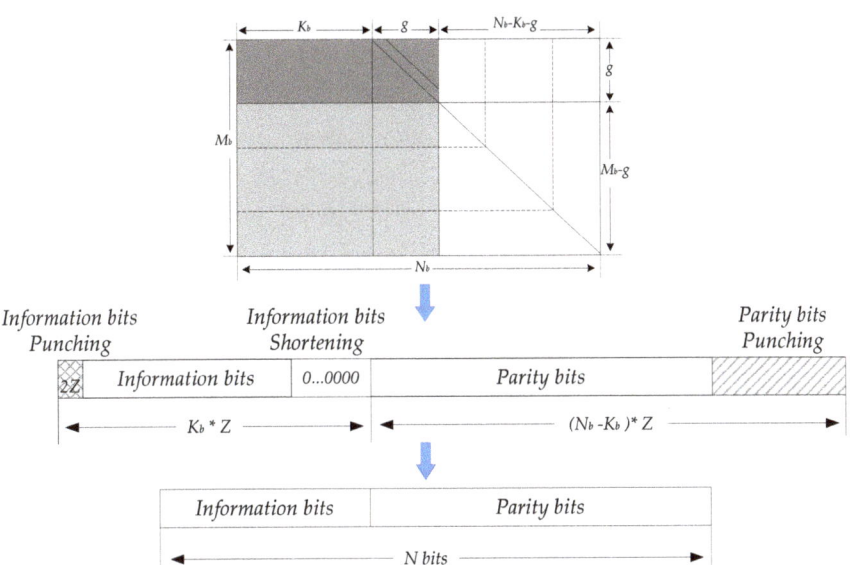

Figure 4. Parity matrix structure and parameters, punching and shortening of 5G LDPC Codes.

3. Design of 5G QC-LDPC Encoder

3.1. QC-LDPC High-Parallel Encoding Algorithm

In [19], an LDPC encoding algorithm for 5G has been proposed. Based on it, this paper optimizes the calculation flow of the parity codeword and arranges the operations in parallel to improve the parallelism of the overall encoding and reduce the latency of the encoder. According to the 3GPP standard, the code block C is divided into information code blocks S, the first group of parity P_1, and the second group of parity P_2, whose lengths are $K_b \times Z$, $4 \times Z$, $(M_b - 4) \times Z$ corresponding to $[A \quad C]^T, [B \quad D]^T, [O \quad I]^T$ of H matrix respectively. K_b is the number of columns of the kernel matrix and M_b is the number of rows of the H matrix, so that C^T can be expressed as

$$c^T = [s|p_1|p_2]^T = \left[s_0, s_1, \cdots, s_{k_b-1} | p_{1,1}, p_{1,2}, p_{1,3}, p_{1,4} | p_{2,1}, p_{2,2}, \cdots, p_{2,m_b-4}\right]^T \tag{1}$$

According to the structure of the parity matrix H shown in Figure 3, the check equation for encoding is represented as

$$HC^T = \begin{bmatrix} A & B & 0 \\ C & D & I \end{bmatrix} \begin{bmatrix} s^T \\ p_1^T \\ p_2^T \end{bmatrix} = 0^T \tag{2}$$

The expansion of (2) denoted as

$$As^T + Bp_1^T + 0p_2^T = 0^T \tag{3}$$

$$Cs^T + Dp_1^T + Ip_2^T = 0^T \tag{4}$$

Simplify and obtain P_1 and P_2 denoted as

$$p_1^T = B^{-1} As^T \tag{5}$$

$$p_2^T = Cs^T + Dp_1^T \tag{6}$$

Divide P_1 into four vectors P_{11}, P_{12}, P_{13}, and P_{14} with length Z and assign the result AS^T as λ, where $a_{i,j}$ is the element of each row of A matrix. s_j is the code word of each segment Z in the information S. This calculation is actually to cyclic shift the Z-length code block corresponding to each element of the PCM, and the number of shifts is the value of the element, that is, the cyclic shift coefficient.

$$\lambda_i = \sum_{j=1}^{k_b} a_{i,j} s_j, i = 1,2,3,4 \tag{7}$$

The encoding operation can thus be divided into two stages: obtaining P_1 and P_2. In this paper, the calculation of AS^T and CS^T is parallelized, and the maximum parallel structures are designed according to the number of columns of A matrix and the number of rows of C matrix respectively. In the process of obtaining P_1, in order to avoid the complexity of matrix inversion, traversing each two B submatrices of H_{BG1} and H_{BG2}, (8–11) shows the four structures of the B matrix, where -1 represents the 0 matrix of $Z \times Z$, 1 and 105 represent the $Z \times Z$ unit matrix that is right cyclic shift once and 105 times, and 0 represents the $Z \times Z$ unit matrix. Under the principle of GF(2) operations, the process of solving (5) can be converted to (12–15), $P_{i,j}^{(\alpha)}$ means the right barrel shift of α bits.

$$H_{BG1\_B1} = \begin{bmatrix} 1 & 0 & -1 & -1 \\ 0 & 0 & 0 & -1 \\ -1 & -1 & 0 & 0 \\ 1 & -1 & -1 & 0 \end{bmatrix} \tag{8}$$

$$H_{BG1\_B2} = \begin{bmatrix} 0 & 0 & -1 & -1 \\ 105 & 0 & 0 & -1 \\ -1 & -1 & 0 & 0 \\ 0 & -1 & -1 & 0 \end{bmatrix} \tag{9}$$

$$H_{BG2\_B1} = \begin{bmatrix} 0 & 0 & -1 & -1 \\ -1 & 0 & 0 & -1 \\ 1 & -1 & 0 & 0 \\ 0 & -1 & -1 & 0 \end{bmatrix} \tag{10}$$

$$H_{BG2\_B2} = \begin{bmatrix} 1 & 0 & -1 & -1 \\ -1 & 0 & 0 & -1 \\ 0 & -1 & 0 & 0 \\ 1 & -1 & -1 & 0 \end{bmatrix} \tag{11}$$

$$P_{11} = \begin{cases} \sum_{i=1}^{4} \lambda_i, \text{when } B = H_{BG1\_B1}, H_{BG2\_B2} \\ (\sum_{i=1}^{4} \lambda_i)^{(105 \bmod Z)}, \text{when } B = H_{BG1\_B2} \\ (\sum_{i=1}^{4} \lambda_i)^{(1)}, \text{when } B = H_{BG2\_B1} \end{cases} \tag{12}$$

$$P_{12} = \begin{cases} \lambda_1 + P_{11}^{(1)}, \text{when } B = H_{BG1\_B1}, H_{BG2\_B2} \\ \lambda_1 + P_{11}, \text{when } B = H_{BG1\_B2}, H_{BG2\_B1} \end{cases} \tag{13}$$

$$P_{13} = \begin{cases} \lambda_2 + P_{12}, \text{when } B = H_{BG2\_B1}, H_{BG2\_B2} \\ \lambda_3 + P_{14}, \text{when } B = H_{BG1\_B1}, H_{BG1\_B2} \end{cases} \tag{14}$$

$$P_{14} = \begin{cases} \lambda_4 + P_{11}^{(1)}, \text{when } B = H_{BG1\_B1} \\ \lambda_4 + P_{11}, \text{when } B = H_{BG1\_B2}, H_{BG2\_B1} \\ \lambda_3 + P_{11}^{(1)}, \text{when } B = H_{BG2\_B2} \end{cases} \tag{15}$$

When P_1 is obtained, the CS^T offers hardware reuse possibility to complete the DP_1^T operation, and the second group of parity P_2 is calculated according to (16), where $c_{i,j}$ is the element of each row of C matrix, d_{i,K_b+j} is the element of each row of D matrix, and s_j is the code word of each segment Z in the information S.

$$P_{2i} = \sum_{j=1}^{k_b} c_{i,j} s_j + \sum_{j=1}^{4} d_{i,k_b+j} P_{1j}, i = 1, 2, \ldots, m_b - 4 \qquad (16)$$

3.2. QC-LDPC Encoder Architecture

The encoding algorithm discussed earlier is based on the structural characteristics of the 5G QC-LDPC code; it has the same linear complexity with the RU method. Herein, this paper uses the proposed algorithm for hardware implementation, not only mapping the algorithm to the circuit architecture but also considering the selection and optimization of the circuit architecture in the mapping process and approaching the limit of the LDPC encoding latency.

The overall hardware structure of the encoder is shown in Figure 5. In this encoder, the memory and functional modules are considered as the major influencing factors of the overall area, latency, and power performance of the hardware design. The encoding algorithm used and the operating frequency of the hardware determine the throughput of the overall architecture.

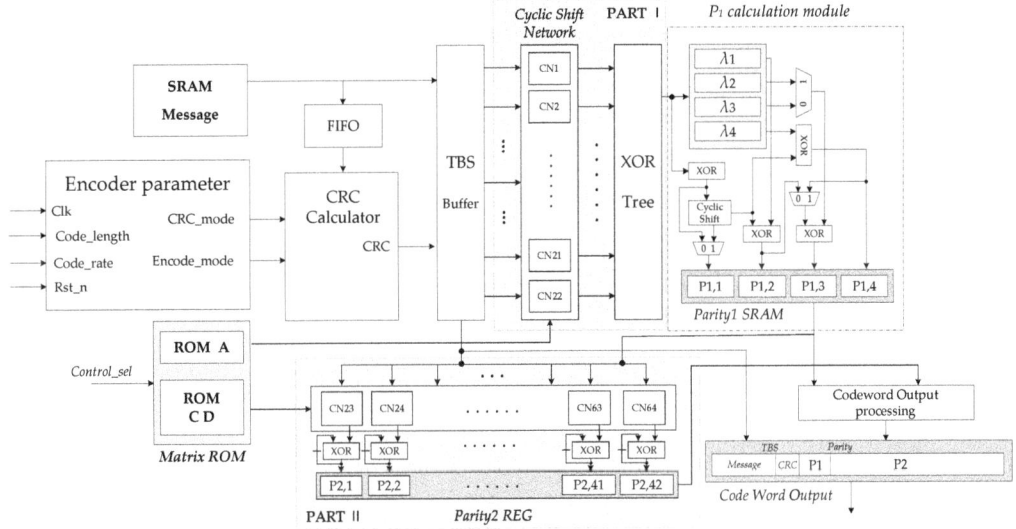

Figure 5. Low latency encoder architecture of 5G QC-LDPC codes.

According to the aforementioned high parallel encoding algorithm, the encoding calculation is actually to complete the multiplication of the PCM and the information vector. PCM is composed of $Z \times Z$ zero matrix and unit cyclic shift matrix; the multiplication of these submatrices and the information vector is actually a bit-level cyclic shift. Thus, the encoder designed in this paper is implemented by cyclic shift network and combinational logic circuits. The encoding calculation is mainly composed of two parts in parallel, Part I calculates AS^T in Equation (5), and Part II calculates CS^T and DP_1^T in Equation (6). In order to realize low latency encoding, 64 (22 + 42) cyclic shift network (CN) modules are used, which are barrel shift logic. The encoder mainly consists of the following functional modules:

(1) Message buffer SRAM: The transmission information of the media access control (MAC) layer is stored in this module; the information is converted through first input first output (FIFO) to perform multi-byte fast CRC check calculation. Then, the information and its generated CRC bits are transferred to the TBS buffer.

(2) Memory blocks: In Figure 5, the matrix ROM stores the cyclic shift coefficient values of the PCM corresponding to the A, C, and D submatrices.

(3) Encoder parameter calculation module: calculating some parameters required by the encoder according to the code length and the original code rate. Meanwhile, the selected encoding parameters will affect the control signal and state machine of the encoder.

(4) CRC calculator module: executing the CRC calculation of the transmission block with high parallelism.

(5) Transport blocks size buffer: combining information bits and CRC into K_b block code words, each code word length is Z.

(6) Cyclic shift network Part I and Part II: cyclic shift network is used to implement the cyclic shift of Z length code words, according to the cyclic shift coefficient provided by the control signal. CNs is a configurable barrel shift register; corresponding to the Z value that does not meet the hardware scale, the input and output of the cyclic shift will be adapted.

(7) P_1 calculation module: this module consists of combinational logic circuit and memory and configurable circular shift registers. Each H_{BG} has two kinds of B submatrices, so this module can flexibly implement different computation processes of different B submatrices. Herein, the calculation of Equations (8)–(11) is also parallelized to speed up the process of obtaining P_1.

(8) Codeword output processing module: punching and shortening the parity code blocks. Connecting the information code block and the parity check code block and output according to the code rate.

According to the column number of matrix A, Part I is designed using 22 CN for K_b code blocks, which are inputs into each CN sub-module. Meanwhile, one row elements in operations have the current value of CN_{1-22}, equaling to a binary addition operation. The execution in 22 parallel CN sub-modules use four clock cycles to get the intermediate variables $\lambda_i (i = 1, 2, 3, 4)$ and to store in memory.

In order to speed up the calculation of (6), Part II may use more CN sub-modules. In each calculation cycle, the same as the execution in each code block of K_b, a codeword is delivered to CN_{23-64}, and a column elements of C matrix is read as the cyclic shift coefficient inputs each CN. When the cyclic shift is completed, the results are kept in registers.

After 22 calculation cycles, 22 column of C matrix is used by 42 CN sub-modules. The 42 CN process the cyclic shift of the information code block in parallel. Finally, the outputs of 42 XOR blocks give the last result. After the CS^T calculation is completed, the 4 column elements of D matrix in ROM are sent into 42 CN in turn, and 4 sets of P_1 vectors are also delivered to CN_{23-64} in parallel; a group of results of DP_1^T are obtained in each cycle. After four times of cyclic shifts and XOR operations, the execution of (12) is completed, and the second group parity P_2 is obtained. When two groups of parities are obtained, the filler invalid bits are removed by the codeword output processing module. Meanwhile, the first two columns of the information code blocks with Z-length are punched out, and the parity codes are punched according to the code rate, then the encoded blocks give output towards the rate matching section.

3.3. Execution Pipeline Scheduling

When the maximum code length is not over the length defined by base graph, the parallel operation process of the encoder is shown in Figure 6, which can be divided into five calculation parts and three steps. The first clock pipeline is for the generation of coding parameters and CRC calculation of TB, the second pipeline is the parallel calculation of AS^T, P_1 and CS^T, and the third pipeline is the calculation of DP_1^T. The latency of the whole encoding process includes CRC calculation and Part II calculation, and the clock cost of LDPC encoding is determined by Part II.

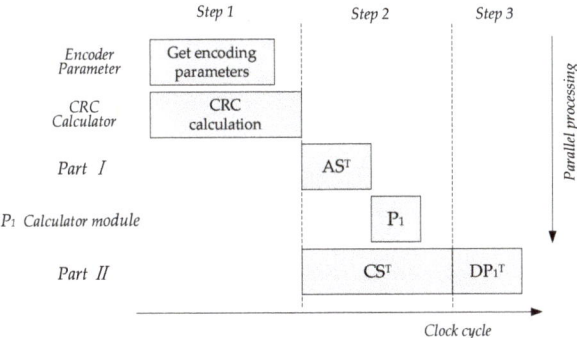

Figure 6. Parallel operation process of encoder.

Figure 7 is the flow chart of 8424 bits data encoding operation under BG1. Firstly, the parameters required for encoding are obtained from the transport block data in the encoding parameter module of the encoder. The bit stream is transmitted to the CRC calculation module through the FIFO module, and the CRC is attached to the TB to form the TBS. Then, the elements of the matrix A and matrix C, D are read to complete the encoding calculation in Part I and Part II respectively. After obtaining two groups of parity code blocks, the filler bits of codeword are processed in the codeword output processing module of the encoder; the invalid bits will be removed and the first two columns of information bits and parity bits are punctured. Finally, the information code blocks and the parity check code blocks are connected as the encoder output.

The control circuit of the encoder issues the overall control of the operation of the encoder, so that each calculation module can orderly perform their own tasks. In this design, the state machine and control signal are used to control the operation of the encoder. It mainly realizes the control signal in sequence to all modules. Figure 8 is the pipeline diagram of the hardware structure of the encoder.

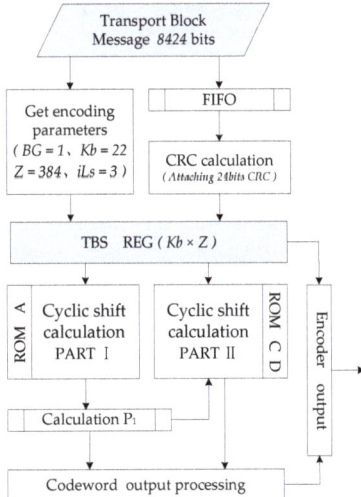

Figure 7. Encoder operation flow chart.

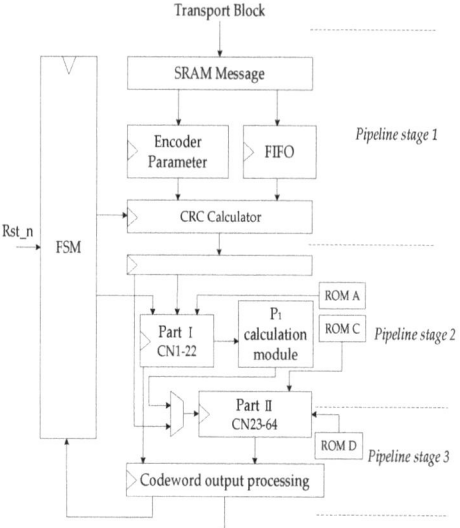

Figure 8. Pipeline of encoder hardware structure.

After the parameters are calculated and information bits are stored in SRAM, finite state machine (FSM) issues CRC calculate enable signal. When CRC calculation is completed, the encoder is enabled, the parity check matrix is read in, and the information encoding is carried out. After completing the Part I operation, the calculation of P_1 starts. After obtaining the first set of parity codes, the hardware waits for the completion of the first round running of Part II, and the input information is switched to P_1 to calculate the second set of parity codes. When all parity codes are obtained, the encoding end signal is enabled to reset the FSM. The encoder returns to the initial state to perform the encoding of the next frame of information data.

4. Encoder Design Details

According to the encoding algorithm and the structure characteristics of the 5G QC-LDPC code, the cyclic shift of encoder and XOR operation in GF(2) is purely logic operations. The hardware complexity of the encoder will increase with the increase of the code length. Especially for CRC calculation, the complexity of encoding hardware will increase linearly with code length. The design of this paper is based on the requirements of 5G NR. In the eMBB scenario, NR requires large-scale data transmission. In the URLLC scenario, NR requires ultra-low latency and high reliability. Hence we need to design an encoder whose performance is close to the latency limit. The solution is to maximize the parallelism of encoding calculations; at the same time, the hardware must be configurable and have reasonable resource utilization. Therefore, this paper optimizes the parallelism of CRC and QC-LDPC encoding and selects a suitable architecture for the flexible configuration.

4.1. CRC Implementation in Parallel

The conventional CRC calculation uses LFSR serial calculation method to calculate bit by bit. The processing in serial has low processing efficiency; it is thus almost impossible to complete CRC calculation for large transmission blocks in 5G communication. In this paper, a high-parallel hardware architecture based on look-up table method is designed for CRC calculation.

The CRC calculation module in the encoder was mainly composed of look up table (LUT) structure and XOR gate circuit. LUT is actually composed of SRAM, the CRC value of each byte of data is stored in it. LUT using bytes as the input to avoid the excessive memory resource occupation caused by the increase in the number of input bits. Therefore, the CRC calculation module is designed to decompose the number of bytes of the input bit stream into the number of LUTs.

The look-up table algorithm pre-calculates the specified CRC value for each data byte and stores it in SRAM; through the LUT structure, fast CRC calculation can be performed for long bit stream data [24]. The CRC calculation module divides the input long bit stream into short bits in bytes and uses the LUT to calculate the CRC value of these bytes. Finally, a multi-byte CRC XOR is used to obtain the CRC value of the long bit stream. There are 2^8 situations for bits byte, so that 256 CRC values are stored in LUT; the input of the LUT structure is 8-bits CRC data as the address to obtain the corresponding stored CRC value in the LUT.

The maximum code length supported by BG1 is 8448 bits. In URLLC scenarios, BG2 is mainly for short code length encoding. As the communication scenario changes, the amount of data transmitted by the data channel also changes. The length of the TB handed over to the CRC calculation module is less than 8424 on the premise of LDPC encoding. Therefore, this paper designs hardware architecture for processing 256 bits data CRC calculation in one clock, as shown in Figure 9. By implementing low latency CRC computing while maintaining low hardware resource overhead, the overall coding time can be further reduced.

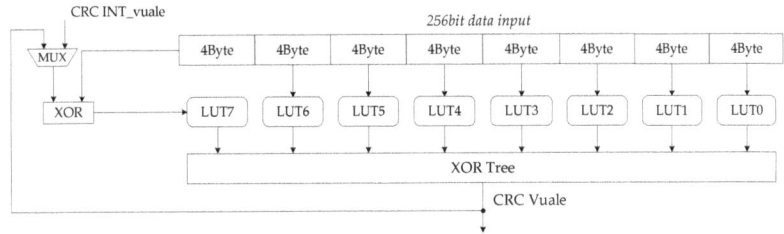

Figure 9. CRC module architecture for 256bits parallel computing.

The design of LUTs is in bytes and decomposition of 256 bits is into 32 bytes. A total of 32 LUT units are thus required. To simplify the number of modules in the architecture, we designed a LUT as a module that can look up CRC values for 4 bytes. Therefore, LUT0-LUT7 can perform CRC calculation for 256 bit data. In the process of calculation, there are two problems worthy of attention: when the input data is less than 256 bits, 0 shall be filled in the high significant bits before the CRC calculation; when the input data is larger than 256 bits and cannot be divided by 256, the calculation module will be based on the information of TB length, 0 filled in the high significant bits. Because the CRC value of 0 is also 0, zero-filling will not change the result. The calculation of long bit stream information also starts from the high significant bit.

In each clock, the architecture uses 32 bytes of 256bits data as the index of each LUT look-up table and obtains 32 values. After XOR logic operation, the CRC value (partial remainder) of the 256 bits input data is obtained. The MSB byte of the next 256bits data is XOR with the partial remainder; the result continues to be calculated until all data calculations are completed and the partial remainder becomes the final remainder. The computing latency of 8428 bits inputs is only 33 clocks. The results demonstrate that the CRC calculation module is a suitable design for the overall encoder, and its high parallelism satisfies the fast CRC calculation and maintains a low hardware complexity.

4.2. Design for Flexible Configuration

To adapt to variable code length and the eight code rates in the standard, we design a configurable circuit. Code length and code rate as dynamic parameters input into module, configuring static parameters for the following encoding calculations. The encoder parameter module performs parameter calculation via selection and output to the remaining modules after receiving code length and code rate information. The parameters are the base graph BG, the number of kernel matrix columns K_b, the lifting size Z, and the corresponding sets i_{Ls} of Z. BG and K_b determine the number of iterations for CN. The lifting size reads the memory module for parity check matrix information used in this encoding based on the group to which Z belongs. The codeword output processing module punches and shortens the information bits according to the code rate and K_b, as well as the parity bits.

The encoder hardware scale is designed according to the maximum parity check matrix under BG1, the matrix H is constructed by $Z \times Z$ size submatrix, and each submatrix is multiplied by the corresponding Z length information vector or P_1 vector. Therefore, the number of CN is set according to the maximum matrix dimension and the fixed length of the barrel shift is set to Z_{max}. Z_{max} is used as the CN hardware length to adapt to multiple $Z \times Z$ size submatrix. A Z-bits as the information or parity is input into CN, if Z is less than Z_{max}, the LSB vacant bits will be filled with 0 bits, only Z significant bits are shifted during cyclic shift, and only Z significant bits of each code word are as the output at the end of encoding. Meanwhile, the parity codeword can be achieved according to Z as a group. It can also meet the redundancy version requirement of QC-LDPC IR-HARQ transmission.

The encoder hardware shall adapt to changes of code rates. When the code rates are less than 2/5, C, D matrix has more rows than columns. In order to design a more parallel P_2 hardware, the multiplication operation between the H matrix and the vector is converted as shown in Figure 10. For high code rate, the encoder uses the code word output processing module to punch the corresponding number of Z-bits parity codes. With $[C\ D]$ matrix row number as the degree of parallelism, the number of Part II calculation modules is configured. The increase of the CN parallelization degree reduces the encoding delay and improves the throughput.

Therefore, the encoder can achieve code rate compatibility, but the encoding latency of different code rate under different BG depends on the encoding time at the lowest code rate. The proposed encoder needs $K_b + 4$ clock cycles to generate parity sequences under BG1 ($K_b = 22$) and BG2 ($K_b = 10$); it also needs one clock to output the encoded codeword. Therefore, the proposed encoder needs a total of K_b and 5 clock cycles to complete the encoding of an information sequence.

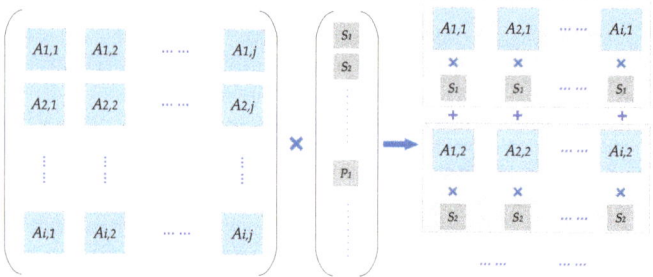

Figure 10. Parallelism improvement of Parities P_2 calculation.

The configurable barrel shift register design allows the encoder to be code length configurable. It avoids the waste caused by changing the hardware scale of the encoder for different lifting size. More CN numbers further shorten the encoding latency. The design of the configurable circuit makes the encoder fully meet the requirements of 5G NR flexibility. Although these schemes increase the hardware complexity of the encoder, they have achieved greater improvements in the performance of the encoder such as latency and throughput. Thus it achieves a balance between hardware complexity and encoder performance. We are constantly approaching the limit of the performance of the encoder within the complexity limit that the IC can achieve.

Based on encoding algorithms, we have studied the dynamic configurable scheme of the encoder in this section. We designed a parameterized encoder module; static parameters are available during power on process, and dynamic parameters are changed by L2/L3 setting via MAC-PHY (Port Physical Layer) API (Application Programming Interface). Then, the encoder schedules the hardware to perform encoding operations. The encoder can thus handle variable code length and rate for LDPC encoding through a fixed hardware architecture, which makes the encoder compatible with all configurations following 5G standard.

5. Results and Discussions

5.1. Discussions and Comparison with Related Work

Presently, there are seldom studies on the hardware implementation of 5G QC-LDPC encoder. In this section, we discuss and compare our proposed scheme with the published state of art to show the differences of related work and explain the novelty of this work.

Reference [19] proposed a 5G QC-LDPC parallel encoding algorithm based on an improved RU method. The encoder uses multiple cyclic shift networks to perform parallel encoding operations. A high throughput and low latency encoding architecture is implemented. Synthesis results on TSMC 65 nm CMOS technology with different submatrix sizes were carried out. The encoding delay is 48 clock cycles, and the throughput ranges from 22.1 to 202.4 Gbps. However, the CRC calculation was not included, and the parallelism of LDPC encoding can be further improved.

Reference [20] adopted the same encoding algorithm as [19] and performs simulation on a single GPU platform. Compared with FPGA and ASIC implementation, GPU-based applications can be flexibly modified and adjusted. The experimental results achieved a maximum throughput of 62.6 Gpbs at the BG2 8/9 code rate. This research verifies the parallelism and throughput of the QC-LDPC encoding algorithm. The implemented encoder is a solution for communication link hardware simulation, which is not applicable to hardware implementation.

For Reference [21], when compared with [19], the maximum encoding latency is reduced by 20 clock cycles. Reference [21] implemented nine encoders for distributed lifting sizes of BG1 and BG2, the application specific integrated circuit (ASIC) synthesis for different lifting sizes. Encoders implemented for different lifting sizes have different performance parameters. Therefore, this work lacks the complete flexibility and configurability for 3GPP standards and cannot meet the needs of all application scenarios.

Reference [22] improved the QC-LDPC encoding algorithm in order to improve the utilization of hardware resources. The proposed architecture is built around the shift network, which improves the original serial encoding structure. The designed flexible shift network has different lifting factors and is divided into three working modes. Partial parallel implementation can provide a compromise between the achievable throughput and the utilization of hardware resources. This paper proposes an optimized coding algorithm and hardware scheduling scheme. Compared with [19,21], the flexibility of the coding architecture has been greatly improved, but the coding delay has not reached the minimum. Under the operating frequency of 580 Mhz, the maximum delay is 875 ns and the peak BG1 throughput is 18.51 Gbps.

In the existing related works, the design of the 5G QC-LDPC encoder is mainly to improve the coding algorithm and design a higher parallel architecture. There are some issues to be solved. There is no design for the complete LDPC encoding chain, such as the design a CRC calculation module. The encoder lacks flexibility and compatibility and the overall architecture cannot satisfy all the lifting sizes, which means that the encoder cannot encode for all PCM.

In the work of this paper, in order to implement a lower latency 5G QC-LDPC encoder, we use more CN modules and increase the calculation speed of the second group of parity check bits (described in Section 4.2). We designed and implemented a higher degree of parallelism encoder architecture. The latency of the proposed encoder is only 33.75 ns at 800 Mhz, compared with the existing work, achieved a significant shortening. Meanwhile, the encoder fully meets the variable code length and code rate in the 5G scenario and improves the compatibility of the CNs to meet all the lifting sizes. Finally, the encoder designed a parallel acceleration structure for CRC calculation, so that the encoder can execute a complete 5G QC-LDPC encoding process.

5.2. Evaluation Results

The RTL code of our designed encoder has been validated using Modelsim, synthesized using Synopsys Design Compiler, and placed and routed using Synopsys IC Compiler. Two scenarios are for simulation. Scenario 1 is encoded under BG1. Two information code block lengths are used, $A_1 = 8424$ bits and $A_2 = 1920$ bits. After attached TB-CRC, and $K_1 = 8448$ bits, $K_2 = 1936$ bits, the initial code rate is $R_1 = 1/3$, $R_2 = 8/9$. Scenario 2 information length is 3824 bits, code rate is 1/5, and encoding is under BG2. The system clock is 800 MHz, the total encoding delay of Scenario 1 is 33.75 ns, and the total encoding delay of Scenario 2 is 18.75 ns.

Similar to [25], Table 1 compares the hardware parameters and performance indicators of the proposed encoder implemented by the ASIC with similar references. Throughput in the table is calculated according to Equation (17), where N represents the total encoded output that has not undergone codeword processing, R is the code rate, f_{max} is the highest frequency of the system clock, and CC is the cycle clocks consumed to obtain all parity checks.

$$Throughput = \frac{N \times R \times f_{max}}{CC} \quad (17)$$

The layout based on the CMOS technology synthesis with SMIC 28nm is shown in Figure 11, because SRAM is replaced by register file; it is a scattered flattening place and routing layout, so the functional module division is not marked in the Figure 11. The silicon layout shows that the total equivalent gates are about 1126K cells, and the total silicon area is 0.712 mm². The peak dynamic power consumption under 800 Mhz is 123.5 mW. The throughput/area is defined as the normalized throughput area ration (TAR), which is 362 Gpbs/mm² in this design. The area shows the resource usage of the encoder, and the number of equivalent gates represents the complexity of the implementation. Under BG2, when $Z = 384$, 3840 information bits are encoded to output 19,200 bits, and the encoder achieves the largest equivalent bit operations per clock: 1280 bit/cycle.

Table 1. Comparison of hardware implementation of 5G QC-LDPC and other standard LDPC encoders.

Encoder	Standard	Technology	Implemented Codes	f_{max} (MHz)	CC	Throughput (Gbps)	Area (Resource) (mm²)	Gate Counts (Complexity)	Equivalent Bit Operations Per Clock (Bit/Cycle)
[19]	5G NR	ASIC 65nm	(BG1,Z144)	645	48	89.0	0.171	214K	198
[19]	5G NR	ASIC 65 nm	(BG1,Z352)	600	48	202.4	0.389	486.4K	484
[19]	5G NR	ASIC 65 nm	(BG1,Z96)	714	48	43.8	0.117	146.3K	132
[20]	5G NR	CUDA GPU	(2178,1936)	1770	48	62.6	-	-	41.5
[21]	5G NR	ASIC 65 nm	(BG1,Z384)	575	28	173.7	0.511	639.5K	905
[21]	5G NR	ASIC 65 nm	(BG2,Z352)	586	16	128.9	0.435	545.2K	1100
[26]	GF(2^2)QC	ASIC 28 nm	(2016,1764)	400	256	6.3	0.007	8.66K	7.875
[27]	IRA-LDPC	ASIC 28 nm	(568,512)	-	57	3.57	-	58.5K + (512 × 64) SRAM	9.96
Proposed [1]	5G NR	ASIC 28 nm	(BG1,25344,8448)	800	27	257.9 *	0.712	1126K	938
Proposed [1]	5G NR	ASIC 28 nm	(BG1,2178,1936)	800	27	62.0 *	0.712	1126K	80.7
Proposed [1]	5G NR	ASIC 28 nm	(BG2,19200,3840)	800	15	213.0 *	0.712	1126K	1280

[1] Encoder implementation satisfies full lifting size Z and includes CRC calculation. * Based on Equation (17), other throughput is derived from references.

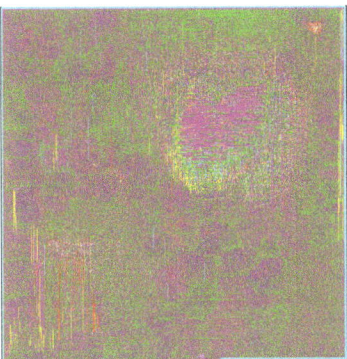

Figure 11. 5G NR QC-LDPC encoder layout.

In the proposed architecture, a configurable barrel shift register uses approximately 13.45K equivalent gates; the encoder uses 64 CNs, so CNs and configurable circuits utilize the largest hardware resources. In addition, the LUT and XOR tree structure of 256-bit parallel CRC calculation uses the remaining resources. Although this design is 40% higher than [21] in terms of resource utilization, the proposed encoder is suitable for full-size Z and includes CRC calculation. In [19,21], ASIC synthesis is performed for different lifting sizes, and five and nine encoders are implemented respectively. Thus these encoders can only work under the specified Z size. Moreover, Refs. [19–22] do not include CRC calculation. Therefore, the work implemented in this paper has more flexibility for various 5G application scenarios. The entire calculation process of data channel coding in the 3GPP standard has also been implemented. Consequently, the design of this paper is a low-latency hardware structure with complete encoding functions.

From the implementation results, the dynamically configurable architecture designed in this paper can directly perform full Z-size encoding operations; it can be seen that this design can be applied to different submatrix sizes. The design has significant silicon area efficiency and encoding throughput, and the design can be applied to a variety of code lengths and code rates.

6. Conclusions

In this paper, a 5G QC-LDPC encoder including CRC calculation is proposed. The designed hardware architecture has high parallelism and flexibility. Through parameter configuration, LDPC codes of various code lengths and code rates in the 5G standard can be encoded. This is achieved by improving the cyclic shift structure, the encoder uses the maximum lifting sizes of the 5G standard as the hardware scale and uses encoding parameters to constrain the hardware to achieve effective compatibility of the encoder.

In addition to architecture innovation, the encoder includes the parallelization of CRC calculations and designed a 256-bit parallel CRC calculation architecture based on look-up tables. Therefore, the encoder can perform the complete process of 5G LDPC encoding, which is an innovation compared to existing work.

The hardware implementation of the encoder is based on SIMC 28 nm CMOS technology. Compared with existing similar LDPC encoders, the proposed encoder achieves higher throughput, lower encoding latency, and the equivalent bit operation of each clock is also improved. Hence, our design achieves a better balance among flexibility, coding efficiency, and hardware power consumption and is suitable for 5G eMBB and URLLC scenarios.

Author Contributions: Conceptualization, D.L. and Y.T.; methodology, D.L. and Y.T.; funding acquisition, D.L. and Y.B.; software, D.L.; validation, Y.T., Y.B. and D.L.; investigation, Y.T.; project administration, D.L.; resources, Y.B. and D.L.; data curation, Y.T.; writing—original draft preparation, Y.T., Y.B. and D.L.; writing—review and editing, Y.B. and D.L. All authors have read and agreed to the published version of the manuscript.

Funding: This research was funded by Hainan University project funding KYQD (ZR)1974, National Natural Science Foundation of China under Grant 61961014, and Hainan Provincial Natural Science Foundation of China under Grant 620RC556.

Institutional Review Board Statement: Not applicable.

Informed Consent Statement: Not applicable.

Data Availability Statement: Not applicable.

Conflicts of Interest: The authors declare no conflict of interest.

References

1. Multiplexing and Channel Coding. Document TS 38.212 V15.0.0, 3GPP. 2017. Available online: https://www.3gpp.org/ftp/Specs/archive/38_series/38.212/ (accessed on 3 January 2018).
2. Wu, H.; Wang, H. A high throughput implementation of QC-LDPC codes for 5G NR. *IEEE Access* **2019**, *7*, 185373–185384. [CrossRef]
3. Wu, X.; Jiang, M.; Zhao, C.; Ma, L.; Wei, Y. Low-rate PBRL-LDPC codes for URLLC in 5G. *IEEE Wirel. Commun. Lett.* **2018**, *7*, 800–803. [CrossRef]
4. Li, L.; Xu, J.; Xu, J.; Hu, L. LDPC design for 5G NR URLLC & mMTC. In Proceedings of the 2020 International Wireless Communications and Mobile Computing (IWCMC), Limassol, Cyprus, 15–19 June 2020; IEEE: New York, NY, USA, 2020; pp. 1071–1076.
5. Liu, Y.; Olmos, P.M.; Mitchell, D.G. Generalized LDPC codes for ultra reliable low latency communication in 5G and beyond. *IEEE Access* **2018**, *6*, 72002–72014. [CrossRef]
6. Richardson, T.J.; Urbanke, R.L. Efficient encoding of low-density parity-check codes. *IEEE Trans. Inf. Theory* **2001**, *47*, 638–656. [CrossRef]
7. Lee, D.U.; Luk, W.; Wang, C.; Jones, C.T. A flexible hardware encoder for low-density parity-check codes. In Proceedings of the 12th Annual IEEE Symposium on Field-Programmable Custom Computing Machines, Napa, CA, USA, 20–23 April 2004; IEEE: New York, NY, USA, 2014; pp. 101–111.
8. Yao, X.; Li, L.; Liu, J.; Li, Q. A Low Complexity Parallel QC-LDPC Encoder. In Proceedings of the 2021 IEEE MTT-S International Wireless Symposium (IWS), Nanjing, China, 23–26 May 2021; IEEE: New York, NY, USA, 2021; pp. 1–3.
9. Theodoropoulos, D.; Kranitis, N.; Tsigkanos, A.; Paschalis, A. Efficient architectures for multigigabit CCSDS LDPC encoders. *IEEE Trans. Very Large Scale Integr. (VLSI) Syst.* **2020**, *28*, 1118–1127. [CrossRef]
10. Wang, X.; Ge, T.; Li, J.; Su, C.; Hong, F. Efficient multi-rate encoder of QC-LDPC codes based on FPGA for WIMAX standard. *Chin. J. Electron.* **2017**, *26*, 250–255. [CrossRef]
11. Mahdi, A.; Kanistras, N.; Paliouras, V. A multirate fully parallel LDPC encoder for the IEEE 802.11 n/ac/ax QC-LDPC codes based on reduced complexity XOR trees. *IEEE Trans. Very Large Scale Integr. (VLSI) Syst.* **2020**, *29*, 51–64. [CrossRef]
12. Goriushkin, R.; Nikishkin, P.; Ovinnikov, A.; Likhobabin, E.; Vityazev, V. FPGA Implementation of LDPC Encoder Architecture for Wireless Communication Standards. In Proceedings of the 2020 9th International Conference on Modern Circuits and Systems Technologies (MOCAST), Bremen, Germany, 7–9 September 2020; IEEE: New York, NY, USA, 2020; pp. 1–4.
13. Wang, R.; Chen, W.; Han, C. Low-complexity encoder implementation for LDPC codes in CCSDS standard. *IEICE Electron. Express* **2021**, 20210128. [CrossRef]
14. Richardson, T.; Kudekar, S. Design of low-density parity check codes for 5G new radio. *IEEE Commun. Mag.* **2018**, *56*, 28–34. [CrossRef]
15. Study on New Radio Access Technology Physical Layer Aspects. Document TR 38.802 V14.2.0, 3GPP. 2017. Available online: https://www.3gpp.org/ftp/Specs/archive/38_series/38.802/ (accessed on 26 September 2017).
16. Hosni, L.Y.; Farid, A.Y.; Elsaadany, A.A.; Safwat, M.A. 5G new radio prototype implementation based on SDR. *Commun. Netw.* **2019**, *12*, 1. [CrossRef]
17. 3GPP Compliant LDPC Encoding/Decoding Chain Hardware IP Core Product Brief. Available online: https://www.accelercomm.com/xilinx-ldpc#resources (accessed on 19 April 2021).
18. 5G LDPC Intel FPGA IP User Guide, Updated for: Intel Quartus Prime Design Suite 21.1. Available online: https://www.intel.sg/content/www/xa/en/programmable/documentation/ond1481066696968.html?countrylabel=Asia%20Pacific (accessed on 29 March 2021).
19. Nguyen, T.T.B.; Nguyen Tan, T.; Lee, H. Efficient QC-LDPC encoder for 5G new radio. *Electronics* **2019**, *8*, 668. [CrossRef]

20. Liao, S.; Zhan, Y.; Shi, Z. A High Throughput and Flexible Rate 5G NR LDPC Encoder on a Single GPU. In Proceedings of the 2021 23rd International Conference on Advanced Communication Technology (ICACT), PyeongChang, Korea, 7–10 February 2021; IEEE: New York, NY, USA, 2021; pp. 29–34.
21. Zhu, Y.; Xing, Z.; Li, Z.; Zhang, Y.; Hu, Y. High Area-Efficient Parallel Encoder with Compatible Architecture for 5G LDPC Codes. *Symmetry* **2021**, *13*, 700. [CrossRef]
22. Petrović, V.L.; El Mezeni, D.M.; Radošević, A. Flexible 5G New Radio LDPC Encoder Optimized for High Hardware Usage Efficiency. *Electronics* **2021**, *10*, 1106. [CrossRef]
23. Wang, W.; Liu, D.; Zhang, Y.; Gong, C. Energy estimation and optimization platform for 4G and the future base station system early-stage design. *China Commun.* **2017**, *14*, 47–64. [CrossRef]
24. Huo, Y.; Li, X.; Wang, W.; Liu, D. High performance table-based architecture for parallel CRC calculation. In Proceedings of the The 21st IEEE International Workshop on Local and Metropolitan Area Networks, Beijing, China, 22–24 April 2015; IEEE: New York, NY, USA, 2015; pp. 1–6.
25. Shao, S.; Hailes, P.; Wang, T.Y.; Wu, J.Y.; Maunder, R.G.; Al-Hashimi, B.M.; Hanzo, L. Survey of turbo, LDPC, and polar decoder ASIC implementations. *IEEE Commun. Surv. Tutorials* **2019**, *21*, 2309–2333. [CrossRef]
26. Zhang, X.; Tai, Y. Low-complexity transformed encoder architectures for quasi-cyclic nonbinary LDPC codes over subfields. *IEEE Trans. Very Large Scale Integr. (VLSI) Syst.* **2017**, *25*, 1342–1351. [CrossRef]
27. Talati, N.; Wang, Z.; Kvatinsky, S. Rate-compatible and high-throughput architecture designs for encoding LDPC codes. In Proceedings of the 2017 IEEE International Symposium on Circuits and Systems (ISCAS), Baltimore, MD, USA, 28–31 May 2017; IEEE: New York, NY, USA, 2017; pp. 1–4.

 *sensors*

Article

Multi-Layer Attack Graph Analysis in the 5G Edge Network Using a Dynamic Hexagonal Fuzzy Method

Hisham A. Kholidy

Department of Networks and Computer Security, College of Engineering, State University of New York (SUNY) Polytechnic Institute, Utica, NY 13502, USA; kholidh@sunypoly.edu; Tel.: +1-(315)-792-7538

Abstract: Overall, 5G networks are expected to become the backbone of many critical IT applications. With 5G, new tech advancements and innovation are expected; 5G currently operates on software-defined networking. This enables 5G to implement network slicing to meet the unique requirements of every application. As a result, 5G is more flexible and scalable than 4G LTE and previous generations. To avoid the growing risks of hacking, 5G cybersecurity needs some significant improvements. Some security concerns involve the network itself, while others focus on the devices connected to 5G. Both aspects present a risk to consumers, governments, and businesses alike. There is currently no real-time vulnerability assessment framework that specifically addresses 5G Edge networks, with regard to their real-time scalability and dynamic nature. This paper studies the vulnerability assessment in the 5G networks and develops an optimized dynamic method that integrates the Technique for Order of Preference by Similarity to Ideal Solution (TOPSIS) with the hexagonal fuzzy numbers to accurately analyze the vulnerabilities in 5G networks. The proposed method considers both the vulnerability and 5G network dynamic factors such as latency and accessibility to find the potential attack graph paths where the attack might propagate in the network and quantifies the attack cost and security level of the network. We test and validate the proposed method using our 5G testbed and we compare the optimized method to the classical TOPSIS and the known vulnerability scanner tool, Nessus.

Keywords: attack graphs; dynamic vulnerability analysis; hexagonal fuzzy number; 5G Edge security; decision-making technique; 5G security testbed

Citation: Kholidy, H.A. Multi-Layer Attack Graph Analysis in the 5G Edge Network Using a Dynamic Hexagonal Fuzzy Method. *Sensors* **2022**, *22*, 9. https://doi.org/10.3390/s22010009

Academic Editor: Giuseppe Caso

Received: 24 September 2021
Accepted: 14 December 2021
Published: 21 December 2021

Publisher's Note: MDPI stays neutral with regard to jurisdictional claims in published maps and institutional affiliations.

Copyright: © 2021 by the author. Licensee MDPI, Basel, Switzerland. This article is an open access article distributed under the terms and conditions of the Creative Commons Attribution (CC BY) license (https://creativecommons.org/licenses/by/4.0/).

1. Introduction

The fifth-generation (5G) wireless technology provides higher speed, lower latency, and greater capacity than 4G LTE networks. It uses Dynamic Spectrum Sharing (DSS) that can support a range of functions—from distance learning to mobile workforces. From emergency response to global payments to next-level gaming and entertainment, the possibilities are virtually limitless. Furthermore, 5G could make drone delivery, cloud-connected traffic control and other applications live up to their potential. It can also work across a wider range of radio frequencies, opening up new possibilities in the ultra-high millimeter-wave bands for carriers to expand their network capabilities [1].

Resultantly, 5G networks require complex security architectures unlike those in prior generations of cellular networks. The architecture of the previous cellular network generations did not account for several attacks such as insider attacks or even attacks on a roaming network. [2] The dynamics of new services and technologies in 5G were not common before, e.g., multi-tenancy and virtualization services share the same mobile network infrastructure. The 5G network integrates cloud computing, Software De-fined Networking (SDN), and Network Function Virtualization (NFV), and inherits their security challenges. Therefore, 5G adds a new trust model, where only the uSIM (Universal Subscriber Identity Module) and UDM (Unified Data Management) with the ARPF (Authentication Credential Repository and Processing Function) are trusted; all intermediate network hosts are not. These 5G networks utilize well-known Internet protocols such as HTTP and TLS. This change can be viewed with some trepidation since, until now, telecom protocols were closed, making them an entry barrier to attackers. Conversely, Internet technologies are open, and they are well known. This emphasizes the need for robust security mechanisms across the entire 5G network.

According to the national strategy to secure 5G implementation plan that was developed by the National Telecommunications and Information Administration (NTIA), the following challenges should be considered to develop an efficient security solution for 5G networks [3]:

(1) The 5G network supports heterogenous infrastructure. Any security solution should use a combination of centralized and distributed, physical and virtual deployments to ensure security at multiple levels (e.g., slices, services, and resources) across multiple domains (i.e., administrative and technological domains where 5G services are orchestrated such as Mobile Virtual Network Operators (MVNOs) for automotive, eHealth, massive IoT, massive multimedia broadband, etc. [4]).

(2) The 5G network requires scalable and higher-performance security solutions. The increase in bandwidth from 4G eNodeB to 5G gNodeB will cause significant increases in performance and scale requirements that the current security infrastructure may not be able to handle. This means the threat detection and vulnerability analysis solutions should be dynamic, consistent, and scalable.

(3) Distributed edge clouds create new attacks surfaces and vulnerability points. If no proper security mechanisms are in place, such as encryption or firewalls, IP connectivity will terminate at the edge of the operator. As a result, edge cloud nodes become susceptible to spoofing, eavesdropping, and other attack [5].

(4) Virtualization and network slicing bring new risks. There must be a method for separating virtualization layers and network slices from one another [6–8].

To the best of our knowledge, none of the current works introduces a real-time vulnerability assessment framework that specifically works for 5G Edge networks and considers these systems' real-time scalability and dynamic features due to the lack of publicly available 5G Edge testbeds, datasets, and attack graphs.

A few works [9–20] study vulnerability analysis and risk assessment in 5G Networks. However, they

(a) are still at an early stage;
(b) focus on either the SDN or NFV security [9,10];
(c) are not accurate enough when they are applied to large-scale systems like the 5G networks;
(d) do not consider the 5G challenges such as performance monitoring, scalability, orchestration and management, heterogeneous network support, and integration of the SDN, NFV, and edge computing;
(e) use generalized attack graph model and do not consider specific 5G attack vectors.

Several 5G threat assessments have been introduced in [11–13] to evaluate threats in 5G networks with a focus on the SDN and NFV technologies to identify the threats to NFV components such as firewalls and IDS and the interfaces between the architectural layers of the data, control and application planes introduced by SDN. In [14], the authors introduced an intrusion prevention system that employed five layers of 5G systems to detect the flow table overloading attack. However, this work is more specific to a particular attack category and does not consider the rest of the 5G attack vectors. Furthermore, it lacks the vulnerability analysis of the 5G core components. The authors of [15] present a graph model for multi-stage attack scenarios relating to the critical assets of the hierarchical network architecture of the 5G. In this work, an automated attack and defense framework is proposed based on the attacker's actions. Although vulnerabilities are generalized in this model rather than hardware or software specific ones, it does nonetheless rely on knowledge of vulnerabilities in the 5G network.

Among promising approaches that proved good performance in the cybersecurity domain is the Multi-Criteria Decision-Making Technique (MCDM) [21] using the TOPSIS [22]. In [23] authors used the TOPSIS to rank various feature selection approaches (e.g., Naive Bayes Classifier, J48 Classifier) that are used for some IDSs to select the important features on network traffic dataset.

In alignment with the NTIA's lines of effort discussed before, we develop a Vulnerability Assessment Approach (VAA) that uses the TOPSIS approach to find the potential attack graph paths where the attack might propagate. The VAA can:

(a) analyze the vulnerabilities in the 5G core components (i.e., SDN, NFV, and cloud Edge servers) and User Equipment (UE) from the attacker perspective especially concerning the dynamic, low latency, and scalable properties of the 5G networks;
(b) generate attack graphs based on the 5G attack vector;
(c) quantify the security level of the network and attack cost by deriving each attack node's minimal effort in the attack tree.

The VAA uses the TOPSIS [22] to compute the shortest attack path by selecting the lowest attacker cost of actions that denotes the lowest attacker efforts to exploit a certain vulnerability. Such shortest paths:

(a) help the Intrusion Response Systems (IRS) predict the position where attacks and exploits will be propagated in the 5G network;
(b) reduce the cardinality exponential growth of the system security state space that any IRS computes and that usually causes the state space explosion problem when applying a mitigation action in large-scale systems such as 5G Edge networks.

The proposed VAA uses two alternative techniques, the classical TOPSIS as discussed in [24] and the integrated TOPSIS with the Hexagonal Fuzzy Numbers (HFN) [25] to find the attack graph paths with the lowest attacker costs where the attack most probably will propagate. The reason for integrating the TOPSIS with the HFN is that the other TOPSIS methods, such as The TOPSIS with triangular, trapezoidal, and pentagonal fuzzy numbers, are found to have some vagueness and are not sufficient to arrive at a solution because of its higher dimensionality [26] particularly when they are used with large systems such as 5G networks. The accuracy, scalability, and performance of the proposed techniques will be tested and evaluated using our new 5G Edge security testbed. The testbed also allows us to develop 5G attack scenarios and attack graphs that are required to evaluate the VAA. We make this testbed in the light of other states of the art such as 5G Playground [27], Cisco [28], AWS [29], and Huawei [30].

The remainder of this paper is organized as follows. Section 2 presents the background and related work. Section 3 describes the 5G Edge attack vectors and scenarios. Section 4 introduces the new 5G Edge security testbed. Section 5 introduces the original VAA using the classic TOPSIS [31] and the optimized VAA using the Hexagonal Fuzzy TOPSIS Method. Section 6 introduces a practical case study for both the original VAA and the optimized one. Section 7 compares the accuracy and performance of the original VAA and the optimized one with the Nessus [32]. Finally, Section 8 draws some concluding remarks and outlines future work.

2. Background and Related Work

Sulaiman et al. [33] introduced qualitative and quantitative analysis of the cyber security issues on LTE and 5G Technologies using the Support Vector Machine (SVM). The proposed approach is capable of classifying the DDoS (Distributed Denial of Service) attack, Man-in-the-middle attack, Phishing attack, SQL Injection, and False Data Injection attacks. Seongmin et al. [34] provided insight into the security challenges in the real 5G NSA network discussed the mitigation techniques. The authors also created an attack tree and developed 15 test cases that can be applied to real networks and identified eight valid vulnerabilities. Gerrit et al. [35] studied possible threats according to the STRIDE threat classification model and derive a risk matrix based on the likelihood and impact of 12 threat scenarios that affect the radio access and the network core. Sullivan et al. [36] categorize security technologies using Open Systems Interconnection (OSI) layers and, for each layer, the authors discuss vulnerabilities, threats, security solutions, challenges, gaps, and open research issues. Weiwei et al. [37] proposed a new channel-based spoofing attack detection scheme in millimeter-wave massive multiple-input multiple-output (mmWave-MIMO) 5G networks using channel virtual representation. Reference [38] introduced new control-aware attack analytics for securing the IoT-based 5G networks. References [16–20,39–42] introduced new vulnerability assessment and attack detection approaches that work specifically for 5G core networks. They studied the new vulnerabilities related to the 5G core network components such as the SDN, NFV, and RAN and introduced new risk assessment and attack graph analysis models using various machine learning approaches.

In the following two subsections, we highlight the techniques used in this paper, namely, the TOPSIS technique and the hexagonal fuzzy number.

2.1. The Technique for Order Preference by Similarity to an Ideal Solution (TOPSIS)

The TOPSIS [22] is a multi-criteria decision-making technique that is based on the concept that the chosen alternative should have the shortest geometric distance from the positive ideal solution and the longest geometric distance from the negative ideal solution. The preferred alternative is the one with the closest distance to the positive ideal solution. The positive ideal solution is formed as a combination of the best points of each criterion. The negative ideal solution is a combination of the worst points of each criterion. The ranking results can be obtained corresponding to the importance weights of the defined criteria. If each characteristic takes on asymptotically raising or lowering variation, then maybe an ideal solution can be easily defined. That solution consists of all possible alternative values to achieve the best attributes since the worst solution consists of all attainable worst attribute values. Assumed a decision-making issue with multiple criteria has n alternatives, $A_1, A_2, \ldots, A_n$ and m criteria, $C_1, C_2, \ldots, C_m$. Each alternative is assessed against the criteria of m. All the values/ratings are allocated to alternatives regarding the decision matrix represented by $X(x_{ij})_{m \times n}$. Let $W = (w_1, w_2, \ldots, w_m)$ be the weight vector of criteria, satisfying $\sum_{j=1}^{m} wj = 1$. The decision Matrix X is shown below.

$$(X)_{m \times n} = \begin{pmatrix} X_{11} & X_{12} & \cdots & X_{1n} \\ X_{21} & X_{22} & & X_{2n} \\ \vdots & & \ddots & \vdots \\ X_{m1} & X_{m2} & \cdots & X_{mn} \end{pmatrix}$$

There are several applications for the TOPSIS in different fields. Dursun and Karsak [43] used a combination of fuzzy information, a 2-tuple linguistic representation model, and fuzzy TOPSIS and gave effective results. Lin and Chang [44] proposed a fuzzy approach for evaluating customers (buyers) and used the assessment results to screen orders by applying the fuzzy TOPSIS. Kamble and Naziya [45] proposed an integrated method of fuzzy AHP and fuzzy TOPSIS and applied it to the staff selection problem. Ashtiani et al. [24] solved Multiple Criteria Decision Making (MCDM) problems using the interval-valued fuzzy TOPSIS method, in which the weights of criteria are unequal.

A few approaches used the TOPSIS method in the cybersecurity domain. For example, Ansari et al. [46] used the Triangular Fuzzy Number TOPSIS approach to select the most suitable security requirements for quality and trustworthy software development based on the security expert's knowledge and experience. Gyumin et al. [47] developed an MCDM approach for flood vulnerability assessment which considers uncertainty. This study uses a modified fuzzy TOPSIS method based on level sets which consider various uncertainties related to weight derivation and crisp data aggregation. However, the proposed flood vulnerability assessment method is limited to support flood management policies. Yazdani et al. [48] developed a framework that extends conventional RAMCAP (Risk Analysis and Management for Critical Asset Protection) by adopting the fuzzy TOPSIS as an MCDM technique to determine the weights of each criterion and the importance of alternatives with respect to criteria.

2.2. Hexagonal Fuzzy Number

A fuzzy number $M^\sim$ is an HFN denoted by six tuples $M^\sim$ $(a_1, a_2, a_3, a_4, a_5, a_6, r, s)$ where $a_1 \leq a_2 \leq a_3 \leq a_4 \leq a_5 \leq a_6$ are real numbers and its membership function $\mu M^\sim (x)$ is given below in Equation (1), where and $0 < r, s < 1$ are interval values of the $\mu M^\sim (x)$. The graphical representation of a HFN for $x \in [0, 1]$ is shown in Figure 1 [25,49].

$$uM(x) = \begin{cases} \frac{1}{2}\left(\frac{(x-a1)}{a2-a1}\right), & a1 \leq x \leq a2 \\ \frac{1}{2} + \frac{1}{2}\left(\frac{(x-a1)}{a3-a2}\right), & a2 \leq x \leq a3 \\ 1, & a3 \leq x \leq a4 \\ 1 - \frac{1}{2}\left(\frac{(x-a4)}{a5-a4}\right), & a4 \leq x \leq a5 \\ \frac{1}{2}\left(\frac{(a6-x)}{a6-a5}\right), & a5 \leq x \leq a6 \\ 0, & otherwise. \end{cases} \quad (1)$$

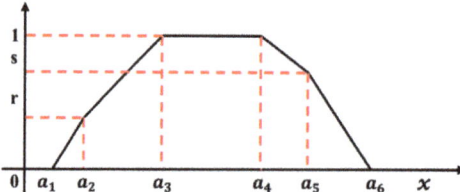

Figure 1. The HFN for $x \in [0, 1]$.

(a) **Operation on Hexagonal Fuzzy Numbers**

Consider two HFNs $M^\sim = (m_1, m_2, m_3, m_4, m_5, m_6)$ and $N^\sim = (n_1, n_2, n_3, n_4, n_5, n_6)$, then the operation on these two HFNs are as follows [50]:

- Addition: $M^\sim \oplus N^\sim = (m_1 + n_1, m_2 + n_2, m_3 + n_3, m_4 + n_4, m_5 + n_5, m_6 + n_6)$;
- Subtraction: $M^\sim - N^\sim = (m_1 - n_6, m_2 - n_5, m_3 - n_4, m_4 - n_3, m_5 - n_2, m_6 - n_1)$;
- Multiplication: $M^\sim \times N^\sim = (m_1 \times n_1, m_2 \times n_2, m_3 \times n_3, m_4 \times n_4, m_5 \times n_5, m_6 \times n_6)$;
- Division: $M^\sim / N^\sim = (m_1/n_6, m_2/n_5, m_3/n_4, m_4/n_3, m_5/n_2, m_6/n_1)$.

(b) **The Distance between Two HFNs**

If $M^\sim = (m_1, m_2, m_3, m_4, m_5, m_6)$ and $N^\sim = (n_1, n_2, n_3, n_4, n_5, n_6)$ are two HFNs, then the hamming distance of $M^\sim$ from $N^\sim$ is given by Equation (2) [50].

$$d(M^\sim, N^\sim) = 1/6 \, (|m_1 - n_1| + |m_2 - n_2| + |m_3 - n_3| + |m_4 - n_4| + |m_5 - n_5| + |m_6 - n_6|) \quad (2)$$

3. The 5G Edge Attack Vector

The attack surface of the 5G edge network is very big, see Figure 2. Dutta and Hammad [31] studied the 5G security challenges, risks, and threats of underlying 5G elements such as the orchestrator, SDN controller, network controller, and the NFV security orchestrator. In the following, we summarize these threat categories.

- Threat 1: Attack from VMs in the same domain. Attackers would manipulate the VM and potentially extend the attack to other VMs. This threat category includes Buffer overflow, DOS, ARP, Hypervisor, and vswitch threats;
- Threat 2: Attack to host, hypervisor, and VMs from applications in host Machine. The attacker exploits vulnerabilities caused by the main poor design of hypervisors and improper configuration and injects malicious software to virtual memory and control VM. This threat category includes the malformed packet attacks to hypervisors;

- Threat 3: Attack from host applications communicating with VMs. This includes attacks that exploit vulnerabilities caused by improper network isolation and improper configuration to application privileges of the host machine;
- Threat 4: Attack to VMs from remote management path. This includes eavesdropping, tampering, DOS attack, and Man-in-the-Middle attack;
- Threat 5: Attack to external communication with third party applications. This includes illegal access to API and DOS attacks to API;
- Threat 6: Attack from external network via network edge node. This includes attacks against Virtualized Firewalls and Residential gateways;
- Threat 7: Attack from host machines or VMs of an external network domain. This includes attacks against the VNF migration and VNF scaling.

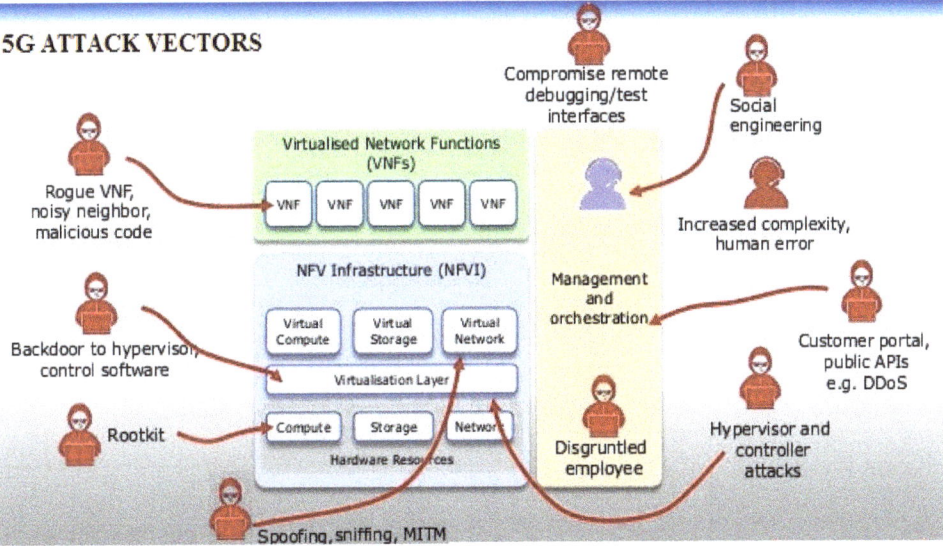

Figure 2. Attack surfaces of the 5G Network.

From our analysis, besides the traditional network, IoT, and cloud attack surfaces that are inherited to the 5G networks, there are additional attacks enabled by the integration of mobile Edge computing (MEC) and 5G networks, as depicted in Figure 3, namely [31]:

1. **(I): Insecure mobile backhaul network.** Data exchanged between MEC nodes often traverse insecure shared backhaul that is vulnerable to MITM attacks, including eavesdropping and spoofing. Such attacks can also come from edge nodes connected to the public internet through the edge Firewall Interfaces (e.g., SGi/N6);
2. **(S): Shared infrastructure with third-party applications.** MEC nodes can be opened to allow authorized participants to deploy applications/services to other users. However, poorly designed applications can create opportunities for attackers to invade the system and pose threats to the network applications running on the platform;
3. **(P): Privacy leakage illegitimate access to the Multi-access MEC system.** In this case, an attacker can compromise the service infrastructure and the network hampering information privacy, and accessing the information stored at the edge system's upper layers that in turns poses a serious concern for privacy leakage. In this paper, we mainly target these attacks using the VAA.

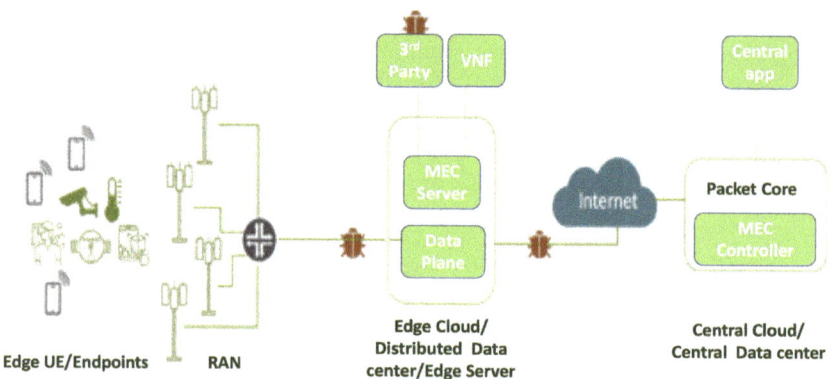

Figure 3. Attack surfaces enabled by the integration of MEC.

4. The New 5G Edge Security Testbed and the Scalable Deployment of the Security Framework

To consider the 5G characteristics, we introduce a hierarchical, scalable, robust, and flexible deployment architecture for our Autonomous Security Management Framework (ASMF) [51–59] see Figure 4. The ASMF framework consists of the following components and processes. The components in yellow, grey, and pink colors are the ones we implemented; the rest of the components are open-source systems that we deployed in the testbed.

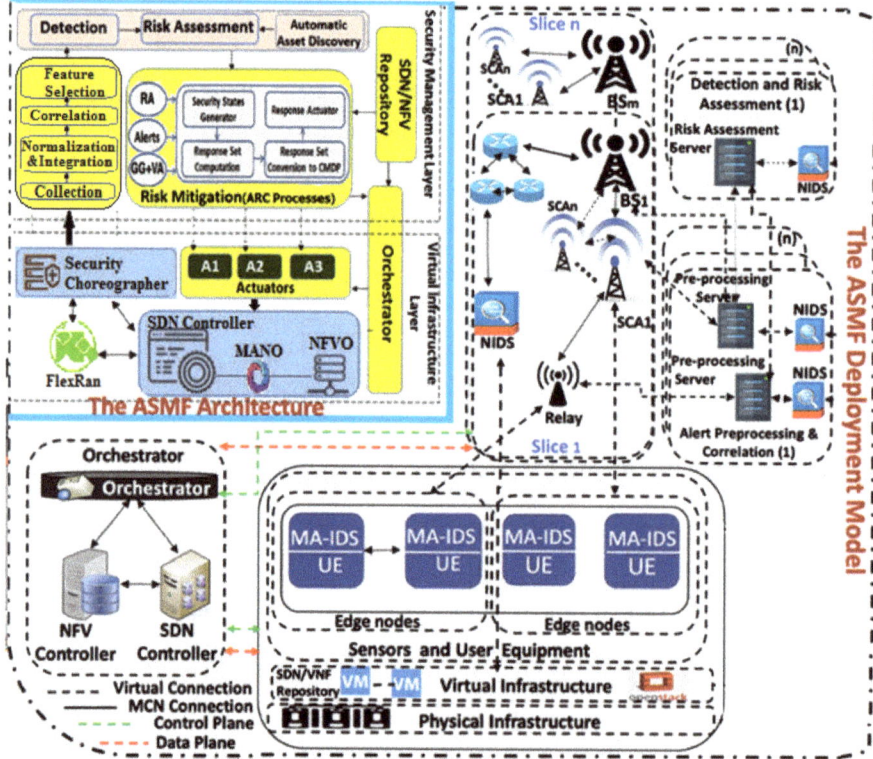

Figure 4. Our 5G Edge security testbed and the ASMF Architecture.

(a) Collection. This process collects events and logs from several IDSs sensors and sends them to the integration process;
(b) Integration. This process integrates distinct events that are collected from distinct sensors through two processes, namely, normalization and prioritization. The former formats any sensor event into the IDMEF protocol format [60] to facilitate the analysis and correlation of these events in the next layer. The latter handles the prioritization systems of distinct detectors i.e., Mobile Agent IDS(MA-IDS) and network-based IDSs (NIDS);
(c) Correlation. It correlates the normalized events from different sensors to highlight the few critical ones. It compares each event against a set of attack rules to discover if it signals a true attack and then it correlates the related events;
(d) Feature Selection. This process extracts a subset of relevant important features from the correlation process to enhance the classification results. More details about this process are listed in [54];
(e) Risk Assessment. The risk assessment model assesses the risk in the 5G infrastructure based on the alert level of different events;
(f) Autonomic Response and Countermeasures Selection Process. This process selects the most suitable set of countermeasures to protect the hosts and the network against a particular attack. More details about this process are listed in [52,53].

Our testbed consists of the following open-source components. Table 1 depicts the capabilities of the resources of the testbed machines.

- OpenStack [61] is an open-source hypervisor platform that uses pooled physical and virtual resources to deliver Infrastructure-as-a-service (IaaS);
- The Open-Source Network Function Virtualization Management and Orchestration (OSM) [62] handles the management and orchestration of NFV layers. OSM enables the creation of network services with programmatic ease. It has two principal elements for building a network service: (1) VNF packages and (2) NS packages;
- The FlexRan [63] platform is made up of two main components: the FlexRAN Control Plane and FlexRAN Agent API. The FlexRAN protocol facilitates the communication between the master controller and the agents;
- Open5GS [64] integrates with 5G New Radio Stand-Alone (SA) base stations and user equipment supporting the current need to have a flexible 5G Core Network.

Table 1. Testbed resource capabilities.

Component	System Parameters			
OSM, OpenStack, and Open5GS	OS: UBUNTU 20.04 LTS GHz SSD: 3TB(RAID 5) OpenStack Version: Wallaby. OAI CN Version: 1.0	RAM: 128 GB OSM Version: 9.1. Open5GS Version: 2.3.		CPU: 32 Cores 2.10 MicroK8s Version: 1.19
FlexRAN	OS: UBUNTU 20.04 LTS. GHz SSD: 2TB(RAID 5)	RAM: 32 GB.		CPU: 4 Cores 2.33
SDR USRP B210	Frequency Range: 70 MHz–6 GHz			Channels: 2TX*2RX

In 5G Edge Networks, UE (e.g., mobile devices) at the edge of a coverage area, or the area where the signal strength of the base station and a Small Cell Access (SCA) point is very low, are connected to a relay which in turn is connected to a Base Station (BS) through SCA. Two or more devices at the relay also establish a direct connection link between each other. In our testbed, the nodes, SCA, relay, and base stations are virtually deployed using the Open5GCore toolkit [27]. Each node/device/user equipment has an MA-IDS deployed to analyze system logs and forwards security alerts to the corresponding dedicated pre-processing server. Each of these servers has a dedicated NIDS to analyze the network traffic. The pre-processing servers run the collection, normalization, integration, and correlation for the alerts forwarded through the relays, SCAs, and/or BS. After that, these servers forward the final correlated alerts to the risk assessment server. In this deployment, we have *m* slices corresponding to *m* BSs. Each slice has *n* risk assessment servers and *n* SCA Security Servers (S3s) for risk mitigation.

The risk assessment server assesses the risks based on all correlated alerts that are received from relays, SCAs, and/or BS. The correlated alerts and risk alert information produced by the VAA are forwarded to a Global BS Security Server (GBSS) which is located at each slice of the deployment. After that, each S3 applies a response against the ongoing attacks in its substation network. S3 forwards log information to the GBSS only if it can mitigate the attacks, otherwise, a response strategy is computed by the GBSS's Autonomous Response Controller (ARC) [52,53] and applied to those substations where the S3 was not able to mitigate the attacks. The response strategy applied by the ARC of the GBSS is of two types, a manual action applied by the 5G administrator, or an automated action against multi-stage attacks requiring that each S3 correlates the alerts signaled from several substations in the 5G.

5. The New Vulnerability Analysis Approach (VAA)

The VAA develops (1) a scalable attack Graph Generator (GG) model, and (2) a new dynamic Vulnerability Analysis (VA) model that hierarchically analyzes the generated attack graphs using the TOPSIS to model the multiple-criteria decision-making problem in the 5G Edge dynamic environment to find the ideal solution that the attacker may consider. The ideal solution in the current context refers to the lowest attacker cost of actions that denotes the lowest attacker efforts to exploit a certain vulnerability, e.g., in Figure 5, if the computed TOPSIS cost of exploitation of the Common Vulnerabilities and Exposures (CVE) [48] security flow with ID CVE2004-0417 is lower than CVE2002-0392 and CVE2004-0415, this means if the attacker started exploiting CVE2004-0417 rather than the other vulnerabilities, this will be considered a positive ideal solution. In the next two sections, we introduce the two alternative TOPSIS techniques that the VAA uses.

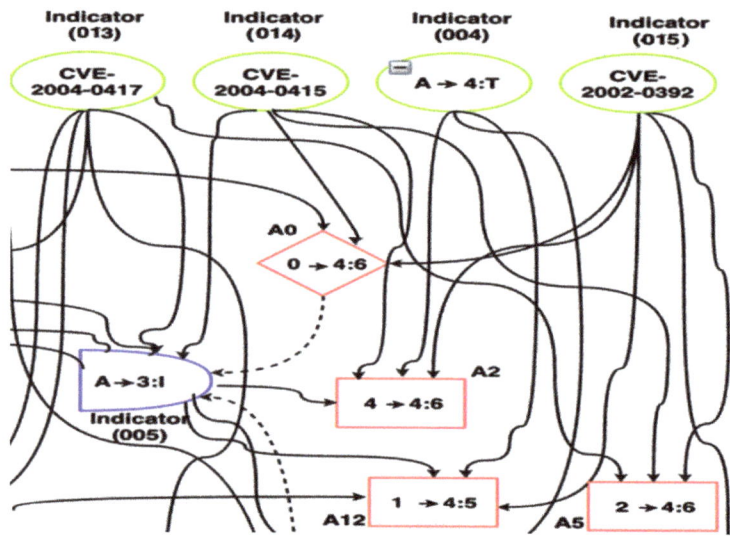

Figure 5. Part of an example of the generated attack Graph.

5.1. Develop the VAA Using the Classical TOPSIS

The following steps summarize the proposed VAA.

Step 1: Develop a scalable attack Graph Generator (GG) model.

This model is based on the security attack vector that focuses on the attacks and threats that may harvest intelligence from the 5G network resources, states, and flows as a result of the integration of the NFV and SDN. The basic idea underlying this model is that the attacker's action cost is under the constraint of certain vulnerability and network dynamic factors/indicators of the 5G network such as latency, accessibility, and other factors described in [65]. The vulnerability factors refer to the Common Vulnerability Scoring System (CVSS) factors/indicators namely Base, Temporal, and Environmental. Each of these factors is a composite of other several factors described in [66]. We model this problem as a multi-objective decision-making problem as follows.

(1) Create the GG three-layer hierarchical model based on the vulnerability and dynamic network factors, see Figure 6.

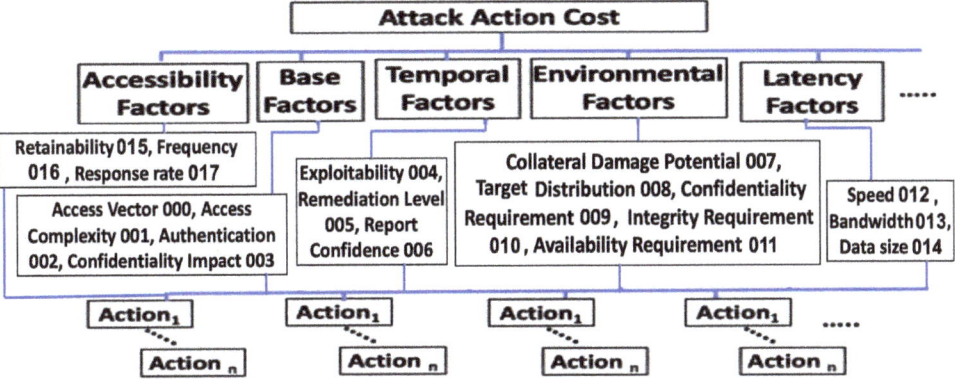

Figure 6. The Hierarchical GG with corresponding factors' codes.

The attack graph is modeled based on these factors. An attack graph is defined as a tuple $G = (A, S, T)$, where A is a set of attack actions, S is a set of system states, T is a set of targets that the attacker tries to achieve. An attack graph GG consists of a set of nodes of four types, see Figure 5: (1) attack-step nodes (circular-shaped AND-nodes). Each node in this set represents a single attack step that can be carried out when all the predecessors (preconditions to the attack which are either configuration settings or network privileges) are satisfied; (2) Privilege nodes (diamond-shaped nodes): Each node in this set represents a single network privilege. The privilege can be achieved through any one of its predecessor AND node which represents an attack step leading to the privilege. Each node in this set represents a fact about the current network configuration that contributes to one or more attack possibilities (sub-action); (3) Configuration nodes (circular-shaped): Each node in this set represents an initial vulnerability, configuration settings, or network privileges that are known to be true and have no variance in probability; (4) Final step nodes (rectangular-shaped): Each node in this set represents a final exploit action against a certain vulnerability.

(2) Construct a pair-wise evaluation matrix M, see Figure 7, based on the attack graph. After that, we compute the combinatorial weights (W^i) which refer to the weight of the impact of each layer's dynamic factors, in the GG three-layer model, on the attacker decision as given in Equation (3).

$$(M)_{n \times n} = \begin{bmatrix} 1 & a_{12} \cdots & a_{1n} \\ a_{21} & 1 \cdots & a_{2n} \\ \cdots & \cdots & \cdots \\ a_{n1} & a_{n2} \cdots & 1 \end{bmatrix}$$

Figure 7. The M pair-wise Matrix.

$$W^i = (W_j^{iL})_{j=1 \to n} W^L \quad (3)$$

where i is the GG hierarchical layer index $\in \{1,2,3\}$, j refers to the dynamic factors, and W^L is the criteria layer combinational weight vector which is computed as given in Equation (4).

$$W^L = M * W \quad (4)$$

where W is the relevant normalized characteristic vector/eigenvector = $\lambda_{max} * W$, for all $w = (w_1, w_2, w_3, \ldots, w_n)$. λ_{max} is the largest eigenvalue of matrix M.

Step 2: Compute the attack cost of actions using the classical TOPSIS.

To compute the attack cost of actions, we will apply the classical TOPSIS approach as follows.

(1) Normalize the pair-wise decision matrix M to form the normalized decision matrix N as given in Equation (5).

$$N_{ij} = (N_{ij})_{m \times n} \quad (5)$$

where, $N_{ij} = \dfrac{M_{ij}}{\sqrt{\sum_{j=1}^{n} M_{ij}^2}}$, $i = 1, 2, \ldots, m$, $j = 1, 2, \ldots, n$

(2) Calculate the weighted normalized decision matrix and the best and worth alternatives.

The weighted normalized decision matrix $E = N \times W$. The best alternative E^+ and the worst alternative E^- are defined in Equations (6) and (7), respectively.

$$E^+ = (E^+_1, E^+_2, E^+_3, \ldots \ldots \ldots, E^+_n) \quad (6)$$

$$E^- = (E^-_1, E^-_2, E^-_3, \ldots \ldots \ldots, E^-_n) \quad (7)$$

Let us define the benefit criteria from the attacker perspective (e.g., high exploitability, high latency, low speed … etc.) as B and the cost criteria as C (e.g., long exploit time, low latency, low speed … etc.). The value of E^+ and E^- can be calculated using Equations (8) and (9), respectively.

$$e_i^+ = [\max_j(E_{ij}) | i \in B], [\min_j(E_{ij}) | i \in C] \quad (8)$$

$$e_i^- = [\min_j(E_{ij}) | i \in B], [\max_j(E_{ij}) | i \in C] \quad (9)$$

(3) Calculate the cost of the attacker's actions. We use the L2-distance defined by the TOPSIS approach to calculate $L2_i^+$, the distance between the target alternative i and the best condition E^+ as given in Equation (10) and $L2_i^-$, the distance between the target alternative i and the worst condition E^- as given in Equation (11).

$$L2_i^+ = \sqrt{\sum_{k=1}^{n} (e_{i,k} - e_k^+)^2} \quad (10)$$

$$L2_i^- = \sqrt{\sum_{k=1}^{n} (e_{i,k} - e_k^-)^2} \quad (11)$$

Based on the $L2_i^+$ and $L2_i^-$ distances, we compute the similarity to the worst condition as the cost of the attacker's actions (Atc_{Cost}) as shown in Equation (12).

$$Atc_{Cost}(i) = \frac{L2_i^-}{L2_i^+ + L2_i^-} \qquad (12)$$

where $i \in \{1, 2, \ldots, m\}$ is the actions the attacker can choose from m possible actions. Using the attack graph in Figure 5, we give a simple demonstration for the decision matrix of the attacker's actions compared to the network indicators (the network components where the attacker may start its exploitation), see Table 2. The full case study of this example is detailed in Section 6. The computed attack graphs, actions, and the costs of these actions can be used by an intrusion response system to model the security reciprocal interaction between it and the attacker and can help in deploying the best countermeasures to mitigate the attacks in the 5G edge networks.

Table 2. Attacker Decision Matrix.

		Exploitation Starting Point		
		CVE-2004-0417	CVE-2004-0415	CVE-2002-0392
Attacker Goal	I: disruption for NFVI Services	A5	A5	A5
	S: illegitimate access to Shared SDN	A12	A0–A12, A12	A12
	P: illegitimate access to the RAN	A2	A0–A2, A2	A2

5.2. Develop the VAA Using the Hexagonal Fuzzy TOPSIS Method

The new proposed approach integrates the TOPSIS with the HFN approach. This approach uses the same attack Graph Generator (GG) and the three-layer hierarchical model that is based on the vulnerability and dynamic network factors described in Section 5.1. In the following, we describe the steps of the proposed approach.

Step 1: Construct the fuzzy decision matrix M. The fuzzy decision matrix has each entry of the HFN as given below:

$$M = \begin{pmatrix} X_{11} & X_{12} & \cdots & X_{1m} \\ X_{21} & X_{22} & & X_{2m} \\ \vdots & & \ddots & \vdots \\ X_{n1} & X_{n2} & \cdots & X_{nm} \end{pmatrix}$$

where $x_{ij} = (x_{ij1}, x_{ij2}, x_{ij3}, x_{ij4}, x_{ij5}, x_{ij6})$, $i = 1, 2, 3, \ldots, m$; $j = 1, 2, 3, \ldots, n$, represents the number of alternatives and criteria, respectively.

Step 2: Construct the normalized decision matrix $\tilde{N}_{ij}$ using M entries as shown in Equation (13).

$$\tilde{N}_{ij} = \frac{x_{ij}}{\sqrt{\sum_{j=1}^{n} \tilde{x}_{ij}^2}}, \quad i = 1, 2, \ldots, m \qquad (13)$$

Step 3: Calculate the weighted normalized decision matrix.

The weighted normalized decision matrix $\tilde{E}_{ij} = \tilde{N}_{ij} \times \tilde{W}_j$, where $i = 1, 2, \ldots, m$ and $j = 1, 2, \ldots, n$. Where $\tilde{W}_j$ is the weight of the criterion which refers to the weight of the impact of each layer's dynamic factors, in the GG three-layer model, on the attacker decision.

Unlike the classical TOPSIS method described in Section 5.1, which uses the λ_{max} (the largest eigenvalue of matrix M) to compute the weight of the criterion, we introduce a special structure of fuzzy numbers, Normalized Fuzzy Weight, that represents a fuzzification of crisp normalized weights that are defined as non-negative real numbers $w_1, w_2, \ldots, w_n$ such that $\sum_{j=1}^{n} w_j = 1$.

Fuzzy numbers $W_1, W_2, \ldots, W_n$ defined on $[0, 1]$ are called normalized fuzzy weights if for any $\alpha \in (0, 1]$ and all $j \in N_n$ the following holds:

For any $w_j \in W_{j\alpha}$ there exist $w_i \in W_{i\alpha}, j \in N_n, i \neq j$, such that $w_j + \sum_{j=1,\, j\neq i}^{n} w_j = 1$.

Normalized fuzzy weights make it possible to model mathematically an uncertain division of a unit into n fractions. Figure 8 illustrates an example of normalized fuzzy weights.

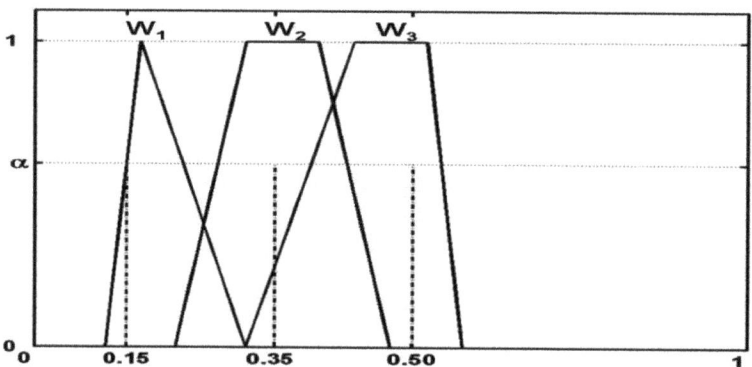

Figure 8. An example of normalized fuzzy weights.

Step 4: Calculate the fuzzy positive ideal alternative $E^{\sim+}$ **and the fuzzy negative ideal alternative** $E^{\sim-}$ as shown in Equations (14) and (15), respectively.

$$E^+ = (E^+{}_1, E^+{}_2, E^+{}_3, \ldots, E^+{}_n) = \left\{ \left(\max_j E_{ij} \Big| i \in B \right), \left(\min_j E_{ij} \Big| i \in C \right) \right\} \quad (14)$$

$$E^- = (E^-{}_1, E^-{}_2, E^-{}_3, \ldots, E^-{}_n) = \left\{ \left(\min_j E_{ij} \Big| i \in B \right), \left(\max_j E_{ij} \Big| i \in C \right) \right\} \quad (15)$$

where $E^{\sim+} i$ is the max value of i for all the alternatives and $E^{\sim-}$ is the min value of i for all the alternatives. B and C represent the positive (based on the benefit criteria) and negative ideal solutions (based on the cost criteria), respectively. The benefit criteria from the attacker perspective include high exploitability, high latency, low speed ... etc. The cost criteria include long exploit time, low latency, low speed ... etc.

Step 5: Determine the distance measures to ideal solutions, since the $E^{\sim+}$ and $E^{\sim-}$ are still HFN, we calculate D_i^+, the distance between the target alternative $i(E_i^{\sim})$ and the best condition in $E^{\sim+}$ from the attacker perspective as given in Equation (16), and D_i^-, the distance between the target alternative $i(E_i^{\sim})$ and the worst condition in $E^{\sim-}$ as given in Equation (17).

$$D_i^+ = \sqrt{\sum_{k=1}^{n} d(E_k^{\sim+}, E_{i,k}^{\sim})^2} \quad i = 1, 2, 3, \ldots, m \quad (16)$$

$$D_i^- = \sqrt{\sum_{k=1}^{n} d(E_k^{\sim-}, E_{i,k}^{\sim})^2} \quad i = 1, 2, 3, \ldots, m \quad (17)$$

where $d\left(E_k^{\sim+}, E_{i,k}^{\sim}\right)$ and $d\left(E_k^{\sim-}, E_{i,k}^{\sim}\right)$ are calculated using the distance equation of HFN in Equation (2).

Step 6: Calculate the cost and benefits of the attacker's actions. Based on the D_i^+ and D_i^- distances, we compute the similarity to the worst condition as the cost of the attacker's actions (Atc_{Cost}) as shown in Equation (18).

$$Atc_{Cost}(i) = \frac{D_i^-}{D_i^+ + D_i^-} \qquad (18)$$

We compute the similarity to the best condition as the benefit of the attacker's actions ($Atc_{benefit}$) as shown in Equation (19).

$$Atc_{benefit}(i) = \frac{D_i^+}{D_i^+ + D_i^-} \qquad (19)$$

where $i \in \{1, 2, \ldots, m\}$ is the actions the attacker can choose from m possible actions.

6. Performance and Accuracy Evaluation: Case Study

To evaluate VAA, we provide a 5G edge case based on the 3GPP architecture [12] in Figure 9 that is deployed in our testbed using the open-source components described in Section 4. This architecture is based on the concepts of control and user planes split, service base architecture, and network slicing. Their main network functionalities are the Network Slice Selection Function (NSSF), the Authentication Server Function (AUSF), the Unified Data Management (UDM), the Access and Mobility Management Function (AMF), the Session Management Function (SMF), the Policy Control Function (PCF), the Application Function (AF), the User Equipment (UE), the Radio Access Network (RAN), the User Plane Function (UPF), and the Data Network (DN). A two-level SDN controllers hierarchy bridges between the functions of the control and user planes, specifically, between the SMFs and the UPFs. The 5G core NFs are implemented as VNFs in an NFVI in which the SDN Controllers are virtualized and implemented. Figure 9 shows the exploited assets in this case study in red color.

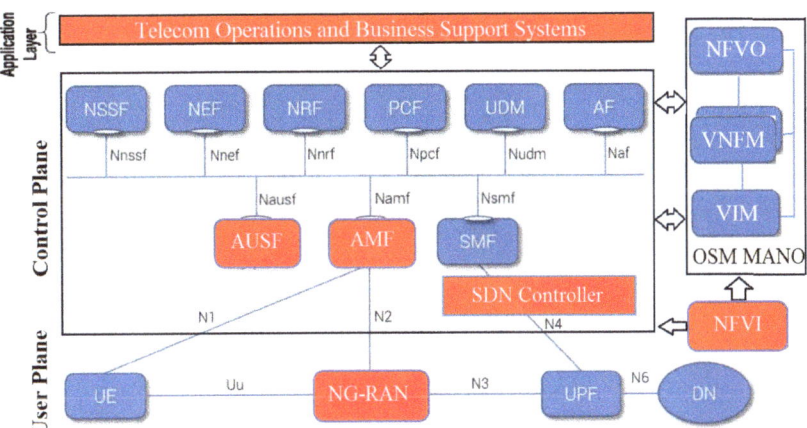

Figure 9. The 5G Edge-based 3GPP planes in our testbed.

Using the Metasploit framework [67], we ran some exploits based on the 5G Edge attack vector described in Section 3. These exploits target six vulnerabilities in the testbed namely, the *CVE-2019-15083* (allows for an XSS injection that leads to control what software is installed on the admin workstation), *CVE-2013-0375* (allows for remote injection of SQL code that leads to bypassing the AUSF), *CVE-2019-16026* (leads to a denial of service (DoS) condition on the AMF), *CVE-2004-0415* (allows for illegitimate access to portions of kernel memory that leads to illegitimate access to the SDN), *CVE-2002-0392* (allows for remote execution of DoS attack that leads to disruption for the NFVI functionalities), *CVE-2004-0417* (allows for an integer overflow in the CVS Apps that leads to illegitimate access to the RAN). Figure 10 shows the attack graph that was created using the aforementioned approach described in Section 5.1. The main target of the attacker is to access and control the RAN module using the aforementioned vulnerabilities that belong to the three attack categories described in Section 3 (i.e., I, S, P).

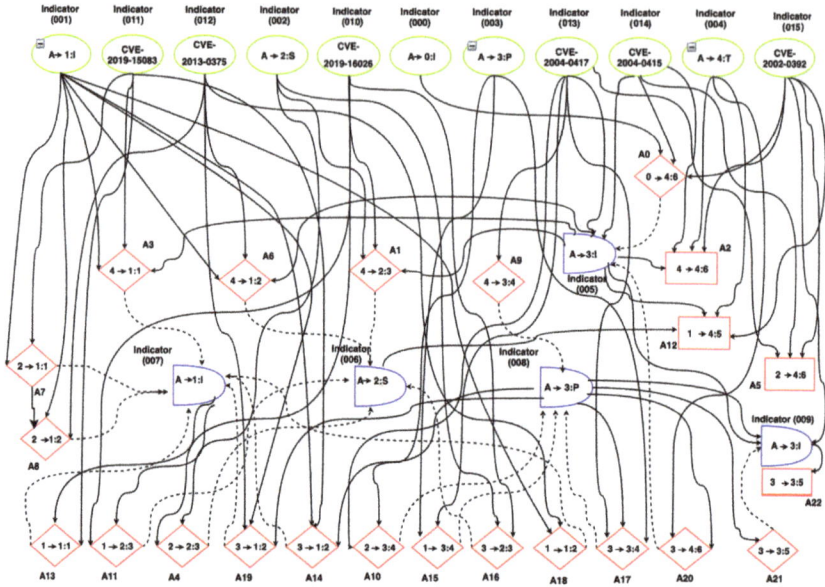

Figure 10. The attack graph with the corresponding factors' codes.

6.1. Evaluating the VAA Using the Classic TOPSIS

Table 3 shows an example of the pair-wise evaluation matrix M of the criteria layer (vulnerability factors) and the indicator layer (network dynamic factors). Using Matrix M, we compute the Atc_{Cost} for each possible path of actions according to Equation (12). We then choose the lowest attacker efforts in three attacking schemes (i.e., I, S, P). As Table 4 depicts the lowest cost is achieved when the attacker exploits the CVE-2004-0417 first. Although the long attacking path increases the attacker's cost, it also enables the attacker to consider more vulnerability and network dynamic factors that in turn reduce the attacker's overall cost. Such long paths reduce the $L2_i^+$ and increase the $L2_i^-$, which in turn reduces the Atc_{Cost}, see Equations (10)–(12). Figure 11 shows the attack costs for all possible paths of the three attacking schemes (i.e., I, S, P).

Table 3. Pair-wise evaluation matrix of the criteria layer.

	001	002	003	004	005	006	007	008	009	011	012	...
001	1	3	2	1/8	1/9	1/7	1/4	1/6	1/7	2	1/4	...
002	1/7	1	3	2	1	1/5	1/3	1/9	2	1/6	1/5	...
003	1/8	1/9	1	1/3	1/2	1/3	1/7	3	1/2	1/4	2	...
004	1/8	1/9	1/2	1	1/8	1/3	1/4	2	1/5	1/3	1/4	...
005	3	1/3	1/6	1/5	1	1/5	1/3	1/5	1/6	1/6	1/9	...
006	1/2	1/7	2	1/3	1/2	1	1/7	3	1/2	1/9	1/3	...
007	1/6	$\frac{1}{2}$	1/7	2	1/3	1/5	1	1/6	1/8	1/7	1/7	...
008	1/2	4	1/2	2	1/7	1/3	1/6	1	3	1/5	4	...
009	1/6	1/5	3	1/6	1/4	1/6	1/3	1/5	1	1/3	4	...
011	3	1	1/6	1/9	2	1/2	1/7	1/3	1/5	1	1/3	...
012	1/5	1/9	1/6	1/7	1	1/8	2	1/7	1/3	2	1	...

Table 4. Attacker cost in three attacking schemes (I, S, P).

		Exploitation Starting Point. Action Paths with the Lowest Costs Are Underlined					
		CVE-2004-0417	CVE-2004-0415	CVE-2002-0392	CVE-2019-15083	CVE-2013-0375	CVE-2019-16026
Attacker Goal	I: Exploit mobile backhaul network.	5. $Atc_{Cost} = 0.63$	5. $Atc_{Cost} = 0.51$	5. $Atc_{Cost} = 0.59$	-	-	-
	S: Access to Shared resources	12, 10-17-20-12, 9-17-20-12, 9-20-12, 15-17-20-12, 15-20-12. $Atc_{Cost} = 0.43$	0-12, 12. $Atc_{Cost} = 0.71$	12. $Atc_{Cost} = 0.67$	3-13-11-12, 3-11-12, 3-4-12, 3-13-4-12, 7-8-4-12, 7-11-12, 7-4-12, 8-4-12, 8-11-12, 14-4-12, 14-11-12. $Atc_{Cost} = 1.06$	8-12, 8-4-12, 8-11-12, 19-11-12, 19-4-12, 6-12, 18-4-12, 18-11-12. $Atc_{Cost} = 0.97$	11-12, 4-12, 1-12, 16-12 $Atc_{Cost} = 0.82$
	P: Access to the RAN and MEC.	2, 22, 10-17-20-22, 10-17-21-22, 10-17-20-2, 10-17-22, 9-17-20-2, 9-17-20-22, 9-17-21-22, 9-17-22, 9-22, 9-20-2, 9-20-12, 9-20-22, 9-21-22, 15-17-20-2, 15-17-20-22, 15-17-21-22, 15-17-22, 15-22, 15-20-2, 15-20-12, 15-20-22, 15-21-22. $Atc_{Cost} = 0.31$	0-2, 2, 0-22. $Atc_{Cost} = 0.39$	2, 22, 0-2, 0-22. $Atc_{Cost} = 0.57$	-	-	-

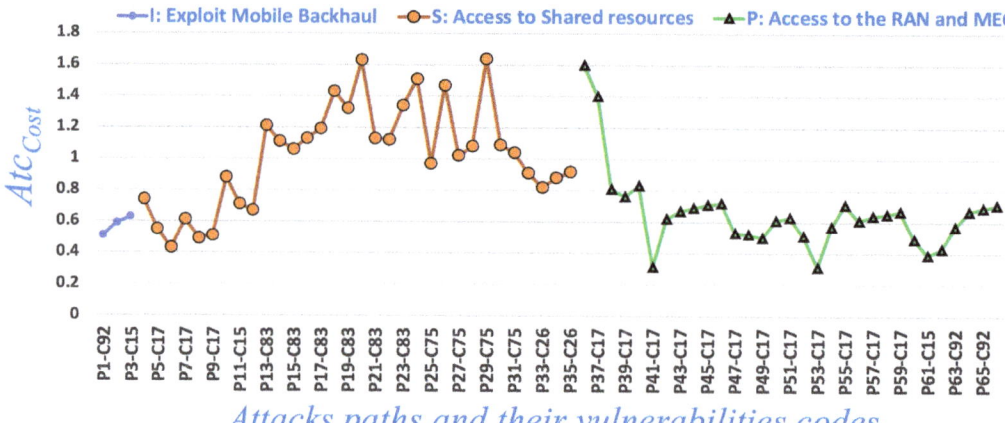

Figure 11. The I, S, and P attack costs and paths.

6.2. Evaluating the VAA Using the Hexagonal Fuzzy TOPSIS Method

In the following steps, we describe the practical implementation of the proposed Hexagonal Fuzzy TOPSIS Method steps that are described in Section 5.2. We use the same use case described in Section 6.1.

Step 1: Construct the fuzzy decision matrix M.

As depicted in Figure 10, the use case involves 16 criteria/indicators/factors and 23 actions. We compute the combinatorial weights (W_i), for $i \in [0, 15]$ which refer to the weight of the impact of each vulnerability CVSS factor/indicator and other dynamic 5G network factors, see Table 5, where i refers to the index of the factor. Further, $A_0, A_2, \ldots, A_{22}$ refer to the alternative attacker's actions associated with the consequences of changing the CVSS and dynamic network factors. We set the initial weights based on their factors' impact on the security, latency, and stability of the 5G network, as Table 5 depicts.

Table 5. The combinatorial weights of the CVSS and dynamic 5G network factors.

Criteria/Indicators/Factors	W_i	Criteria/Indicators/Factors	W_i	Criteria/Indicators/Factors	W_i
Access Vector 000	$W_0 = 0.03$	Report Confidence 006	$W_6 = 0.01$	Speed 012	$W_{12} = 0.08$
Access Complexity 001	$W_1 = 0.04$	Collateral Damage 007	$W_7 = 0.06$	Bandwidth 013	$W_{13} = 0.08$
Authentication 002	$W_2 = 0.09$	Target Distribution 008	$W_8 = 0.01$	Data Size 014	$W_{14} = 0.08$
Confidentiality impact 003	$W_3 = 0.09$	Confidentiality req. 009	$W_9 = 0.09$	Retainability 015	$W_{15} = 0.03$
Exploitability 004	$W_4 = 0.11$	Integrity req. 010	$W_{10} = 0.09$	-	-
Remediation level 005	$W_5 = 0.02$	Availability req. 011	$W_{11} = 0.09$	-	-

The criteria and alternative attacker's actions are compared with linguistic terms as Tables 6 and 7 depict. The rating of the alternative attacker's actions given in Table 7 is computed based on the weight/impact of the CVSS and dynamic 5G network factors/indicators on the attackers' actions based on the generated attack graph in Figure 10. For instance, w_1, w_5, and w_{11} have a Very High (VH) impact on Action 3 (A_3) because there is a direct impact of indicators 1, 5, and 11 on A_3. Similarly, w_{13} and w_{14} have Medium-High (MH) impact on A_3 because there is an indirect impact of indicators 13 and 14 on A_3 through indicator 5. W_3 has Low (L) impact on A_3 because there is an indirect impact of indicators 3 on A_3 through a longer path (I3-A15-I8-A20-I5-A3).

Table 6. Linguistic terms and their corresponding HFN.

Linguistic Variables	Hexagonal Fuzzy Numbers	Linguistic Variables	Hexagonal Fuzzy Numbers
Very low (VL)	(1, 2, 3, 4, 5, 6)	Medium high (MH)	(3, 4, 5, 6, 7, 8)
Low (L)	(1.5, 2.5, 3.5, 4.5, 5.5, 6.5)	High (H)	(3.5, 4.5, 5.5, 6.5, 7.5, 8.5)
Medium low (ML)	(2, 3, 4, 5, 6, 7)	Very high (VH)	(4, 5, 6, 7, 8, 9)
Neutral (N)	(2.5, 3.5, 4.5, 5.5, 6.5, 7.5)		

Table 7. Rating the alternative attacker's actions with respect to the weights of the indicators.

	W_0	W_1	W_2	W_3	W_4	W_5	W_6	W_7	W_8	W_9	W_{10}	W_{11}	W_{12}	W_{13}	W_{14}	W_{15}
A_0	VH	VL	VL	VL	VL	VL	VL	VL	VL	VL	VL	VL	VL	VL	VH	VH
A_1	N	VL	VH	VL	VL	VH	VL	VL	VL	VL	VH	VL	VL	H	H	N
A_2	VL	VL	L	VL	VH	VH	VL	VL	VL	VL	VL	VL	L	MH	VH	VH
A_3	N	VH	VL	L	ML	VH	VL	VL	VL	VL	VL	VH	VL	MH	MH	N
A_4	L	N	L	VL	L	N	VL	H	VL	VL	VL	N	L	ML	ML	L
A_5	VL	VL	VL	VL	VL	VL	VL	VL	VL	VL	VL	VL	VL	VL	VH	VH
⋮	⋮	⋮	⋮	⋮	⋮	⋮	⋮	⋮	⋮	⋮	⋮	⋮	⋮	⋮	⋮	⋮
A_{22}	L	L	VL	VL	L	N	VL	VL	ML	VH	VL	VL	L	ML	ML	H

Using the information in Table 7 and the HFN in Table 6, we construct a decision matrix M, see Table 8.

Table 8. The decision matrix using the HFN.

	W_0	W_1	W_2	W_3	W_4	W_5	
A_0	(4, 5, 6, 7, 8, 9)	(1, 2, 3, 4, 5, 6)	(1, 2, 3, 4, 5, 6)	(1, 2, 3, 4, 5, 6)	(1, 2, 3, 4, 5, 6)	(1, 2, 3, 4, 5, 6)	...
A_1	(2.5, 3.5, 4.5, 5.5, 6.5, 7.5)	(1, 2, 3, 4, 5, 6)	(4, 5, 6, 7, 8, 9)	(1, 2, 3, 4, 5, 6)	(1, 2, 3, 4, 5, 6)	(4, 5, 6, 7, 8, 9)	...
A_2	(1, 2, 3, 4, 5, 6)	(1, 2, 3, 4, 5, 6)	(1.5, 2.5, 3.5, 4.5, 5.5, 6.5)	(1, 2, 3, 4, 5, 6)	(4, 5, 6, 7, 8, 9)	(4, 5, 6, 7, 8, 9)	...
A_3	(2.5, 3.5, 4.5, 5.5, 6.5, 7.5)	(4, 5, 6, 7, 8, 9)	(1, 2, 3, 4, 5, 6)	(1.5, 2.5, 3.5, 4.5, 5.5, 6.5)	(2, 3, 4, 5, 6, 7)	(4, 5, 6, 7, 8, 9)	...
A_4	(1.5, 2.5, 3.5, 4.5, 5.5, 6.5)	(2.5, 3.5, 4.5, 5.5, 6.5, 7.5)	(1.5, 2.5, 3.5, 4.5, 5.5, 6.5)	(1, 2, 3, 4, 5, 6)	(1.5, 2.5, 3.5, 4.5, 5.5, 6.5)	(2.5, 3.5, 4.5, 5.5, 6.5, 7.5)	...
A_5	(1, 2, 3, 4, 5, 6)	(1, 2, 3, 4, 5, 6)	(1, 2, 3, 4, 5, 6)	(1, 2, 3, 4, 5, 6)	(1, 2, 3, 4, 5, 6)	(1, 2, 3, 4, 5, 6)	...
⋮	⋮	⋮	⋮	⋮	⋮	⋮	⋮
A_{22}	(1.5, 2.5, 3.5, 4.5, 5.5, 6.5)	(1.5, 2.5, 3.5, 4.5, 5.5, 6.5)	(1, 2, 3, 4, 5, 6)	(1, 2, 3, 4, 5, 6)	(1.5, 2.5, 3.5, 4.5, 5.5, 6.5)	(2.5, 3.5, 4.5, 5.5, 6.5, 7.5)	...

Step 2: Construct the normalized decision matrix.

We construct the normalized decision matrix $\tilde{N}_{ij}$ using Equation (13) as Table 9 depicts.

Step 3: Calculate the weighted normalized decision matrix.

We create the weighted normalized decision matrix $\tilde{E}_{ij}$ as described in Section 5.2. The following example explains the way the weighted normalized decision matrix in Table 10 is calculated.

$\tilde{E}_{ij} = \tilde{N}_{ij} \times \tilde{W}_j$, where $i = 0, 1, \ldots, 15$ and $j = 0, 2, \ldots, 22$.

$\tilde{E}_{00} = (0.24, 0.3, 0.36, 0.42, 0.48, 0.54) \times 0.03 = (0.0072, 0.009, 0.0108, 0.0126, 0.0144, 0.0162)$.

Table 9. The normalized decision matrix.

	W_0	W_1	W_2	W_3	W_4	W_5	
A_0	(0.24, 0.30, 0.36, 0.42, 0.48, 0.54)	(0.10, 0.20, 0.31, 0.41, 0.52, 0.62)	(0.10, 0.20, 0.31, 0.41, 0.52, 0.62)	(0.10, 0.20, 0.31, 0.41, 0.52, 0.62)	(0.10, 0.20, 0.31, 0.41, 0.52, 0.62)	(0.10, 0.20, 0.31, 0.41, 0.52, 0.62)	...
A_1	(0.19, 0.27, 0.34, 0.42, 0.50, 0.57)	(0.10, 0.20, 0.31, 0.41, 0.52, 0.62)	(0.24, 0.30, 0.36, 0.42, 0.48, 0.54)	(0.10, 0.20, 0.31, 0.41, 0.52, 0.62)	(0.10, 0.20, 0.31, 0.41, 0.52, 0.62)	(0.24, 0.30, 0.36, 0.42, 0.48, 0.54)	...
A_2	(0.10, 0.20, 0.31, 0.41, 0.52, 0.62)	(0.10, 0.20, 0.31, 0.41, 0.52, 0.62)	(0.14, 0.23, 0.32, 0.42, 0.51, 0.61)	(0.10, 0.20, 0.31, 0.41, 0.52, 0.62)	(0.24, 0.30, 0.36, 0.42, 0.48, 0.54)	(0.24, 0.30, 0.36, 0.42, 0.48, 0.54)	...
A_3	(0.19, 0.27, 0.34, 0.42, 0.50, 0.57)	(0.24, 0.30, 0.36, 0.42, 0.48, 0.54)	(0.10, 0.20, 0.31, 0.41, 0.52, 0.62)	(0.14, 0.23, 0.32, 0.42, 0.51, 0.61)	(0.16, 0.25, 0.33, 0.42, 0.50, 0.59)	(0.24, 0.30, 0.36, 0.42, 0.48, 0.54)	...
A_4	(0.14, 0.23, 0.32, 0.42, 0.51, 0.61)	(0.19, 0.27, 0.34, 0.42, 0.50, 0.57)	(0.14, 0.23, 0.32, 0.42, 0.51, 0.61)	(0.10, 0.20, 0.31, 0.41, 0.52, 0.62)	(0.14, 0.23, 0.32, 0.42, 0.51, 0.61)	(0.19, 0.27, 0.34, 0.42, 0.50, 0.57)	...
A_5	(0.10, 0.20, 0.31, 0.41, 0.52, 0.62)	(0.10, 0.20, 0.31, 0.41, 0.52, 0.62)	(0.10, 0.20, 0.31, 0.41, 0.52, 0.62)	(0.10, 0.20, 0.31, 0.41, 0.52, 0.62)	(0.10, 0.20, 0.31, 0.41, 0.52, 0.62)	(0.10, 0.20, 0.31, 0.41, 0.52, 0.62)	...
⋮	⋮	⋮	⋮	⋮	⋮	⋮	⋮
A_{22}	(0.14, 0.23, 0.32, 0.42, 0.51, 0.61)	(0.14, 0.23, 0.32, 0.42, 0.51, 0.61)	(0.10, 0.20, 0.31, 0.41, 0.52, 0.62)	(0.10, 0.20, 0.31, 0.41, 0.52, 0.62)	(0.14, 0.23, 0.32, 0.42, 0.51, 0.61)	(0.19, 0.27, 0.34, 0.42, 0.50, 0.57)	...

Table 10. The weighted normalized decision matrix.

	W_0	W_1	W_2	W_3	W_4	W_5	
A_0	(0.0072, 0.009, 0.0108, 0.0126, 0.0144, 0.0162)	(0.004, 0.008, 0.0124, 0.0164, 0.0208, 0.0248)	(0.009, 0.018, 0.0279, 0.0369, 0.0468, 0.0558)	(0.009, 0.018, 0.0279, 0.0369, 0.0468, 0.0558)	(0.011, 0.022, 0.0341, 0.0451, 0.0572, 0.0682)	(0.002, 0.004, 0.0062, 0.0082, 0.0104, 0.0124)	...
A_1	(0.0057, 0.0081, 0.0102, 0.0126, 0.015, 0.0171)	(0.004, 0.008, 0.0124, 0.0164, 0.0208, 0.0248)	(0.0216, 0.027, 0.0324, 0.0378, 0.0432, 0.0486)	(0.009, 0.018, 0.0279, 0.0369, 0.0468, 0.0558)	(0.011, 0.022, 0.0341, 0.0451, 0.0572, 0.0682)	(0.0048, 0.006, 0.0072, 0.0084, 0.0096, 0.0108)	...
A_2	(0.003, 0.006, 0.0093, 0.0123, 0.0156, 0.0186)	(0.004, 0.008, 0.0124, 0.0164, 0.0208, 0.0248)	(0.0126, 0.0207, 0.0288, 0.0378, 0.0459, 0.0549)	(0.009, 0.018, 0.0279, 0.0369, 0.0468, 0.0558)	(0.0264, 0.033, 0.0396, 0.0462, 0.0528, 0.0594)	(0.0048, 0.006, 0.0072, 0.0084, 0.0096, 0.0108)	...
A_3	(0.0057, 0.0081, 0.0102, 0.0126, 0.015, 0.0171)	(0.0096, 0.012, 0.0144, 0.0168, 0.0192, 0.0216)	(0.009, 0.018, 0.0279, 0.0369, 0.0468, 0.0558)	(0.0126, 0.0207, 0.0288, 0.0378, 0.0459, 0.0549)	(0.0176, 0.0275, 0.0363, 0.0462, 0.055, 0.0649)	(0.0048, 0.006, 0.0072, 0.0084, 0.0096, 0.0108)	...
A_4	(0.0042, 0.0069, 0.0096, 0.0126, 0.0153, 0.0183)	(0.0076, 0.0108, 0.0136, 0.0168, 0.02, 0.0228)	(0.0126, 0.0207, 0.0288, 0.0378, 0.0459, 0.0549)	(0.009, 0.018, 0.0279, 0.0369, 0.0468, 0.0558)	(0.0154, 0.0253, 0.0352, 0.0462, 0.0561, 0.0671)	(0.0038, 0.0054, 0.0068, 0.0084, 0.01, 0.0114)	...
A_5	(0.003, 0.006, 0.0093, 0.0123, 0.0156, 0.0186)	(0.004, 0.008, 0.0124, 0.0164, 0.0208, 0.0248)	(0.009, 0.018, 0.0279, 0.0369, 0.0468, 0.0558)	(0.009, 0.018, 0.0279, 0.0369, 0.0468, 0.0558)	(0.011, 0.022, 0.0341, 0.0451, 0.0572, 0.0682)	(0.002, 0.004, 0.0062, 0.0082, 0.0104, 0.0124)	...
⋮	⋮	⋮	⋮	⋮	⋮	⋮	⋮
A_{22}	(0.0042, 0.0069, 0.0096, 0.0126, 0.0153, 0.0183)	(0.0056, 0.0092, 0.0128, 0.0168, 0.0204, 0.0244)	(0.009, 0.018, 0.0279, 0.0369, 0.0468, 0.0558)	(0.009, 0.018, 0.0279, 0.0369, 0.0468, 0.0558)	(0.0154, 0.0253, 0.0352, 0.0462, 0.0561, 0.0671)	(0.0038, 0.0054, 0.0068, 0.0084, 0.01, 0.0114)	...

Step 4: Calculate the positive and the negative alternatives.

Computing the positive and negative ideal solution using Equations (14) and (15), respectively. Using the weighted normalized decision matrix of Table 10, we compute the positive and negative ideal solutions as the largest and smallest HFN of each column of the indicator's weights respectively. For simplicity, we consider the first six factors only, which are w_0, w_1, w_2, w_3, w_4, and w_6. See Table 11.

Table 11. The positive and negative ideal solution.

Positive Ideal Solutions	Negative Ideal Solutions
$\tilde{E}^+{}_0 = (0.0072, 0.009, 0.0108, 0.0126, 0.0144, 0.0162)$	$\tilde{E}^-{}_0 = (0.003, 0.006, 0.0093, 0.0123, 0.0156, 0.0186)$
$\tilde{E}^+{}_1 = (0.0096, 0.012, 0.0144, 0.0168, 0.0192, 0.0216)$	$\tilde{E}^-{}_1 = (0.004, 0.008, 0.0124, 0.0164, 0.0208, 0.0248)$
$\tilde{E}^+{}_2 = (0.0216, 0.027, 0.0324, 0.0378, 0.0432, 0.0486)$	$\tilde{E}^-{}_2 = (0.009, 0.018, 0.0279, 0.0369, 0.0468, 0.0558)$
$\tilde{E}^+{}_3 = (0.0171, 0.0243, 0.0306, 0.0378, 0.04, 0.0513)$	$\tilde{E}^-{}_3 = (0.009, 0.018, 0.0279, 0.0369, 0.0468, 0.0558)$
$\tilde{E}^+{}_4 = (0.0264, 0.033, 0.0396, 0.0462, 0.0528, 0.0594)$	$\tilde{E}^-{}_4 = (0.011, 0.022, 0.0341, 0.0451, 0.0572, 0.0682)$
$\tilde{E}^+{}_5 = (0.0048, 0.006, 0.0072, 0.0084, 0.0096, 0.0108)$	$\tilde{E}^-{}_5 = (0.002, 0.004, 0.0062, 0.0082, 0.0104, 0.0124)$

Step 5: Determine the distance measures to ideal solutions.

The distance of each alternative from positive and negative ideal is calculated using Equations (14) and (15), then using Equations (16) and (17). For example, we compute the distance measure $D_0{}^+$ to ideal positive solutions for alternative A_0 for the first six factors only for simplicity w_0, w_1, w_2, w_3, w_4, and w_6 is computed as follows: $D_0{}^+ = \sqrt{(d((0.0072, 0.009, 0.0108, 0.0126, 0.0144, 0.0162), (0.0072, 0.009, 0.0108, 0.0126, 0.0144, 0.0162))^2}$ + $d((0.0096, 0.012, 0.0144, 0.0168, 0.0192, 0.0216), (0.004, 0.008, 0.0124, 0.0164, 0.0208, 0.0248))^2$ + $d((0.0216, 0.027, 0.0324, 0.0378, 0.0432, 0.0486), (0.009, 0.018, 0.0279, 0.0369, 0.0468, 0.0558))^2$ + $d((0.0264, 0.033, 0.0396, 0.0462, 0.0528, 0.0594), (0.011, 0.022, 0.0341, 0.0451, 0.0572, 0.0682))^2$ + $d((0.0048, 0.006, 0.0072, 0.0084, 0.0096, 0.0108), (0.002, 0.004, 0.0062, 0.0082, 0.0104, 0.0124))^2$ = 0.129. In the same way, we compute $D_0{}^- = 0.0458$ using the negative ideal solutions values in Table 11. In the same way we can compute the other $D_i{}^+$ and $D_i{}^-$ for all 22 attacker's actions using the 16 indicators, see Table 12.

Table 12. The cost and benefits of the attacker's actions.

Action	$D_i{}^+$	$D_i{}^-$	$Atc_{Cost}(i)$	$Atc_{Benefit}(i)$
A_0	0.0111	0.0021	0.1591	0.8409
A_1	0.0092	0.0066	0.4177	0.5823
A_2	0.0071	0.0080	0.5298	0.4702
A_3	0.0080	0.0051	0.3893	0.6107
A_4	0.0086	0.0033	0.2773	0.7227
A_5	0.0114	0	0.0000	1.0000
⋮	⋮	⋮	⋮	⋮
A_{22}	0.0098	0.0024	0.1967	0.8033

Step 6: Calculate the cost and benefits of the attacker's actions.

The cost (Atc_{Cost}) and benefits ($Atc_{Benefit}$) of each attacker's action are computed using Equations (18) and (19). See Table 13.

Table 13. The cost and benefits of the attack paths for two exploitation starting points.

		Exploitation Starting Point. Action Paths with the Lowest Costs Are Underlined.	
		CVE-2004-0415	CVE-2002-0392
Attacker Goal	I: Exploit mobile backhaul network.	– <u>I14-A5</u>. Atc$_{Cost}$ = 0.025 + 0 = 0.025	– <u>I15-A5</u>. Atc$_{Cost}$ = 0.031 + 0 = 0.031
	S: Access to Shared resources	– I14-A0-I5-A12. Atc$_{Cost}$ = 0.025 + 0.1591 + 0.1 + 0.6515 = 0.9356 – I14-A0-I5-A3-I7-A4-I6-A12, Atc$_{Cost}$ = 0.025 + 0.1591 + 0.1 + 0.3893 + 0.175 + 0.2773 + 0.6515 = 1.7772. – I14-A0-I5-A1-I6-A12, Atc$_{Cost}$ = 0.025 + 0.1591 + 0.1 + 0.4177 + 0.125 + 0.6515 = 1.4783. – I14-A0-I5-A3-I7-A4-I6-A12, Atc$_{Cost}$ = 0.025 + 0.1591 + 0.1 + 0.3893 + 0.175 + 0.2773 + 0.125 + 0.6515 = 1.9022 – I14-A0-I5-A6-I6-A12, Atc$_{Cost}$ = 0.025 + 0.1591 + 0.1 + 0.2593 + 0.125 + 0.6515 = 1.3199. – I14-I5-A1-I6-A12, Atc$_{Cost}$ = 0.025 + 0.1 + 0.4177 + 0.125 + 0.6515 = 1.3192. – I14-I5-A3-I7-A4-I6-A12, Atc$_{Cost}$ = 0.025 + 0.1 + 0.3893 + 0.175 + 0.0.2773 + 0.125 + 0.6515 = 1.49353. – <u>I14-I5-A6-I6-A12</u>, Atc$_{Cost}$ = 0.025 + 0.1 + 0.2593 + 0.125 + 0.6515 = 1.1608	– <u>I15-A12</u>. Atc$_{Cost}$ = 0.031 + 0.6515 = 0.6825 – I15-A0-I5-A12. Atc$_{Cost}$ = 0.031 + 0.1591 + 0.1 + 0.6515 = 0.9416. – I15-A0-I5-A3-I7-A4-I6-A12, Atc$_{Cost}$ = 0.031 + 0.1591 + 0.1 + 0.6107 + 0.175 + 0.7227 + 0.125 + 0.6515 = 2.02537 – I15-A0-I5-A1-I6-A12, Atc$_{Cost}$ = 0.031 + 0.1591 + 0.1 + 0.4177 + 0.125 + 0.6515 = 1.4843. – I15-A0-I5-A3-I7-A4-I6-A12, Atc$_{Cost}$ = 0.031 + 0.1591 + 0.1 + 0.3893 + 0.175 + 0.2773 + 0.6515 = 1.7832 – I15-A0-I5-A6-I6-A12, Atc$_{Cost}$ = 0.031 + 0.1591 + 0.1 + 0.2593 + 0.125 + 0.6515 = 1.3259.
	P: Access to the RAN and MEC.	– I14-A0-I5-A2, Atc$_{Cost}$ = 0.025 + 0.1591 + 0.1 + 0.5298 = 0.8139 – I14-A2, Atc$_{Cost}$ = 0.025 + 0.5298 = 0.5548 – I14-I5-A2, Atc$_{Cost}$ = 0.025 + 0.1 + 0.5298 = 0.6548 – I14-A0-I5-I9-A22, Atc$_{Cost}$ = 0.025 + 0.1591 + 0.1 + 0.11 + 0.1967 = 0.5908 – <u>I14-I5-I9-A22</u>. Atc$_{Cost}$ = 0.025 + 0.1 + 0.11 + 0.1967 = 0.4317	– I15-A2, Atc$_{Cost}$ = 0.031 + 0.5298 = 0.5608 – <u>I15-A0-I5-A2</u>. Atc$_{Cost}$ = 0.031 + 0.1591 + 0.1 + 0.5298 = 0.8199. – <u>I15-I9-A22</u>. Atc$_{Cost}$ = 0.031 + 0.11 + 0.1967 = 0.3377 – I15-A0-I5-I9-A22. Atc$_{Cost}$ = 0.031 + 0.1591 + 0.1 + 0.11 + 0.1967 = 0.5968

Step 7: Compute the Shortest Attack Path.

To compute the shortest attack path, we calculate the total attack cost of all attack actions that form each possible attack path. After that, we rank the attack paths based on the total attack paths costs and select the path with the lowest cost. Table 13 demonstrates how the attack paths costs are calculated for two vulnerability starting points *CVE-2004-0415* and *CVE2002-0392*. Intuitively, the cost of exploitation of *CVE-2004-0415* is less expensive than *CVE2002-0392* for attacks that target the goal 'I: Exploit mobile backhaul network'. So, the attack that is launched from "*CVE-2004-0415*" to exploit the mobile backhaul network is easier and has lower attack efforts than that is initiated from *CVE2002-0392*. However, the cost of exploitation of *CVE2002-0392* is less expensive than *CVE-2004-0415* for attacks that target the goal '*S: Access to Shared resources*' or '*P: Accessing the RAN or MEC*'. Thus, the attacker's goals and the change of the 5G network factors decide which path the attack will potentially go through.

7. Compare the Accuracy and Performance of the VAA with the Nessus

The underlying idea behind the VEA-bility metric [48] is that the security of a network is influenced by many factors, including the severity of existing vulnerabilities, distribution of services, connectivity of hosts, and possible attack paths. These factors are modeled into three network dimensions: Vulnerability, Exploitability, and Attackability. The overall VEA-bility score, a numeric value in the range (0, 10), is a function of these three dimensions, where a lower value implies better security. The VEA-bility metric uses data from three sources: the 5G Edge testbed topology, attack graphs, and scores as assigned by the Common Vulnerability Scoring System (CVSS) [66]. To adjust the VEA-bility metric to validate the accuracy of the vulnerability assessment of the VAA and Nessus, we modify this metric by replacing the asset Attackability factor with the $Atc_{Cost}(i)$ value at Equation (19) for each set of actions i. We let each vulnerability v, which corresponds to a set of actions i, have an impact score, exploitability score, and temporal score as defined by the CVSS. Impact and exploitability subscores are automatically generated for each common vulnerability identifier based on its CVE name defined by the CVSS, whereas the temporal score requires user input. We then define the severity, S, of a vulnerability to be the average of the impact and temporal scores, Equation (20):

$$S(v) = (Impact\ Score(v) + Temporal\ Score(v))/2 \qquad (20)$$

The Vulnerability score (V) of a 5G Edge testbed asset, e.g., UE, MEC server, SDN, NFV, ... etc., is an exponential average of the severity scores of the vulnerabilities on the 5G Edge asset, or 10, whichever is lower. The asset Exploitability score (E) is the exponential average of the exploitability score for all asset vulnerabilities multiplied by the ratio of network services on the asset. The asset Attackability score (A) refers to the toral CP values for all vulnerabilities at a certain asset. The Attackability score is multiplied by a factor of 10 to produce a number in the range (0, 10), ensuring that all dimensions have the same range. For an asset, a, let v be an asset vulnerability. We then define the three asset dimensions as shown in Equations (21)–(23):

$$V(a) = min(10, \ln \sum e^{S(v)}) \qquad (21)$$

$$E(a) = (min(10, \ln \sum e^{Exploitability\ Score(v)}))\ (\#\ services\ on\ a)/(\#\ network\ services) \qquad (22)$$

$$A(t) = (10) * \sum_{i=1}^{n} a_{CP(e_i)} \qquad (23)$$

The overall *VEA-bility* equation for an asset a is then computed as in Equation (24).

$$VEA\text{-}bility_a = 10 - ((V + E + A)_a/3) \qquad (24)$$

To test the performance of the proposed *VEA-bility* metric for both the VAA and Nessus, we developed an extensive set of scenarios described in Sections 3 and 6 and used the vulnerabilities observed by the Nessus scan [32] and our VAA results after running the attacks scenarios. Figure 12 shows the overall average *VEA-bility* scores observed in our experiments for the 5G Edge testbed assets. A higher score indicates a more secure configuration, which we call more "VEA-ble". Figure 12 shows that the VAA using the classical TOPSIS, on average, is 31.35% more VEA-ble than Nessus. Whereas, the VAA using the Hexagonal Fuzzy TOPSIS method, on average, is 9.65% and 37.84% more VEA-ble than the VAA with the classical TOPSIS and Nessus, respectively.

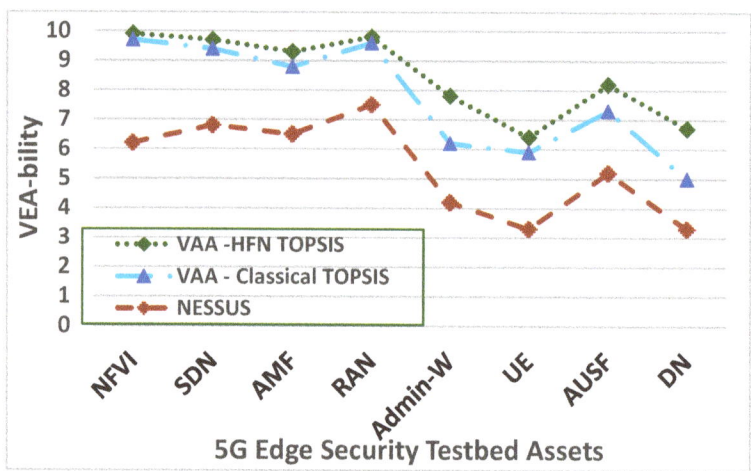

Figure 12. The VEA-bility metric of the VAA and the Nessus.

To compare the performance of the VAA and Nessus, we run the experiment based on the above-mentioned six vulnerabilities. Figure 13 shows the performance of the VAA and Nessus in milliseconds. The VAA using the classical TOPSIS, on average, outperforms Nessus and the VAA using the Hexagonal Fuzzy TOPSIS by 27.14% and 11.15%, respectively. The VAA using the classical TOPSIS takes 6151ms to compute the cost related to all possible paths of the six vulnerabilities while Nessus and the VAA using the Hexagonal Fuzzy TOPSIS take 8445 ms and 6837 ms, respectively, to assess the same six vulnerabilities. The VAA using the Hexagonal Fuzzy TOPSIS outperforms Nessus by 19.02%. This shows that our VAA introduces a more scalable and faster assessment.

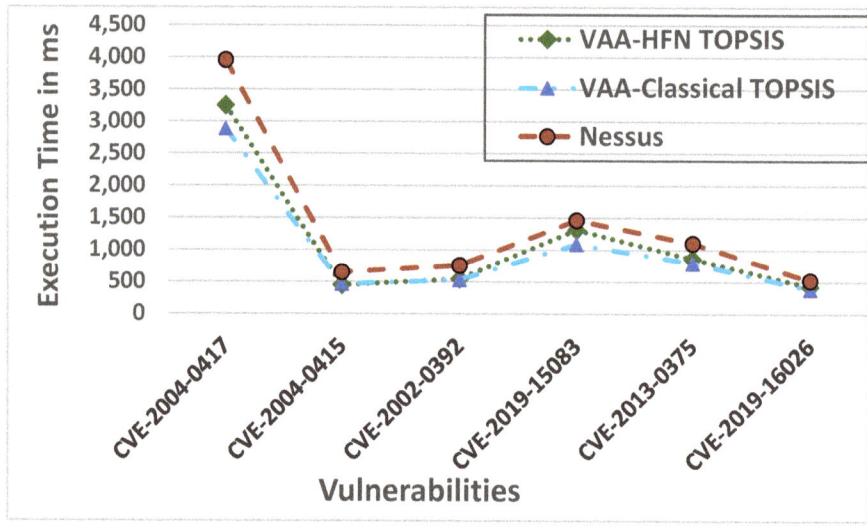

Figure 13. Execution time of the VAA and Nessus.

To evaluate the scalability of the VAA, we run one of the aforementioned six vulnerability analysis experiments using the *CVE-2004-0417* that takes the longest execution time as shown in Figure 13. As shown in Figure 14, the VAA using the Hexagonal Fuzzy TOPSIS method outperforms the Nessus and the VAA using classic TOPSIS when the number of participating UEs is larger than 50. This indicates that the Hexagonal Fuzzy TOPSIS method is more scalable than the other methods when the size of the 5G network increases. However, the other methods outperform the Hexagonal Fuzzy TOPSIS method for a small size 5G network. The reason underlying this is that the HFN uses the linguistic scale and quantization method that reduces the size of the processed data by mapping several HFNs into a single linguistic variable as depicted in Table 6.

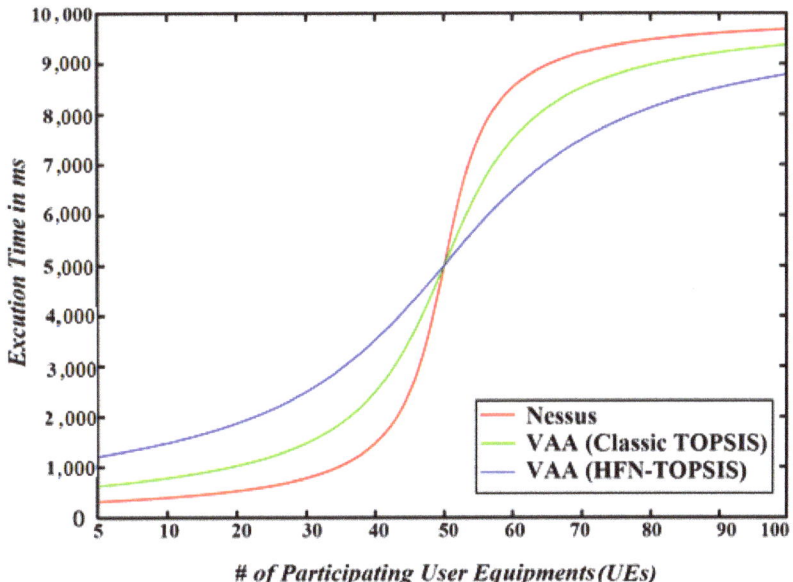

Figure 14. The scalability of the VAA and Nessus using a variant number of UEs.

8. Conclusions and Future Work

The 5G system improves the bandwidth and capabilities of the current telecommunication infrastructure. However, it introduces new threats and attacks. In this paper, we introduced a scalable and accurate vulnerability analysis approach that was tested and evaluated using our newly developed 5G Edge testbed. The experiment results depict that VAA successfully analyzed the vulnerabilities with a low error rate. The VAA using the classical TOPSIS, on average, is 31.35% more VEA-ble than Nessus. Whereas, the VAA using the Hexagonal Fuzzy TOPSIS method, on average, is 9.65% and 37.84% more VEA-ble than the VAA with the classical TOPSIS and Nessus, respectively. From a performance perspective, the VAA using the classical TOPSIS outperforms Nessus and the VAA using the Hexagonal Fuzzy TOPSIS by 27.14% and 11.15%, respectively. This is due to the Hexagonal fuzzy number computational time. The VAA using the Hexagonal Fuzzy TOPSIS is more scalable than the other methods when it is used in a large-scale 5G network.

In future work, we will integrate the VAA with an autonomous intrusion response system that considers the vulnerability assessment values of VAA to deploy countermeasures against cyberattacks. We will also integrate the model with a secure network slicing approach to decide which resources can be used by the network slices based on their risk assessment evaluation and block resources that are under attack.

Funding: This research was generously supported in part by the SUNY Polytechnic Institute Research Seed Grant Program. This research was also supported in part by the Air Force Research Laboratory through the Information Directorate's Information Institute® CPO# FA8750-20-3-1003 contract # SA1003202109E0410.

Institutional Review Board Statement: Not applicable.

Informed Consent Statement: Not applicable.

Data Availability Statement: Not applicable.

Conflicts of Interest: The author declares no conflict of interest.

References

1. Norrman, K.; Nakarmi, P.K.; Fogelstrm, E. 5G Security Enabling a Trust-Worthy 5g System. 2018. Available online: https://www.ericsson.com/en/reports-and-papers/white-papers/5g-security---enabling-a-trustworthy-5g-system (accessed on 5 September 2021).
2. 5G Security Issues, White Paper by Positive-Tech. Co. 2019. Available online: https://positive-tech.com/expert-lab/research/5g-security-issues/ (accessed on 5 September 2021).
3. The National Strategy to Secure 5g Implementation Plan. The National Telecommunications and Information Administration (NTIA). 2020. Available online: https://www.govinfo.gov/content/pkg/FR-2020-06-16/pdf/2020-12960.pdf (accessed on 5 September 2021).
4. Afolabi, I.; Ksentini, A.; Bagaa, M.; Taleb, T.; Corici, M.; Nakao, A. Towards 5G Network Slicing over Multiple-Domains. *IEICE Trans. Commun.* **2017**, *E100-B*, P1992–P2006. [CrossRef]
5. Vijayan, J. 4 Ways Edge Computing Changes Your Threat Model. May 2020. Available online: https://www.csoonline.com/article/3543191/4-ways-edge-computing-changes-your-threat-model.html (accessed on 10 October 2021).
6. Subedi, P.; Alsadoon, A.; Prasad, P.W.C.; Rehman, S.; Giweli, N.; Imran, M.; Arif, S. Network slicing: A next generation 5G perspective. *J. Wirel. Commun. Netw.* **2021**, *2021*, 102. [CrossRef]
7. Fernandez, J.-M.; Vidal, I.; Valera, F. Enabling the Orchestration of IoT Slices through Edge and Cloud Microservice Platforms. *Sensors* **2019**, *19*, 2980. [CrossRef] [PubMed]
8. Makris, N.; Zarafetas, C.; Valantasis, A.; Korakis, T. Service Orchestratidoion Over Wireless Network Slices: Testbed Setup and Integration. *IEEE Trans. Netw. Serv. Manag.* **2021**, *18*, 482–497. [CrossRef]
9. Rodrigo, R.; Javier Lopez, M.M. Mobile edge computing, Fog et al.: A survey and analysis of security threats and challenges. *Future Gener. Comput. Syst.* **2018**, *78*, 680–698.
10. Fan, Z.; Xiao, Y.; Nayak, A.; Tan, C. An improved network security situation assessment approach in software defined networks. *Peer-to-Peer Netw. Appl.* **2019**, *12*, 295–309. [CrossRef]
11. Khan, R.; Kumar, P.; Jayakody, D.N.K.; Liyanage, M. A survey on security and privacy of 5g technologies: Potential solutions, recent advancements and future directions. *IEEE Commun. Surv. Tutor.* **2019**, *22*, 196–248. [CrossRef]
12. Rudolph, H.C.; Kunz, A.; Iacono, L.L.; Nguyen, H.V. Security challenges of the 3gpp 5g service based architecture. *IEEE Commun. Stand. Mag.* **2019**, *3*, 60–65. [CrossRef]
13. Enisa Threat Landscape for 5G Networks, Report, European Union for Cybersecurity. 2019. Available online: https://www.enisa.europa.eu/publications/enisa-threat-landscape-report-for-5g-networks (accessed on 10 December 2020).
14. Abdulqadder, I.; Zou, D.; Aziz, I.; Yuan, B.; Dai, W. Deployment of robust security scheme in sdn based 5g network over nfv enabled cloud environment. *IEEE Trans. Emerg. Top. Comput.* **2018**, *9*, 866–877. [CrossRef]
15. Tian, Z.; Sun, Y.; Su, S.; Li, M.; Du, X.; Guizani, M. Automated attack and defense framework for 5g security on physical and logical layers. *arXiv* **2019**, arXiv:1902.04009.
16. Luo, S.; Wu, J.; Li, J.; Guo, L.; Pei, B. Toward Vulnerability Assessment for 5G Mobile Communication Networks. In Proceedings of the 2015 IEEE International Conference on Smart City/SocialCom/SustainCom (SmartCity), Chengdu, China, 19–21 December 2015; pp. 72–76. [CrossRef]
17. Batalla, J.M.; Andrukiewicz, E.; Gomez, G.P.; Sapiecha, P.; Mavromoustakis, C.X.; Mastorakis, G.; Zurek, J.; Imran, M. Security Risk Assessment for 5G Networks: National Perspective. *IEEE Wirel. Commun.* **2020**, *27*, 16–22. [CrossRef]
18. Khan, J.A.; Chowdhury, M.M. Security Analysis of 5G Network. In Proceedings of the 2021 IEEE International Conference on Electro Information Technology (EIT), Mt. Pleasant, MI, USA, 14–15 May 2021. [CrossRef]
19. Sun, Y.; Tian, Z.; Li, M.; Zhu, C.; Guizani, N. Automated Attack and Defense Framework toward 5G Security. *IEEE Netw.* **2020**, *34*, 247–253. [CrossRef]
20. Xu, H.; Dong, M.; Ota, K.; Wu, J.; Li, J. Toward Software Defined Dynamic Defense as a Service for 5G-Enabled Vehicular Networks. In Proceedings of the 2019 International Conference on Internet of Things (iThings) and IEEE Green Computing and Communications (GreenCom) and IEEE Cyber, Physical and Social Computing (CPSCom) and IEEE Smart Data (SmartData), Atlanta, GA, USA, 14–17 July 2019; pp. 880–887. [CrossRef]
21. Kumar, A.; Sah, B.; Singh, A.R.; Deng, Y.; He, X.; Kumar, P.; Bansal, R. Chapter 1—Multicriteria decision-making methodologies and their applications in sustainable energy system/microgrids. In *Decision Making Applications in Modern Power Systems*; Academic Press: Cambridge, MA, USA, 2020; pp. 1–40, ISBN 9780128164457.
22. Behzadian, M.; Khanmohammadi Otaghsara, S.; Yazdani, M.; Ignatius, J. A state-of the-art survey of TOPSIS applications. *Expert Syst. Appl.* **2012**, *39*, 13051–13069. [CrossRef]

23. Dursun, M.; Ertugrul Karsak, E. A fuzzy MCDM approach for personnel selection. *Expert Syst. Appl.* **2010**, *37*, 4324–4330. [CrossRef]
24. Ansari, M.T.J.; Al-Zahrani, F.A.; Pandey, D.; Agrawal, A. A fuzzy TOPSIS based analysis toward selection of effective security requirements engineering approach for trustworthy healthcare software development. *BMC Med. Inform. Decis. Mak.* **2020**, *20*, 236. [CrossRef] [PubMed]
25. Chakraborty, A.; Maity, S.; Jain, S.; Mondal, S.P.; Alam, S. Hexagonal fuzzy number and its distinctive representation, ranking, defuzzification technique and application in production inventory management problem. *Granul. Comput.* **2021**, *6*, 507–521. [CrossRef]
26. Fathi, M.R.; Matin, H.Z.; Zarchi, M.K.; Azizollahi, S. The application of fuzzy TOPSIS approach to personnel selection for Padir Company. *Iran. J. Manag. Res.* **2011**, *3*, 1–14. [CrossRef]
27. Gheorghe-Pop, E.D. FOKUS, 5G Ready Testbeds: Enabling Early Prototyping and Experimentation, In Proceedings of the IEEE 5G and Beyond Testbed Workshop, Toronto, ON, Canada, 24 September 2017.
28. Geller, M.; Nair, P. 5G Security Innovation White Paper. Available online: .https://www.netsync.com/2019/05/03/white-paper-5g-security-innovation-with-cisco/ (accessed on 5 April 2019).
29. 5G Network Evolution with AWS. 2020. Available online: https://d1.awsstatic.com/whitepapers/5g-network-evolution-with-aws.pdf (accessed on 5 April 2019).
30. Huawei 5G Security White Paper. Available online: https://www-file.huawei.com/-/media/corporate/pdf/trust-center/huawei-5g-security-white-paper-4th.pdf (accessed on 10 December 2020).
31. Dutta, A.; Hammad, E. 5G Security Challenges and Opportunities: A System Approach. In Proceedings of the 2020 IEEE 3rd 5G World Forum (5GWF), Bangalore, India, 10–12 September 2020; pp. 109–114. [CrossRef]
32. Nessus Vulnerability Scanner. Available online: http://www.nessus.org (accessed on 10 December 2020).
33. Park, S.; Kim, D.; Park, Y.; Cho, H.; Kim, D.; Kwon, S. 5G Security Threat Assessment in Real Networks. *Sensors* **2021**, *21*, 5524. [CrossRef]
34. Holtrup, G.; Lacube, W.; David, D.P.; Mermoud, A.; Bovet, G.; Lenders, V. 5G System Security Analysis. *arXiv* **2021**, arXiv:2108.08700.
35. Sullivan, S.; Brighente, A.; Kumar, S.A.P. 5G Security Challenges and Solutions: A Review by OSI Layers. *IEEE Access* **2021**, *9*, 116294–116314. [CrossRef]
36. Li, W.; Wang, N.; Jiao, L.; Zang, K. Physical Layer Spoofing Attack Detection in MmWave Massive MIMO 5G Networks. *IEEE Access* **2021**, *9*, 60419–60432. [CrossRef]
37. Singh, R.; Kumar, H.; Singla, R.K. TOPSIS Based Multi-Criteria Decision Making of Feature Selection Techniques for Network Traffic Dataset. *Int. J. Eng. Technol.* **2013**, *5*, 4598–4604.
38. Haque, N.; Rahman, M.; Chen, D.; Kholidy, H. BIoTA: Control-Aware Attack Analytics for Building Internet of Things. In Proceedings of the 18th IEEE International Conference on Sensing, Communication and Networking (SECON), Rome, Italy, 6–9 July 2021.
39. Kholidy, H.A.; Karam, A.; Sidoran, J.L.; Rahman, M.A. 5G Core Security in Edge Networks: A Vulnerability Assessment Approach. In Proceedings of the 26th IEEE Symposium on Computers and Communications (ISCC), Athens, Greece, 5–8 September 2021; pp. 1–6. [CrossRef]
40. Steele, B.; Kholidy, H.A. 5G Networks Security: Attack Detection Using the J48 and the Random Forest Tree Classifiers. DSPACE and SDR Open Access Repository. Available online: https://soar.suny.edu/handle/20.500.12648/1604 (accessed on 10 December 2020).
41. Ferrucci, R.; Kholidy, H.A. A Wireless Intrusion Detection for the Next Generation (5G) Networks: DSPACE and SOAR Open Access Repository. 2020. Available online: https://soar.suny.edu/handle/20.500.12648/1607 (accessed on 11 May 2020).
42. Borgesen, M.L.; Kholidy, H.A. Evaluating Variant Deep Learning and Machine Learning Approaches for the Detection of Cyberattacks on the Next Generation 5G Systems. The SUNY Digital Repository, SUNY Open Access Repository. Available online: https://dspace.sunyconnect.suny.edu/handle/1951/71327 (accessed on 10 December 2020).
43. Lin, H.T.; Chang, W.L. Order selection and pricing methods using flexible quantity and fuzzy approach for buyer evaluation. *Eur. J. Oper. Res.* **2008**, *187*, 415–428. [CrossRef]
44. Kamble, P.N.; Parveen, N. An application of integrated fuzzy AHP and fuzzy TOPSIS method for staff selection. *J. Comput. Math. Sci.* **2018**, *9*, 1161–1169. [CrossRef]
45. Ashtiani, B.; Haghighirad, F.; Makui, A.; Montazer, G.A. Extension of fuzzy TOPSIS method based on interval-valued fuzzy sets. *Appl. Soft Comput.* **2008**, *9*, 457–461. [CrossRef]
46. Gyumin, L.; Chung, E.S.; Jun, K.S. MCDM Approach for Flood Vulnerability Assessment using TOPSIS Method with a Cut Level Sets. *J. Korea Water Resour. Assoc.* **2013**, *46*. [CrossRef]
47. Yazdani, M.Y.M.; Alidoosti, A.; Basiri, M.H. Risk Analysis for Critical Infrastructures Using Fuzzy TOPSIS. *J. Manag. Res.* **2012**, *4*, 1–19. [CrossRef]
48. Tupper, M.; Zincir-Heywood, A. VEA-bility security metric: A network security analysis tool. In Proceedings of the 2008 Third International Conference on Availability, Reliability and Security, Barcelona, Spain, 4–7 March 2008.
49. Leela-apiradee, W.; Thipwiwatpotjana, P. A Ranking Method of Hexagonal Fuzzy Numbers Based on Their Possibilistic Mean Values. Available online: https://link.springer.com/chapter/10.1007/978-3-030-21920-8_29 (accessed on 10 December 2020).

50. Ghosh, A.; Ghorui, N.; Mondal, S.P.; Kumari, S.; Mondal, B.K.; Das, A.; Gupta, M.S. Application of Hexagonal Fuzzy MCDM Methodology for Site Selection of Electric Vehicle Charging Station. *Mathematics* **2021**, *9*, 393. [CrossRef]
51. Kholidy, H.A.; Erradi, A.; Abdelwahed, S.; Baiardi, F. A hierarchical, autonomous, and forecasting cloud IDS. In Proceedings of the 5th International Conference on Modelling, Identification and Control (ICMIC), Cairo, Egypt, 31 August–2 September 2013; pp. 213–220.
52. Kholidy, H.A. Autonomous mitigation of cyber risks in the Cyber–Physical Systems. *Future Gener. Comput. Syst.* **2020**, *115*, 171–187. [CrossRef]
53. Kholidy, H.A.; Erradi, A.; Abdelwahed, S.; Baiardi, F. A risk mitigation approach for autonomous cloud intrusion response system. *Computing* **2016**, *98*, 1111–1135. [CrossRef]
54. Kholidy, H.A.; Erradi, A. VHDRA: A Vertical and Horizontal Intelligent Dataset Reduction Approach for Cyber-Physical Power Aware Intrusion Detection Systems. Available online: https://www.hindawi.com/journals/scn/2019/6816943/ (accessed on 10 December 2020).
55. Kholidy, H.A. Towards A Scalable Symmetric Key Cryptographic Scheme: Performance Evaluation and Security Analysis. In Proceedings of the 2019 2nd International Conference on Computer Applications & Information Security (ICCAIS), Riyadh, Saudi Arabia, 1–3 May 2019; IEEE: Piscataway Township, NJ, USA, 2019.
56. Kholidy, H.A. Detecting impersonation attacks in cloud computing environments using a centric user profiling approach. *Gener. Comput. Syst.* **2021**, *117*, 299–320. [CrossRef]
57. Kholidy, H.A. Correlation-based sequence alignment models for detecting masquerades in cloud computing. *IET Inf. Secur.* **2020**, *14*, 39–50. [CrossRef]
58. Kholidy, H.A.; Baiardi, F.; Hariri, S. DDSGA: A Data-Driven Semi-Global Alignment Approach for Detecting Masquerade Attacks. *IEEE Trans. Depend. Sec. Comput.* **2015**, *12*, 164–178. [CrossRef]
59. Kholidy, H.A.; Abdelkarim, E. A Cost-Aware Model for Risk Mitigation in Cloud Computing Systems. In Proceedings of the 2015 IEEE/ACS 12th International Conference of Computer Systems and Applications (AICCSA), Marrakech, Morocco, 17–20 November 2015; IEEE: Piscataway Township, NJ, USA, 2015.
60. Debar, H.; Curry, D. The Intrusion Detection Message Exchange Format (IDMEF). Available online: https://datatracker.ietf.org/doc/html/rfc4765 (accessed on 6 August 2021).
61. OpenStack. Available online: https://www.openstack.org/ (accessed on 1 July 2021).
62. Open-Source MANO (OSM). Available online: https://osm.etsi.org/ (accessed on 10 December 2021).
63. FlexRAN (Mosaic5G). Available online: https://mosaic5g.io/flexran/ (accessed on 13 May 2021).
64. Open5GS. Available online: https://open5gs.org/ (accessed on 10 June 2021).
65. Bräuning, F.; Koopman, J.S. The dynamic factor network model with an application to international trade. *J. Econom.* **2019**, *216*, 494–515. [CrossRef]
66. Common Vulnerability Scoring System (CVSS) Factors. Available online: https://www.first.org/cvss/specification-document (accessed on 8 November 2021).
67. The Metasploit Framework. Available online: https://www.metasploit (accessed on 2 October 2021).

Article

Random Access Using Deep Reinforcement Learning in Dense Mobile Networks

Yared Zerihun Bekele [1] and Young-June Choi [2,*]

1 Department of Artificial Intelligence, Ajou University, Suwon 16499, Korea; yaredzerihun@ajou.ac.kr
2 Department of Software and Computer Engineering, Ajou University, Suwon 16499, Korea
* Correspondence: choiyj@ajou.ac.kr

Abstract: 5G and Beyond 5G mobile networks use several high-frequency spectrum bands such as the millimeter-wave (mmWave) bands to alleviate the problem of bandwidth scarcity. However high-frequency bands do not cover larger distances. The coverage problem is addressed by using a heterogeneous network which comprises numerous small and macrocells, defined by transmission and reception points (TRxPs). For such a network, random access is considered a challenging function in which users attempt to select an efficient TRxP by random access within a given time. Ideally, an efficient TRxP is less congested, minimizing delays in users' random access. However, owing to the nature of random access, it is not feasible to deploy a centralized controller estimating the congestion level of each cell and deliver this information back to users during random access. To solve this problem, we establish an optimization problem and employ a reinforcement-learning-based scheme. The proposed scheme estimates congestion of TRxPs in service and selects the optimal access point. Mathematically, this approach is beneficial in approximating and minimizing a random access delay function. Through simulation, we demonstrate that our proposed deep learning-based algorithm improves performance on random access. Notably, the average access delay is improved by 58.89% from the original 3GPP algorithm, and the probability of successful access also improved.

Keywords: machine learning; optimization; random access

Citation: Bekele, Y.Z.; Choi, Y.-J. Random Access Using Deep Reinforcement Learning in Dense Mobile Networks. *Sensors* **2021**, *21*, 3210. https://doi.org/10.3390/s21093210

Academic Editor: Giuseppe Caso

Received: 15 March 2021
Accepted: 29 April 2021
Published: 5 May 2021

Publisher's Note: MDPI stays neutral with regard to jurisdictional claims in published maps and institutional affiliations.

Copyright: © 2021 by the authors. Licensee MDPI, Basel, Switzerland. This article is an open access article distributed under the terms and conditions of the Creative Commons Attribution (CC BY) license (https://creativecommons.org/licenses/by/4.0/).

1. Introduction

In 5G and Beyond 5G cellular networks, random access (RA) protocols maneuver multiple users to negotiate over a small portion of bandwidth before they assent to transmit data on a radio resource. In RA protocols, TRxPs send preambles at the start of the network. Users randomly choose one out of the preambles for negotiating with the TRxP. A preamble is a radio resources for RA consisting of both time and frequency resources and appears in each random access opportunity (RAO) periodically broadcast by TRxPs (i.e., base stations), as depicted in Figure 1 [1]. When users need to connect to the network, they randomly select one out of a set of possible preambles in a given RAO. In the case that two or more users select the same preamble, a collision may occur, and a back-off procedure is initiated. The process repeats until the users succeed in their access attempt, or the network is unreachable after the maximum number of retrials.

RA resources can be requested and re-requested by users under different cases, such as accessing the network for the first time, the loss of system information, change of attachment from the current access point to another due to mobility, etc. [1–4]. In LTE systems, RA has a long four-step procedure. These systems are exposed to the RA delay issue, which is not beneficial in terms of meeting the stringent latency requirement of 5G mobile network use cases, such as ultra-reliable and low-latency communications (URLLC) services. The delay issue in RA becomes more serious for vehicle-to-everything (V2X) communications, where highly mobile users or vehicles cross a network of dense millimeter-wave (mmWave) TRxPs deployed to relieve a coverage problem.

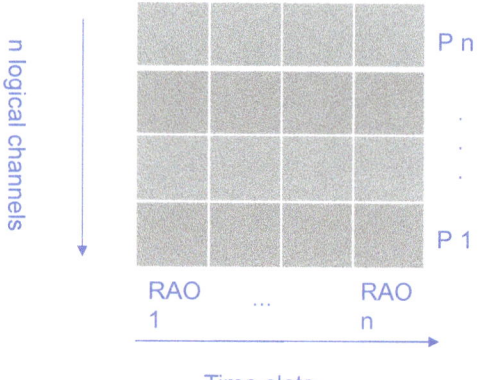

Figure 1. The frame structure of RA typically employed in mobile networks. Preambles (P_1 up to P_n) are rotated in every RAO.

Recently, a two-step procedure has been proposed to reduce the RA delay, where a request for RA is transmitted in the first step, and the second step is completed with a scheduling decision, as illustrated in Figure 2. This is applicable to 5G New Radio (NR). However, the search for protocols and algorithms that further reduce the RA delay remains an area of active research. In this paper, we focus on the most significant factor contributing to RA delay, which is the congestion that occurs at the TRxPs due to the influx of 5G and Beyond 5G traffic. Mobile nodes are associated with TRxPs frequently and near-instantaneously, thus triggering RA consecutively. As a result, some TRxPs may become congested by excessive requests from too many users, even if they have enough RA preambles to accommodate users in a given RAO.

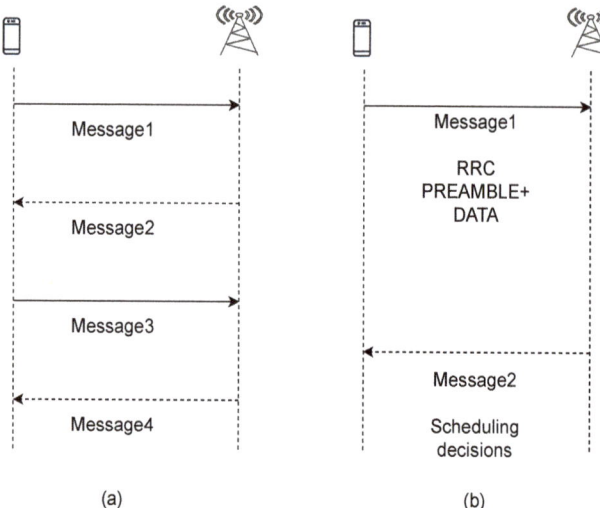

Figure 2. Procedure of RA: (**a**) LTE; (**b**) 5G NR.

Because these networks include many heterogeneous cells (small and macro-cells), users can leverage this feature and intelligently choose a TRxP by estimating the random access delay caused by congestion. A smart user application able to estimate the current congestion level of a TRxP before connecting to it is expected to reduce delay and reduce congestion. Previous methodologies reach maximum signal-to-noise ratios for network access, or implement an access class barring (ACB) scheme for machine-type communications [5,6].

We consider mathematical optimization of the RA delay. One must assume a model representation of the network environment to proceed with RA; this is a strong assumption. For example, to minimize the RA delay, an exact analytical expression that captures the context of the communication system should be given. The RA delay is a stochastic variable with options for consistent approximations. However, machine learning techniques are relatively new approaches still being researched for the optimization of such network procedures, which do not require an exact postulation of a complex mathematical function, but rather stimulate an approximation. Therefore, a machine learning approach to find less congested access points helps users learn over time from experience and try to develop a decision strategy (policy) without requiring the strong assumptions for RA delay [7–12]. In this paper, we test how reinforcement learning (RL) strategies allow for optimization of the RA procedure when the network model is fully represented as a Markov decision process (MDP).

The main reason for experimenting with reinforcement learning is that transition probabilities are not known in advance in the MDP model described in this paper, due to the lack of a labeled data-set. The partial model of the random access environment with no predefined labeled data-set is such that our agents (users) observe the status of the network, take actions by selecting random access points, and collect rewards and punishments in the form of the environment's key performance indicators. For value approximation over finitely many states (i.e., many-dimensional input), powerful neural network approximations, as well as deep RL, have recently been proposed to solve the convergence problem [13–15].

In light of this, to further reduce the RA delay of users and to overcome the current inefficiency of TRxP selection, we propose a novel deep RL technique where users learn over time, through training, to select an efficient TRxP among available covering access points (TRxPs), then satisfy their RA performance expectations. In particular, the main contributions of this paper are outlined as follows:

- Formulate the random access selection task as a mathematical optimization formulation.
- Define the random access selection task in terms of MDP.
- Propose a novel deep reinforcement learning algorithm that solves the random access selection problem formulated as MDP. This is performed by designing the system states, defining actions that are taken by agents, and defining a reward function.
- Test and compare the performance of the proposed deep reinforcement learning algorithm against another learning algorithm and baseline approaches.

The remainder of this paper is organized as follows. In Section 2, we assess relevant and up-to-date enhancements on RA performance proposed for delay-sensitive use cases of 5G and Beyond 5G (B5G) networks. We discuss the system model and problem formulation in Section 3. Section 4 presents an analysis of our proposed approach and model in terms of feasibility. In Section 5, we present experimental results by simulation. Finally, Section 6 concludes the paper.

2. AI and Recent RA Enhancements in Literature

In this section, we discuss literature regarding artificial intelligence. We also revisit some recent proposals for RA enhancement. These recent advancements mainly address some architectural modifications of the procedure and are also specific to each B5G use case.

2.1. AI for Wireless Networking

Artificial Intelligence (AI) algorithms act in a way the human mind functions. Cognition and learning are simulated into machines (agents) that interact with their environment to learn meaningful experiences. This is in contrast to the conventional computation paradigms, where algorithms are given a specific set of instructions to operate on inputs to give an output. In AI, however, algorithms start to function from the output and work towards finding the implicit patterns that resulted in the outputs. AI has seen a lot of interesting results in different research domains. The wireless domain is no exception to this.

A survey of AI techniques is given in [16], where authors discuss how AI can be leveraged to improve the design and operation of future generation wireless networks including 5G. It is discussed that the problems found in the design of these networks are unstructured, and hence AI techniques can be helpful. Some discussed techniques are divided according to the problems found in each layer of the protocol stack. A more detailed discussion and survey about these techniques, however, is found in [17]. As an example of such techniques, [18] proposed a fast machine learning algorithm by modeling the problem as a contextual multi-armed bandit one. Authors in [19] proposed a combination of Support Vector Machine(SVM) and Deep Belief Network(DBN) to solve a joint cross-layered problem: scheduling and power allocation.

In particular, for deep learning, a subset of AI [20], one can find its application in all layers of the protocol stack including network security (intrusion detection systems) [21]. Deep learning models allow learning from the data they are trained upon. However, in wireless tasks where an agent has to actively interact with the environment and a reward/punishment signal is available, reinforcement learning can be applied. In the recent advancement in the field of AI, deep reinforcement learning is proposed where deep learning is combined with reinforcement learning. The surveys given in [22,23] discusses deep reinforcement learning applications for wireless networks. For instance, Ref. [24] applied deep reinforcement learning for the resource allocation problem.

2.2. Information Redundancy for RA

3GPP first introduced the concept of redundant preambles for narrowband (NB)-IoT, and the authors in [25] tested the feasibility of the proposal in improving initial access probability for 5G mmWave networks for a massive V2X use case, where a massive number of sensors were deployed on vehicles, and subsequently, massive machine-type communications (mMTC) are no longer commonly spatially static. In practice, mMTC traffic tends to flow in bursts, and beam alignment problems along with the harsh propagation conditions of mmWaves are huge challenges to the reliability of the RA process.

Redundant preamble transmission aims to quickly acquire data transmission opportunities in addition to improving the reliability (successful access probability). The mmWave base stations (eNodeBs, gNodeBs, and access points) send variable j in addition to ACB and uniform back-off window (UBW) variables. Here j denotes the number of times a user is allowed to send a selected preamble after selecting o from the set of preambles available. However, the major concern is to dynamically allocate j based on the traffic load. For this, the authors in [26] adopted a previously developed algorithm calculating an optimal j by solving an optimization problem.

Other studies in [27,28] considered an information redundancy approach in which RA response (RAR) messages are redundantly sent to users to reduce the collision rate and hence support an envisioned a large number of users. In the legacy system, if more than one user gets the same preamble, they collide or one of them obtains a RAR response. Owing to the redundant RAR responses, a user randomly selects a single RAR message as they are different from each other and has a chance to proceed further in the procedure. They experimentally demonstrated that the performance of RA increases as the number of redundant RAR messages increases. This tends to occur when user density is very high. 5G NR adopted the legacy RA procedure from LTE; however, a beam selection enhancement was added. Users are expected to synchronize with a selected beam to perform the procedure.

The authors in [29–33] suggested an interesting analysis that can be applied to various RA processes. Users participating in the RA procedure are considered analogous to stochastic experiments involving the computation of a probability distribution and expectations of some of the random variables involved in the analysis. The random variables are the control parameters discussed in this paper. Assuming the RA channel (RACH) as a queueing system, probabilistic upper bounds for performance metrics have also been suggested in [34]. However, in this analysis process, some questionable assumptions were made. For instance, a Poisson-type arrival process for bursty machine-type communication traffic was assumed. These initial assumptions are critical as they influence the final results.

2.3. Architectural Improvements for RA

The unpredictable channel condition of mmWave networks results in a significant challenge of RA preamble detection in the physical layer. 5G and B5G services, including mMTC, evolved mobile broadband (eMBB), and URLLC, require efficiency and reliability of the initial attachment point. Because of severe congestion resulting from different mixed traffic sources originating from 5G networks, especially from mMTC, 3GPP introduced the concept of access class barring (ACB), where some users that would request access are barred from the service. The major concern regarding RA is the methods in which the access point dynamically selects RA control parameters, such as the number of preambles/number of consecutive preambles sent by users, ACB, and UBW, depending on the load size of the cell. The load is estimated based on past channel history, and the ACB parameter should be updated dynamically depending on the load size of each cell. The calculation of load estimation and the barring rate was proposed in [5,6].

To reduce RA delay, proposals have considered shortening the RA procedure from a four-way handshaking system to a two-way handshaking system, as illustrated in Figure 2. For example, the authors in [35] introduced the concept of a grant-free RA (one-shot) system, where data signals are sent along with the RA request. This is a viable solution where the data size is low for mMTC. A two-phase RA was proposed in [36] where users are first grouped according to the selected random preamble; for instance, users who select a certain preamble are in one group. No collision occurs across the group; thus, in the second phase, a dedicated channel is assigned for each group to request access. The concept allows the base station to decide the number of channels that should be assigned.

2.4. Perspective

Machine learning techniques do not assume predefined analytical formulation but rather help approximate complex stochastic functions based on stored information in the case of supervised learning, and trial-and-error setups in the case of reinforcement learning (RL), or a mixture of both. From the literature overview, we note that proposals have been developed on four-way handshaking for the RA procedure, and we believe that our machine learning procedure can be applied to any of the proposed architectural changes, depending on the considered use cases. To the best of our knowledge, it remains difficult to find machine learning techniques allowing users to predict congestion and thus select an appropriate access point without the help of a centralized controller. In light of this, the next section elaborates the problem formulation and our proposed system model.

3. Problem Formulation and System Model

The system model is illustrated in Figure 3. The network model describes a scenario where multiple TRxPs $\{A_1, A_2, \ldots, A_N\}$ are deployed to cover a large area. The TRxPs could be femto-cells, pico-cells, macro-cells, or gNodeBs. User devices $\{T_1, T_2, \ldots, T_K\}$ requesting access should select one to proceed with the RA step. The users are moving within the network and therefore are constantly hopping among the TRxPs.

Users can receive a signal from one or more TRxP depending on their position. We do not assume a centralized controller managing the handover because it is unrealistic. In this case, users must identify TRxPs within the transmission range. Once the selection is performed, users participate in contention-based RA. The selection would be performed by using the deep reinforcement learning algorithm proposed in this paper. The TRxPs will rotate RAOs, which are the preambles periodically selected by the users. A four-way handshake or modified one-shot procedure can work with the considered system model.

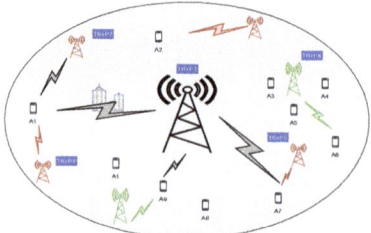

Figure 3. Users moving through the network have single or multiple selection options to perform a RA request depending on their position.

3.1. Traffic Model

To evaluate the effectiveness of the proposed approach, we include a more congested scenario in the experiment using 3GPP's synchronized traffic model 2 [37]. This refers to many machine-type devices accessing the network almost simultaneously. The traffic model from 3GPP allows us to experimentally model a congested network. The probability density function of the beta distribution is given as follows.

$$g(t) = \frac{t^{\alpha-1}(T-t)^{\beta-1}}{T^{(\alpha+\beta-1)}B(\alpha,\beta)}, \quad (1)$$

$$B(\alpha,\beta) = \int_0^1 t^{\alpha-1}(1-t)^{\beta-1}dt, \quad (2)$$

where t is the time of access opportunity at a given time, T is the duration of the activation of the devices, α and β are shape parameters of the beta distribution.

3.2. Combined Channel Model

Because of the tendency toward harsh channel statuses in mmWaves due to impairments such as obstructions, considerable research effort has been devoted to designing an accurate channel model for mmWave communications. The channel status is further degraded by the high mobility of users who frequently make handoffs between base stations. For this reason, a channel model accurately representing the network environment should be considered to capture and analyze the network scenario.

Based on real-world statistical measurements at frequencies of 28 and 73 GHz in New York City, the authors in [38] presented a channel model for dense urban deployment. The path loss measurements adopted in this paper are as follows.

$$PL_{LOS}(dB) = \alpha + \beta 10\log_a(d) + \xi_c, \\ \xi_c \sim N(0,\theta), \quad (3)$$

where d is the distance, α and β are the least-square fits of floating intercept and slope over a covered distance, respectively. ξ_c is the log–normal shadowing. The shadowing variance is given by θ.

3.3. Problem Formulation

Any of the models proposed for RA enhancement can be assumed. In a four-way handshake RA, users send preambles at the first step. In three subsequent steps, TRxPs and users exchange control information leveraging resource reservation and collision resolution. For a one-shot-based and two-way RA, data can be sent along with the RA request in two steps. For these models, prior works required separate mathematical analyses to provide an analytical expression of the RA delay. However, in this work, we do not assume a predefined expression, and the analysis presented can be applied to any of these models.

As shown in the system model in Figure 3, when a user moves through a TRxP's coverage area, it receives a signal from a single TRxP or some subset depending on the position. It also contends with other users to seize an RA preamble opportunity. We consider a selection problem where the goal is to connect with a less congested TRxP; therefore, to reduce the amount of time the users spend to perform the RA. We also assessed other RA performance metrics.

The problem statement is that we need to select an optimal policy that maximizes the probability of selecting a single best performing TRxP in a given spatial and temporal situation out of the K TRxPs available for the users to choose from. In such a situation where the user receives multiple signals from the available access points, the user can estimate the congestion level indirectly by ranking the TRxPs according to a delay variable representing an expectation of RA completion time for each. Considering this, users can select the optimal access point.

We consider that as users move throughout a network of dense TRxPs, $\{A_1, A_2, \ldots, A_n\}$, where at any given RAO time, t_i, and position in the network, a user has some subset of TRxP choices of which to consider requesting RA, one TRxP is selected. Weights for each TRxP are assigned by the users for the purpose of the selection; thus, the higher the weight of a TRxP, the higher the chance of it being selected. Therefore, the probability that h-TRxP is selected depends on its weight and is given by:

$$\frac{w_i}{\sum_{\forall i} w_i}. \tag{4}$$

We consider four strategies to obtain a policy that maximizes the selection strategy, which is equivalent to maximizing the probability of selecting a better-performing TRxP. Four strategies for selection are considered, including (1) A strategy that randomly selects one of the available TRxPs, where each has an equal probability of selection, (2) a strategy that considers a channel quality metric based on reference signal received power (RSRP) measurements of users at the current time slot, ranking the TRxPs accordingly, (3) a weight ranking strategy, where weights are assigned based on the previous time slot experiences of a user, and (4) a strategy that considers any combination of the above strategies. A subset of the n TRxPs are available for a user to select at a given point, and the following weights are assigned to those members: $\{w_1, w_2, \ldots, w_n\}$.

If we consider the users' experience to rank TRxPs, a weight, w_i, of any TRxP can be calculated from the equation given below.

$$w_i = d_{t-1, a_i} = \begin{cases} T_{4a_i} - T_{1a_i}, & \text{in four way RA,} \\ T_{2a_i} - T_{1a_i}, & \text{in two way RA,} \end{cases} \tag{5}$$

where d_{t-1,a_i} is the user delay experience at a given RAO slot with TRxP i, T_{4a_i} is the time the user completed step four, T_{2a_i} is the time the user completed step two, and T_{1a_i} is the time the user initiated the RA procedure. Let D_t represent a function encoding all the weights from all available TrXPs as follows.

$$D_t = x_1 d_{t-1,a_1} + x_2 d_{t-1,a_2} + \cdots + x_n d_{t-1,a_n}. \tag{6}$$

The variables $x_1, x_2, \ldots, x_n$ are natural numbers such that:

$$\begin{aligned} x_1 + x_2 + \cdots + x_n &= 1, \\ x_1 x_2 \ldots x_n &= 0. \end{aligned} \tag{7}$$

The optimal TRxP selection strategy is given by the following optimization equation.

$$\arg\min_{a \in A} D_t$$
$$\text{subject to} \quad (1) P_{a_1} \geq P_{t_1},$$
$$(2) P_{a_2} \geq P_{t_2},$$
$$\vdots \qquad\qquad\qquad\qquad (8)$$
$$(3) P_{a_n} \geq P_{t_n},$$
$$(4) R_\alpha \geq P_\alpha,$$
$$(5) P(W \geq t) \leq \delta.$$

The parameters in the constraints are defined as follows. Constraints (1)–(3) are related to the power strength received from the available TrXPs. P_{a_i} is the power received from TRxP a_i, which should be at least equal to the threshold value P_t. This constraint requires that users receive an acceptable power level from the TRxP to consider it for selection and later perform RA through it. In constraint (4), users draw a random number, R_α, that should be greater than the system parameter, P_α, broadcast by the TRxP, enforcing a prohibition on excessively massive connection scenarios for accepted RA requests. Before considering the current TRxP for selection, users must first make sure they pass this requirement.

Constraint (5) describes the delay-budget of the user. Weight (delay) estimation is another task in solving the equation given in (8). An exact analytical expression representing the weights first depends on the RACH model, and second, considers strong assumptions from queuing theory. In this study, however, we employ learning techniques that enable the proposed method to predict (estimate) the weights, which also can be advantageous in that they do not assume a predefined RACH model. A deep RL formulation for the delay is provided in the next section.

4. RL Based Selection of TRxPs for RA

In this section we present a comprehensive analysis in which we sequentially address the initial steps of RA, along with some of the proposals suggested to optimize RA channel performance.

4.1. TRxPs Search and Selection

(1) The cell search procedure is initiated when a user has a buffer to send/receive data to/from the TRxPs. Cell search and selection criteria depend on the users' RSRP and reference signal received quality (RSRQ) measurements. Based on these measurements, users can select from the available TRxPs and monitor system parameters through the system information block (SIB2) signal. A user can attach to a selected TRxP given that its current RSRP measurement is higher than a threshold value provided according to the following equation.
$$\text{RSRP} > \text{RSRP}_{\min}. \qquad (9)$$

4.2. System Parameters through SIB2

(2) UBW and ACB are random variables that are initially broadcast by the TRxPs and later selected by the users to reduce the occurrence of collision and congestion, respectively. UBW is the original standard of RA. ACB is a recently adopted mechanism to control congestion in massive RA scenarios. They become important inference variables for learning because it is shown that proper selection of these parameters allows reduction of collision and congestion, and therefore has a direct impact on estimating the RA delay. Once users select the proper system parameters, the available resources for RA are made known to them according to the configuration from the TRxPs.

4.3. Proposed RL Based Selection for RA

In the RL algorithm, users learn the selection policy through interaction with the RA environment, as depicted in Figure 4. When a user needs to establish/re-establish a network connection with a TRxP or the buffer is ready, the learning algorithm selects a TRxP before proceeding to the RA procedure. This is done before exchanging message 1 in the RA protocol procedure, illustrated in Figure 2. The user observes the state, takes an action, receives a reward, and observes the next state along with their current connection status. The reward is a factor of the RA's key performance indicators (KPIs), explained in detail in Section 4.4.2. In general, it combines values from both the state and action sets with KPIs. This can be represented by using a Markov decision process, as in a simple tuple (S, A, r, S'), where S is the state space, A is the action space, r is the reward, and S' is the new state. An agent is initially at a given state. It takes action and receives a reward. After that, it transits to the next state. Transition probabilities are not predetermined.

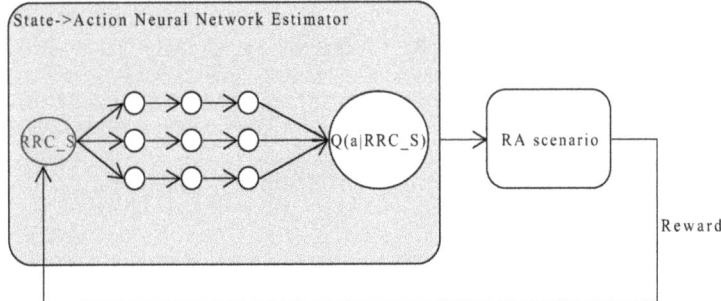

Figure 4. The Deep Q-Network (DQN)-based agent interacts with the random access network environment to receive rewards.

The goal of such users is to maximize their expected long-term reward value. The KPI values can be accumulated to measure whether users are maximizing their reward. Starting from a certain position, where the network starts, the expected long-term reward can be formulated as in the following equation.

$$E[r] = \sum_{i=0}^{\infty}(\gamma_i S_i | S = S_0), \tag{10}$$

where S_0 is the initial state, S_i is the ith state, and $\gamma < 1$.

The action value function estimation is based on a neural network (thus deep RL) and allows the selection of the best action, which refers to the selection of the better performing access point. In the case of Q-based tabular learning, we can store the values in a Q-table initialized to null or infinity values. As the agent traverses through the network and gains information, the table is updated progressively. For deep RL, the algorithm itself approximates this action value function.

We approach the problem by solving the deep RL task for two main reasons. First, the difficulty of the Q-based tabular algorithm in estimating new unseen positions, and second, the complexity of maintaining the table with increasing network size. Therefore, instead of using empty tables for the value-function approximation or using only Q tables, our neural network approach estimates the state-action-value function without the need for Q tables.

The agent performs neural-network-based RL. It selects the optimal actions; that is, a user must be attached to a nearby cell based on the stored experience and current state. The agent also performs exploration with a certain probability and receives rewards in terms of the delay experienced by the user during the RA request. The reward is then recorded to update past experiences. In this manner, the agent makes predictions as well as learns from past experiences.

Finally, we can find the optimal policy by evaluating the optimal Q value, given in Equation (11) below. $Q(S, a)$ measures the importance of taking action a in state S. Out of the many actions listed, the optimal policy selects the optimal Q value in the following manner. During exploitation, it selects an action with a probability of $(1 - \epsilon)$, and during exploration, with a probability of ϵ. Exploration is performed at the beginning of the training. As the agent advances through training, ϵ decays with a decaying factor so that exploitation of the experiences observed so far begins to be utilized. To summarize, $Q(S, a)$ is updated as follows.

$$Q(S, a) = \alpha(r + \gamma \arg \min Q(S', a)) + (1 - \alpha) Q(S, a). \tag{11}$$

As we are considering the RA delay as a factor for determining the reward values, the policy optimization can be safely written as a minimization function given as

$$\pi = \arg \min_{a \in A} Q^*(S, a). \tag{12}$$

In deep RL, we approximate the above Q function by minimizing the error between the estimator and the Q function given below.

$$Error = (Q(s, a, \theta) - Q(s, a))^2, \tag{13}$$

where θ is the weights from the neural network.

4.4. Design

The architecture of the proposed neural network-based RL model is depicted in Figure 4. The agents running the deep RL algorithm interact with the RA environment by taking action from the action set. The RA environment in turn responds by returning a reward, which is a factor of the RA KPIs. The input to the network is the current state of the user from RRC_IDLE, RRC_INACTIVE or RRC_CONNECTED. To rearrange the dataset, we associate simple numerical values to the various RA states a node can occupy. We seek to obtain estimates of state-value action as an output, and the learning algorithm uses these metrics to select the best performing access point for an RA request.

As with a typical RL design, we list the entities as follows.

4.4.1. States

A single state in our design is further composed of three entities. These are the initial criteria, system parameter criteria, and set of TRxPs. We further elaborate on the entities as follows:

A. Initial criteria: In the RA selection problem, user nodes are allowed to participate in the RA selection problem if they are in the RRC_IDLE RA mode and have a full buffer to send data in the uplink, or a request from a TRxP to receive data in the downlink. Mathematically, we use an indicator variable as follows.

$$I = \begin{cases} 1 & if \quad \text{user has full buffer,} \\ 0 & else. \end{cases} \tag{14}$$

B. System parameters criteria: Once users pass the above criteria, the next step is to pass the ACB system parameter criteria that they receive from the serving cell. The ACB flag indicates whether users are barred from performing RA in case of insufficient resources. Initially, this parameter is represented as a real number. We use another indicator variable to check whether a user has passed this parameter as follows.

$$A = \begin{cases} 1 & if \quad 0 < a < t < 1, \\ 0 & else, \end{cases} \tag{15}$$

where a is the ACB factor the user randomly selects and sends to the serving cell, and t is a threshold factor for admission control by the cell. Finally, the user is allowed to perform RA if the above two criteria are successfully met, which is mathematically presented as

$$E = \begin{cases} 1 & if \quad I==1 \& A==1, \\ 0 & else. \end{cases} \quad (16)$$

C. Set of TRxPs: We encode the set consisting of the TRxPs from which user nodes can obtain a pilot signal and measure the RSRP representing potential candidates for RA channel selection. This is given as follows.

$$A = <A_1, A_2, ..., A_n>, \quad (17)$$

where

$$A_i = \begin{cases} 1 & if \quad T_i \text{ is within reach,} \\ 0 & else. \end{cases} \quad (18)$$

Finally, the state is represented by the vector as:

$$S = [E, A]. \quad (19)$$

4.4.2. Reward Function

The reward obtained from the RA environment can be thought of as having an inverse relationship with the RA delay in successfully completing a procedure. A higher reward value means that the user completed the RA procedure with less delay and even within a shorter time before the delay budget expires. The reward value also encodes the delay budget given below. For instance, if a user cannot complete a random access within the delay limit, the reward value approaches zero. Otherwise, the reward is calculated as the inverse of the completion time. Mathematically, it is given by the following equation:

$$r = 1/D, \begin{cases} D = D_i & if \quad P(W \geq t) \leq \delta, \\ D \to \infty & else, \end{cases} \quad (20)$$

where D_i is the delay user experienced from TRxP i. W is the waiting time of the user, and δ, a delay threshold.

4.4.3. Using Replay Buffer for Stability

We use experience replay for efficiently running the stochastic gradient descent algorithm updating weights in the neural network. This approximates the Q function given in Equation (11) by minimizing the loss function given in Equation (21) below. In addition, the channel condition of the network is dynamic. The state-action values used for initial training may change over time, and therefore, it is more appropriate to sample experiences. Therefore, we store some state-action-value pairs annexed by time slots as given in Equations (22)–(24) in which the agent samples from at a later point in time to decide on the actions to perform.

$$Loss = \sum_{i=1}^{n}(Q(s,a,\theta) - Q(s,a))^2, \quad (21)$$

where θ is the weights from the neural network.

$$s_1 = <E, T, T_1, D_1, RRC\_C, t_1>, \quad (22)$$
$$s_2 = <E, T, T_2, D_2, RRC\_C, t_2>, \quad (23)$$
$$\vdots$$
$$s_n = <E, T, T_n, D_n, RRC\_C, t_n>. \quad (24)$$

Because the nature of the network is dynamic, it is not sufficient if only the last experience is considered for making predictions; rather, a random batch of experiences is selected from storage and helps the machine agent learn from long-term experiences.

4.5. Algorithms

In this section, we present the pseudocode for the four algorithms proposed and analyze their performance through a comparison. Algorithms 1 and 2 describe our proposals in this work. Algorithm 3 is a Q-based algorithm [39], and Algorithm 4 is a random TRxP selector. The baseline algorithm is the original 3GPP selection algorithm, which selects a TRxP based solely on the RSRP measurement, i.e., a user ranks and assigns a numerical weight to each TRxP that it receives a pilot signal from. Finally, the TRxP that returned the highest rank was selected for the RA procedure.

Algorithm 1 DQN-based Intelligent TRxPs Selector Algorithm: Training.

1: Initialize discount rate ($\gamma \in (0,1)$), ϵ-greedy ($\epsilon \in (0,1)$) rate value, and the range of an episode
2: Start RA in a mobile network
3: **while** (Episode is not finished) **do**
4:     **while** (Not every position is explored or step is reached) **do**
5:         Get the visible TRxPs at the current position according to Equation (9)
6:         Select a TRxP based on the ϵ-greedy policy; predict a TRxP returning the minimum RA delay from the deep neural network or select a random TRxP.
7:         Receive the reward according to Equation (20)
8:         Remember (CurrentPosition, selectedTRxP, reward, nextSelectedPosition, trainingEndMarker)
9:         Replay by sampling the experiences obtained from the above steps from 5 to 8
10:        Train by updating the weights of the DQN
11:    **end while**
12: **end while**

Algorithm 2 DQN-based Intelligent TRxPs Selector Algorithm: Online.

1: **while** (getRRCState() == RRC_IDLE && UE has buffer) **do**
2:     Get the visible TRxPs at the current position according to Equation (9) and calculate the state
3:     Feed the state input to Algorithm 1
4:     Get the Q values of every TRxPs and select the maximum
5:     Perform RA with selected TRxP and receive reward
6:     Store reward
7: **end while**
8: **while** (getRRCState() == RRC_IDLE) **do**
9:     Run Algorithm 1
10: **end while**

The online algorithm given in Algorithm 3 is based on a tabular Q value function. It updates each access point (TRxP here) according to Equation (25) given below. In Algorithm 1, the agent is trained for a number of episodes. In each step of a single episode, it aims to explore as many user positions as possible to gain an understanding of the network environment. Each selection decision moves the state of the agent from RRC_IDLE mode to RRC_Connected and then back to the former, to explore more positions.

The Deep Q-Network (DQN) algorithm has two neural networks in the implementation. One estimates the Q value and transfers the learned weights to the other neural network. Finally, a mini-batch of experiences is sampled, and the neural network is trained on the updated information. The online algorithm given in Algorithm 2 makes use of the output obtained from Algorithm 1. Algorithm 2 executes when the user needs to perform the RA (i.e., it has a full buffer and passed system parameter criterion). To further minimize delay, additional training on the updated environment experiences is run only when the user is in RRC_IDLE mode. Here, $Q(s,a)$ is updated as follows.

$$Q(S,a) = \alpha r + (1-\alpha)Q(S,a). \tag{25}$$

Algorithm 3 Q-Based Intelligent TRxPs Selector Algorithm: Online.

1: Initialize discount rate ($\gamma \in (0,1)$), ϵ-greedy ($\epsilon \in (0,1)$) rate value, and the range of an episode
2: Start the RA network
3: **while** (Episode is not finished) **do**
4:     **while** (Not every position is explored or steps is reached) **do**
5:         Get the visible TRxPs at the current position according to the equation given in (9)
6:         **if** (empty Q table) **then**
7:             Select a random TRxP
8:             Perform RA with selected TRxP, receive reward and update the Q value of that TRxP
9:         **else**
10:            Select a TRxP based on an ϵ-greedy policy; get the TRxP that returned highest Q value or select a random TRxP.
11:            Receive the reward according to Equation (20)
12:            Update Q value and get the next state
13:         **end if**
14:     **end while**
15: **end while**

Algorithm 4 Random TRxPs Selector Algorithm: Online.

1: **while** (getRRCState() == RRC_IDLE && UE has buffer) **do**
2:     Get the visible TRxPs at the current position according to Equation (9) and calculate the state
3:     Select a random TRxP
4:     Perform RA with selected TRxP and receive reward
5: **end while**

5. Evaluation

For the purpose of evaluating the proposed algorithm and analyzing the performance gains compared to other algorithms, we conduct experiments with a well-known simulator, ns-3 [40]. We also used Python to implement the proposed RL algorithm. The main simulation and analytical parameters are explained in the following subsections. We consider two main criteria: (1) learning performance and (2) the algorithms' relative performance compared to other previous proposals, including Q-based algorithms, RSRP-based selection algorithms, and random selection algorithms.

5.1. Experimental Setup

For simulation, we used ns-3. We simulated a random access network environment, and Table 1 presents some of the main parameters used. We consider the contention-based RA, where the TRxPs do not pre-allocate resources for users, users compete to seize an RA opportunity, and collisions occur in doing so. We also assume that users frequently trigger the RA and re-establish connections as in highly mobile environments. The mobility pattern follows a random uniform distribution. Each RA slot includes six physical resource blocks (PRBs), totaling 1.08 MHz. The number of available RA preambles in an RAO is 64. Users send a maximum of 50 preambles before they assume that the network is unavailable and then withdraw. The average tolerable delay is 100 slots, and the TRxPs can use any scheduler. In our case, we adopt the proportional fair scheduler. The main parameters used for the deep RL algorithm are summarized in Table 2. We use keras over Tensor-flow for the implementation. There are four connected layers. Each hidden layer has 48 neurons. Neurons are activated according to a Relu activation function.

Table 1. Simulation parameters.

Parameter	Value
Maximum number of retrials	50
Number of available preambles	64
Number of access points	5
Tolerable delay	100 slots
Scheduler	Proportional Fair
Channel frequency	28 GHz
Total number of users	900
Number of TRxPs	5
Mobility pattern	ConstantVelocityMobilityModel
Position allocator	Random uniform distribution allocator
Scheduler	Proportional Fair

Table 2. The parameters used for DQN.

Parameter (Description)	Value
m (Replay memory size)	500,000
M (Mini-batch size)	32
γ (Discount factor)	0.95
ϵ	(0.01, 1.0)
ϵ_{decay}	0.0001
α (Learning rate)	0.0001
τ (Copy rate)	0.05
Optimizer	Adam
Activation	0.05
Episodes	1000
Steps	500
Connected layers	4

5.2. Performance Metric Measures

The performance was obtained from the perspective of RA delay, successful access probability (SP), and waiting time distribution. Delay measures the time difference between when users seize an RAO, and when the decision notification by the access point arrives. More technically, in a four-way RA, it is the time difference between messages 1 and 4; and in a two-way RA, it is the difference between messages 1 and 2 of the RA procedure. SP measures the chance of successful transmission of a user given that many users are competing to seize an RA request preamble (opportunity). The number of RA preambles sent gives the number of times the user has been keeping retrials before access is granted.

A normalized cumulative reward function for a number of episodes can be formulated as follows:

$$R = 1/\sum_{i=1}^{|E|} 1/D_i, \qquad (26)$$

where $|E|$ represents the magnitude of the episodes per iteration.

5.3. Learning Performance

The goal of each learning user is to choose the best serving TRxP among the many TRxPs from which it gets an RAO advertisement. Selecting the best serving TRxP allows the user to perform the RA procedure quickly, and transition into the phase of radio resource scheduling. Intuitively, this will be the least congested TRxP. Figure 5a shows the performance of the learning algorithm. It is observed that the performance increases and the reward becomes stable.

We averaged the reward values for every other episode. The algorithm quickly reaches its peak reward value around the 20th episode. Subsequently, it tries to maintain this value despite the randomness of the environment. The algorithm's performance does not dip any lower than the initial reward value afterwards. The effect of the learning rate on the DQN algorithm is shown in Figure 5b. A lower learning rate eventually allows for better performance improvement despite the initial penalty. Initially, it is desirable that the algorithm relies on learning instead of exploiting its inadequate experience, and thus it shows a low performance. After a while, the learning rate should be smaller, and the users should be able to exploit their experience for better performance.

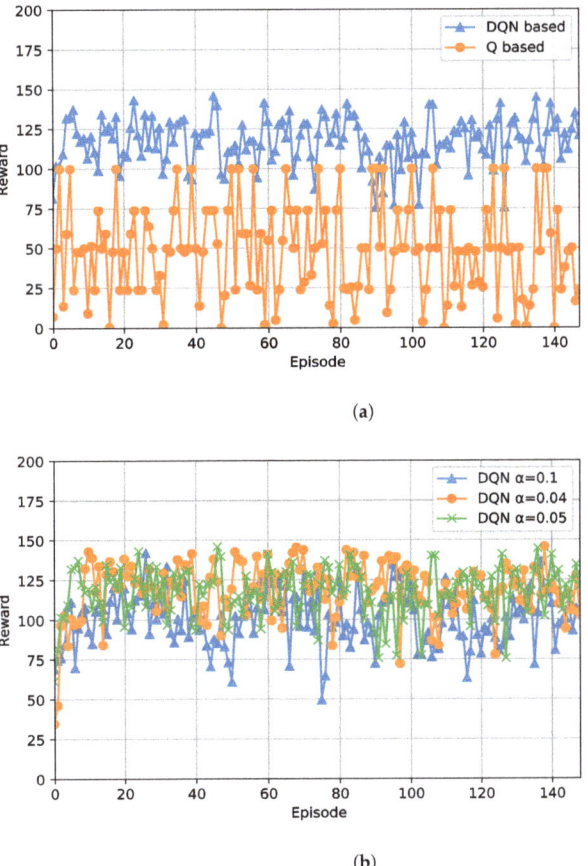

Figure 5. Convergence plot of Q-based and DQN-based algorithms: stability of reward values despite a random access network environment. Reward values are computed for every other episode. (a) Comparison between RL approaches for reward values in random access network environment; (b) reward values for DQN-based algorithm: different learning rates.

5.4. Impact of Proposed Algorithm on RA KPIs

In this subsection, the impact of the DQN on the RA delay, SP, and waiting time distribution is analyzed.

5.4.1. Reliability

Figure 6 depicts the SP of the proposed algorithm against the others. To describe the test results for the learning curve as well as the performance on improving SP, the figure shows different positions where the metric is calculated. The position can be random;

however, we test the initial position as well to test how the SP improves, which helps to also visualize how the algorithm is learning. We observe that, in the initial positions, because the network is starting, and previously-stored information is not available, the deep RL algorithm proceeds to exploit as expected, and in the remaining positions, we observe that the deep RL method outperforms the other algorithms in terms of reliability. The increase in SP is attributed to the algorithm's efficient way of selecting a less congested TRxP by exploiting its own stored knowledge.

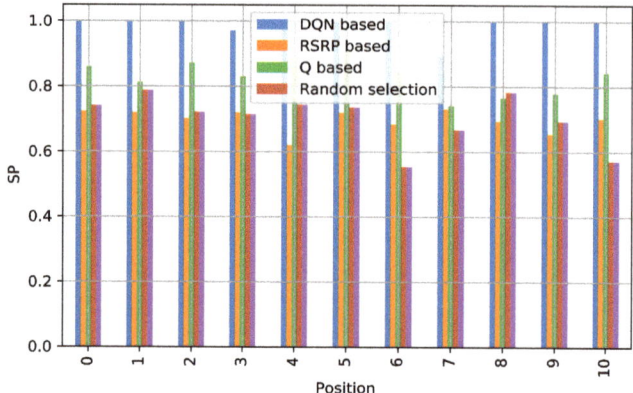

Figure 6. Comparison of successful access probability: DQN-based vs. others in random access network environment.

5.4.2. RA Delay

We also test the RA delay, measured from different positions. We find that the DQN-based algorithm has superior performance compared to algorithms for different positions, as shown in Figure 7. The same reasoning follows from that described for the reliability metrics. Generally, some performance degradation is observed for DQN at some locations. This is because of the dynamic environment, as expected. Although the Q-based algorithm shows a reasonable performance, DQN shows the most promising performance on average. Particularly, in comparison with the current 3GPP's methodology of selection, The DQN-based algorithm reduced the RA delay by 58.89%.

5.4.3. Waiting Time Distribution

The dropped packet rate can be explained in terms of the waiting time distribution. It could be defined as the probability that the waiting time of a request does not exceed the delay budget of the user. We measured the waiting time distribution for different delay budgets of packets at different time points. In Figure 8, we grouped the episodes into 50 units. Group 3 requires more training time. The DQN allowed the waiting time to decrease sharply, which also means fewer drop rates. The sharp decrease is more pronounced for the latter groups. In addition, Figure 9 illustrates the comparison between DQN and the other algorithms on the waiting time distribution. DQN again shows the best results.

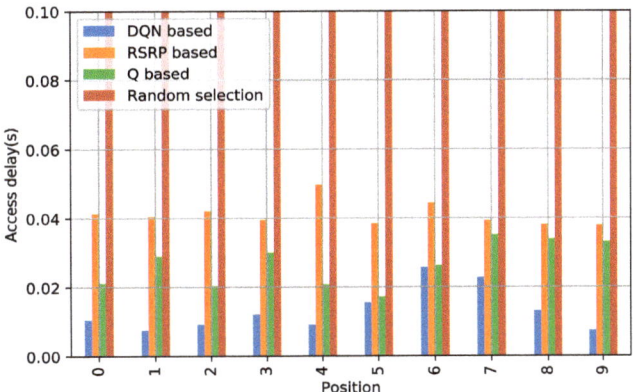

Figure 7. Comparison of access delay: DQN based vs. others in random access network environment.

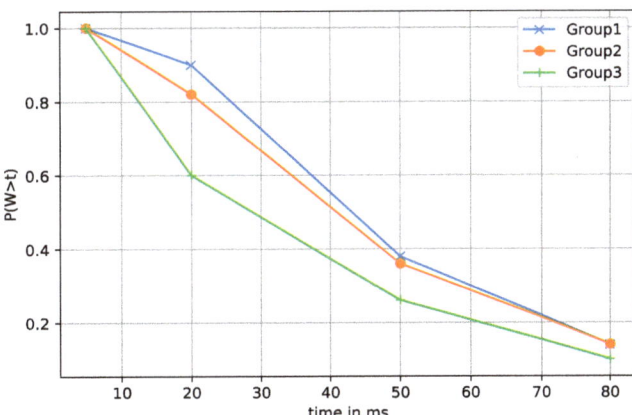

Figure 8. DQN's waiting time distribution measured at different groups of episodes in random access network environment.

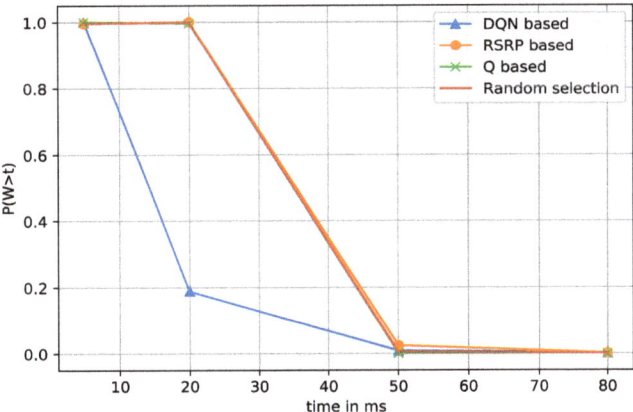

Figure 9. Comparison of waiting time distribution: DQN-based vs. others in random access network environment.

5.4.4. Algorithm Overhead Analysis

Generally, the potential drawback of learning algorithms is the resulting overhead from implementation when the algorithm makes an inference. We discuss the overhead of the proposed DQN algorithm in terms of the storage(space) and running time. Our deep reinforcement learning algorithm, as applied to the aforementioned environment, has a possible advantage in terms of memory overhead over other algorithms, such as Q learning. This is because it does not store the increasing number of state and action pairs for training. It rather approximates that function, and we use replay memory for storing experiences as Algorithm 1 illustrates. Then, a min-batch size of the memory is used for experience replay. Therefore, space complexity is minimal.

In spite of that, we need to store samples of experiences. This depends on the selected batch memory size, which can be fixed (the size doesn't grow) because of being overwritten frequently and storing the most recent batch of experiences. Allowing more size helps the agent to sample from more experiences and cancels correlation, which is helpful for the stability of the algorithm. Therefore, the memory overhead is upper bounded by the replay memory size M. Let M represent the memory replay size, and the number of bits required to store our current state, next state, the action taken is B bits. Therefore, the RAM memory overhead R_m of the devices is given by the following equation.

$$R_m = M * B. \tag{27}$$

For inference, Each layer has a matrix of weights. The size reserved for one of the matrices can be used for the next multiplication operation performed at the next layer. Therefore, space is bounded by the size of the biggest weight matrix. It is given by:

$$\mathcal{O}(nk),$$

where n and k are the dimensions of the rows and columns of the matrix respectively. Time overhead in forward-propagation constitutes matrix multiplication operations. Suppose n is the number of layers. Matrix multiplication operation performed at each layer is in the $\mathcal{O}(n^3)$ time complexity. The overall time overhead is given by:

$$(n-1)layers * n^3 = O(n^4). \tag{28}$$

6. Conclusions

For random access in 5G and B5G networks, users have the opportunity to receive pilot signals from a number of neighboring TRxPs. This paper proposes and tests the feasibility of recent machine learning approaches, in particular RL, to solve a random access network control problem. If we allow users to have stored knowledge (through training) in terms of the service points that show better performance, they can opportunistically choose the optimal access point, which helps optimize their expected RA performance. We conducted an experiment using ns-3 to prove the efficacy of our proposed RL method in a dynamic network scenario with channel conditions varying over time.

There are significant implications of applying the reinforcement learning method for wireless networking. For example, it allows us to estimate the random access delay that occurs at a given TRxP without requiring an exact model of the random access environment since users learn about the environment through their own experience. Another benefit for future networks is that users can intelligently determine the optimal attachment points in such a way that their QoS can be met without requiring a central agent to calculate their expectations and provide resources accordingly.

The next step after random access is a data exchange. Such a learning algorithm, for example, reduces the congestion that can occur at the would-be overloaded access points. Hence, access request load is shared among the access points. Learning algorithms will determine the load-sharing strategy without requiring a model. In this way, efficient resource distribution and allocation are realized throughout the whole coverage area.

The potential drawback of learning algorithms is the overhead. Space complexity is minimal. However, despite a slight training time penalty, the deep RL algorithm increases the overall long-term reward values for the users. We further analyze such learning algorithms to achieve better convergence and performance results in fewer iterations, and also reduce the associated computational overhead, which is left as an avenue for our future work.

Author Contributions: Conceptualization, Y.Z.B. and Y.-J.C.; formal analysis, Y.Z.B.; funding acquisition, Y.-J.C.; methodology, Y.Z.B. and Y.-J.C.; project administration, Y.-J.C.; resources, Y.-J.C.; supervision, Y.-J.C.; validation, Y.Z.B.; writing—original draft, Y.Z.B.; writing—review & editing, Y.Z.B. and Y.-J.C. All authors have read and agreed to the published version of the manuscript.

Funding: This research received no external funding.

Institutional Review Board Statement: Not applicable.

Informed Consent Statement: Not applicable.

Data Availability Statement: Not applicable.

Acknowledgments: This work was supported by the National Research Foundation of Korea (NRF) grant funded by the Korea government (MSIT) (No. 2019R1A2C1008530).

Conflicts of Interest: The authors declare no conflict of interest.

References

1. 3rd Generation Partnership Project; Technical Specification Group Radio Access Network; Evolved Universal Terrestrial Radio Access (E-UTRA); Radio Resource Control (RRC); Protocol Specification. September 2011. Available online: https://www.3gpp.org/ftp/Specs/archive/36_series/36.331 (accessed on 10 March 2021).
2. 3rd Generation Partnership Project; Radio Resource Control (RRC); Protocol Specification. September 2011. Available online: https://www.3gpp.org/ftp/Specs/archive/38_series/38.331 (accessed on 10 March 2021).
3. 3rd Generation Partnership Project; Technical Specification Group Radio Access Network; Evolved Universal Terrestrial Radio Access (E-UTRA) User Equipment (UE) Procedures in Idle Mode. September 2011. Available online: https://www.3gpp.org/ftp/Specs/archive/36_series/36.304 (accessed on 10 March 2021).
4. 3rd Generation Partnership Project; Technical Specification Group Core Network; NAS Functions related to Mobile Station (MS) in idle Mode. September 2011. Available online: https://www.3gpp.org/ftp/Specs/archive/23_series/23.122 (accessed on 10 March 2021).
5. Wan, C.; Sun, J. Access Class Barring Parameter Adaptation Based on Load Estimation Model for mMTC in LTE-A. In Proceedings of the 2019 International Conference on Communications, Information System and Computer Engineering (CISCE), Haikou, China, 5–7 July 2019; pp. 512–515.
6. Tello-Oquendo, L.; Vidal, J.R.; Pla, V.; Guijarro, L. Dynamic access class barring parameter tuning in LTE-A networks with massive M2M traffic. In Proceedings of the 2018 17th Annual Mediterranean Ad Hoc Networking Workshop (Med-Hoc-Net), Capri, Italy, 20–22 June 2018; pp. 1–8.
7. Sutton, R.S.; Barto, A.G. *Reinforcement Learning: An Introduction*; MIT Press: Cambridge, MA, USA, 13 November 2018.
8. Watkins, C.J.; Dayan, P. Q-learning. *Mach. Learn.* **1992**, *8*, 279–292. [CrossRef]
9. Mnih, V.; Kavukcuoglu, K.; Silver, D.; Rusu, A.A.; Veness, J.; Bellemare, M.G.; Graves, A.; Riedmiller, M.; Fidjeland, A.K.; Ostrovski, G.; et al. Human-level control through deep reinforcement learning. *Nature* **2015**, *518*, 529–533. [CrossRef] [PubMed]
10. Kaelbling, L.P.; Littman, M.L.; Moore, A.W. Reinforcement learning: A survey. *J. Artif. Intell. Res.* **1996**, *4*, 237–285. [CrossRef]
11. Puterman, M.L. *Markov Decision Processes: Discrete Stochastic Dynamic Programming*; John Wiley & Sons: Hoboken, NJ, USA, 2014.
12. Russell, S.; Norvig, P. Artificial Intelligence: A Modern Approach. Available online: https://storage.googleapis.com/pub-tools-public-publication-data/pdf/27702.pdf (accessed on 10 March 2021).
13. Mnih, V.; Kavukcuoglu, K.; Silver, D.; Graves, A.; Antonoglou, I.; Wierstra, D.; Riedmiller, M. Playing atari with deep reinforcement learning. *arXiv* **2013**, arXiv:1312.5602.
14. Lillicrap, T.P.; Hunt, J.J.; Pritzel, A.; Heess, N.; Erez, T.; Tassa, Y.; Silver, D.; Wierstra, D. Continuous control with deep reinforcement learning. *arXiv* **2015**, arXiv:1509.02971.
15. Van Hasselt, H.; Guez, A.; Silver, D. Deep reinforcement learning with double q-learning. In Proceedings of the AAAI Conference on Artificial Intelligence 2016, Phoenix, AZ USA, 12–17 February 2016; Volume 30.
16. Wang, C.X.; Di Renzo, M.; Stanczak, S.; Wang, S.; Larsson, E.G. Artificial intelligence enabled wireless networking for 5G and beyond: Recent advances and future challenges. *IEEE Wirel. Commun.* **2020**, *27*, 16–23. [CrossRef]
17. Kulin, M.; Kazaz, T.; De Poorter, E.; Moerman, I. A survey on machine learning-based performance improvement of wireless networks: PHY, MAC and network layer. *Electronics* **2021**, *10*, 318. [CrossRef]

18. Asadi, A.; Müller, S.; Sim, G.H.; Klein, A.; Hollick, M. FML: Fast machine learning for 5G mmWave vehicular communications. In Proceedings of the IEEE INFOCOM 2018—IEEE Conference on Computer Communications, Honolulu, HI, USA, 16–19 April 2018; pp. 1961–1969.
19. Cao, X.; Ma, R.; Liu, L.; Shi, H.; Cheng, Y.; Sun, C. A Machine Learning-Based Algorithm for Joint Scheduling and Power Control in Wireless Networks. *IEEE Internet Things J.* **2018**, *5*, 4308–4318. [CrossRef]
20. Zhang, C.; Patras, P.; Haddadi, H. Deep learning in mobile and wireless networking: A survey. *IEEE Commun. Surv. Tutor.* **2019**, *21*, 2224–2287. [CrossRef]
21. Khan, M.A.; Kim, J. Toward Developing Efficient Conv-AE-Based Intrusion Detection System Using Heterogeneous Dataset. *Electronics* **2020**, *9*, 1771. [CrossRef]
22. Luong, N.C.; Hoang, D.T.; Gong, S.; Niyato, D.; Wang, P.; Liang, Y.C.; Kim, D.I. Applications of deep reinforcement learning in communications and networking: A survey. *IEEE Commun. Surv. Tutor.* **2019**, *21*, 3133–3174. [CrossRef]
23. Xiong, Z.; Zhang, Y.; Niyato, D.; Deng, R.; Wang, P.; Wang, L.C. Deep reinforcement learning for mobile 5G and beyond: Fundamentals, applications, and challenges. *IEEE Veh. Technol. Mag.* **2019**, *14*, 44–52. [CrossRef]
24. Wang, J.; Zhao, L.; Liu, J.; Kato, N. Smart resource allocation for mobile edge computing: A deep reinforcement learning approach. *IEEE Trans. Emerg. Top. Comput.* **2019**. [CrossRef]
25. Orsino, A.; Galinina, O.; Andreev, S.; Yilmaz, O.N.; Tirronen, T.; Torsner, J.; Koucheryavy, Y. Improving initial access reliability of 5G mmWave cellular in massive V2X communications scenarios. In Proceedings of the 2018 IEEE International Conference on Communications (ICC), Kansas City, MO, USA, 20–24 May 2018; pp. 1–7.
26. Galinina, O.; Turlikov, A.; Andreev, S.; Koucheryavy, Y. Multi-channel random access with replications. In Proceedings of the 2017 IEEE International Symposium on Information Theory (ISIT), Aachen, Germany, 25–30 June 2017; pp. 2538–2542.
27. Grassi, A.; Piro, G.; Boggia, G. A look at random access for machine-type communications in 5th generation cellular networks. *Internet Technol. Lett.* **2018**, *1*, e3. [CrossRef]
28. Alavikia, Z.; Ghasemi, A. Pool resource management based on early collision detection in random access of massive MTC over LTE. *Ad Hoc Netw.* **2019**, *91*, 101883. [CrossRef]
29. Sinitsyn, I.E.; Zaripova, E.R.; Gaidamaka, Y.V.; Shorgin, V.S. Success Access Probability Analysis Using Virtual Preambles Via Random Access Channel. In *CEUR Workshop Proceedings*; CEUR: Budapest, Hungary, 2018.
30. Yuan, J.; Huang, A.; Shan, H.; Quek, T.Q.; Yu, G. Design and Analysis of Random Access for Standalone LTE-U Systems. *IEEE Trans. Veh. Technol.* **2018**, *67*, 9347–9361. [CrossRef]
31. Agiwal, M.; Qu, M.; Jin, H. Abstraction of Random Access Procedure for Bursty MTC Traffic in 5G Networks. In Proceedings of the 2018 24th Asia-Pacific Conference on Communications (APCC), Ningbo, China, 12–14 November 2018; pp. 280–285.
32. Park, S.; Lee, S.; Choi, W. Markov Chain Analysis for Compressed Sensing based Random Access in Cellular Systems. In Proceedings of the 2019 International Conference on Computing, Networking and Communications (ICNC), Honolulu, HI, USA, 18–21 February 2019; pp. 34–38.
33. Bekele, Y.Z.; Choi, Y.J. Scheduling for Machine Type Communications in LTE Systems. In Proceedings of the 2018 International Conference on Information and Communication Technology Convergence (ICTC), Jeju, Korea, 17–19 October 2018; pp. 889–891.
34. Vilgelm, M.; Schiessl, S.; Al-Zubaidy, H.; Kellerer, W.; Gross, J. On the reliability of LTE random access: Performance bounds for machine-to-machine burst resolution time. In Proceedings of the 2018 IEEE International Conference on Communications (ICC), Kansas City, MO, USA, 20–24 May 2018; pp. 1–7.
35. Lee, J.Y.; Noh, H.; Lee, K.; Choi, J. Comparison of one-shot and handshaking systems for MTC in 5G. In Proceedings of the 2018 IEEE 87th Vehicular Technology Conference (VTC Spring), Porto, Portugal, 3–6 June 2018; pp. 1–5.
36. Cheng, R.G.; Becvar, Z.; Huang, Y.S.; Bianchi, G.; Harwahyu, R. Two-Phase Random Access Procedure for LTE-A Networks. *IEEE Trans. Wirel. Commun.* **2019**, *18*, 2374–2387. [CrossRef]
37. 3GPP. *Study on RAN Improvements for Machine-Type Communications*; Technical Report, TR 37.868; SGPP: Paris, France, 2014.
38. Akdeniz, M.R.; Liu, Y.; Samimi, M.K.; Sun, S.; Rangan, S.; Rappaport, T.S.; Erkip, E. Millimeter wave channel modeling and cellular capacity evaluation. *IEEE J. Sel. Areas Commun.* **2014**, *32*, 1164–1179. [CrossRef]
39. Bekele, Y.Z.; June-Choi, Y. Access Point Selection Using Reinforcement Learning in Dense Mobile Networks. In Proceedings of the 2020 International Conference on Information Networking (ICOIN), Barcelona, Spain, 7–10 January 2020; pp. 676–681.
40. NSNAM. Ns-3: A Discrete-Event Network Simulator for Internet Systems, 2006–2020. Available online: https://www.nsnam.org/ (accessed on 10 March 2021).

Short Biography of Authors

Yared Zerihun Bekele received the B.Sc degree in Computer Science from Addis Ababa University in 2013 and the M.Sc degree in Computer Science and Engineering from Ajou University in 2016. Currently, he is with the Intelligence Platform, Network, and Security (Intelligence PLANETs) Lab at Ajou University. His research area revolves around Artificial Intelligence, Internet of Things, and Computer Networks.

Young-June Choi received his B.S., M.S., and Ph.D. degrees from the Department of Electrical Engineering and Computer Science, Seoul National University, in 2000, 2002, and 2006, respectively. From 2006 to 2007, he was a post-doctoral researcher with the University of Michigan, Ann Arbor, MI, USA. From 2007 to 2009, he was with NEC Laboratories America, Inc., Princeton, NJ, USA, as a Research Staff Member. He is currently a Professor at Ajou University, Suwon, South Korea. His research interests include beyond-mobile wireless networks, radio resource management, and cognitive radio networks. He was a recipient of the Gold Prize at the Samsung Humantech Thesis Contest in 2006, Haedong Young Researcher Award in 2015, and Best Paper Award from Journal of Communications and Networks in 2015.

Article

Implementation of Deep-Learning-Based CSI Feedback Reporting on 5G NR-Compliant Link-Level Simulator [†]

Daniel Gaetano Riviello [1,*], Riccardo Tuninato [2], Elisa Zimaglia [3], Roberto Fantini [3] and Roberto Garello [2]

[1] Department of Electrical, Electronic, and Information Engineering, University of Bologna, 40136 Bologna, Italy
[2] Department of Electronics and Telecommunications (DET), Politecnico di Torino, 10129 Torino, Italy; riccardo.tuninato@polito.it (R.T.); roberto.garello@polito.it (R.G.)
[3] TIM S.p.A., 10148 Torino, Italy; elisa.zimaglia@telecomitalia.it (E.Z.); roberto.fantini@telecomitalia.it (R.F.)
* Correspondence: daniel.riviello@unibo.it
[†] This manuscript is an extended version of the conference paper: Zimaglia, E.; Riviello, D.G.; Garello, R.; Fantini, R. A Novel Deep Learning Approach to CSI Feedback Reporting for NR 5G Cellular Systems. In Proceedings of the 2020 IEEE Microwave Theory and Techniques in Wireless Communications (MTTW), Riga, Latvia, 1–2 October 2020.

Abstract: Advances in machine learning have widened the range of its applications in many fields. In particular, deep learning has attracted much interest for its ability to provide solutions where the derivation of a rigorous mathematical model of the problem is troublesome. Our interest was drawn to the application of deep learning for channel state information feedback reporting, a crucial problem in frequency division duplexing (FDD) 5G networks, where knowledge of the channel characteristics is fundamental to exploiting the full potential of multiple-input multiple-output (MIMO) systems. We designed a framework adopting a 5G New Radio convolutional neural network, called NR-CsiNet, with the aim of compressing the channel matrix experienced by the user at the receiver side and then reconstructing it at the transmitter side. In contrast to similar solutions, our framework is based on a 5G New Radio fully compliant simulator, thus implementing a channel generator based on the latest 3GPP 3-D channel model. Moreover, realistic 5G scenarios are considered by including multi-receiving antenna schemes and noisy downlink channel estimation. Simulations were carried out to analyze and compare the performance with current feedback reporting schemes, showing promising results for this approach from the point of view of the block error rate and throughput of the 5G data channel.

Keywords: 5G; New Radio; deep learning; convolutional neural network; CSI reporting

1. Introduction

New Radio (NR) wireless networks are anticipated to support very high data rates and new applications that will create opportunities for a radically new radio technology paradigm [1]. In this context, machine learning (ML) has regained attention for its achievements especially in the upper layers, such as in cognitive radio [2,3], self-organizing networks (SONs) [4] and resource management [5,6]. However, the authors of [7] claim that the potential use of deep learning (DL) to the physical layer will be increasingly recognized. This appears to be reasonable considering the new features of next-generation communications, such as complex scenarios, with a consequent lack of information about the channel model, high data rates and accurate processing requirements [7].

Studies on ML applications to the physical layer have been carried out, for example, for modulation recognition [8,9], signal classification [10], multiple input multiple output (MIMO) detection [11], channel state information (CSI) feedback reduction [12,13], non-orthogonal multiple access (NOMA) [14], hybrid precoding [11,15], encoding and decoding [16], and channel estimation and equalization [17–20]. Researchers have presented a range of arguments to support the adoption of DL techniques in contemporary communication environments [7,11,16]:

- deep networks are very good and adaptable function approximators—they learn the weights of the model optimizing the overall performance through a training process, instead of requiring a rigorous mathematical description that could be hard to extract in complex scenarios;
- DL-based systems could replace manual feature extractors and learning features automatically, flexibly adapting the structure and the parameters of the model, with considerable improvement to the end-to-end performance;
- DL-based algorithms work very well with large amounts of data due to their intrinsic parallel and distributed computing, leading to speeding up of computation;
- DL models can overcome the block structure to provide a complete view of the system and optimize it end-to-end.

This paper proposes a DL-based solution for CSI feedback improvement in 5G-based communication systems. The availability of information about the colorful characteristics of the communication channels has a fundamental impact on many transmission features in most modern radio-access technologies [21]. This framework of information can vary from a rough estimate of the radio link path loss, which is useful for adjusting the transmitted power, to very precise knowledge of the channel amplitude and phase [21]. Measurements and estimates can be performed by either the transmitter or the receiver side. Focusing on the downlink case, the knowledge of the channel characteristics can be acquired by means of device measurements or by the network itself, depending on the particular scenario:

- when working in frequency division duplexing (FDD) mode, downlink and uplink could potentially be significantly different. In consequence, to obtain reliable information about the downlink channel, measurements must necessarily be acquired by the user device and then reported to the network; the network will exploit this feedback to properly set the transmission parameters for future downlink transmissions;
- in time-division duplexing (TDD) communications, when downlink and uplink transmissions experience the same channel characteristics, feedback from the device is not necessary, since the network itself can obtain useful information about the downlink features of interest by measuring them in the uplink transmissions.

In general, the evaluation of the radio environment is referred to as channel sounding and requires the adoption of specific reference signals (RS) on which the receiver can perform measurements.

The adoption of appropriate channel modelling is critical when performing simulations involving signal processing, such as channel sensing. Several channel models have been reported in the literature, with two main approaches described: stochastic and statistical. The former relies on the definition of the probability density function (PDF) of the channel parameters depending on the geometry of the environment, while the latter exploits real measures on which to base the definition of the channel. Each of these solutions has possible drawbacks, but a hybrid approach can be chosen, firstly, stochastically, characterizing the channel parameters through their PDF, and subsequently leveraging real data to confirm and eventually adapt them. In this investigation, we rely on the latest 3D stochastic channel model for 5G mmWave massive MIMO communications released by 3GPP in TR 38.901 [22,23]. It covers the entire range of 0.5–100 GHz, with particular relevance to the new challenges represented by mmWave communications, where some phenomena, such as path attenuation, noise, interference, and atmospheric attenuation, can seriously impact the signal transmission. One of its main characteristics is the modelling of the channel through a certain number of clusters distributed over the area, which groups the scatterers and so produces different replicas of the propagated signal (i.e., different rays). It is categorised as a clustered delay line (CDL) model. Moreover, while, in 4G, the propagation waves were considered only in the horizontal plane, thus producing a 2D channel model, mmWave communications (and thus 5G) require a 3D channel model, characterising the signal propagation depending on the elevation coordinate. The channel model generation is performed inside a link-level simulator designed by TIM, which also provides the resource blocks generation, transmission and reception for a 5G 3GPP-compliant communication, with evaluation of the primary downlink shared channel (PDSCH) throughput and the block error rate (BER).

1.1. Literature Review

Several studies, such as [12,13,24,25], suggest that, with the introduction of massive MIMO technologies in 5G systems, the potential gain from an accurate estimation of channel characteristics will considerably increase, with channel sounding becoming a critical issue. Moreover, as the authors of [12,13] point out, the most-used approaches to reduce the feedback overhead, based on codebooks or vector quantization, process feedback quantities whose dimensions scale with the number of antennas, making these techniques unsuitable in massive MIMO scenarios. These criticisms have stimulated new studies aimed at overcoming the difficulties associated with traditional approaches with DL-based solutions.

The authors of [12] designed an autoencoder based on neural networks to compress and then reconstruct the channel state information, called CsiNet. This paper stimulated significant interest among researchers who sought to expand the applicability and improve the performance. In [26], the authors present two different structures, ConvCsiNet and ShuffleCsiNet, both able to outperform CsiNet from an NMSE point of view. Even though the latter has reduced complexity with respect to the first structure, it is still more complex than CsiNet. One of the most recent advancements in DL is the concept of attention, which is exploited in [27,28]. In the former, long short-term memory (LSTM) is adopted to learn the temporal correlation of channels, while an attention mechanism is developed to perceive local information and automatically weight feature information. This kind of solution can further improve the reconstruction capabilities, but comes at a higher cost that could not be supported in terms of user equipment. A solution to effectively decrease the complexity of CsiNet was proposed in [29], which identified a lighter, fully connected (FC) layer as the key to encoder compression. The network parameters are transformed from a 32-bit floating point number to a 1-bit binary number, optimizing a positive scale factor that minimises the distance between standard weights and binary weights. In [30], a DL-based CSI feedback framework is described for beam-forming (BF) design, CsiBFnet. Its goal is to maximize the BF performance gain rather than the feedback accuracy, including with respect to single-cell or multi-cell scenarios. Another interesting solution is the CQNet described in [31], which focuses on the impact of quantisation on the channel estimation coefficients and exploits radial coordinates to improve quantisation scheme efficiency.

1.2. Paper Contribution and Organization

The solutions presented in the papers referred to above increase the possibilities of DL-based solutions for CSI; however, there is a lack of studies focusing on the characteristics of a system based on 5G NR and, therefore, the channel model and performance in terms of the BLER of the data channel. In this article, we extend our findings in [32] and propose a DL-based technique for channel state information feedback reporting in FDD transmission mode, based on the implementation of a convolutional neural network, called NR-CsiNet. The improvements in our approach with respect to [12] can be summarized in terms of the following new features:

1. provision of MIMO capabilities through the use of antenna arrays at both the transmitter and receiver sides;
2. addressing the estimation of the downlink channel affected by noise;
3. testing the system with a 5G NR fully compliant simulator with a clustered delay line channel model.

The remainder of this paper is organized as follows: Section 2 introduces CSI-RS, which are reference signals used for downlink channel sounding. Section 3 provides a description of the New Radio link simulator software developed for all our experiments in order to outline the simulation environment. Section 4 presents the NR-CsiNet DL model, describing its internal structure and the data-processing steps required. The simulation results are presented in Section 5. Section 6 concludes the article with some observations and suggestions for potential future research directions.

2. Channel State Information Reference Signals

One of the key design principles of NR is to avoid, as far as possible, "always-on" signals [21,33]. In release 8 of the LTE standard, channel sounding for downlink transmissions is performed by means of device measurements on cell-specific reference signals (CRS) [34], which are transmitted over the whole transmission bandwidth in each subframe. From release 10 on [35], these reference signals are complemented by another type of reference signal called CSI-RS, which, in contrast to the first, is not expected to be continuously transmitted. The main reason for this upgrade lays in the necessity to support spatial multiplexing with more than four layers; however, as [21] points out, CSI-RS introduction has opened the way to further technological extensions, such as coordinated multi-point (CoMP) [36] operations and interference estimation.

In 3GPP specifications [37], the channel quality indicator (CQI), rank indicator (RI), precoding matrix indicator (PMI), and several other quantities, are jointly referred to as channel state information (CSI). The precoding matrix indicator is reported by the user equipment (UE) to the base station (BS); it represents an indication of what the user considers to be a suitable precoding matrix to be applied on downlink transmissions. In particular, the PMI is no more than a set of indexes or a single index pointing to a specific entry in the precoding codebook, which contains a list of all the possible precoding matrices W that the device can select and report to the network. There exists at least one codebook for each permitted combination of N_T (number of antenna ports) and N_L (number of layers) associated with the configured CSI-RS.

It is important to stress that precoding codebooks play a role only in the context of PMI reporting and do not impose any restriction in the choice of the precoding matrix to be applied by the network [21]. In some cases, it is convenient for the network to select the precoding matrix suggested by the device, but, when, for example, the network is in possession of additional information, the precoding computation may lead to a different choice.

As [21] reports, the typical use case of multi-antenna precoding is multi-user MIMO (MU-MIMO) [38–40]. In this case, the main purposes are to direct the energy towards the device and simultaneously limit the interference towards the other users scheduled on the same time-frequency resource. In this kind of scenario, it is clear that the network needs more detailed information about the channel experienced by different UEs so that it can take into account the PMI reported by all simultaneously scheduled devices when selecting the precoding matrix [21].

The NR standard defines two types of CSI reporting, each characterized by a different size and structure of the codebook [37]:

- Type I CSI codebooks: designed for single user-MIMO (SU-MIMO) scenarios, where a single user is scheduled within a certain time-frequency resource, transmitting on a potentially large number of layers in parallel;
- Type II CSI codebooks: designed for MU-MIMO scenarios, where many users are scheduled within the same time-frequency resource, each transmitting on a limited number of layers in parallel (two at most).

For fast time-varying wireless channels, the adoption of delayed CSI at the transmitter can help reduce the feedback frequency of the channel estimates [41].

3. New Radio Link-Level Simulator

New Radio link simulator software was used for all the experiments conducted and described in this paper. The simulator was developed in Telecom Italia laboratories with an engine implemented in MATLAB®. The most critical blocks in terms of execution speed were, instead, implemented in C language and linked to the MATLAB engine via MEX. The purpose was to model a radio interface which was fully compliant with 3GPP specification and to evaluate the link-level performances of 5G-based point-to-point communications. The simulator is a link-level simulator and targets scenarios with a single next-generation base station or gNodeB and a single UE for a SU-MIMO scenario where the UE can deploy an antenna array.

The various blocks of the simulator provide a bit-level model of the 5G NR physical layer, as described in the 38 series of the 3GPP specifications [37,42–44]. The physical downlink shared channel (PDSCH) transmission chain can be represented as the block scheme of Figure 1, which also reflects the 5G NR simulator structure. The red blocks are those which exploit the C language to speed-up the computations.

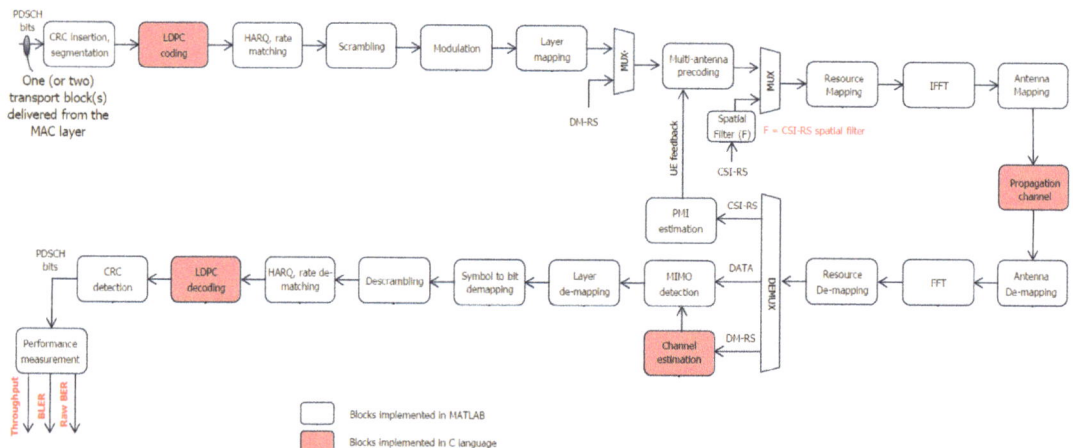

Figure 1. New Radio link-level simulator scheme.

3.1. Transmission Chain

A detailed description of the main blocks is provided as follows.

Transport Block generator Data are generated as a sequence of bits. Depending on the transport size (A) and the modulation and coding scheme (MCS), in particular, on the code rate (R), the LPDC base graph selection is performed:

- if $A \leq 292$, or if $A \leq 3824$ and $R \leq 0.67$, or if $R \leq 0.25$, LDPC base graph 2 is used;
- otherwise, LDPC base graph 1 is used.

Input bits are then segmented into different blocks; the CRC parity bits are calculated on and attached to each block. Depending on the LPDC base graph, the maximum dimension of blocks can change. The lowest order information bit is mapped to the most significant bit of the transport block (i.e., parity bits are found at the end of the block).

LDPC encoder LPDC coding is applied to the bit sequence for a given code block. N encoded bits are obtained as output, where $N = 66\,Z_c$ for LDPC base graph 1 and $N = 50\,Z_c$ for LDPC base graph 2 (Z_c value can be found in subclause 5.2.2 of TR 38.212 [42]).

Rate-matching block A rate-matching block is required to adapt the size of the transport block after LDPC coding to the size of the allocated resources that can be used for PDSCH transmission. PDSCH coded bits must be rate-matched around the resource elements occupied by the CSI-RS and other reference signals, otherwise the coding rate may exceed the unit value (i.e., the REs in the slot available for PDSCH are not sufficient to transmit the information bits). In practice, it is expected that the gNB scales down the MCS in the slots where the CSI-RS transmission causes an LDPC coding rate higher than about 0.95. This approach is also modelled in the link simulator. The throughput calculation must consider this effect, re-scaling the formula accordingly.

Scrambling operation Before modulation, the codewords (up to two) are scrambled, as in subclause 7.3.1 of [42], resulting in a block of scrambled bits.

QAM modulation The block of scrambled bits for each codeword are QAM-modulated using one of the modulation schemes (selected by the MCS) from table 7.3.1.2-1 [42], resulting in a block of complex-valued modulation symbols.

Layer and subcarrier mapping The modulated symbols are mapped to one or more layers (if multi-layer transmission is enabled), by splitting the codewords (one or two) among them. Then, the symbols are inserted into the actual resource elements of the physical resource block, through a predefined look-up table, based on the 3GPP resource allocation procedure.

MIMO processing The precoding matrix is applied to the PDSCH channel, i.e., subcarriers containing data. If PMI reporting is enabled, the precoding matrix F_j is selected by the transmitter at the gNB as the j-th element of the codebook, where j is the PMI index reported by the UE. The digital beam-forming scheme implemented in the simulator is wideband; that is, the same beam-forming matrix F_j is applied to all the PRBs. If, instead, the channel estimate is given through feedback by the UE, (e.g., SRS transmission in uplink), downlink beam-forming schemes based on the channel matrix can be applied exploiting the downlink/uplink channel reciprocity.

CSI-RS mapping The transmission of CSI-RS signals in the link-level simulator is modelled in a realistic way. The CSI-RS signals are generated and mapped in the time frequency-grid and configuration parameters set the number of ports and the transmission period, denoted as *CSI-RS period*, which can take the set of values defined in the 3GPP TS 38.331 [45] specifications. The CSI-RS signals are transmitted once every [4, 5, 8, 10, 16, 20, 32, 40, 64, 80, 160, 320, 640] slots.

OFDM modulator The OFDM modulation is performed through the IFFT Operation. Before the IFFT, an IFFT shift must be applied to properly translate the spectrum into the positive frequency domain. The IFFT must be applied on an OFDM symbol-basis. The channel bandwidth and sub-carrier spacing (SCS) determine the size of the IFFT and the number of samples for each OFDM symbol. At this point a cyclic prefix is added at the beginning of each OFDM symbol, through a look-up table, with a duration selected between "normal" or "extended". The "normal" option is selected for the simulations according to the used sub-carrier spacing of 30 kHz. This value is compatible with the maximum delay of the channel that falls into the selected CP length.

Oversampling and filtering An oversampling step increases the number of samples for each symbol by a selected factor and the sampling frequency is increased accordingly. A raised cosine filter is used as the transmitting filter.

Receiver side At the receiver side, a finite impulse response filter is applied to remove the undesired frequencies and a down-sampler stage re-samples the signal to the normal frequency, by the same factor as the up-sampler. To account for the delay due to the signal transmission and FIR filter, at each iteration, the signal at the receiver side is buffered and processed on a block basis, where the block length in time is equal to the slot duration. The receiver must then reverse all the signal-processing applied by the transmitter with suitable blocks, such as an OFDM signal demodulator, a sub-carrier demapper, and so on. The MIMO processing consists of the application of a combining matrix over the received symbols to exploit the antenna array at the receiver if more than one antenna is configured. The combining matrix can be used for various purposes, i.e., improving the SINR or for separating the different layers if more than one data stream is transmitted using spatial multiplexing. The LDPC decoder applies the offset min-sum (OMS) decoding algorithm. The performance measurements are applied on the CRC detection for the BLER, while the raw BER is computed on the number of actual erroneous bits before the LDPC decoding. The approximate peak throughput of the simulated NR configuration can be calculated by means of the formula provided in the TS 38.306 3GPP [46] specification:

$$\text{data rate [Mbps]} = 10^{-6} \cdot \sum_{j=1}^{J} \left(v_L^{(j)} \cdot Q_m^{(j)} \cdot f^{(j)} \cdot R_{max} \cdot \frac{N_{PRB}^{BW(j),\mu} \cdot 12}{T_s^{\mu}} \cdot \left(1 - OH^{(j)}\right) \right) \quad (1)$$

where:

- J is the number of aggregated component carriers in a band or band combination.
- $R_{max} = 948/1024$ is the maximum LDPC code rate.
- $v_L^{(j)}$ is the maximum number of layers.
- $Q_m^{(j)}$ is the maximum modulation order
- $f^{(j)}$ is the scaling factor (it can take the values 1, 0.8, 0.75 and 0.4) and is signalled per band or per band combination).
- μ is the numerology.
- T_s^{μ} is the average OFDM symbol duration in a subframe for numerology μ and normal CP, i.e., $T_s^{\mu} = \frac{10^{-3}}{14 \cdot 2^{\mu}}$.
- $N_{PRB}^{BW(j),\mu}$ is the maximum RB allocation in maximum UE supported bandwidth BW(j) with numerology μ.
- $OH^{(j)}$ is the overhead (0.14 for DL FR1-0.18 for DL FR2-0.08 for UL FR1-0.10 for UL FR2).

3.2. Channel Model Generation

The key element of this simulation framework is clearly the fading channel block: for an NR-compliant link simulator, the 3GPP has two defined models for NR link and system evaluation purposes [22,47]:

- Tapped delay line (TDL): for this channel model, the correlation between different antennas is defined statically by a correlation matrix. The TDL model is based on the description of the impulse response of the channel;
- Clustered delay line (CDL): with this channel model the direction of the signal in the space is modelled. The model is based on the description of the main departure and arrival directions of the signal in the space and the number of clusters corresponds to the number of channel reflections.

The CDL channel model is adopted for all the simulations presented in this article due to its importance for practical applications. In particular, we select the CDL-B profile. This CDL profile is specific for non-line-of-sight (NLOS) transmissions and can be used for sub 6 GHz frequency, where line-of-sight (LOS) is not mandatory. A characterising property is that the first path in time is also the strongest one.

The channel between the user and the BS depends on the environment geometry. In our scenario, the user is placed at a distance of 100 m from the BS, with a height of 1.5 m, while the BS has a height of 10 m. The UE direction could be defined as DOMINANT_PATH (the same direction of the main azimuth of arrival (AoA) direction), RANDOMLY (uniformly generated around $[-180°, +180°]$) and ARBITRARY (statically selecting a UE direction). The delay spread can be selected among the set ('VERY SHORT', 'SHORT', 'NOMINAL',

'LONG', 'VERY_LONG'). NOMINAL is fixed for our set of simulations, which corresponds to 100 ns. The coherence time of the channel depends on the Doppler spread and on the user speed, which is fixed at 3 km/h (i.e., a walking pedestrian). The CDL profile channel requires the generation of N_c clusters. Each cluster n will be assigned a different delay (depending on the delay spread times), a set of angular orientations, including AoA, azimuth of departure (AoD), zenith of departure (ZoD) and zenith of arrival (ZoA), and a power gain P_n. The azimuth angle spread of departure and arrival (ASD and ASA, respectively) and the zenith angle spread of departure and arrival (ZSD and ZSA, respectively), characterize the entire set of clusters. These values are used for the generation of the M rays that form each cluster. The direction of a certain ray is given by the angular orientation of its own cluster, the angular spreads and a different coefficient for each ray. The angle for azimuth is ϕ, while the angle for zenith is θ. At both the gNB and UE side, three levels of antenna correlation are possible: LOW, MEDIUM and HIGH. The level of correlation is inversely related to the angle spread (i.e., larger angle spreads correspond to lower correlation and vice versa). The CDL model for cluster n, transmitter antenna element u and receiver antenna element s is, thus, a combination of M NLOS rays and a LOS ray when the UE is in a LOS condition:

$$H_{u,s,n}^{NLOS} = \sqrt{\frac{P_n}{M}} \sum_{m=1}^{M} \begin{bmatrix} F_{rx,u,\theta}(\theta_{n,m,ZoA}, \phi_{n,m,AoA}) \\ F_{rx,u,\phi}(\theta_{n,m,ZoA}, \phi_{n,m,AoA}) \end{bmatrix}^T \begin{bmatrix} e^{(j\Phi_{n,m}^{\theta\theta})} & \sqrt{\kappa_{n,m}^{-1}} e^{(j\Phi_{n,m}^{\theta\phi})} \\ \sqrt{\kappa_{n,m}^{-1}} e^{(j\Phi_{n,m}^{\phi\theta})} & e^{(j\Phi_{n,m}^{\phi\phi})} \end{bmatrix}$$
$$\begin{bmatrix} F_{tx,s,\theta}(\theta_{n,m,ZoD}, \phi_{n,m,AoD}) \\ F_{tx,s,\phi}(\theta_{n,m,ZoD}, \phi_{n,m,AoD}) \end{bmatrix} \exp\left(\frac{j2\pi \hat{r}_{rx,n,m}^T \cdot \bar{d}_{rx,u}}{\lambda_0}\right) \exp\left(\frac{j2\pi \hat{r}_{tx,n,m}^T \cdot \bar{d}_{tx,s}}{\lambda_0}\right) \exp\left(\frac{j2\pi \hat{r}_{rx,n,m}^T \cdot \bar{v}}{\lambda_0}\right) \quad (2)$$

$$H_{u,s}^{LOS} = \begin{bmatrix} F_{rx,u,\theta}(\theta_{LOS,ZoA}, \phi_{LOS,AoA}) \\ F_{rx,u,\phi}(\theta_{LOS,ZoA}, \phi_{LOS,AoA}) \end{bmatrix}^T \begin{bmatrix} 1 & 0 \\ 0 & -1 \end{bmatrix} \begin{bmatrix} F_{tx,s,\theta}(\theta_{LOS,ZoD}, \phi_{LOS,AoD}) \\ F_{tx,s,\phi}(\theta_{LOS,ZoD}, \phi_{LOS,AoD}) \end{bmatrix} \exp\left(\frac{-j2\pi d_{3D}}{\lambda_0}\right)$$
$$\exp\left(\frac{j2\pi \hat{r}_{rx,LOS}^T \cdot \bar{d}_{rx,u}}{\lambda_0}\right) \exp\left(\frac{j2\pi \hat{r}_{tx,LOS}^T \cdot \bar{d}_{tx,s}}{\lambda_0}\right) \exp\left(\frac{j2\pi \hat{r}_{rx,LOS}^T \cdot \bar{v}}{\lambda_0}\right) \quad (3)$$

where F is the field pattern in the vertical or horizontal plane; $\hat{r}_{tx,n,m}$ and $\hat{r}_{rx,n,m}$ are the ray m direction vectors in spherical units, heading from the BS and reaching the UE, respectively; $\bar{d}$ is the location vector of the antenna elements; $\bar{d}_{3D}$ is the distance between the BS and the UE; $\bar{v}$ is the user speed; and λ_0 is the wavelength corresponding to the carrier frequency. Moreover, $\{\Phi_{n,m}^{\theta\theta}, \Phi_{n,m}^{\theta\phi}, \Phi_{n,m}^{\phi\theta}, \Phi_{n,m}^{\phi\phi}\}$ are the random initial phases for each ray m of each cluster n and for four different polarization combinations $(\theta\theta, \theta\phi, \phi\theta, \phi\phi)$, with distribution $\sim \mathcal{U}(-180°, +180°)$, and $\kappa_{n,m}$ is the cross-polarization power ratio (XPR) for each ray m of each cluster n (7.5-21 in [22]).

The channel generation implementation in the link-level simulator is obtained by several blocks. All the blocks launch the same mex-file with a different configuration:

- *cdlModelInit*: during the configuration of the link simulator parameters, the channel is initialized and the memory is allocated on the basis of parameter selection (e.g., the allocated memory grows with the number of antenna elements). The *mexLock()* function is used to reserve memory to the mex application.
- *cdlModelRegen*: during both the initialization and running phase, the main AoA/AoD of the clusters can be modified to analyze multiple MIMO configurations in a single simulation.
- *cdlModelRun*: the CDL is generated each slot and is applied to the input data. The time-to-frequency conversion of the channel is applied to report the generated channel matrix as a function of the frequency.
- *cdlModelDelete*: at the end of the simulation, the memory reserved to the mex application is deallocated using the *mexUnlock()* function.

The simulator can then operate in two different modes: the frequency domain or the time domain. In the time domain mode, the channel is applied on the oversampled OFDM signal after the IFFT. In the frequency domain mode, the channel is applied in the frequency domain on the OFDM signal before the IFFT. In this case, the OFDM modulator and demodulator are by-passed, as are all the blocks between them, allowing a significant reduction in the computational load. However, the frequency domain mode is applicable only in scenarios characterized by low mobility (i.e., when the channel is nearly constant within the OFDM symbol duration) and when the maximum delay of the channel is lower than the cyclic prefix length. In the simulations presented in the following, the time domain mode is selected and an impulse response is generated after a certain time interval, defined as an integer multiple of the slot length, and then interpolated in the time domain. For the frequency domain, an impulse response would be generated for each OFDM symbol.

4. A Deep Learning-Based CSI Feedback for New Radio

To obtain the optimal precoder for MIMO communications, the channel knowledge is required by the transmitter (i.e., the BS). In the frequency division duplexing (FDD) mode, the uplink and downlink transmissions occur in different frequency bands, so there is no channel reciprocity. Thus, the UE must estimate the downlink channel and send this estimation back to the BS. This procedure is the channel state information feedback. The drawback of this system is the unbearable overhead resulting from the higher number of antenna elements, both in transmission and reception, as highlighted in [12]. The only way to adopt the FDD mode for MIMO transmission is to significantly reduce the feedback overhead—machine learning represents one viable solution to address the problem. In [12], the author designed a DL-based CSI sensing and recovery mechanism, named CsiNet. The main difference from previous DL-based investigations was consideration of the recovery stage. The CsiNet model is based on two main modules:

- Encoder: the encoder generates compressed codewords by learning a proper mapping from the estimated channel matrices (dimensionality reduction). It is implemented by the UE.
- Decoder: the decoder tries to recover the original CSI from the codewords generated by the encoder, learning the inverse mapping. It is implemented at the BS sides, whereas the codewords are received from the UE through a feedback channel.

In this paper, we extend the CsiNet model for CSI information reduction and recovery in a 5G context, producing a deep convolutional neural network (CNN), named NR-CsiNet. The additional features are intended to widen the applicability of the model to a more practical range of use cases:

- We sought to make the model compatible with the typical 5G NR MIMO communications, in contrast to the single receiving antenna limitation of [12]. Practically, this introduces a third dimension to the channel matrices due to the different channel coefficients for each receiving antenna.
- We also considered the downlink channel estimation, whereas this additional step was beyond the scope of [12]. This means that, instead of feeding our NR-CsiNet with perfect channel matrices, we provide as input, noisy matrices, estimated through the CSI-RS.

The CNN is built and trained via Tensorflow's Keras API [48]. To make this DL-based system work with the 5G NR simulator, the traditional feedback reporting blocks are rearranged. A new block imports the pre-trained encoder and uses it to elaborate an encoded version of the channel matrix, previously estimated from the CSI-RS. Then, at the transmitter side, we insert a specular decoding block which imports the pre-trained decoder model and uses the reconstructed channel matrix at its output to determine the optimal precoding vector.

4.1. System Model

While the authors of [12] adopted a multiple-input single-output (MISO) system, i.e., a transmitter deploying an antenna array of N antennas with only one antenna at the receiver side, here, we consider a 5G NR-compliant MIMO system, with M receiving antennas. For the c-th sub-carrier at the m-th receiving antenna, the received signal can be expressed as

$$y_{m,c} = \mathbf{h}_{m,c}^H \mathbf{v}_c x_c + z_{m,c} \tag{4}$$

where:
- $\mathbf{h}_{m,c}$ is the complex channel vector relative to the c-th sub-carrier and to the m-th receiving antennas of size $N \times 1$;
- $\mathbf{v}_c$ is the complex precoding vector of size $N \times 1$;
- x_c is the complex data symbol transmitted on the c-th sub-carrier;
- $z_{m,c}$ denotes the additive noise on the c-th sub-carrier relative to the m-th receiving antenna.

The precoding vector $\mathbf{v} = \{\mathbf{v}_c : c = 1, \ldots, \widetilde{C}\}$, with $\widetilde{C}$ the number of sub-carriers of the OFDM system, is computed by the BS once it receives the CSI feedback information $\mathbf{H}_c = [\mathbf{h}_1, \ldots, \mathbf{h}_M] \in \mathbb{C}^{N \times M}$. The amount of coefficients the UE must feedback is then $N \times M \times \widetilde{C}$, which can easily become too demanding from a complexity point of view, since resource elements must be dedicated to the channel reporting, instead of data packets (i.e., a capacity drop). The M $y_{m,c}$ symbols received per sub-band are then combined at the receiver side and the final estimated symbol $\hat{y}_c$ on the c-th sub-carrier is obtained as follows:

$$\hat{y}_c = \mathbf{u}_c^H \mathbf{y}_c \tag{5}$$

where $\mathbf{u}_c$ is an $M \times 1$ combiner and $\mathbf{y}_c = [y_{1,c}, \ldots, y_{M,c}]^T$ is an $M \times 1$ vector containing all the received symbols on the c-th sub-carrier.

4.2. The Channel Estimation Task

When considering massive MIMO systems, the channel estimation task is fundamental and many studies have addressed the issue [19,20] since beam-forming techniques strongly depend on the outcome of this phase. In [12], the main focus is the compression task, i.e, the model in [12] takes as input a perfect channel matrix and learns efficient encoding and decoding algorithms to compress and decompress it with minimum error. Our model, instead, aims to deal also with the challenging downlink channel estimation task. This means that the compression and decompression process is not performed on the ideal channel matrix generated by the CDL channel module, but on a noisy estimation of it, coming from the CSI-RS compensation. The model is expected to learn efficient encoding and decoding algorithms that, besides compressing and decompressing the input matrices, must be able to remove the noisy contributions and reconstruct the clean channel matrices with minimum error. It should be noted that, to simplify the experiments, we decided to consider only the noise affecting the downlink transmission to avoid simulating the uplink channel.

To include this channel estimation task, we need to define two different instances of the channel matrix $\mathbf{H}$:

- an ideal channel matrix $\mathbf{H}^{id}$, generated by the CDL module of the software simulator. It represents the desired output of the NR-CsiNet model;
- a noisy version of the perfect channel matrix $\mathbf{H}^{CSI\text{-}RS}$, estimated from the CSI-RS pilots by means of a simple interpolation. It represents the input of the NR-CsiNet model.

To obtain a first raw estimation of the complete downlink complex channel matrix for each transmitting/receiving antenna pair, we performed a cubic radial basis function (RBF) interpolation on the real and the imaginary parts separately, using a MATLAB predefined library.

An example of the result obtained is shown in Figure 2, where n and m are the transmitting and receiving antenna indexes, respectively. The estimated $\mathbf{H}^{CSI\text{-}RS}$ matrices are collected by simulating different conditions of the channel; practically, we select a couple of different SNR values, 10 dB and 20 dB, and train a different NR-CsiNet model for each of these values. Then, we test the behavior of these models at different levels of channel quality; to be precise, simulations are performed with SNR values varying between −5 dB and 35 dB, with a 5 dB granularity. To simplify the notation, in the following subsections, we refer to the two channel instances $\mathbf{H}^{id}$ and $\mathbf{H}^{CSI\text{-}RS}$ as a single matrix $\mathbf{H}$, meaning that all the processing steps described have to be performed on both.

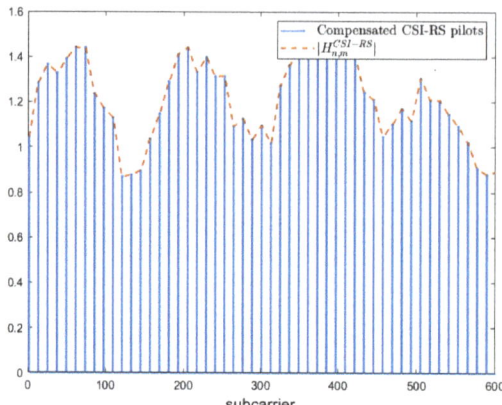

Figure 2. Module of interpolated channel matrix $|\mathbf{H}_{n,m}^{CSI\text{-}RS}|$.

4.3. DFT-Based Preprocessing of CSI Information

The first processing that is applied to the estimated channel matrix in the feedback task is the 2D discrete Fourier transform (DFT), with the goal of sparsifying the coefficients of **H** in the angular-delay domain, as proposed in [12]. To deal with more antennas at the receiver, this operation is iterated M times, thus producing a different transformed spatial-frequency channel matrix $\tilde{\mathbf{H}}_m$ for each receiving antenna:

$$\tilde{\mathbf{H}}_m = \mathbf{F}_d \mathbf{H}_m \mathbf{F}_a^H \tag{6}$$

where $\mathbf{F}_d$ and $\mathbf{F}_a$ are $\tilde{C} \times \tilde{C}$ and $N \times N$ DFT matrices, respectively. $\mathbf{H}_m$ has size $\tilde{C} \times N$ and m is the index of the receiving antenna. Figure 3 shows an instance of $\mathbf{H}_m$ with $N = 8$ and $\tilde{C} = 600$.

As the inter-arrival time between rays only spans a certain range, only a few elements of the matrix $\tilde{\mathbf{H}}_m$ contain significant information, while the vast majority of the matrix elements are made up of coefficients close to zero; thus, DFT processing is necessary. It is obvious that the remaining columns of $\tilde{\mathbf{H}}_m$ can be eliminated and that only the core $C < \tilde{C}$ columns are significant (Figure 4).

A truncated version of $\tilde{\mathbf{H}}_m$ is then obtained as a first step to decrease the feedback overhead, denoted as $\hat{\mathbf{H}}_m^t$ and having size $C \times N$.

Successively, we obtain the spatial-frequency domain version of the truncated matrix in the angular-delay domain $\tilde{\mathbf{H}}_m^t$, through an an inverse DFT (IDFT). This matrix, denoted $\mathbf{H}_m^t$, eases the compression and reconstruction task of the CNN, since, in the spatial-frequency domain, the "image" representation of the matrix is characterized by a smoother profile (Figure 3), whereas, in the angular-delay domain, it is recognizable as a composite of crisp and sharp lines (Figure 4). This last step is not considered in the DFT processing addressed in [12]; we anticipate that it will improve the overall system behaviour.

Lastly, the matrix $\mathbf{H}_m^t$ is normalised to assume values only inside the interval $[0, 1]$. This can help the training of the CNN by reducing the effect of outliers.

In a specular way, at the output of the decoder implemented at the BS, a rescaling operation, followed by a DFT and an inverse DFT operation, must be performed.

4.4. Multiple Receiving Antennas

While the authors of paper [12] limit their DL-based solution to single receiving antenna scenarios ($M = 1$), our purpose is to make the model applicable also to MIMO contexts. With this in mind, the downlink channel information relative to each distinct receiving antenna must, in some way, be organized at the input of the CNN. We decided to maintain only two input channels, one for the real and one for the imaginary parts of the matrices $\mathbf{H}_m^{\text{CSI-RS},t}$; this means that the matrices relative to distinct receiving antennas are conveyed through the CNN on the same input channels.

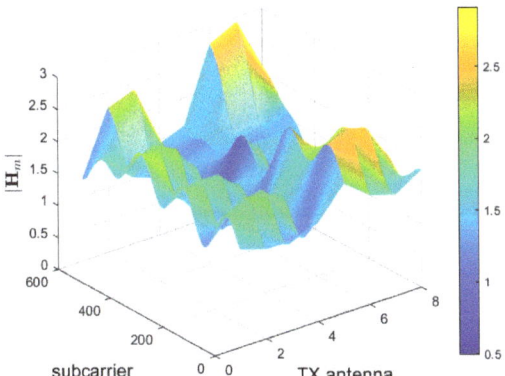

Figure 3. Module of channel matrix $|\mathbf{H}_m|$ [32].

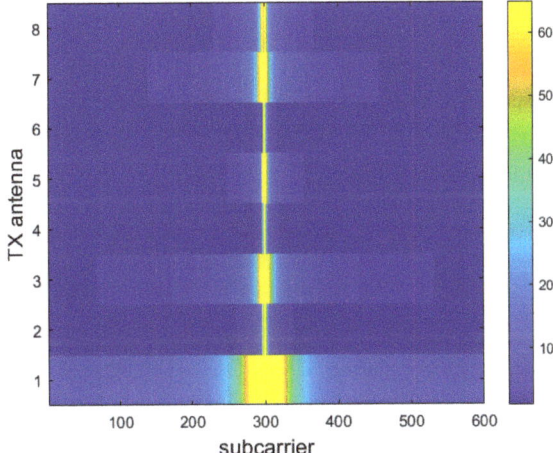

Figure 4. Module of DFT-transformed channel matrix $|\tilde{\mathbf{H}}_m|$ [32].

The reasons behind this approach are several:
- we do not need to train a different CNN model for each distinct receiving antenna;
- the number of parameters learned by the CNN is not affected by the number of receiving antennas M. This means that in massive MIMO scenarios, where $M \gg 1$, the complexity of the model does not increase with M and, thus, the risk of running into overfitting phenomena remains limited;
- if the different receiving antennas were spatially correlated, this correlation could be exploited during the learning process and, probably, smaller training datasets would be sufficient to obtain effective and generalized models.

4.5. NR-CsiNet Encoder

The structure of the encoder of the NR-CsiNet (Figure 5a) is based on the encoder designed for the CsiNet proposed in [12]. It consists of a deep convolutional neural network, where the input has size $C \times N \times 2$, corresponding to the real and imaginary parts of the truncated matrices $\mathbf{H}_m^{\text{CSI-RS},t}$. The first layer of the CNN is a convolutional layer adopting a filter of size 3 × 3 that generates 2 feature maps. A reshape process vectorizes the two feature maps into a vector of size $T \times 1$, where $T = 2 \cdot C \cdot N$. The last block is a fully connected layer which outputs the actual codeword **s**, one for each receiving antenna, as a vector of size R. The overall compressing ratio is $K = \frac{R}{C \cdot N}$.

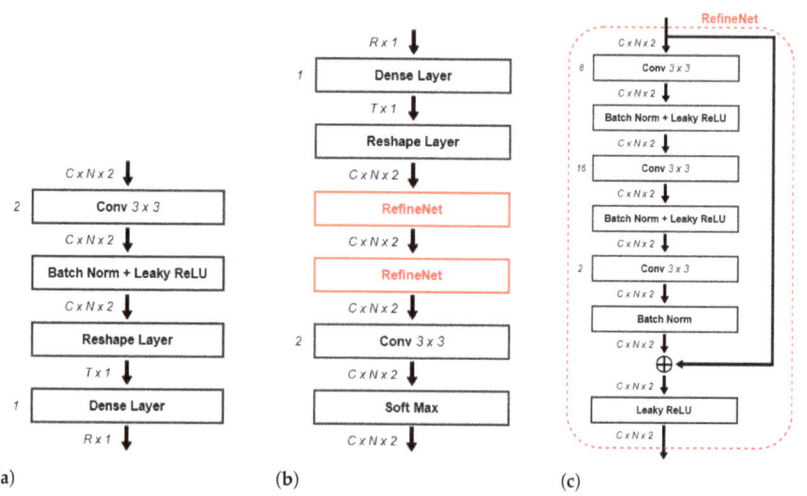

Figure 5. NR-CsiNet representation. (**a**) Block scheme of the NR-CsiNet encoder. (**b**) Block scheme of the NR-CsiNet decoder. (**c**) Block scheme of the RefineNet unit.

4.6. NR-CsiNet Decoder

As for the encoder, the NR-CsiNet decoder (Figure 5b) utilizes the implementation scheme of the CsiNet decoder presented in [12]. The first layer is a fully connected layer which receives as input the codeword **s** produced by the encoder at the UE side, sent to the BS. The result of this layer is a coarse reconstruction of the real and imaginary part of the channel matrix $\mathbf{H}_m^{id,t}$ in the form of a vector of size $T \times 1$. A reshape layer transforms the vector back to the two matrices corresponding to the real and imaginary part of the channel, i.e., two matrices of size $C \times N$ each. In order to improve these initial estimates, a particular set of blocks, called the RefiNet Unit (Figure 5c), is inserted in the decoder. Each RefineNet unit is composed of three convolutional layers using a kernel of size 3 × 3. The first and second layers generate 8 and 16 feature maps, respectively, while the third outputs the final reconstruction of the $\mathbf{H}_m^{id,t}$ matrices (in the form of two feature maps). The feature maps produced by the three layers of a RefineNet unit are forced by a zero-padding technique to have the same size as the input channel matrix ($C \times N$). Moreover, each layer is followed by a rectified linear unit (ReLU) [49,50] and a batch normalisation layer [50,51]. Before the last leaky ReLU computation, the input of the RefiNet is added to the output of the last CNN (after proper batch normalisation). This step is necessary since, as reported in the literature [52], the sequence of many CNN layers may lead to a vanishing gradient problem. To identify a suitable trade-off between the complexity and reconstruction capabilities, the authors of [12] investigated the impact of the number of RefiNet units, determining that two RefineNet units were sufficient. In our work, we investigated the effect of adopting different numbers of RefiNet units and observed that exploiting more than two RefiNet units did not significantly impact the reconstruction quality, though at the expense of greater complexity. An additional convolutional layer follows the RefiNet Units and, finally, a softmax layer [50,53] scales the reconstructed coefficients into the $[0, 1]$ range.

4.7. Training Process

Using the same notation adopted in [12], the set of trainable parameters is denoted as $\Theta = \{\Theta_{en}, \Theta_{de}\}$. The truncated input and output of the NR-CsiNet model for the i-th patch are denoted as $\mathbf{H}_i^{CSI\text{-}RS,t}$ and $\hat{\mathbf{H}}_i^t = f(\mathbf{H}_i^{CSI\text{-}RS,t}; \Theta) = f_{de}(f_{en}(\mathbf{H}_i^{CSI\text{-}RS,t}; \Theta_{en}); \Theta_{de})$, respectively. The loss function is defined as

$$L(\Theta) = \frac{1}{S}\sum_{i=1}^{S} ||f(\mathbf{H}_i^{CSI\text{-}RS,t}; \Theta) - \mathbf{H}_i^{id,t}||_2^2 \qquad (7)$$

where S denotes the number of training samples and $||.||_2$ is the Euclidean norm operator.

5. Simulation Results

In this section, we report the main results collected from the NR-CsiNet model and described in the previous sections. The assessment of the performance is carried out through simulation trials exploiting the NR link-level simulator presented in Section 3 by substituting the blocks for CSI feedback definition and reporting with our DL-based models. The transmitter precoding matrix is obtained by a single value decomposition (SVD) operation on the recovered channel matrix, which is generated from the compressed feedback sent back by the UE. This means selecting the eigenvector that corresponds to the higher eigenvalue as the precoding vector for the subsequent downlink transmission. Taking advantage of the spatial diversity given by the M receiving antennas, a maximal ratio combiner (MRC) is used at the receiving side.

Table 1 reports the main parameters of interest concerning the simulator settings:

Table 1. Simulation parameters for NR-CsiNet training.

NR Simulator Parameters	
System bandwidth	5 MHz
Subcarrier spacing	15 kHz
Time slot	1 ms
Carrier frequency	3.64 GHz
iMCS	21
(Modulation, coding rate)	(64-QAM, 0.694)
TBS	19,968 bit
NFFT	512
$\tilde{C}$	300
Transmission layers	1
Codewords	1
CSI-RS Tx period	4 slots
CSI reporting type	Type I
Channel model	CDL-B
Delay spread model	Nominal

More details on some of the main parameters are provided below:

Time slot Time duration of the transport block of data transmission, corresponding to 14 OFDM symbols.

Modulation and coding scheme (MCS) Configuration parameter of the system to determine the coding rate and the order and type of modulation to be adopted for the transmission.

Transport block size (TBS) Value corresponding to the number of bits transmitted in one slot.

NFFT Smaller power of two greater than the number of sub-carriers used by the system to be used by FFT and IFFT operations.

Number of sub-carriers for data transmission $\tilde{C}$ Computed as the difference between the NFFT value and the number of sub-carriers composing the band guards. In our system $\tilde{C} = 512 - 106 - 106$.

Delay spread model Parameter that determines the delay profile, affecting the scaling factor for the time of arrival of each cluster signal, leading to a shorter or longer delay spread.

It should be noted that the adopted bandwidth is smaller than the one commonly expected for a 5G NR network. Behind this choice are considerations of computational complexity since a larger bandwidth would lead to a significant increase in simulation and training time.

Table 2 shows the hyperparameters adopted for the training and testing process of our model.

Table 2. NR-CsiNet model parameters [32].

NR-CsiNet Parameters	
Training set	1000 sim of 100 slots
Validation set	100 sim of 100 slots
Testing set	100 sim of 100 slots
Learning rate	0.001
Loss function	MSE
Optimizer	Adam
Epochs	300
RefineNet units	2
K_{DFT}	3

The DFT-compression factor K_{DFT}, which should not be confused with the final compression factor K introduced in Section 4.5, is defined as:

$$K_{DFT} = \frac{\tilde{C}}{C} \qquad (8)$$

where $\tilde{C}$ and C are the same parameters defined in Section 4.

The transmitting antenna system consists of a 2×2 planar array formed of dual-polarized antenna components, while the receiver is equipped with a single dual-polarized antenna; thus, we have $N = 8$ transmitting antennas and $M = 2$ receiving antennas. Since there are a relatively small number of antennas, it is obvious that this is not a massive MIMO scenario. This decision was forced by considerations solely related to computational complexity because adding more antennas will increase simulation times proportionately. Larger values of N and/or M should be envisioned for future research.

In our system, the DFT-compression factor is fixed at $K_{DFT} = 3$. The training process of the neural network is performed for two different SNR levels: 10 dB and 20 dB. Figures 6 and 7 highlight how the normalised mean square error (NMSE) of the channel reconstruction for the NR-CsiNet model does not depend on the training data SNR level, except for the lowest compression value K ($K = 1/120$).

The PDSCH throughput results for SNR training values of 10 dB and 20 dB are reported in Figures 8 and 9, respectively. The relevant SNR range is $[-5, 23]$ dB. The results for the second evaluation metric, BLER1, i.e., BLER at the first transmission attempt, are reported in Figures 10 and 11 for the $[0, 23]$ dB SNR range. The performance of the NR-CsiNet is compared with the PMI reporting technique, referred to here as follow PMI. This procedure requires channel measurements by the UE from CSI-RS, in addition to which a PMI is determined [37]. The PMI is an index that the UE sends back to the BS to suggest the preferable precoding vector corresponding to that index from a predefined precoding matrix.

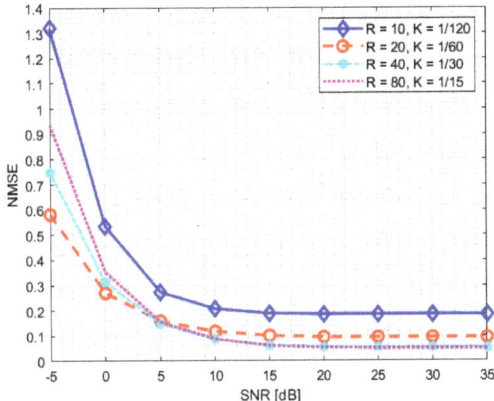

Figure 6. NMSE statistics for NR-CsiNet model trained at SNR = 10 dB.

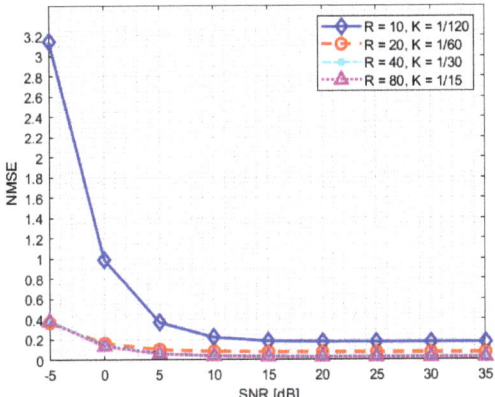

Figure 7. NMSE statistics for NR-CsiNet model trained at SNR = 20 dB.

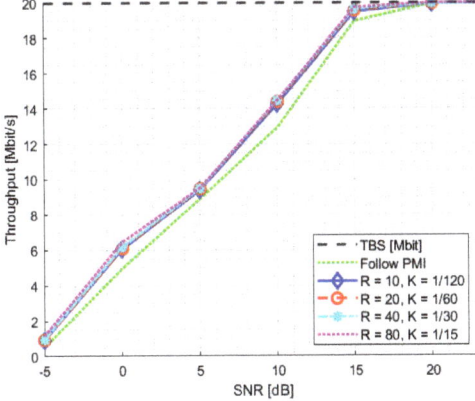

Figure 8. Throughput statistics for NR-CsiNet model trained at SNR = 10 dB.

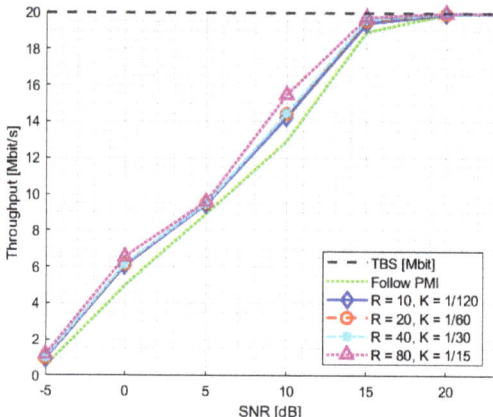

Figure 9. Throughput statistics for NR-CsiNet model trained at SNR = 20 dB [32].

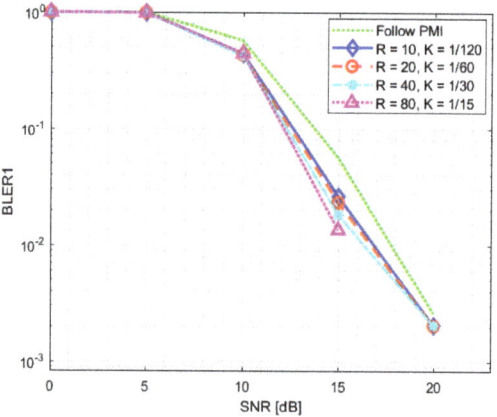

Figure 10. BLER1 statistics for NR-CsiNet model trained at SNR = 10 dB.

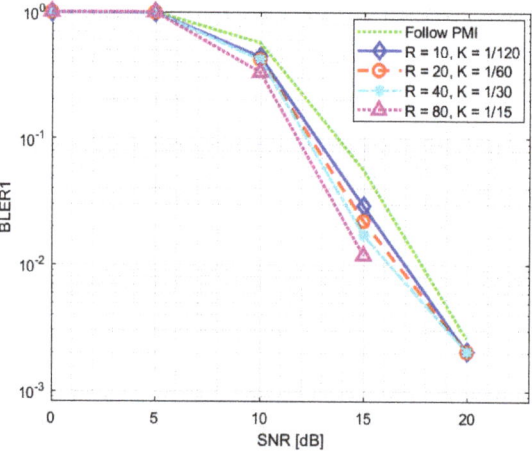

Figure 11. BLER1 statistics for NR-CsiNet model trained at SNR = 20 dB [32].

It is possible to infer from the graphs that, even when dealing with noisy channel estimates rather than ideal channel matrices, our DL-based technique performs better than the follow PMI algorithm in 8 × 2 cases. The plots specifically illustrate that over 20 dB of SNR, both the NR-CsiNet and follow PMI throughput curves achieve the transport block size (TBS) maximum limit; however at lower SNR, all the variations of our DL solution perform better. It is important to note that, in all of our experiments, we used the same channel model configuration. The simulation results demonstrated that, despite being intended for multipath contexts, this type of channel model typically presents a dominant path, which implicitly defines a preferential direction for signal transmission. It is obvious that the follow PMI is expected to function well when taking into account such a channel model. In fact, among a range of potential beams, the PMI index merely determines which one is most precisely pointed to the receiver. Our hypothesis is that our DL-based technique has the best chance of outperforming the follow PMI algorithm in "richer" channel realizations when the multipath is not dominated by a single LOS cluster.

The complexity of DL-based solutions is one of the main shortcomings in their implementation at the user equipment side, characterized by limited power and hardware resources. In Table 3, we report the number of parameters and FLOPs required for the NR-CsiNet encoder, which are greatly dependent on the choice of the factor K. For the CNN layer, the number of learnable parameters are computed as $par_{CNN} = \text{\# filters} \cdot (filter\ width \cdot filter\ height \cdot input\ feature\ maps + 1)$ while the FLOPs are $FLOP_{CNN} = 2 \cdot \text{\# filters} \cdot filter\ width \cdot filter\ height \cdot Output\ size$; for the FC layer, the parameters are $par_{FC} = (Input\ size + 1) \cdot Output\ size$, while the FLOPs are $FLOP_{FCL} = 2 \cdot Input\ size \cdot Output\ size$.

Table 3. Complexity of the encoder in terms of learnable parameters and FLOPs.

K	Parameters	FLOPs
1/120	5.381	179.200
1/60	10.725	243.200
1/30	21.411	371.200
1/15	42.785	627.200

The FLOP amount is of the same order of magnitude for both the CNN and the FC, while the FC requires a significantly higher number of parameters since it needs a weight for each input-output node link (plus the bias). The advanced hardware designed specially for neural network operations can significantly help the deployment of such technology. For the follow PMI, the parameters required are almost negligible, since the DFT codebook can be generated whenever required. Nonetheless, the complexity from a FLOPs perspective is almost zero at the base station; however, at the user side it can be quite significant, since it requires a full search over all the DFT beam-forming codewords in each frequency position to maximize the capacity. Thus, the number of FLOPs can be estimated as the multiplication between two complex matrices of size $M \times N$ and $N \times C_s$: $FLOP_{followPMI} = 8MC_sNL$; where C_s is the codebook size and L is the number of frequency bins where the PMI is computed. In our tests, a different PMI is required for each PRB; thus, $L = 25$ and we use as the codebook a DFT beamspace with an oversampling factor $O_F = 4$; therefore, $C_s = O_F N = 32$. The final number of FLOPs with follow PMI is equal to $FLOP_{followPMI} = 102.400$. The use of a system such as NR-CsiNet instead of the simpler follow PMI demands higher complexity; however, unlike follow PMI, it can allow the BS to apply advanced precoding techniques that exploit complete CSI, which is not achievable through simplified codebooks (e.g., in the case of users in NLOS and/or who could interfere with each other). We aim to investigate NR-CsiNet capabilities for more sophisticated MIMO scenarios in future studies.

6. Conclusions

The CSI feedback for FDD transmission is an open problem and DL-based techniques have made a new tool available to attempt to solve it. The channel state information availability is of crucial importance for MIMO communications and for 5G New Radio. In this paper, we investigated the potential of a neural network technique to serve as an alternative to the traditional feedback reporting block. From the work of the authors reported in [12], we obtained a NR-CsiNet model, able to deal with SU-MIMO systems and providing channel estimation capabilities. Simulations were performed by exploiting a 5G NR-compliant physical layer simulator with a CDL channel model, which enables modelling of the complex environment envisioned by the 5G network. The results showed that our DL-based feedback system can achieve performances comparable to those obtained with a traditional PMI-based reporting technique and clearly outperformed it in some cases. The framework and the data collected in this study provide a solid basis for more in-depth tests of the capabilities of DL for CSI feedback in 5G NR, enabling investigation of a larger number of scenarios and different configurations, such as larger MIMO systems (i.e., massive MIMO), and exploitation of the channel matrix to support spatial division multiplexing solutions, that are currently difficult to obtain in FDD mode.

Moreover, our objective was to highlight useful aspects of research on this topic, which is of significant interest considering the fundamental role that MIMO systems play in network performance improvement.

Author Contributions: Conceptualization, R.G. and R.F.; formal analysis, E.Z., D.G.R. and R.G.; investigation, E.Z., D.G.R. and R.T., software, E.Z. and R.F.; supervision, D.G.R. and R.G.; writing—original draft preparation, R.T. and E.Z.; writing—review and editing, D.G.R., R.T. and R.G. All authors have read and agreed to the published version of the manuscript.

Funding: This research received no external funding.

Data Availability Statement: The data that support the findings of this study are available from TIM S.p.A. Restrictions apply to the availability of these data, which were used under licence for this study. Data are available from the corresponding author, D.G.R., with the permission of TIM S.p.A., upon reasonable request.

Acknowledgments: Riccardo Tuninato acknowledges support from TIM S.p.A. through the Ph.D. scholarship.

Conflicts of Interest: The authors declare no conflict of interest.

References

1. Jiang, C.; Zhang, H.; Ren, Y.; Han, Z.; Chen, K.; Hanzo, L. Machine Learning Paradigms for Next-Generation Wireless Networks. *IEEE Wirel. Commun.* **2017**, *24*, 98–105. [CrossRef]
2. Bkassiny, M.; Li, Y.; Jayaweera, S.K. A Survey on Machine-Learning Techniques in Cognitive Radios. *IEEE Commun. Surv. Tutor.* **2013**, *15*, 1136–1159. [CrossRef]
3. Sharma, V.; Bohara, V. Exploiting machine learning algorithms for cognitive radio. In Proceedings of the 2014 International Conference on Advances in Computing, Communications and Informatics (ICACCI), Delhi, India, 24–27 September 2014; pp. 1554–1558.
4. Murudkar, C.V.; Gitlin, R.D. Optimal-Capacity, Shortest Path Routing in Self-Organizing 5G Networks using Machine Learning. In Proceedings of the 2019 IEEE 20th Wireless and Microwave Technology Conference (WAMICON), Cocoa Beach, FL, USA, 8–9 April 2019; pp. 1–5.
5. Khan Tayyaba, S.; Khattak, H.A.; Almogren, A.; Shah, M.A.; Ud Din, I.; Alkhalifa, I.; Guizani, M. 5G Vehicular Network Resource Management for Improving Radio Access Through Machine Learning. *IEEE Access* **2020**, *8*, 6792–6800. [CrossRef]
6. Hussain, F.; Hassan, S.A.; Hussain, R.; Hossain, E. Machine Learning for Resource Management in Cellular and IoT Networks: Potentials, Current Solutions, and Open Challenges. *IEEE Commun. Surv. Tutor.* **2020**, *22*, 1251–1275. [CrossRef]
7. Wang, T.; Wen, C.; Wang, H.; Gao, F.; Jiang, T.; Jin, S. Deep learning for wireless physical layer: Opportunities and challenges. *China Commun.* **2017**, *14*, 92–111. [CrossRef]
8. Zhou, R.; Liu, F.; Gravelle, C.W. Deep Learning for Modulation Recognition: A Survey With a Demonstration. *IEEE Access* **2020**, *8*, 67366–67376. [CrossRef]

9. Zhang, M.; Zeng, Y.; Han, Z.; Gong, Y. Automatic Modulation Recognition Using Deep Learning Architectures. In Proceedings of the 2018 IEEE 19th International Workshop on Signal Processing Advances in Wireless Communications (SPAWC), Kalamata, Greece, 25–28 June 2018; pp. 1–5.
10. Rajendran, S.; Meert, W.; Giustiniano, D.; Lenders, V.; Pollin, S. Deep Learning Models for Wireless Signal Classification With Distributed Low-Cost Spectrum Sensors. *IEEE Trans. Cogn. Commun. Netw.* **2018**, *4*, 433–445. [CrossRef]
11. Huang, H.; Guo, S.; Gui, G.; Yang, Z.; Zhang, J.; Sari, H.; Adachi, F. Deep Learning for Physical-Layer 5G Wireless Techniques: Opportunities, Challenges and Solutions. *IEEE Wirel. Commun.* **2020**, *27*, 214–222. [CrossRef]
12. Wen, C.; Shih, W.; Jin, S. Deep Learning for Massive MIMO CSI Feedback. *IEEE Wirel. Commun. Lett.* **2018**, *7*, 748–751. [CrossRef]
13. Wang, T.; Wen, C.; Jin, S.; Li, G.Y. Deep Learning-Based CSI Feedback Approach for Time-Varying Massive MIMO Channels. *IEEE Wirel. Commun. Lett.* **2019**, *8*, 416–419. [CrossRef]
14. Gui, G.; Huang, H.; Song, Y.; Sari, H. Deep Learning for an Effective Nonorthogonal Multiple Access Scheme. *IEEE Trans. Veh. Technol.* **2018**, *67*, 8440–8450. [CrossRef]
15. Huang, H.; Song, Y.; Yang, J.; Gui, G.; Adachi, F. Deep-Learning-Based Millimeter-Wave Massive MIMO for Hybrid Precoding. *IEEE Trans. Veh. Technol.* **2019**, *68*, 3027–3032. [CrossRef]
16. O'Shea, T.; Hoydis, J. An Introduction to Deep Learning for the Physical Layer. *IEEE Trans. Cogn. Commun. Netw.* **2017**, *3*, 563–575. [CrossRef]
17. Ye, H.; Li, G.Y.; Juang, B. Power of Deep Learning for Channel Estimation and Signal Detection in OFDM Systems. *IEEE Wirel. Commun. Lett.* **2018**, *7*, 114–117. [CrossRef]
18. Soltani, M.; Pourahmadi, V.; Mirzaei, A.; Sheikhzadeh, H. Deep Learning-Based Channel Estimation. *IEEE Commun. Lett.* **2019**, *23*, 652–655. [CrossRef]
19. Fascista, A.; De Monte, A.; Coluccia, A.; Wymeersch, H.; Seco-Granados, G. Low-Complexity Downlink Channel Estimation in mmWave Multiple-Input Single-Output Systems. *IEEE Wirel. Commun. Lett.* **2022**, *11*, 518–522. . LWC.2021.3134826. [CrossRef]
20. Kebede, T.; Wondie, Y.; Steinbrunn, J. Channel Estimation and Beamforming Techniques for mm Wave-Massive MIMO: Recent Trends, Challenges and Open Issues. In Proceedings of the 2021 International Symposium on Networks, Computers and Communications (ISNCC), Dubai, United Arab Emirates, 31 October–2 November 2021; pp. 1–8. [CrossRef]
21. Dahlman, E.; Parkvall, S.; Skold, J. *5G NR: The Next Generation Wireless Access Technology*; Elsevier Science: 2018.
22. 3GPP. *Study on Channel Model for Frequencies from 0.5 to 100 GHz*; Version 14.3.0; Technical Report (TR) 38.901; 3rd Generation Partnership Project (3GPP): Valbonne, France, 2018.
23. Riviello, D.G.; Di Stasio, F.; Tuninato, R. Performance Analysis of Multi-User MIMO Schemes under Realistic 3GPP 3-D Channel Model for 5G mmWave Cellular Networks. *Electronics* **2022**, *11*, 330. [CrossRef]
24. Xie, H.; Gao, F.; Jin, S.; Fang, J.; Liang, Y. Channel Estimation for TDD/FDD Massive MIMO Systems With Channel Covariance Computing. *IEEE Trans. Wirel. Commun.* **2018**, *17*, 4206–4218. [CrossRef]
25. Han, Y.; Hsu, T.; Wen, C.; Wong, K.; Jin, S. Efficient Downlink Channel Reconstruction for FDD Multi-Antenna Systems. *IEEE Trans. Wirel. Commun.* **2019**, *18*, 3161–3176. [CrossRef]
26. Cao, Z.; Shih, W.T.; Guo, J.; Wen, C.K.; Jin, S. Lightweight Convolutional Neural Networks for CSI Feedback in Massive MIMO. *IEEE Commun. Lett.* **2021**, *25*, 2624–2628. [CrossRef]
27. Li, Q.; Zhang, A.; Liu, P.; Li, J.; Li, C. A Novel CSI Feedback Approach for Massive MIMO Using LSTM-Attention CNN. *IEEE Access* **2020**, *8*, 7295–7302. [CrossRef]
28. Ji, D.J.; Cho, D.H. ChannelAttention: Utilizing Attention Layers for Accurate Massive MIMO Channel Feedback. *IEEE Wirel. Commun. Lett.* **2021**, *10*, 1079–1082. [CrossRef]
29. Lu, Z.; Wang, J.; Song, J. Binary Neural Network Aided CSI Feedback in Massive MIMO System. *IEEE Wirel. Commun. Lett.* **2021**, *10*, 1305–1308. [CrossRef]
30. Guo, J.; Wen, C.K.; Jin, S. Deep Learning-Based CSI Feedback for Beamforming in Single- and Multi-Cell Massive MIMO Systems. *IEEE J. Sel. Areas Commun.* **2021**, *39*, 1872–1884. [CrossRef]
31. Liu, Z.; Zhang, L.; Ding, Z. An Efficient Deep Learning Framework for Low Rate Massive MIMO CSI Reporting. *IEEE Trans. Commun.* **2020**, *68*, 4761–4772. [CrossRef]
32. Zimaglia, E.; Riviello, D.G.; Garello, R.; Fantini, R. A Novel Deep Learning Approach to CSI Feedback Reporting for NR 5G Cellular Systems. In Proceedings of the 2020 IEEE Microwave Theory and Techniques in Wireless Communications (MTTW), Riga, Latvia, 1–2 October 2020; Volume 1, pp. 47–52. [CrossRef]
33. Ahmadi, S. *5G NR: Architecture, Technology, Implementation, and Operation of 3GPP New Radio Standards*; Elsevier Science: 2019.
34. 3GPP. *Evolved Universal Terrestrial Radio Access (E-UTRA); Physical Channels and Modulation (Release 8)*; Version 8.9.0; Technical Specification (TS) 36.211; 3rd Generation Partnership Project (3GPP): Valbonne, France, 2009.
35. 3GPP. *Evolved Universal Terrestrial Radio Access (E-UTRA); Physical Channels and Modulation (Release 10)*; Version 10.7.0; Technical Specification (TS) 36.211; 3rd Generation Partnership Project (3GPP): Valbonne, France, 2013.
36. 3GPP. *Evolved Universal Terrestrial Radio Access (E-UTRA); Further Advancements for E-UTRA Physical Layer Aspects (Release 9)*; Version 9.0.0; Technical Specification (TS) 36.814; 3rd Generation Partnership Project (3GPP): Valbonne, France, 2010.
37. 3GPP. *NR; Physical Layer Procedures for Data (Release 15)*; Version 15.9.0; Technical Specification (TS) 38.214; 3rd Generation Partnership Project (3GPP): Valbonne, France, 2020.

38. Roy, R.H. Spatial division multiple access technology and its application to wireless communication systems. In Proceedings of the 1997 IEEE 47th Vehicular Technology Conference. Technology in Motion, Phoenix, AZ, USA, 4–7 May 1997; Volume 2, pp. 730–734.
39. Liu, L.; Chen, R.; Geirhofer, S.; Sayana, K.; Shi, Z.; Zhou, Y. Downlink MIMO in LTE-advanced: SU-MIMO vs. MU-MIMO. *IEEE Commun. Mag.* **2012**, *50*, 140–147. [CrossRef]
40. Spencer, Q.H.; Peel, C.B.; Swindlehurst, A.L.; Haardt, M. An introduction to the multi-user MIMO downlink. *IEEE Commun. Mag.* **2004**, *42*, 60–67. [CrossRef]
41. Zhang, T.; Wang, R. Achievable DoF Regions of Three-User MIMO Broadcast Channel With Delayed CSIT. *IEEE Trans. Commun.* **2021**, *69*, 2240–2253. [CrossRef]
42. 3GPP. *NR; Physical Channels and Modulation*; Version 15.6.0; Technical Specification (TS) 38.211; 3rd Generation Partnership Project (3GPP): Valbonne, France, 2019.
43. 3GPP. *NR; Multiplexing and Channel Coding*; Version 15.6.0; Technical Specification (TS) 38.212; 3rd Generation Partnership Project (3GPP): Valbonne, France, 2019.
44. 3GPP. *NR; Physical Layer Procedures for Control*; Version 15.6.0; Technical Specification (TS) 38.213; 3rd Generation Partnership Project (3GPP): Valbonne, France, 2019.
45. 3GPP. *Radio Resource Control (RRC); Protocol Specification*; Version 16.1.0; Technical Report (TR) 38.331; 3rd Generation Partnership Project (3GPP): Valbonne, France, 2020.
46. 3GPP. *User Equipment (UE) Radio Access Capabilities*; Version 15.3.0; Technical Report (TR) 38.306; 3rd Generation Partnership Project (3GPP): Valbonne, France, 2018.
47. 3GPP. *NR; Study on Test Methods*; Version 2.4.0; Technical Report (TR) 38.810; 3rd Generation Partnership Project (3GPP): Valbonne, France, 2018.
48. Tensorflow Keras Module. Available online: https://www.tensorflow.org/api_docs/python/tf/keras (accessed on 5 January 2023).
49. ReLU Keras API. Available online: https://keras.io/api/layers/activation_layers/relu/ (accessed on 5 January 2023).
50. Goodfellow, I.; Bengio, Y.; Courville, A. *Deep Learning (Adaptive Computation and Machine Learning)*; MIT Press: Cambridge, MA, USA, 2016.
51. Batch Normalization Keras API. Available online: https://keras.io/api/layers/normalization_layers/batch_normalization/ (accessed on 5 January 2023).
52. Szegedy, C.; Liu, W.; Jia, Y.; Sermanet, P.; Reed, S.; Anguelov, D.; Erhan, D.; Vanhoucke, V.; Rabinovich, A. Going deeper with convolutions. In Proceedings of the 2015 IEEE Conference on Computer Vision and Pattern Recognition (CVPR), Boston, MA, USA, 7–12 June 2015; pp. 1–9. [CrossRef]
53. Softmax Keras API. Available online: https://keras.io/api/layers/activation_layers/softmax/ (accessed on 5 January 2023).

Disclaimer/Publisher's Note: The statements, opinions and data contained in all publications are solely those of the individual author(s) and contributor(s) and not of MDPI and/or the editor(s). MDPI and/or the editor(s) disclaim responsibility for any injury to people or property resulting from any ideas, methods, instructions or products referred to in the content.

Article

Machine Learning-Based Methods for Enhancement of UAV-NOMA and D2D Cooperative Networks

Lefteris Tsipi [1,*], Michail Karavolos [1], Petros S. Bithas [2] and Demosthenes Vouyioukas [1]

[1] Department of Information and Communication Systems Engineering, School of Engineering, University of the Aegean, 83200 Samos, Greece
[2] Department of Digital Industry Technologies, National and Kapodistrian University of Athens, Thesi Skliro, 34400 Evia, Greece
* Correspondence: ltsipis@aegean.gr

Abstract: The cooperative aerial and device-to-device (D2D) networks employing non-orthogonal multiple access (NOMA) are expected to play an essential role in next-generation wireless networks. Moreover, machine learning (ML) techniques, such as artificial neural networks (ANN), can significantly enhance network performance and efficiency in fifth-generation (5G) wireless networks and beyond. This paper studies an ANN-based unmanned aerial vehicle (UAV) placement scheme to enhance an integrated UAV-D2D NOMA cooperative network. The proposed placement scheme selection (PSS) method for integrating the UAV into the cooperative network combines supervised and unsupervised ML techniques. Specifically, a supervised classification approach is employed utilizing a two-hidden layered ANN with 63 neurons evenly distributed among the layers. The output class of the ANN is utilized to determine the appropriate unsupervised learning method—either k-means or k-medoids—to be employed. This specific ANN layout has been observed to exhibit an accuracy of 94.12%, the highest accuracy among the ANN models evaluated, making it highly recommended for accurate PSS predictions in urban locations. Furthermore, the proposed cooperative scheme allows pairs of users to be simultaneously served through NOMA from the UAV, which acts as an aerial base station. At the same time, the D2D cooperative transmission for each NOMA pair is activated to improve the overall communication quality. Comparisons with conventional orthogonal multiple access (OMA) and alternative unsupervised machine-learning based-UAV-D2D NOMA cooperative networks show that significant sum rate and spectral efficiency gains can be harvested through the proposed method under varying D2D bandwidth allocations.

Keywords: machine learning; UAV placement; artificial neural network (ANN); deep neural network (DNN); NOMA; cooperative communications; D2D

Citation: Tsipi, L.; Karavolos, M.; Bithas, P.S.; Vouyioukas, D. Machine Learning-Based Methods for Enhancement of UAV-NOMA and D2D Cooperative Networks. *Sensors* **2023**, *23*, 3014. https://doi.org/10.3390/s23063014

Academic Editors: Giuseppe Caso, Anna Brunstrom, Özgü Alay, Harilaos Koumaras, Almudena Díaz Zayas and Valerio Frascolla

Received: 20 December 2022
Revised: 6 March 2023
Accepted: 7 March 2023
Published: 10 March 2023

Copyright: © 2023 by the authors. Licensee MDPI, Basel, Switzerland. This article is an open access article distributed under the terms and conditions of the Creative Commons Attribution (CC BY) license (https://creativecommons.org/licenses/by/4.0/).

1. Introduction

Undoubtedly, the utilization of unmanned aerial vehicles (UAVs) as UAV flying base stations (UFBSs) is of potential interest in the context of new-generation wireless communication systems. UAV-enabled wireless communication systems can provide wireless coverage extension, capacity enhancement, communication restoration during disaster events, and aerial data collection within the framework of Internet of Things (IoT) applications [1,2]. In contrast to conventional wireless communication systems that depend on fixed terrestrial infrastructures, UFBSs are dynamic and simple to deploy and reconfigure. Thus, their use introduces several degrees of freedom in terms of flexibility, wide coverage, and communication restoration during a disaster and temporary events. However, the anticipated advantages of deploying UFBSs are heavily contingent on their precise location within the region of interest to offer terrestrial users reliable and high-quality communication [3].

1.1. Background

Identifying the proper horizontal and vertical locations of UFBSs concerning other ground or flying objects is one of the most challenging parts of establishing UAV-based communication systems that achieve optimal or near-optimal performance. Hence, several research attempts in the technical literature have proposed various UFBSs placement techniques to maximize the aerial network communication performance and exploit the advantages provided [4–10]. The authors in [4] proposed a low-complexity method that optimizes UAVs' 2D location, admission control, and power allocation using penalty function and successive convex approximation techniques. This approach maximizes the quality of service for terrestrial users and is effective, as confirmed by simulation results. Furthermore, the authors in [5] jointly optimized the 2D locations and the transmit power of multiple UFBSs to maximize the system sum rate using a distributed learning method that achieves stochastic stability. Collisions between the UFBSs were prevented by determining their respective heights in advance. Moreover, in [6], the 2D placement and the power allocation of the UFBSs are jointly optimized to increase the UAV network's performance. The proposed method consists of two sub-processes. The first sub-process finds the optimal 2D position, while the second further determines the optimal power allocation to maximize the terrestrial users' total sum rate.

The works [4–6] have presented conventional optimization methods to determine the optimal location of the UFBSs. Notwithstanding, other approaches focus on leveraging the machine learning (ML) advantages to deal with the UFBSs placement problem [7–10]. More specifically, the authors in [7] suggested a UAV-aided offloading approach for terrestrial networks that uses an unsupervised ML method to optimize UFBS deployment in high-traffic areas. The proposed method is divided into two sub-processes—user clustering employing the k-medoids algorithm and cluster selection scheme for identifying the UFBSs with the highest offloading factor. Another ML-based solution that aims to offload terrestrial base stations (TBSs) is proposed in [8]. The proposed scheme is based on the weighted expectation–maximization algorithm and estimates both the user distribution and the downlink traffic demand to determine the optimal UFBSs location. Similarly, the authors of [9] studied the joint 3D placement and UAV-user associations in UAV-assisted networks. For the 2D positioning of UAVs, a modified version of the k-means algorithm is utilized, while for the altitude optimization problem, they propose a game theoretic approach. Simulation results have shown that the proposed scheme outperforms other trivial cases where users are associated, over iterations, with the closest UAV. Lastly, in [10], UFBSs are treated as long-term evolution (LTE)-advanced heterogeneous networks (HetNet) to cover safety incidents. In this approach, the UFBSs are deterministically positioned on a precalculated hexagonal grid with fixed placement points, restricting the placement optimality.

UFBS optimal placement increases the possibility of obtaining LoS conditions, thus enhancing the physical communication link quality. Therefore, effective resource management techniques should be utilized to optimally exploit the improved physical links and provide highly spectral efficient communication to several ground users. Towards the goal of intelligent integration of the UFBSs into fifth-generation (5G), beyond 5G (B5G), and sixth-generation (6G) communication systems, non-orthogonal multiple access (NOMA) is expected to be a fundamental radio access technique [11,12]. The basic principle of NOMA is to serve multiple users simultaneously in a single resource block (space/time/frequency) by multiplexing them in the power domain. To accomplish this objective, superposition coding (SC) is performed at the transmitter and successive interference cancellation (SIC) at the receiver [13]. Moreover, combining NOMA with high spectral efficient multiple-input multiple-output (MIMO) techniques, such as quadrature spatial modulation (QSM) [14,15], can further enhance the spectral efficiency and increase the capacity of non-terrestrial wireless networks [3].

Recent research attempts have investigated the use of NOMA to enhance the performance of UAV-enabled communication systems [16–18]. The authors of [16] have studied a NOMA-based UAV-enabled communication network. Specifically, a path-following algorithm is proposed to solve the max-min rate optimization problem, which is subjected to the constraints of the total power, available bandwidth, UAV altitude, and antenna beamwidth. The numerical results have shown that the NOMA scheme outperforms OMA, in terms of achievable rate, for different system parameters. Subsequently, the authors in [17] developed a novel NOMA UAV-assisted offloading architecture for cellular networks to significantly enhance the system's spectrum efficiency. Specifically, the 3D trajectory design and power allocation optimization problem are formulated to maximize the system sum rate. For this purpose, ML-based methods, namely k-means and mutual deep Q-network (MDQN), are utilized to deal with this problem. Another strategy [18] proposes a resource allocation scheme for a UAV-assisted full-duplex (FD) NOMA system to improve spectrum efficiency, reduce terrestrial users' power requirements, and maintain quality of service (QoS) requirements. The method utilizes a joint uplink/downlink stepwise optimization approach to solve the NP-hard optimization problem. Simulation results demonstrate that the proposed method outperforms other methods in terms of spectrum and energy efficiency.

Besides the optimal placement of the UFBS and the selection of an efficient radio access technique, leveraging physical transmission techniques can further enhance the overall UAV communication quality. Device-to-device (D2D) communication is one such technique. For instance, in highly dense urban areas where several devices coexist within a distance of a few meters, they can benefit through the utilization of a cooperative transmission scheme. Consequently, integrating D2D communications into UAV networks has recently attracted a lot of attention, and related issues have also been studied in the literature [19–23]. In [19], the authors have derived the closed-form expressions for the outage probability in a UAV-assisted NOMA network with D2D communication capabilities. Also, they have formulated a power control optimization problem to maximize the D2D sum rate while ensuring a minimum rate for each UAV-connected user. The proposed method is computationally efficient but has a lower sum rate than other methods, as this has been confirmed via the simulation results. Furthermore, the energy-efficient resource allocation problem in D2D communications underlying UAV-enabled networks is investigated in [20]. Especially, this study attempts to optimize the overall energy efficiency of all D2D pairs while ensuring the secrecy rates of all users via combined power control and channel allocation. Accordingly, the Lagrangian dual and Kuhn–Munkres algorithms are utilized to solve this problem. The simulation results have shown that the proposed approach performs better than other benchmark methods. Moreover, the authors of [21] exploited the advantages that UAV-assisted communications offer and effectively combined with the NOMA technique. Particularly, they present a D2D-enhanced UAV-NOMA network architecture in which D2D is added to improve the dispatching efficiency of files. So, a graph-based file dispatching protocol is provided to decrease the UAV-assisted file dispatching mission time and control interference. Simulation results confirm the benefits of the proposed D2D-enhanced UAV NOMA network architecture and the efficacy of the planned protocol. The research presented in [22] proposed a novel approach to address disaster management issues utilizing a UAV-assisted SWIPT-enabled NOMA-based D2D network. They formulated a nonlinear power allocation optimization problem that maximized the system's energy efficiency performance and solved it using the Dinkelbach approach. Simulation results show that the advanced NOMA system outperforms the ordinary NOMA scheme. Alternately, ref. [23] has investigated a sequential optimization problem for resource allocation and communication mode selection in a UAV-assisted D2D cellular network to improve energy efficiency and ensure satisfactory transmission rates for all ground UEs. They proposed a reinforcement learning-based scheme to solve this problem, which has been shown to be effective through simulated results.

1.2. Contributions

As presented in the previously detailed literature review, several studies on standalone UAV networks utilize unsupervised machine learning methods such as k-means and k-medoids to place the UAV in the region of interest. However, applying these algorithms individually to a UAV-NOMA and D2D cooperative network might degrade the overall network quality while rendering the D2D network unnecessary. Hence, to achieve enhanced network quality, it is vital to consider the interactions and trade-offs between the two algorithms and the network elements and adopt an integrated approach [7,24].

Concerning the operation of the two placement methods, both k-means and k-medoids are centroid-based clustering techniques. The two methods are fed with the terrestrial users' coordinates as an input feature to find the point where the UFBS should be placed. In such scenarios, k-means behaves well when the terrestrial users form spherical clusters without outliers [24]. In contrast, k-medoids is robust to the outliers and correctly represents the cluster center [7]. Hence, by efficiently combining k-means and k-medoids algorithms, the UAV can be positioned in the most suitable location to ensure effective coverage for D2D communication. This combined approach considers both the similarities in the data points as well as the actual data points themselves and potential outliers or noise in the data. As a result, it leads to a more precise and reliable UAV placement. Thus conspicuously, the combination of these two algorithms exploits the strengths of both k-means and k-medoids in determining the ideal UAV placement [25].

Nevertheless, whenever the UFBS needs to be relocated, it is necessary to determine the most suitable placement method by comparing the results obtained from both clustering algorithms, i.e., k-means and k-medoids. This decision-making process requires the real-time execution of both ML methods, thus increasing the overall time complexity. Also, k-means and k-medoids are clustering algorithms that can be used to group data points together based on their similarities. However, deciding which algorithm to use can be complex and may depend on several factors. Essentially, when the dataset contains non-spherical clusters, outliers, or clusters of different sizes, it is difficult to model a decision-making approach with a simple threshold boundary. Hence, this can make it challenging to identify the unsupervised ML method that should be utilized.

Inspired by this observation, the placement scheme selection (PSS) can be regarded as a supervised classification problem, which can be handled through a fully connected artificial neural network (ANN) to enhance the overall system QoS. ANNs can be used to predict which clustering algorithm to use between k-means and k-medoids because they are able to learn the underlying patterns in the data and identify which algorithm is better suited for the given dataset. Moreover, ANNs can capture complex relationships between the input data and the output cluster labels, which can be difficult to model with a simple threshold boundary. Consequently, this paper presents and analyzes an ANN-based UAV placement scheme to enhance the network performance of an integrated UAV-NOMA and D2D cooperative network. The proposed method intelligently integrates the UFBS into the cooperative network by efficiently combining the k-means and k-medoids unsupervised ML algorithms. Concerning the UAV-NOMA and D2D cooperative network, pairs of users are simultaneously served through the UFBS, which utilizes a NOMA optimal user pairing and power allocation strategy. At the same time, terrestrial cooperation is enabled by adopting the D2D communication paradigm, thus improving the overall communication quality. To the authors' knowledge, this is the first time supervised machine learning techniques, such as the ANN, and unsupervised machine learning algorithms, such as k-means and k-medoids, are combined to improve the integrated UAV-NOMA D2D cooperative network. Specifically, the following major contributions are provided:

- An ANN-based UFBS placement framework is established in order to improve the overall communication quality of a UAV-NOMA and D2D cooperative network. Towards this end, supervised ML algorithms (ANN) and unsupervised ML algorithms (k-means and k-medoids) are combined.
- State-of-the-art data mining strategies are presented to transform raw data into an intelligible format for ANN algorithms and avoid underfitting and overfitting drawbacks. To the best of our knowledge, it is the first time that specific strategies have been provided in the field of UAV-NOMA and D2D cooperative networks.

- A step-by-step approach on how to handle the issue of hyperparameter tuning in ANN models is provided to enhance the predictability of the UFBS placement procedure.
- For the UFBS NOMA transmission, an optimal power allocation and user pairing strategy is considered [26]. Also, the proposed scheme promotes the cooperation between aerial and D2D networks.

1.3. Structure

The remainder of this paper is organized as follows. Section 2 presents the considered system model, while Section 3 outlines the unsupervised machine-learning-based methods for the UFBS placement procedure. Next, the data collection, data pre-processing, learning, validation, and testing procedures, and the performance metrics of the proposed ANN-based placement scheme selection are outlined in Section 4. Finally, simulation results are given in Section 5, followed by conclusions and future directions in Section 6.

2. System Model

From the system point of view, we consider a cooperative UAV and D2D-aided wireless communication system, where the UFBS is mainly responsible for communication. The D2D scheme is employed between the ground mobile terminals (GMTs) to achieve higher data rates and spectral efficiency without the involvement of any additional terrestrial or flying base station.

The wireless network architecture is depicted in Figure 1, where a two-tier heterogeneous network is formed, operating in two different and non-overlapping spectrum bands. From now on, these two ways of communication will be referred to as UFBS NOMA transmission when the GMTs receive the data directly from the UFBS through the NOMA scheme and the D2D cooperative transmission when the GMTs cooperate to improve the overall communication quality. Concerning the UFBS NOMA transmission, all GMTs are served by the UFBS via the air-to-ground (A2G) link, utilizing the NOMA technique according to an optimal power allocation and user pairing strategy [27,28]. More specifically, the total available UFBS' bandwidth B_u is divided into K slots, equally distributed to the GMT pairs, as depicted in Figure 1. Each GMT pair k ($1 \leq k \leq K$) consists of a strong GMT_i and a weak GMT_j ground terminal, with $i \neq j$, which are sharing the same sub-channel in the frequency/time domain. The UFBS classifies the GMTs of each pair as either weak or strong based on the A2G channel conditions. Following the NOMA principle, in each pair of users the strong GMT_i first decodes the signal of the weak GMT_j from the received superposition-coded signal and then performs successive interference cancellation (SIC) to retrieve its signal. Hence, leveraging this knowledge, the utilization of the D2D cooperative transmission scheme on the ground can further enhance the communication quality of the weak users of the system. Concerning the D2D ground communication procedure, each strong GMT_i decodes and forwards (DF) the received UFBS's signal to the weak GMT_j of its pair, thus providing reception diversity through the ground assistance. Consequently, each weak GMT_j in each pair will receive two different copies of the same signal, one from the UFBS and the other from its pair, i.e., the strong GMT_i, which acts as a relay.

From a technical standpoint, the communication system consists of $N = 2K$ GMTs, where K is the number of GMT pairs and a UFBS located in an R-radius circle region of interest A. Each GMT_l ($1 \leq l \leq N$) is randomly placed in the region of interest, and its location is expressed as $u_l = (x_l^u, y_l^u, z_l^u) \in A$. The 3D location of the UFBS is denoted as $p_1 = (x_1^p, y_1^p, z_1^p) \in A$. The UFBS is equipped with an antenna with transmit gain G_t^u, and total available transmit power P_u. Also, the downlink operating frequency of the UFBS is F_u. Furthermore, the operating frequency, the total available bandwidth, and the transmit power for the D2D transmission are denoted as F_d, B_d, and P_d, respectively. Moreover, the GMTs are equipped with two antennas, one for the reception of the UFBS's signals with reception gain G_r^u, and the other for D2D communication, i.e., for transmission and reception, with transmit and receive gain $G_t^d = G_r^d$. We consider that the common antenna for transmission and reception regarding D2D communication is implemented through a radio frequency (RF) switch. Hence, each GMT can only transmit or receive during a D2D frequency/time slot.

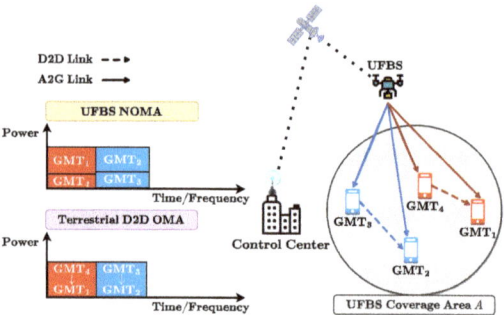

Figure 1. System model.

Finally, the seamless communication between the UFBS and the GMTs requires a reliable and efficient backhaul network. In this regard, we propose the use of zero-touch commissioning (ZTC) cloud radio access network (C-RAN) for the UAV backhaul, as it can provide efficient and automated network management [25,29]. The ZTC-C-RAN model comprises a control element that performs the ZTC procedures, including the instantiation, configuration, and synchronization of the UAV and D2D cooperative network as well as the placement of the UFBS in the region of interest A. Furthermore, the proposed ZTC-C-RAN is benefited from the satellite communication as a backhaul relay between the UFBS and the control center, providing ultra-reliable low latency communication (URLLC) and enhanced mobile broadband (eMBB) network slices responsible for routing the control and data plane information to the terrestrial and aerial segments of the proposed scheme.

2.1. Air-to-Ground and Device-to-Device Channels

The channel between UFBS and its associated GMTs is characterized as an A2G channel. To conduct performance analysis, the channel complex coefficient for each GMT_l ($1 \leq l \leq N$) is denoted as h_l^u, and follows the complex Gaussian distribution with zero mean and unit variance $\sim \mathcal{CN}(0,1)$. Additionally, the path loss attenuation of the UFBS signal is modeled using the elevation angle-based path loss model [25] in an urban environment, and is represented as follows:

$$\text{PL}_l^u(h, r_l) = \text{FSL}_l + \eta_{\text{LoS}} P_{\text{LoS}}(h, r_l) + \eta_{\text{NLoS}}(1 - P_{\text{LoS}}(h, r_l)), \quad (1)$$

where FSL_l is the free space pathloss given by $\text{FSL}_l = 20 \log\left(\frac{4\pi d_l F_u}{c}\right)$, d_l is the transmission distance between UFBS and each GMT_l ($1 \leq l \leq N$), and c is the speed of light. In addition, the η_{LoS} and η_{NLoS} coefficients reflect the extra losses for LoS and Non-LoS (NLoS) air-to-ground transmission links, and they depend on the propagation environment. Moreover, P_{LoS} denotes the probability of the LoS component between the UFBS and each GMT_l and is modelled as a function of the altitude h of the UFBS and the 2D Euclidean distance r_l between the UFBS and each GMT_l. Hence, P_{LoS} can be expressed as follows [30]:

$$P_{\text{LoS}}(h, r_l) = \frac{1}{1 + a \exp(-b(\arctan(\frac{h}{r_l}) - a))}, \quad (2)$$

where a, b are parameters determined by the propagation environment. Regarding the D2D link between the strong GMT_i and weak GMT_j of each pair k ($1 \leq k \leq K$) the multipath fading is modeled by the complex Gaussian distribution with zero mean and unit variance $\sim \mathcal{CN}(0,1)$. The complex channel coefficient for the D2D link is denoted as h_k^d. Moreover the path loss model for the D2D communication of each pair k ($1 \leq k \leq K$), used from [27], is as follows:

$$\mathrm{PL}_k^d(d_k^e) = 157 + \log_{10}(d_k^e), \quad (3)$$

where d_k^e is the distance in km between the strong GMT_i and the weak GMT_j of each pair k ($1 \leq k \leq K$). Furthermore, the A2G and the D2D links under consideration are assumed to be degraded by additive white Gaussian noise (AWGN), which is statistically modeled by the normal distribution $\sim \mathcal{N}\left(0, \sigma_q^2\right)$ with $q = \{u, d\}$. The noise power of the A2G and D2D receivers are given by $N_u = k_B T_u B_u$ and $N_d = k_B T_d B_d$, respectively; where k_B is the Boltzmann constant, and T_u, T_d are the A2G and D2D receiver system noise temperatures, respectively. Therefore, the corresponding noise variances for each receiver type are $\sigma_u = \sqrt{N_u}$ and $\sigma_d = \sqrt{N_d}$.

2.2. Transmission and Reception Structure

As previously stated, the UFBS forms K user pairs, where each pair k ($1 \leq k \leq K$) consists of one strong GMT_i and one weak GMT_j. Therefore, the wireless communication system under consideration comprises K strong GMTs and K weak GMTs (2K GMTs in total). Additionally, we assume that the UFBS transmits to the N GMTs without any delays. Such an assumption is acceptable for a broadcast system in which the UFBS transmits the information repeatedly, and the GMTs get this information immediately. Thus, the superimposed NOMA signal, transmitted to each pair k by the UFBS, is expressed as:

$$x_k^u = \sqrt{G_t^u}\left(\sqrt{\alpha_i P_u} s_i + \sqrt{\alpha_j P_u} s_j\right), \quad (4)$$

where $s_i, s_j \in \mathbb{C}$ are the signals of GMT_i and GMT_j, respectively. Also, α_i and α_j denote the fraction of the total UFBS transmit power P_u allocated to each GMT, with $\alpha_i + \alpha_j = 1$.

The signals received by the strong GMT_i and the weak GMT_j for each k pair are obtained as follows:

$$y_i^u = \sqrt{\frac{G_r^u}{\mathrm{PL}_i^u}} h_i^u x_k^u + z^u, \quad (5)$$

$$y_j^u = \sqrt{\frac{G_r^u}{\mathrm{PL}_j^u}} h_j^u x_k^u + z^u, \quad (6)$$

where $z^u \sim \mathcal{N}(0, \sigma_u^2)$ represents the AWGN of the A2G link. Simultaneously, the received signal at the weak GMT_j when the D2D cooperative transmission is activated, is given by the following expression:

$$y_j^d = \sqrt{\frac{G_r^d}{\mathrm{PL}_k^d}} h_k^d x_j^d + z^d, \quad (7)$$

where $z^d \sim \mathcal{N}(0, \sigma_d^2)$ stands for the AWGN noise in the D2D link. Since we have considered the decode and forward (DF) operation regarding the D2D links, the strong user GMT_i of each pair k immediately decodes the received UFBS NOMA signal x_k^u and then estimates the weak user's signal $\hat{s}_j$. Subsequently, the strong user GMT_i forwards $\hat{s}_j$ to the weak user GMT_j through transmitting the signal:

$$x_j^d = \sqrt{G_t^d P_d}\, \hat{s}_j. \quad (8)$$

2.3. Signal-to-Interference-Plus-Noise Ratio (SINR) Analysis

In general, for each GMT$_l$ $(1 \leq l \leq N)$ in the considered communication system, the A2G channel gain is calculated as:

$$\Gamma_l^u = \frac{G_t^u G_r^u}{PL_l^u N_u} |h_l^u|^2, \qquad (9)$$

including additional gains, losses, and the noise power of the UFBS receiver N_u. Hence, using (5), the instantaneous signal-to-noise ratio (SNR) γ_i^u of the strong GMT$_i$ to detect its own signal s_i, assuming perfect SIC, is given as follows:

$$\gamma_i^u = \alpha_i P_u \Gamma_i^u \qquad (10)$$

where Γ_i^u is the A2G channel gain of the strong GMT$_i$, which involves the noise power of the UFBS receiver N_u, as it can be observed in (9). Furthermore, the instantaneous signal-to-interference plus noise ratio (SINR) γ_k^u, for detecting the signal s_j of the weak user GMT$_j$ on the strong user GMT$_i$, is expressed as:

$$\gamma_k^u = \frac{\alpha_j P_u \Gamma_i^u}{\alpha_i P_u \Gamma_i^u + 1}. \qquad (11)$$

Moreover, the SINR γ_j^u at the weak user GMT$_j$, for detecting its own signal s_j from the UFBS is obtained by:

$$\gamma_j^u = \frac{\alpha_j P_u \Gamma_j^u}{\alpha_i P_u \Gamma_j^u + 1}, \qquad (12)$$

where Γ_j^u is the A2G channel gain for the weak GMT$_j$. Furthermore, the SINR γ_k^d at the weak user GMT$_j$ for detecting its signal, which is relayed by the strong user GMT$_i$ in the same pair k, equals:

$$\gamma_k^d = P_d \Phi_k, \qquad (13)$$

where Φ_k is the channel gain of the D2D link between the strong GMT$_i$ and the weak GMT$_j$ belonging to the same NOMA pair k $(1 \leq k \leq K)$ and is expressed as:

$$\Phi_k = \frac{G_t^d G_r^d}{PL_k^d N_d} |h_k^d|^2, \qquad (14)$$

2.4. Achievable Rates Analysis

As the SINR expressions of the strong GMT$_i$ and the weak GMT$_j$ for each pair k have been determined, it is straightforward to compute the corresponding achievable rates. The theoretical achievable rate of each GMT$_l$, when we consider a conventional UAV-OMA transmission scheme, can be mathematically expressed as:

$$R_l^o = \frac{B_u}{2K} \log_2(1 + P_u \Gamma_l^u), \qquad (15)$$

In contrast, in the case of a UAV-NOMA scheme, the maximum downlink NOMA achievable rates which succeed by the strong GMT$_i$ and the weak GMT$_j$ through the A2G channel are:

$$R_i^u = \frac{B_u}{K} \log_2(1 + \gamma_i^u), \qquad (16)$$

$$R_j^u = \frac{B_u}{K} \log_2\left(1 + \gamma_j^u\right), \qquad (17)$$

respectively. Moreover, for the strong GMT$_i$, the achievable rate of the weak GMT$_j$'s signal is equal to:

$$R_k^u = \frac{B_u}{K} \log_2(1 + \gamma_k^u). \tag{18}$$

Also, the maximum achievable rate R_k^d concerning the established D2D link between the strong user GMT$_i$ and the weak user GMT$_j$ is expressed as:

$$R_k^d = \frac{B_d}{K} \log_2\left(1 + \gamma_k^d\right), \tag{19}$$

Since the weak GMT$_j$ can receive its signal directly from the UFBS or via the strong GMT$_i$ of the pair it belongs to utilizing the D2D communication capabilities, GMT$_j$'s device always chooses to be served by the link that offers the highest achievable rate. Thus, it holds that the maximum achievable rate of each weak GMT$_j$ that belongs to the NOMA pair k, combining the UAV-NOMA with cooperative D2D scheme, can be calculated as follows:

$$R_j^{\text{COPD2D}} = \max\left(R_j^u, \Lambda_j\right), \tag{20}$$

where Λ_j is the achievable rate through the D2D communication with the strong GMT$_i$. In fact, the weak GMT$_j$'s signal is decoded on the strong GMT$_i$, and the D2D communication provides the channel to forward this decoded signal from the strong GMT$_i$ to the weak GMT$_j$. As a result, the weak GMT$_j$ can never receive a rate greater than R_k^u, meaning that $\Lambda_j \leq R_k^u$. Essentially, the quality of the D2D communication will determine whether the weak GMT$_j$ will enjoy the maximum possible rate R_k^u or less. Specifically, we can recognize the following cases:

Case 1. *The D2D channel is profitable for the weak user, i.e., $R_k^d \geq R_k^u$, and the achievable rate of the weak user is $\Lambda_j = R_k^u$. This happens because the weak user can never receive a rate greater than the achievable decoding rate of its signal on the strong user.*

Case 2. *The D2D channel is not profitable for the weak user, i.e., $R_k^d < R_k^u$, and the achievable rate of the weak user is equal to the transmission rate that the D2D communication can provide, i.e., $\Lambda_j = R_k^d$. In this case, we observe that the achievable rate of the weak user is limited based on the capabilities of the D2D communication channel.*

Based on the above cases concerning the use of D2D communication for receiving the signal on the weak user, we observe that the minimum rate between the achievable rates R_k^d and R_k^u is always selected. Therefore, in the case where D2D communication is used, it follows that the achievable rate of the weak user is equal to $\Lambda_j = \min\left(R_k^u, R_k^d\right)$. By substituting Λ_j in (20):

$$R_j^{\text{COPD2D}} = \max\left(R_j^u, \min\left(R_k^u, R_k^d\right)\right). \tag{21}$$

Utilizing the UAV-NOMA and D2D-aided scheme the total sum rate which is succeeded on each pair k is equal to:

$$R_k = R_i^u + R_j^{\text{COPD2D}}. \tag{22}$$

Therefore, the total system sum rate that can be achieved by utilizing the aforementioned cooperative scheme is:

$$R_s = \sum_{k=1}^{K} R_k \tag{23}$$

2.5. User Pairing Policy

So far, we have noted that the system's GMTs are separated into K groups of two members each, but we have not specified how the GMTs are allocated to each group. Hence, in this sub section, we propose the maximum weight perfect matching (MWPM) pairing policy which takes into account both the A2G and D2D channel conditions. The primary objective is to maximize the system's total sum rate. Therefore, a matching technique must be implemented between the GMTs in order to discover those user pairs that optimize the system's overall sum rate. The MWPM method generates $\binom{N}{2}$ pairings between the N GMTs and retains the K that maximize the system sum rate. For this purpose, it is necessary to define a binary matrix Θ that represents the pairing relationship between the GMTs as follows:

$$\theta_{i,j} = \begin{cases} 1 & \text{GMT}_i \quad \text{paired with} \quad \text{GMT}_j \\ 0 & \text{otherwise} \end{cases} \quad (24)$$

The dimension of the pairing matrix Θ that is retrieved from the MWPM method is equal to $N \times N$. Moreover the diagonal elements of the pairing matrix Θ are all equal to zero because one GMT cannot pair itself. Also, due to the fact that the matrix components $\theta_{i,j}$ and $\theta_{j,i}$ both pertain the same GMT pairing, it can also be argued that $\theta_{i,j} = \theta_{j,i}$. Therefore, the MWPM pairing policy can be expressed as the following maximization problem:

$$\begin{aligned} \max_{\theta_{i,j}} \quad & \sum_{i=1}^{N} \sum_{j=i+1}^{N} \theta_{i,j} \left(R_i^u + R_j^{COPD2D} \right), \\ \text{s.t.} \quad & \sum_{j=1}^{i-1} \theta_{j,i} + \sum_{j=i+1}^{N} \theta_{i,j} = 1, \forall i = 1,2,3, \cdots, N \\ & \theta_{i,j} \in \{0,1\}, \quad 1 \leq i,j \leq N. \end{aligned} \quad (25)$$

The maximization problem (25) can be regarded as a matching problem in a fully connected undirected graph $G(V, E)$, where the total number of vertices is equal to the total number of GMTs $|V| = N$. E is the set of all feasible edges $\theta_{i,j}$, connecting all users to each other with $i \neq j$ and $i,j = \{1,2,...,N\}$. In order to solve this issue optimally, we use the Blossom algorithm to obtain an optimal pairing strategy between the GMTs [31].

2.6. Power Allocation Strategy

Concerning the UFBS NOMA transmission, the objective is to maximize the sum rate of each pair of GMTs under the condition that both GMTs enjoy at least the rate utilizing the conventional UFBS OMA transmission. This is an optimization problem which is mathematically expressed as follows:

$$\begin{aligned} \max_{\alpha_i} \quad & R_i^u + R_j^u, \\ \text{s.t.} \quad & R_i^u \geq R_i^o, \\ & R_j^u \geq R_j^o, \\ & 0 \leq \alpha_i \leq 1. \end{aligned} \quad (26)$$

The solution to this problem has been obtained in [26,27] by identifying the optimal value of α_i, as:

$$\alpha_i = \frac{\sqrt{1 + \Gamma_j^u P_u} - 1}{\Gamma_j^u P_u}. \quad (27)$$

To conclude, in Table 1, the definitions of most of the parameters involved in this study are included.

Table 1. System model parameters definition.

Parameter	Definition
A	Circle region of interest
u_l	3D location of each GMT_l
p_1	3D location of UFBS
N	Total number of GMTs
K	Total number of GMT pairs
G_t^u	UFBS transmit antenna gain
B_u	UFBS bandwidth.
P_u	UFBS transmit power
F_u	UFBS operating frequency
B_d	D2D bandwidth
P_d	D2D transmit power
F_d	D2D operating frequency
G_t^d	D2D transmit antenna gain
G_r^d	D2D receive antenna gain
N_u	A2G receivers noise power
N_d	D2D receivers noise power
PL_l^u	A2G path loss for each GMT_l ($1 \leq l \leq N$)
PL_k^d	D2D path loss for each k pair of users ($1 \leq k \leq K$)
x_k^u	Superimposed NOMA signal of each k pair~(1 k K)
α_i	Power allocation factor of the strong GMT_i
Γ_l^u	A2G channel gain for each GMT_l ($1 \leq l \leq N$)
y_i^u	The received signal by the strong GMT_i from the UFBS
y_j^u	The received signal by the weak GMT_j from the UFBS
y_j^d	The received signal by the weak GMT_j from his pair's strong GMT_i when the D2D cooperative transmission is activated.
γ_i^u	SNR of the A2G link of the strong GMT_i assuming perfect SIC
γ_k^u	SINR of the A2G link of the strong GMT_i for detecting the signal s_j from his pair's weak GMT_j
γ_j^u	SINR of the A2G link of the strong GMT_i for detecting its own signal
γ_k^d	SINR of the D2D link of the weak GMT_j for detecting its own signal, which is relayed by his pair's strong GMT_i
Φ_k	D2D channel gain for the weak GMT_j when the D2D cooperative transmission is activated
R_i^u	Maximum downlink NOMA achievable rate which succeed by the strong GMT_i through the A2G channel
R_j^u	Maximum downlink NOMA achievable rate which succeed by the weak GMT_j through the A2G channel
R_k^u	Maximum downlink NOMA achievable rate of the weak GMT_j's signal which succeed by his pair's strong GMT_i through the A2G channel
R_k^d	Maximum achievable rate which succeed by the weak GMT_j through the D2D channel

3. UFBS Placement Procedure

In this section, we analyze the placement procedure of the UFBS in the region of interest A. For this purpose, we propose an UFBS placement procedure that is divided into two sub-processes. The first sub-process aims to find the 2D plane position of the UFBS. For this purpose, k-means and k-medoids algorithms are exploited and assessed [7,9]. The second sub-process seeks to discover the UFBS's height aiming to improve coverage and communication quality, thus determining its location in the three-dimensional space.

3.1. 2D UFBS Placement

3.1.1. k-Means Analysis and Setup

This sub-subsection describes the UFBS 2D placement procedure utilizing the k-means algorithm. In more detail, the k-means algorithm is fed with the coordinates u_l ($1 \leq l \leq N$) of all GMTs located within the region of interest A. Subsequently, the algorithm groups the users into a cluster and returns as output the centroid point $p_1^c \in A$ where $p_1^c = (x_1^{p_1^c}, y_1^{p_1^c}, z_1^{p_1^c})$. The goal of the k-means method is to minimize the centroid-point to group distances metric, expressed as $\sum_{u_l \in U} \|u_l - p_1^c\|^2$. In particular, this expression represents the objective function of the following minimization problem:

$$\arg\min_{p_1^c \in A} \sum_{u_l \in U} \|u_l - p_1^c\|^2. \tag{28}$$

Therefore, the UFBS should be placed in p_1^c to achieve improved communication quality. The operation of the 2D UFBS placement process using the k-means algorithm is summarized in Algorithm 1.

Algorithm 1 2D UFBS placement process through the k-means algorithm

---

1: **input:** The set of coordinates of all GMTs $U = \{u_1, u_2, \ldots, u_N\}$, and the number of UFBSs Y
2: $\epsilon = 10^{-6}$
3: $t = 0$
4: Initialize Y centroid points $C^t = \{p_1^c, p_2^c, \ldots, p_Y^c\} \subseteq U$, randomly
5: **repeat**
6:     $S_k = \emptyset, \forall k = 1, 2, \cdots, Y$
7:     **for** $i \leftarrow 1$ to N **do**
8:         $k^* = \arg\min_{k=1\ldots Y} \|u_i - C_k^t\|$
9:         $S_{k^*} = S_{k^*} \cup \{u_i\}$
10:    **end for**
11:    **for** $k \leftarrow 1$ to Y **do**
12:        $C_k^t = \frac{1}{|S_k|} \sum_{u_l \in S_k} u_l$.
13:    **end for**
14:    $t = t + 1$
15: **until** $C^t - C^{t-1} \leq \epsilon$
16: **output:** A set of centroid points that the Y UFBSs will be deployed C^t.

For simplicity, it is assumed that the number of UFBS $Y = 1$. However, as can be shown in Algorithm 1, the k-means algorithm can be straightforwardly applied to scenarios with $Y > 1$. Hence, in our case, the centroid p_1^c is given by the following three steps:

Step 1: Determine the coordinate Y_u of the UFBS as follows: $Y_u = \frac{\sum_{i=1}^{N} y_i^u}{N}$

Step 2: Determine the coordinate X_u of the UFBS as follows: $X_u = \frac{\sum_{i=1}^{N} x_i^u}{N}$

Step 3: Configure the point p_1^c that the UFBS should be placed as follows: $p_1^c = (X_u, Y_u, h)$, where h is the initial height of the UFBS before the 3D UFBS placement procedure.

Finally, it is essential to acknowledge that the choice of the optimal number of clusters for a clustering problem is not straightforward and may be influenced by a range of factors, including the specific requirements and objectives of the analysis, as well as the inherent properties of the data. Within the context of our system model, the user locations are randomly distributed within a circular region of interest, forming a single cluster. This characteristic of the data renders the choice of Y equal to 1 in k-means clustering a sensible and appropriate decision, as it adequately captures the underlying structure of the data. The resulting cluster is representative of the overall distribution of users and adequately reflects the inherent properties of the dataset. In this particular scenario, using a single cluster is sufficient to accurately and effectively represent the nature of the user distribution and therefore is a suitable approach to analyze the data [32].

3.1.2. k-Medoids Analysis and Setup

In this sub-subsection, the basic principles of the k-medoids algorithm are presented. The k-medoids method can be used for the 2D placement of the UFBS in A in the same fashion as k-means. However, the way that the UFBS placement point p_1 is selected differs between the two approaches. As previously stated, in the k-means UFBS placement scheme, the centroid point p_1^c is the empirical mean of the coordinates U of the GMTs in A. However, in k-medoids, it is one of the actual GMT$_l$ ($1 \leq l \leq N$), and it is called medoid point p_1^m. Specifically, in k-means, the point-to-group-centroid distance is assessed concerning a virtual point $p_1^c \in A$, while in k-medoids, it is measured concerning one of the actual data points $u_l \in A$ ($p_1^m = u_l$) where ($1 \leq l \leq N$), i.e., actual GMTs location. Similarly to the k-means algorithm, the goal of the k-medoid method is to minimize the medoid-point to group distances metric, expressed as $\sum_{u_l \in U} \|u_l - p_1^m\|^2$ by solving the following minimization problem:

$$\arg\min_{p_1^m \in A} \sum_{u_l \in U} \|u_l - p_1^m\|^2. \tag{29}$$

The operation of the 2D UFBS placement process using the k-medoids algorithm is summarized in Algorithm 2.

In the same manner with k-means, it is assumed that the number of UFBS Y = 1. However, as can be shown in Algorithm 2, the k-medoids algorithm can be straightforwardly applied to scenarios with Y > 1. Additionally, Algorithm 3 is the modified version of Algorithm 2 for the special case where $Y = 1$.

3.2. 3D UFBS Placement

Following the determination of the UFBS's 2D deployment location, the 3D UFBS placement procedure adjusts the UFBS's altitude to provide the highest quality of service to GMTs within the area of interest A. Thus, the farthest GMT$_l$ from the point p_1 where the UFBS is finally placed should be identified, according to the horizontal two-dimensional distance r_l. After that, the convenient height for the critical point p_1 is found by solving the following equation using (1):

$$\frac{\partial \text{PL}_l^u(h, r_l^{p_1})}{\partial h} = 0. \tag{30}$$

For the considered A2G path-loss model, as the altitude of the UFBS increases the path loss initially decreases and then increases again. This behavior can be attributed to the dependence of the particular A2G model on the elevation angle and the distance between the UFBS and each GMT$_l$. As the height of the UFBS increases the elevation angle also increases, leading to an increased probability of line-of-sight, i.e., obscurance by buildings and other surrounding objects is reduced. Based on this behavior, the A2G path loss PL$_l^u$ function is convex [25]. Thus, it can be deduced that the global minimum is consistently located at the critical point which can be derived through the Equation (30).

Algorithm 2 2D UFBS placement process through the k-medoids algorithm

1: **input:** The set of coordinates of all GMTs $U = \{u_1, u_2, \ldots, u_N\}$, and the number of UFBSs Y
2: $\epsilon = 10^{-6}$
3: $t = 0$
4: Initialize Y medoid points $C^t = \{p_1^m, p_2^m, \ldots, p_Y^m\} \subseteq U$, randomly
5: $S_k = \emptyset, \forall k = 1, 2, \cdots, Y$.
6: **for** $i \leftarrow 1$ to N **do**
7:     $k^* = \arg\min_{k=1\ldots Y} \|u_i - C_k^t\|$
8:     $S_{k^*} = S_{k^*} \cup \{u_i\}$
9: **end for**
10: $A^t = \sum_{k=1}^{Y} \sum_{u_i \in S_k} \|u_i - C_k^t\|^2$
11: **repeat**
12:     **for** $k \leftarrow 1$ to Y **do**
13:         **for** $i \leftarrow 1$ to N **do**
14:             **if** $u_i \notin C^t$ **then**
15:                 Swap the role of C_k^t with u_i
16:                 Repeat steps 6 to 9
17:                 $B = \sum_{k=1}^{Y} \sum_{u_i \in S_k} \|u_i - C_k^t\|^2$
18:                 **if** $B < A^{[t]}$ **then**
19:                     $t = t + 1$
20:                     $C_k^t = u_i$
21:                     $A^t = B$
22:                 **end if**
23:             **end if**
24:         **end for**
25:     **end for**
26: **until** $C^t - C^{t-1} \leq \epsilon$
27: **output:** A set of centroid points that the Y UFBSs will be deployed C^t.

Algorithm 3 2D UFBS placement process through the k-medoids algorithm with Y = 1

1: **input:** The set of coordinates of all GMTs $U = \{u_1, u_2, \ldots, u_N\}$
2: $B_k = 0, \forall k = 1, 2, \cdots, N$
3: **for** $i \leftarrow 1$ to N **do**
4:     $B_i = \sum_{j=1}^{N} \|u_i - u_j\|^2$
5: **end for**
6: $j^* = \arg\min_{i=1\ldots N} B_i$
7: **output:** The medoid point that the UFBS will be deployed u_{j^*}.

3.3. Computational Complexity of k-Means and k-Medoids Algorithms

Another crucial aspect is to estimate the computational complexity of the examined k-means and k-medoids algorithms based on their respective methods as described in Algorithms 1 and 2, respectively. K-means is a centroid-based algorithm, and k-medoids is a medoid-based algorithm.

The computational complexity of the k-means algorithm has been proven to be $O(nkId)$, where n is the number of data points, k is the number of clusters, I is the number of iterations, and d is the number of dimensions [33]. It uses the mean of the data points to calculate the cluster centroid and updates the assignment of the data points to the closest cluster centroid. The algorithm requires multiple iterations until convergence. The time complexity of the k-means algorithm is affected by the number of data points, the number of clusters and the number of dimensions.

The computational complexity of the k-medoids algorithm has been proven to be $O(k(n-k)^2 I)$, where n is the number of data points, k is the number of clusters, and I is the number of iterations [34]. K-medoids selects a single data point as the representative of a cluster, known as the medoid, and updates the assignment of the data points to the closest medoid. The algorithm requires multiple iterations until convergence. The time complexity of the k-medoids algorithm is affected by the number of data points, clusters, iterations, and the distance metric used.

In summary, both algorithms have a polynomial time complexity, and the main difference is that k-means use centroids, and k-medoids use medoids as the center of the cluster. As a result, the k-means is sensitive to the initial choice of centroids, while k-medoids is less sensitive and tends to find the global optimum more quickly.

4. ANN-Based Placement Scheme Selection

The main difference between the two algorithms mentioned before, is that the virtual centroid point $p_1^c \in A$ given from the k-means where the UFBS will be placed, will be equidistant from all GMTs. Conversely, the medoid point $p_1^m \in A$ given from the k-medoids will be a GMT location within the region of interest that will minimize the objective function (see (29)). Consequently, if the GMTs are spread equally in the area of interest, the p_1^c point provided by k means will improve the channel quality of GMTs, since the distances of the GMTs from the UFBS will be almost identical and the LoS probability will be significantly high. On the contrary, if a GMT is remote (outlier), the k-means algorithm will try to find the point p_1^c equidistant from every GMT, detaching it quite a bit from the majority of GMTs and thus increasing the GMTs' propagation losses. In contrast, the k-medoids through the proposed p_1^m point reduce the point-to-group-centroid distances, achieving higher A2G channel gains and increasing the QoS of the overall system.

To better highlight the advantages of each algorithm, let us consider a toy network with GMTs located in the 2D plane as depicted in Figure 2. Focusing on Figure 2 on the right, the group of GMTs in the right form a cluster, while the rightmost GMT is an outlier. The $p_1^c \in A$ point proposed by the k-means is greatly influenced by the outlier and thus cannot represent the correct cluster center. In contrast, the medoid point $p_1^m \in A$ provided by k-medoids is robust to the outlier and correctly represents the cluster center. On the contrary, regarding Figure 2 on the left, we notice that there is no remote GMT, and everyone is close to each other, forming a cluster of GMTs. Consequently, the $p_1^c \in A$ proposed from the k-means is equidistant from all GMTs, thus increasing the channel gain compared to the $p_1^m \in A$, which is not equidistant from all GMTs offered from the k-medoids algorithm.

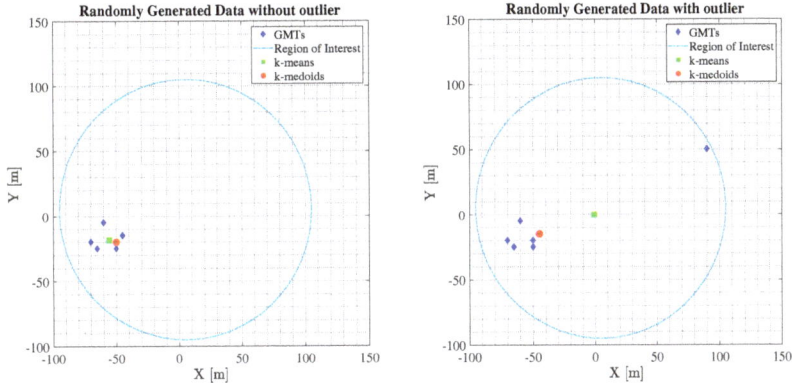

Figure 2. Comparisons between the k-means and k-medoids regarding the UFBS placement procedure.

Motivated by this observation, the PSS can be regarded as a supervised classification problem, where it can be approximated through the utilization of a fully connected artificial neural network (ANN) to enhance the overall system QoS. Since an ANN model learns how to efficiently match predictions to patterns seen during the training method, a data set containing various features that affect the A2G transmission should be created. To this end, this section presents the data set generation procedure, the date prepossessing, and the hyper-parameter tuning of the ANN model.

4.1. Data Set Generation

In this subsection, the dataset generation procedure concerning the training of the ANN model is presented. The objective of the ANN model is to predict the UFBS placement method to enhance the overall communication quality according to specific key performance indicator (KPI). In this work, the considered KPI that should be improved is the total system sum rate, R_s, given in expression (23). Hence, the optimization problem that the ANN model aims to solve is represented by Equation (23), which expresses the objective function that the ANN model seeks to maximize. This can be achieved through the ability of a well trained ANN model to recognize patterns, indicating when each method should be conducted to achieve the highest system sum rate. Using Equation (23) as a KPI for dataset generation ensures that the generated data is relevant and valuable for training and evaluating ANN models. Furthermore, incorporating a KPI directly aligned with the problem being addressed can guarantee that the model is configured optimally for the targeted classification task and exhibit superior performance for the specific issue [35]. Hence, considering the k-means and the k-medoids algorithms, the ANN should determine which of these two UFBS placement methods will achieve the highest R_s. Furthermore, the calculation of R_s involves various transmission parameters of the considered wireless communication system presented in Section 2, such as the 3D location of the UFBS, as well as the A2G propagation model. Therefore, all these aspects should be carefully considered during the training procedure of the ANN model.

In general, optimizing the total system sum rate, i.e., the R_s, can offer valuable insights into the optimal allocation of system resources, including bandwidth and transmit power [36]. In the context of a UAV-NOMA and D2D cooperative network, optimizing R_s can help identify the most effective resource allocation strategies for achieving optimal system performance. For instance, optimizing the total system sum rate allows the cooperative scheme to allocate bandwidth and power to UAVs and D2D users to maximize the total data rate transmitted over a given period. In addition, this optimization process can consider the physical layer parameters of the UAV and D2D users, including their communication requirements. For example, UAVs may require higher power allocations to maintain stable connections due to their altitude. Additionally, the distance of D2D users from the UFBS can impact their channel conditions and overall communication performance. Considering these physical layer parameters during the optimization process, the system can allocate resources more efficiently and effectively, leading to improved overall performance. In summary, optimizing the sum rate in a UAV-NOMA and D2D cooperative network can help achieve the best use of resources and enhance the system's overall performance. It is noted that the proposed capacity based optimization of the R_s can be considered as the upper bound on the maximum amount of data that can be reliably transmitted over a communication channel as the size of the channel goes to infinity. However, achieving this limit is often difficult in real world scenarios due to practical constraints such as noise and interference in the channel.

Focusing on the data set generation process, Monte Carlo simulations were carried out using Matlab© (MATLAB (Version R2021a) [Computer software]. MathWorks, Natick, MA, USA) software to conduct the entire training data set D, following the system model described in Section 2 and depicted in Figure 1. More specifically, in each simulated transmission frame, the GMTs are generated randomly following the uniform distribution into the circular region of interest, while the UFBS is placed through the two unsupervised algorithms mentioned above. It is noted that all GMTs are served by the UFBS via the A2G link, utilizing the NOMA technique, while the D2D cooperative transmission is activated to improve the overall communication quality. The A2G and D2D channel gains are generated based on expressions (9) and (14), respectively, while the urban environment parameters are given in Section 5. Concerning the dataset format, it can be expressed as $D = \{(\mathbf{x_i}, y_i)\}$ with $i = 1, \ldots, d$, where d is the total number of instances. Also, $\mathbf{x_i} \in R^w$ is the input vector of the i-th instance comprised of w features and $y_i \in \{k-\text{means}, k-\text{medoids}\}$ is the class of $\mathbf{x_i}$. In the following, the input features vector $\mathbf{x_i}$ consists of eight parameters, i.e., $w = 8$, that affect the placement procedure of the UFBS and are presented in detail in Table 2. Moreover, for the computation of class y_i, we evaluate the total system sum rate R_s in each simulated frame (see Equation (23)) for each UFBS placement procedure. Thus, the class value of the i-th instance, y_i, is determined as the placement method that achieved the highest R_s.

To precisely train the ANN model and to prevent over-fitting and under-fitting issues, the entire data set D is divided into training, validation, and testing subsets using the data splitting approach. A popular strategy for data partitioning is to use 70–80% of the entire dataset for training, with the remaining proportion used to improve and assess the trained models. Consequently, 70% of the total samples are chosen for the training phase, 15% for validation, and the remaining 15% for testing the proposed ANN model [37]. The training set is used to train the ANN, the validation set is used to evaluate the performance of the ANN during training, and the testing set is used to evaluate the performance of the ANN after training.

Table 2. The features utilized in the developed ANN model.

Feature	Description
D_{ptc}	The sum of distances between each GMT_l ($1 \leq l \leq N$) and the UFBS located in the centroid point $p_1^c \in A$
D_{ptm}	The sum of distances between each GMT_l ($1 \leq l \leq N$) and the UFBS located in the medoid point $p_1^m \in A$
$r_{\min}^{p_1^c}$	The minimum 2D distance of the GMTs from the point $p_1^c \in A$
$r_{\max}^{p_1^c}$	The maximum 2D distance of the GMTs from the point $p_1^c \in A$
$r_{\min}^{p_m}$	The minimum 2D distance of the GMTs from the point $p_1^m \in A$
$r_{\max}^{p_m}$	The maximum 2D distance of the GMTs from the point $p_1^m \in A$
$\text{PL}_{\text{sum}}^{p_c}$	The sum of the propagation losses of the GMTs in the case of placing the UFBS at the point $p_1^c \in A$
$\text{PL}_{\text{sum}}^{p_m}$	The sum of the propagation losses of the GMTs in the case of placing the UFBS at the point $p_1^m \in A$

4.2. Data Pre-Processing

The effectiveness of an ANN is highly dependent on the quantity and quality of training data. Consequently, regardless of which classifier is used, inferior models are generated if the training data are inaccurate. In light of the above assertion, stratified sampling and data normalization procedures are utilized to obtain the most incredible performance of the ANN model.

As an essential data pre-processing step, instance selection is employed not only to cope with the infeasibility of learning from massive data sets, but also to reduce the risk of the ANN model tending towards the majority and avoid coming up with what is known as the accuracy paradox [38]. For this purpose, stratifying sampling is applied. Hence, the overall training set is reduced, and the class values are uniformly distributed in the training sets, as shown in Figure 3. After removing redundant instances per class values, 3000 data samples were collected, which means a 50% reduction of the initial 6000 raw data samples. In addition, an ANN model cannot attain optimal performance if the feature values are in different units and scales.

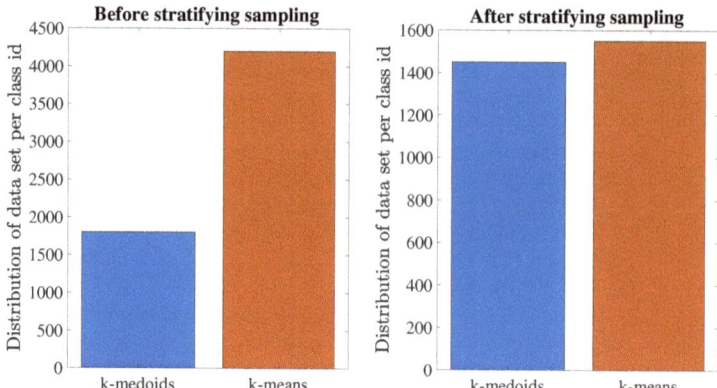

Figure 3. Distribution of data set per class.

In order to resolve these challenges, it is necessary to use a normalizing technique that eliminates the effects of those mismatches. Using this approach, the values of the dataset's features are scaled into a given range while keeping the original dataset's overall distribution and ratios. Hence, before the training phase, all input features were normalized for this purpose. The formula for normalizing is as follows:

$$X_{norm} = \frac{X - X_{min}}{X_{max} - X_{min}} \quad (31)$$

where X is a value of the corresponding feature under normalization, X_{max} and X_{min} are the maximum and the minimum value of this feature, respectively, and $X_{norm} \in [0, 1]$ is the final normalized value [37].

4.3. ANN Model Construction

ANN has the most hyper-parameters to be tuned among all the ML algorithms. Consequently, this subsection provides a concise but adequate description of the standard hyperparameters of an ANN model and their tuning.

The first step in hyperparameter tuning is finding the layer type [39]. Since non-linear data collection is used in this study, we investigate a fully connected multi-layer perceptron (MLP) network in which the input from the dataset propagates in one direction through one or more hidden layers. Therefore, using the normalized feature vectors obtained through (31) and their corresponding labels, we can build an ANN model consisting of one input layer, $l_i = 1$, $l_h \in \{1, 2, ..., L\}$ hidden layers, and one output layer $l_o = 1$ for the PSS prediction. The l_i layer consists of $m_i = 8$ neurons which represent the input features vector $\mathbf{x_i}$ for the ANN:

$$\mathbf{x_i} = \left[D_{ptc}, D_{ptm}, r_{min}^{p_c}, r_{max}^{p_c}, r_{min}^{p_m}, r_{max}^{p_m}, PL_{sum}^{p_c}, PL_{sum}^{p_m} \right]. \quad (32)$$

Each term mentioned in (32) is a real number and is described in detail in Table 2. Moreover, the l_o consists of $m_o = 2$ neurons, which is the total number of classes that we want to predict. The number of neurons m_h per hidden layer can be determined as [40]:

$$m_h = \left\lceil \frac{m_i + \sqrt{d}}{l_h} \right\rceil \quad (33)$$

Consequently, if there is one hidden layer ($l_h = 1$), the number of neurons is 63 according to (33). Similarly, the number of neurons for two hidden layers ($l_h = 2$) is 31.5 per layer, resulting in the selection of 32 and 31 neurons for the first and second hidden layers. Additionally, we model ANN with $l_h = 3$ and $l_h = 4$ hidden layers, and the number of neurons per each hidden layer is listed in Table 3.

Table 3. Examined ANN layouts.

l_h	m_h	Layout	Converged Epoch	Minimum Loss Score	Training Time (s)
1	63	ANN_{8-63-2}	26	0.09	0.81
2	32/31	$ANN_{8-32-31-2}$	37	0.06	0.92
3	21/21/21	$ANN_{8-21-21-21-2}$	56	0.08	1.4
4	16/16/16/15	$ANN_{8-16-16-16-15-2}$	58	0.15	1.6

The following step in hyperparameter tuning concerning ANN models is to determine the activation and the loss function. In this study, the rectified linear unit (ReLU) activation function is employed in hidden layers. It is easy to build and overcome the constraints of widely used activation functions like Sigmoid and Tanh. Furthermore, since PSS may be seen as a binary classification problem, the output layer activation function is SoftMax. Regarding the loss function, cross-entropy is utilized since it is the most widely used for classification problems. Therefore, in order to find the best ANN hyperparameters, the selected loss function should be minimized. The minimization of the loss function is achieved through gradient descent (GD) with momentum backpropagation. The momentum term navigates the GD along the relevant direction and softens the oscillations in irrelevant directions. For this purpose, the grid search method is utilized. Accordingly, the momentum is tested for values between 0.2 and 1 with a step of 0.1. In the last phase of hyperparameter tuning, the learning rate and the number of epochs are chosen. The learning rate is evaluated for values between 0.001 and 0.1 with a step of 0.001, while the number of epochs range is set to be from 1 to 1000. In addition, the early stopping criterion is used to improve the model's generalization capability and minimize overfitting. Finally, in Table 4, all the finalized hyperparameters are listed for ANNs methods derived throughout the training, validation, and testing process.

Figure 4 presents the evaluation of the training, validation, and testing phases in terms of the loss function versus the number of epochs. In essence, the number of epochs directly affects the adopted method's convergence. The low number of epochs entails that the algorithm may converge at a local minimum. Nonetheless, too many epochs may lead to over-learning. The results in Figure 4 concerning the modelled ANNs prove that the loss function for all processes, i.e., training, validation, and testing, converges smoothly, obtaining constant loss values and reaching the global minimum in a short period. The acquired global minimum loss for the convergence during the testing phase, and the corresponding epoch values are listed in Table 3. According to Table 3, ANN with two hidden layers demonstrates the best performance among all the examined ANN techniques, providing the minimum loss score of 0.06. Furthermore, for each ANN layout, the training time is also recorded. Specifically, the training times for ANN with one, two, three, and four hidden layers are 0.81, 0.92, 1.4, and 1.6 seconds, respectively. Comparing the training time of the assessed ANNs models, it is evident that the training time depends directly on the applied layout structure. Finally, the conventional time complexity (TTC) for any ANN layout is $O(n^3)$ [37]. The TTC represents the standard theoretical asymptotic complexity, which takes into account only the training samples n. It only examines training samples, since the training phase is the most time-consuming operation in ML algorithms and occurs offline, and not in real-time scenarios.

Table 4. Chosen hyperparameters values for ANNs models.

Parameters	Values
Activation functions	ReLU and SoftMax
Training algorithm	Gradient Descent
Learning rate	0.01
Maximum number of epochs to train	1000
Loss function	cross-entropy
Minimum performance gradient	10^{-6}

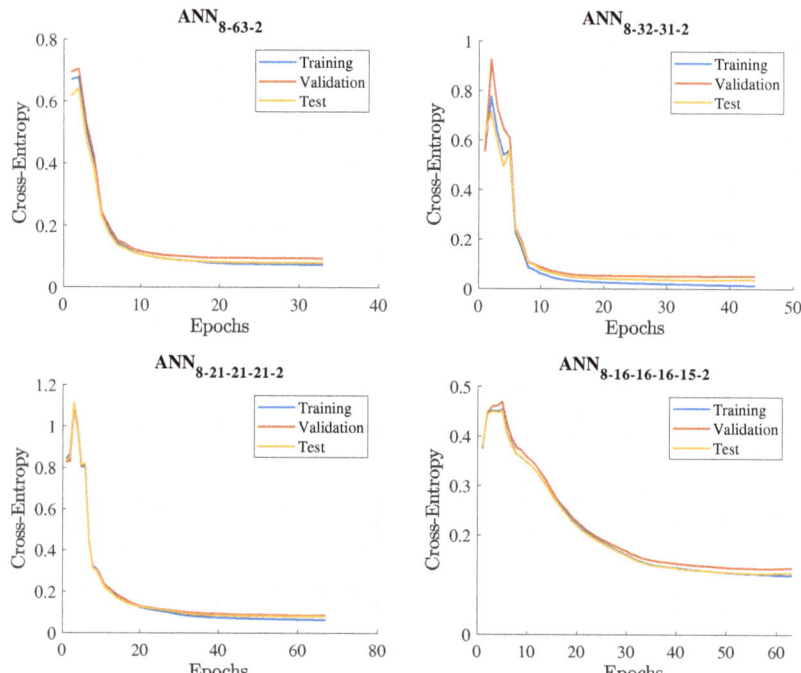

Figure 4. Loss convergence progression versus epochs for the training, validation, and testing phase of all the introduced ANNs.

4.4. ANN Model Selection

This section presents the evaluation results obtained from the ANNs methods for the testing set. The evaluation of the ANNs methods and, by extension, the choice of the ANN algorithm to solve the PSS classification problem is achieved based on the accuracy, precision, recall, and F1 score performance metrics.

Specifically, accuracy, precision, recall, and F1 score are commonly used evaluation metrics for assessing the performance of ML models, particularly in classification tasks. These metrics are calculated based on the number of true positive (TP), true negative (TN), false positive (FP), and false negative (FN) predictions made by the model. Accuracy is the proportion of correct predictions made by the model out of all predictions made. In the context of sum-rate maximization, a high accuracy score would indicate that the ANN can predict the best PSS more often accurately, and it is calculated as follows:

$$\text{Accuracy} = \frac{\text{TP} + \text{TN}}{\text{TP} + \text{TN} + \text{FP} + \text{FN}} \quad (34)$$

Precision is the proportion of true positive predictions made by the model out of all positive predictions made. For example, in the context of sum-rate maximization, a high precision score would indicate that when the ANN predicts a PSS, it is more likely to be the best prediction that maximizes the system sum rate, and it can be expressed as follows:

$$\text{Precision} = \frac{TP}{TP + FP} \quad (35)$$

Recall (also known as sensitivity or true positive rate) is the proportion of true positive predictions made by the model out of all actual positive cases. In term of sum-rate maximization, a high recall score would indicate that the ANN is able to find more of the actual PSS solutions, and it is calculated as follows:

$$\text{Recall} = \frac{TP}{TP + FN} \quad (36)$$

F1 score is a harmonic mean of precision and recall. In the context of sum-rate maximization, a high F1 score would indicate that the ANN has a good balance of precision and recall, making fewer false PSS predictions while also identifying most of the relevant cases. It is calculated as:

$$F1 = 2 \times \frac{\text{Precision} \times \text{Recall}}{\text{Precision} + \text{Recall}} \quad (37)$$

Figures 5 and 6 present the evaluation results obtained from the ANN methods for the testing set. Accuracy, precision, recall, and the F1 score are used to evaluate the ANN's approaches. More specifically, the accuracy of each ANN model is depicted in Figure 5, while Figure 6 illustrates the mean precision, recall, and F1-score obtained from each ANN method. The classification accuracy in Figure 5 reveals that the best prediction is achieved through the ANN with two hidden layers $ANN_{8-32-31-2}$. Comparing the performance of the different ANN layouts, the prediction accuracy decreases until the neural network reaches two hidden layers in depth. Then, by extending the depth of the ANNs to more than two hidden layers, the accuracy is diminished. Specifically, the prediction accuracy increases from 92.5% for a single hidden layer (ANN_{8-63-2}) to 95.32% for a two-layered ($ANN_{8-32-31-2}$) and then decreases to 92.3% and 92.7% for a three ($ANN_{8-21-21-21-2}$) and four-layered ($ANN_{8-16-16-16-15-2}$) structure, respectively. As can be observed in Figure 6, the assessed ANN models exhibit exceptional performance with an F1-score greater than 91%, maintaining an average accuracy and average recall greater than 91%. Among the evaluated ANNs, the neural network with two hidden layers $ANN_{8-32-31-2}$ achieves the best prediction result. The specific model yields a mean precision of 94.12%, a mean recall of 93.14%, and an average F1-score of 93.63%. Hence this level of accuracy in a balanced data set implies that the model has recognized and formed strong correlations between features and class and has avoided overfitting issues. Moreover, this success is related to the two-layered neural network's ability to effectively approximate nonlinear functions and reliably predict the PSS class value. Hence the ANN with two hidden layer is chosen to solve the PSS classification problem.

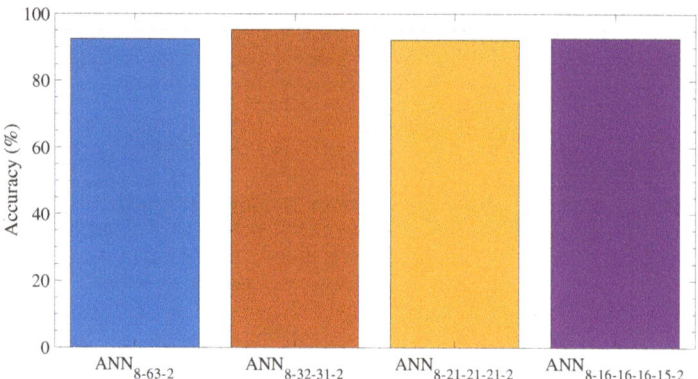

Figure 5. Accuracy comparison between the different ANN layouts.

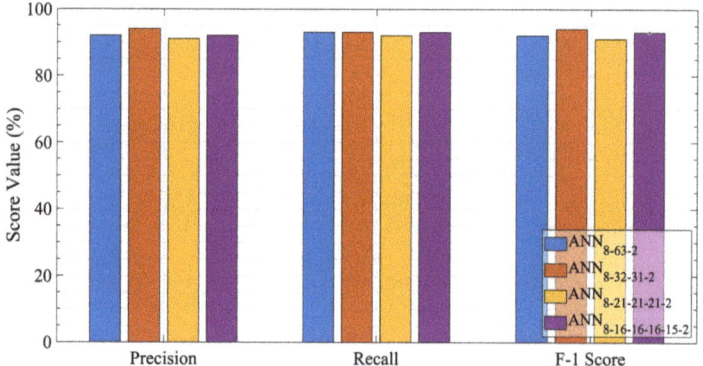

Figure 6. F1-score, precision, and recall performance measurements of all ANN layouts.

5. Performance Evaluation

In this section, the system sum rate and the spectral efficiency results from Monte Carlo simulations conducted in Matlab© are presented to evaluate the performance of the proposed ANN-based PSS. The simulations were executed on a computer consisting of a Windows 10 64-bit operating system, Intel Core i7-8700 CPU, and 16 GB of RAM. Moreover, the impact of various system parameters, such as D2D bandwidth allocation and the UFBS transmit power P_u, on the performance of the proposed method is studied.

Furthermore, the proposed ANN-based PSS is compared against the standalone UFBS placement schemes k-medoids and k-means [7,9]. These two methods will be referred to as the k-means deployment process (MEA-DP) and the k-medoids deployment process (MED-DP). More specifically, comparisons are made between different networks schemes, such as the cooperative UAV-NOMA and D2D scheme termed as NOMA-D2D, and two standalone UAV transmission schemes without D2D communication capabilities between the GMTs, the UAV-NOMA optimal user pairing scheme [26], called NOMA, and the time domain UAV-OMA scheme, termed as OMA. In order to assess the performance of the proposed scheme as well as the compared ones, we define the spectral efficiency as:

$$SE = \frac{R_{ach}}{B_{occ}}, \tag{38}$$

where R_{ach} is the achievable system sum rate and B_{occ} denotes the total utilized network bandwidth. Concerning both the standalone OMA and NOMA transmission scheme, $B_{occ} = B_u$, while for the NOMA-D2D scheme, $B_{occ} = B_d + B_u$. The rest of the selected parameters regarding the abovementioned scenarios are listed in Table 5.

Table 5. Simulation parameters.

Parameters	Values
Simulated frames	100,000
Number of GMTs N	20
Region of interest circle radius R	500 m
UFBS downlink frequency F_u	1.8 GHz
D2D operating frequency F_d	2 GHz
UFBS transmit power P_u	0–24 dBm
GMT transmit power P_d	24 dBm
UFBS Tx antenna gain G_t^u	0 dBi
GMT Rx antenna gain G_r^g with $g = \{u, d\}$	0 dBi
GMT Tx antenna gain G_t^d	0 dBi
Terrestrial environment	Urban
Urban environment parameters	$a = 9.61, b = 0.16, \eta_{LoS} = 1, \eta_{NLoS} = 20$
UFBS bandwidth B_u	5 MHz
Receiver noise temperature T_g with $g = \{u, d\}$	24.6 dBK

Figure 7 presents the spectral efficiency performance of the proposed ANN-based PSS for different terrestrial D2D bandwidth values and between the different network schemes. As it can be observed, the proposed ANN-based PSS scheme combined with the NOMA-D2D transmission technique for $B_d = 0.2$ provides significant spectral efficiency gains compared to the other NOMA-D2D cooperative networks with $B_d \neq 0.2$ and the standalone NOMA and OMA schemes. It is noteworthy that the proposed strategy, utilizing a B_d equal to 0.1 MHz, exhibits comparable performance with a B_d equals to 0.2 MHz for low UFBS transmit power values. Conversely, for high UFBS transmit power, the proposed strategy utilizing a B_d equals to 0.2 MHz is determined to result in the near optimal spectral efficiency. Also, regarding the NOMA-D2D cooperative network with $B_d \leq 1.2$ MHz, the proposed method achieves higher spectral efficiency gain than the standalone NOMA and the OMA scheme for all UFBS power transmission values. In contrast, for $B_d > 1.2$ MHz, the suggested method's spectral efficiency in a NOMA-D2D cooperative network is inferior to that of NOMA. This occurs because there is no need for additional bandwidth since the weak users' rates are always constrained by the decoding rates of their signals at the strong users (21). Therefore, regarding the communication network, B_d values greater than 1.2 MHz are considered a waste of resources. Additionally, for $B_d = 1.2$ MHz, a switch case statement can be established. More specifically, in the case where the P_u is lower than 20 dBm, the NOMA-D2D cooperative network outperforms the NOMA scheme, while for $P_u > 20$ dBm, the standalone NOMA outperforms the NOMA-D2D cooperative scheme. This phenomenon occurs for large P_u values since the A2G channel between the weak GMTs and the UFBS is strengthened, resulting in greater achievable rates for the weak GMTs via the direct A2G connection. Hence the D2D communication between the K pairs is mainly avoided, as the offered data rates via the D2D links are lower than those that can arise through the A2G links. This claim can be verified by expression in (21). Moreover, spectral efficiency degradation is observed when the terrestrial D2D bandwidth B_d is greater than 1.2 MHz. In this case, the weak users can not efficiently exploit the capabilities offered by the wireless D2D channel link, as the rate received through the terrestrial cooperation is restricted by the decoding rates achieved by the strong users of each pair. This observation is derived as a result of the constraints imposed by (17)–(19), as well as from the explanation of cases 1 and 2 in Section 2.4. As an illustrative case for this phenomenon, the baseline standalone OMA scheme behaves better than the NOMA-D2D scheme with $B_d = 3.0$ MHz in terms of spectral efficiency. Therefore, in the case of cooperative NOMA schemes such as the proposed one, the value of the terrestrial D2D bandwidth B_d should be carefully chosen to avoid wasting spectrum resources. Also, in the NOMA-D2D cooperative network, for UFBS transmit power in the range of 0 to 12 dBm, it can be observed that the spectral efficiency is approximately the same for B_d values equal to 0.1 and 0.2 MHz. However, for UFBS transmit power higher than 12 dBm, the proposed method with $B_d = 0.2$ MHz achieves higher spectral efficiency than the others. In other words, $B_d = 0.2$ MHz is a near-optimal D2D bandwidth value for the considered communication system.

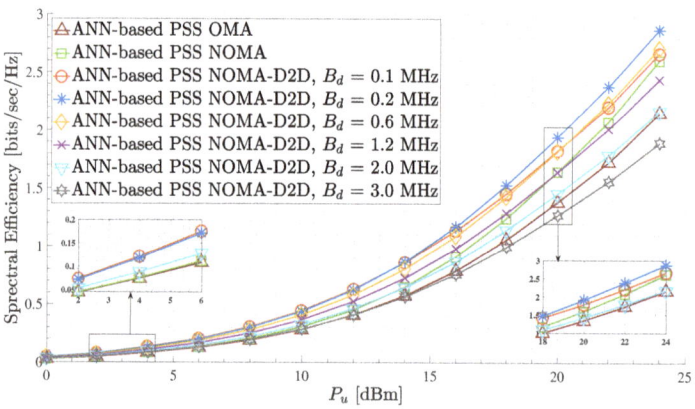

Figure 7. Spectral efficiency for the ANN-based PSS and different terrestrial D2D bandwidth values.

In Figure 8, the sum rate performance of the proposed ANN-based PSS is examined for the different network schemes. It can be easily observed that the employment of the suggested PSS technique in the NOMA-D2D cooperative network readily outperforms OMA and NOMA schemes for all UFBS transmit power values and regardless of the D2D bandwidths value allocations. Moreover, for the NOMA-D2D cooperative network, we observe that the sum rate is approximately the same for any value of $B_d > 0.1$ MHz. This can be supported by (21), which demonstrates that there is no need to devote more bandwidth to D2D transmission. Also, for UFBS transmit power in the range of 0 to 12 dBm, it can be observed that the sum rate is approximately the same for all B_d values. Hence, large B_d values for low-to-medium UFBS transmit powers are thus seen as a waste of resources. Therefore, for that UFBS transmit power range, there is a maximum value B_d, which should not be exceeded to avoid wasting resources. Nevertheless, the findings from Figures 7 and 8 demonstrate that dynamic bandwidth allocation is required for D2D out-band communication to improve both the sum rate and spectral efficiency performance.

Figures 9 and 10 show the effects caused by the different placement methods on the spectral efficiency and the system sum rate, respectively. More specifically, Figure 9 illustrates the spectral efficiency performance of the different communication schemes, NOMA-D2D with $B_d = 0.2$ MHz, NOMA, and OMA, utilizing the different placement procedures. As can be observed, the ANN-based PSS applied to the NOMA-D2D cooperative network scheme achieves significant spectral efficiency gains compared to MEA-DP and MED-DP for all UFBS power transmission values. Also, observing all the network schemes individually (i.e., NOMA-D2D, NOMA, and OMA), the proposed ANN-based PSS outperforms the other two methods for all UFBS power transmission values. This results from the ability of the ANN to recognize patterns, indicating when each method should be conducted. Furthermore, regardless of the placement method, the cooperation between the aerial and D2D networks is promoted, i.e., the NOMA-D2D method, since it achieves the maximum spectral efficiency rates compared to standalone NOMA and OMA schemes. Moreover, for all UFBS transmission power values, the MEA-DP outperforms the

MED-DP scheme in all three network configurations. This is justified by the explanation given in Section 4. Specifically, as the GMTs are placed randomly and uniformly in the region of interest, the probability of an outlying user appearing is very low. Consequently, in most cases, the k-means algorithm places the UFBS at such a point that it is equidistant by the users, thus improving the quality of channels gains against k-medoids. Lastly, the spectral efficiency of the ANN-based PSS applied to the standalone NOMA scheme is higher than that of MED-DP in the NOMA-D2D cooperative network scheme for P_u values of approximately up to 22 dBm. This phenomenon occurs due to the improvement of the A2G channels through the proposed placement scheme. Consequently, in contrast to other cooperative systems, such as satellite D2D cooperative networks [27], the success of aerial and D2D cooperative networks strongly relies on the UFBS placement procedure. Hence, an inaccurate prediction concerning UAV's position might degrade the overall network quality and lay the D2D network unnecessary.

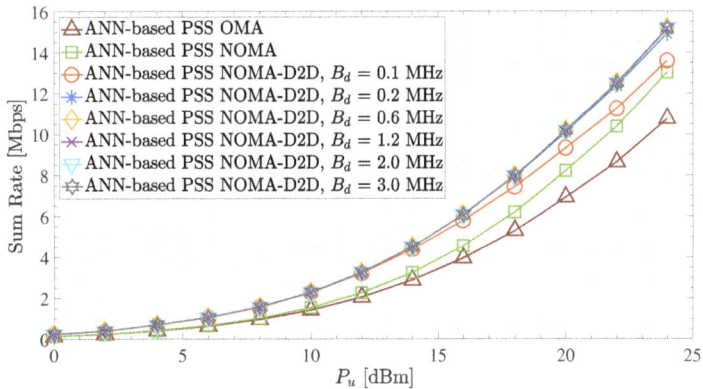

Figure 8. Sum rate for the ANN-based PSS and different terrestrial D2D bandwidth values.

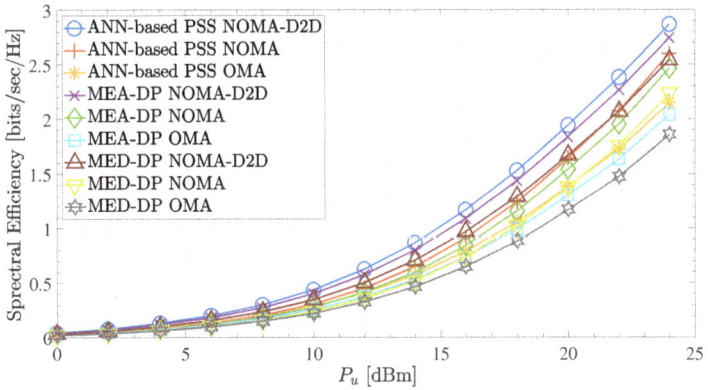

Figure 9. Spectral efficiency for $B_d = 0.2$ MHz and different UFBS placement schemes.

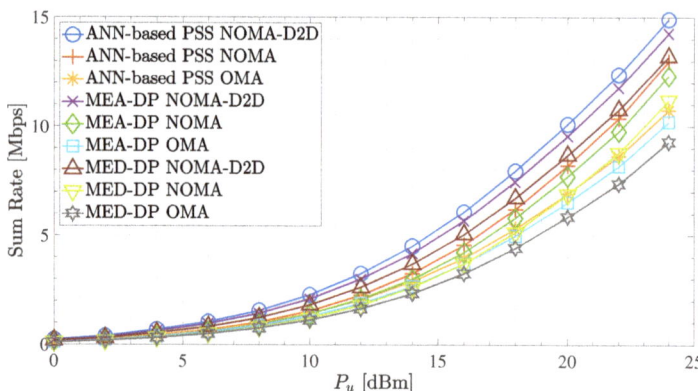

Figure 10. Sum rate for $B_d = 0.2$ MHz and different UFBS placement schemes.

Next, Figure 10 presents the sum rate for $B_d = 0.2$ MHz and different placement procedures for NOMA-D2D, NOMA, and OMA network schemes. Throughout the P_u range and regardless of the placement method scheme, it can be shown that the sum rate of the NOMA-D2D cooperative network is superior to that of NOMA and OMA, respectively. Similarly, as in spectral efficiency in Figure 9, the proposed ANN-based PSS outperforms the other two placement procedures for all network schemes. Moreover, it is observed that the proposed method, when applied in a NOMA scheme, can achieve higher spectral efficiency gains for the MED-DP applied in NOMA-D2D for $P_u > 22$ dBm. Therefore, in such a scenario, with the deployment of the proposed method, we could avoid D2D transmission and save the entire D2D bandwidth.

Overall, the sum rate results of the NOMA-D2D cooperative scheme in all placement procedures indicate that the weak user's achievable rate can be significantly improved. This advantage results from strong users cooperating with weak users of the system through out-band D2D communication. However, the sum rate and the spectral efficiency in all network schemes are heavily contingent on the UFBS placement within the region of interest. Regarding the results in Figures 7–10, the proposed ANN-based PSS outperforms the other two methods in all network schemes and can offer terrestrial users reliable and high-quality communication.

Finally, Table 6 summarizes the key characteristics of the proposed ANN-based PSS and the compared MEA-DP and MED-DP schemes. Specifically, our method is less sensitive to outliers compared to MEA-DP, making it more robust in noisy environments. It also has higher reliability compared to both MEA-DP and MED-DP. Regarding spectral efficiency and sum rate, our method outperforms both MEA-DP and MED-DP, indicating that it may be a better choice for optimizing the utilization of resources and achieving higher data transmission rates in the given scenario.

Table 6. Comparison of the main properties of ANN-based PSS and MEA-DP and MED-DP schemes.

Performance indicator	ANN-Based PSS	MEA-DP	MED-DP
Sensitive to outliers	No	Yes	No
Reliability	High	Medium	Medium
Spectral efficiency	High	Medium	Medium
Sum rate	High	Medium	Medium
Influenced by the distribution of GMTs in A	Medium	High	Medium
Fairness	High	High	Low

6. Conclusions and Future Directions

Summarizing this paper, we proposed an ANN-based PSS method that maximizes the spectral efficiency and the sum rate in a NOMA-D2D cooperative network. It is the first time supervised ML methods are combined with unsupervised ones to enhance the placement procedure of the UFBS; the examples demonstrate the improvements achieved. To evaluate the performance of the ANN-based PSS policy, we compared it with two stand-alone unsupervised ML methods schemes. The results showed that the proposed method outperforms the other two in different network scenarios, such as NOMA-D2D cooperative, NOMA, and OMA schemes, regarding sum rate and spectral efficiency terms. Furthermore, the results show that utilizing the proposed method in a UAV-aided D2D-NOMA-cooperative network can offer terrestrial users reliable and high-quality communication compared with stand-alone NOMA or OMA schemes.

Possible future directions include studying various machine learning models as base learners and forming ensemble approaches to enhance the predictability of the placement procedure. Furthermore, in future work, we consider examining machine learning methods to identify the optimal D2D bandwidth value that achieves the maximum sum rate and, simultaneously, the maximum spectral efficiency regarding a UAV-aided D2D-NOMA-cooperative network. Finally, of potential interest is the integration of virtual MIMO in the context of aerial–terrestrial networks to improve communication between UAVs and other devices. Specifically, UAVs typically have limited size, weight, and power constraints, which can make it challenging to install multiple antennas and radio resources on them. By using virtual MIMO, various UAVs can work together as a single MIMO system and share their antennas and radio resources, increasing the range and capacity of the communication [41,42]. In addition, virtual MIMO can also improve the robustness of communication in UAV networks, as it can reduce the impact of fading and interference caused by the dynamic and often hostile environment in which UAVs operate.

Author Contributions: Conceptualization, L.T., M.K., P.S.B. and D.V.; methodology, L.T and M.K.; software, L.T. and M.K.; validation, L.T., M.K., P.S.B. and D.V.; formal analysis, L.T. and M.K.; investigation, L.T. and M.K.; resources, L.T.; data curation, L.T.; writing—original draft preparation, L.T. and M.K.; writing—review and editing, D.V. and P.S.B.; visualization, L.T. and M.K.; supervision, D.V. and P.S.B. All authors have read and agreed to the published version of the manuscript.

Funding: This research received no external funding.

Institutional Review Board Statement: Not applicable.

Informed Consent Statement: Not applicable.

Data Availability Statement: The data that support the findings of this study are available from the corresponding author upon reasonable request.

Conflicts of Interest: The authors declare no conflict of interest.

Abbreviations

The following abbreviations are used in this manuscript:

5G	Fifth Generation
6G	Sixth Generation
A2G	Air-to-Ground
ANN	Artificial Neural Network
AWGN	Additive White Gaussian Noise
B5G	Beyond 5G
D2D	Device-to-Device
DDPG	Deep Deterministic Policy Gradient
eICIC	Enhanced Inter-Cell Interference Coordination

FD	Full-Duplex
FSL	Free Space Pathloss
GD	Gradient Descent
GMT	Ground Mobile Terminal
HetNet	Heterogeneous Network
IoT	Internet of Things
KPI	Key Performance Indicator
LoS	Line of Sight
LTE	Long Term Evolution
MDQN	Mutual Deep Q-Network
MEA-DP	k-Means Deployment Process
MED-DP	k-Medoids Deployment Process
MIMO	Multiple-Input Multiple Output
ML	Machine Learning
MLP	Multi-Layer Perceptron
NLoS	Non Line of Sight
NOMA	Non-Orthogonal Multiple Access
OMA	Orthogonal Multiple Access
PSS	Placement Scheme Selection
QoS	Quality-of-Service
QSM	Quadrature Spatial Modulation
RF	Radio Frequency
SC	Superposition Coding
SIC	Successive Interference Cancellation
TBS	Terrestrial Base station
UAV	Unmanned Aerial Vehicle
UFBS	UAV Flying Base Station

References

1. Shahzadi, R.; Ali, M.; Khan, H.Z.; Naeem, M. UAV assisted 5G and beyond wireless networks: A survey. *J. Netw. Comput. Appl.* **2021**, *189*, 103114. [CrossRef]
2. Elnabty, I.A.; Fahmy, Y.; Kafafy, M. A survey on UAV placement optimization for UAV-assisted communication in 5G and beyond networks. *Phys. Commun.* **2022**, *51*, 101564. [CrossRef]
3. Bithas, P.S.; Michailidis, E.T.; Nomikos, N.; Vouyioukas, D.; Kanatas, A.G. A Survey on Machine-Learning Techniques for UAV-Based Communications. *Sensors* **2019**, *19*, 5170. [CrossRef] [PubMed]
4. Tang, R.; Cheng, J.; Cao, Z. Joint Placement Design, Admission Control, and Power Allocation for NOMA-Based UAV Systems. *IEEE Wirel. Commun. Lett.* **2020**, *9*, 385–388. [CrossRef]
5. Dai, H.; Zhang, H.; Hua, M.; Li, C.; Huang, Y.; Wang, B. How to Deploy Multiple UAVs for Providing Communication Service in an Unknown Region? *IEEE Wirel. Commun. Lett.* **2019**, *8*, 1276–1279. [CrossRef]
6. Liu, X.; Wang, J.; Zhao, N.; Chen, Y.; Zhang, S.; Ding, Z.; Yu, F.R. Placement and Power Allocation for NOMA-UAV Networks. *IEEE Wirel. Commun. Lett.* **2019**, *8*, 965–968. [CrossRef]
7. Tsipi, L.; Karavolos, M.; Vouyioukas, D. An Unsupervised Machine Learning Approach for UAV-Aided Offloading of 5G Cellular Networks. *Telecom* **2022**, *3*, 86–102. [CrossRef]
8. Zhang, Q.; Saad, W.; Bennis, M.; Lu, X.; Debbah, M.; Zuo, W. Predictive Deployment of UAV Base Stations in Wireless Networks: Machine Learning Meets Contract Theory. *IEEE Trans. Wirel. Commun.* **2021**, *20*, 637–652. [CrossRef]
9. El Hammouti, H.; Benjillali, M.; Shihada, B.; Alouini, M.S. A Distributed Mechanism for Joint 3D Placement and User Association in UAV-Assisted Networks. In Proceedings of the 2019 IEEE Wireless Communications and Networking Conference (WCNC), Marrakesh, Morocco, 15–18 April 2019; pp. 1–6. [CrossRef]
10. Kumbhar, A.; Guvenc, I.; Singh, S.; Tuncer, A. Exploiting LTE-Advanced HetNets and FeICIC for UAV-Assisted Public Safety Communications. *IEEE Access* **2018**, *6*, 783–796. [CrossRef]
11. Makki, B.; Chitti, K.; Behravan, A.; Alouini, M.S. A Survey of NOMA: Current Status and Open Research Challenges. *IEEE Open J. Commun. Soc.* **2020**, *1*, 179–189. [CrossRef]
12. Ding, Z.; Lei, X.; Karagiannidis, G.K.; Schober, R.; Yuan, J.; Bhargava, V.K. A Survey on Non-Orthogonal Multiple Access for 5G Networks: Research Challenges and Future Trends. *IEEE J. Sel. Areas Commun.* **2017**, *35*, 2181–2195. [CrossRef]
13. Ghafoor, U.; Ali, M.; Khan, H.Z.; Siddiqui, A.M.; Naeem, M. NOMA and future 5G & B5G wireless networks: A paradigm. *J. Netw. Comput. Appl.* **2022**, *204*, 103413. [CrossRef]

14. Li, J.; Dang, S.; Yan, Y.; Peng, Y.; Al-Rubaye, S.; Tsourdos, A. Generalized Quadrature Spatial Modulation and its Application to Vehicular Networks with NOMA. *IEEE Trans. Intell. Transp. Syst.* **2021**, *22*, 4030–4039. [CrossRef]
15. Li, J.; Dang, S.; Huang, Y.; Chen, P.; Qi, X.; Wen, M.; Arslan, H. Composite Multiple-Mode Orthogonal Frequency Division Multiplexing with Index Modulation. *IEEE Trans. Wirel. Commun.* **2022**, 1. [CrossRef]
16. Nasir, A.A.; Tuan, H.D.; Duong, T.Q.; Poor, H.V. UAV-Enabled Communication Using NOMA. *IEEE Trans. Commun.* **2019**, *67*, 5126–5138. [CrossRef]
17. Zhong, R.; Liu, X.; Liu, Y.; Chen, Y. NOMA in UAV-aided cellular offloading: A machine learning approach. In Proceedings of the 2020 IEEE Globecom Workshops, Taipei, Taiwan, 7–9 December 2020; pp. 1–6. [CrossRef]
18. Shi, W.; Sun, Y.; Liu, M.; Xu, H.; Gui, G.; Ohtsuki, T.; Adebisi, B.; Gacanin, H.; Adachi, F. Joint UL/DL Resource Allocation for UAV-Aided Full-Duplex NOMA Communications. *IEEE Trans. Commun.* **2021**, *69*, 8474–8487. [CrossRef]
19. Selim, M.M.; Rihan, M.; Yang, Y.; Huang, L.; Quan, Z.; Ma, J. On the Outage Probability and Power Control of D2D Underlaying NOMA UAV-Assisted Networks. *IEEE Access* **2019**, *7*, 16525–16536. [CrossRef]
20. Chen, P.; Zhou, X.; Zhao, J.; Shen, F.; Sun, S. Energy-Efficient Resource Allocation for Secure D2D Communications Underlaying UAV-Enabled Networks. *IEEE Trans. Veh. Technol.* **2022**, *71*, 7519–7531. [CrossRef]
21. Wang, B.; Zhang, R.; Chen, C.; Cheng, X.; Yan, L. Graph-Based File Dispatching Protocol With D2D-Aided UAV-NOMA Communications in Large-Scale Networks. In Proceedings of the 2020 IEEE Wireless Communications and Networking Conference (WCNC), Seoul, Republic of Korea, 25–28 May 2020; pp. 1–6. [CrossRef]
22. Ghosh, S.; Roy, S.D.; Kundu, S. UAV Assisted SWIPT Enabled NOMA Based D2D Network for Disaster Management. *Wirel. Pers. Commun.* **2022**, *128*, 2341–2362. [CrossRef]
23. Xu, Y.H.; Sun, Q.M.; Zhou, W.; Yu, G. Resource allocation for UAV-aided energy harvesting-powered D2D communications: A reinforcement learning-based scheme. *Ad Hoc Netw.* **2022**, *136*, 102973. [CrossRef]
24. Mandloi, D.; Arya, R. Seamless connectivity with 5G enabled unmanned aerial vehicles base stations using machine programming approach. *Expert Syst.* **2022**, *39*, e12828. [CrossRef]
25. Karavolos, M.; Tsipi, L.; Bithas, P.S.; Vouyioukas, D.; Mathiopoulos, P.T. Satellite Aerial Terrestrial Hybrid NOMA Scheme in 6G Networks: An Unsupervised Learning Approach. In Proceedings of the 2022 1st International Conference on 6G Networking (6GNet), Paris, France, 6–8 July 2022; pp. 1–5. [CrossRef]
26. Zhu, L.; Zhang, J.; Xiao, Z.; Cao, X.; Wu, D.O. Optimal User Pairing for Downlink Non-Orthogonal Multiple Access (NOMA). *IEEE Wirel. Commun. Lett.* **2019**, *8*, 328–331. [CrossRef]
27. Karavolos, M.; Nomikos, N.; Vouyioukas, D. Enhanced Integrated Satellite-Terrestrial NOMA with Cooperative Device-to-Device Communication. *Telecom* **2020**, *1*, 10. [CrossRef]
28. Karavolos, M.; Nomikos, N.; Vouyioukas, D.; Mathiopoulos, P.T. HST-NNC: A Novel Hybrid Satellite-Terrestrial Communication With NOMA and Network Coding Systems. *IEEE Open J. Commun. Soc.* **2021**, *2*, 887–898. [CrossRef]
29. Angui, B.; Corbel, R.; Rodriguez, V.Q.; Stephan, E. Towards 6G zero touch networks: The case of automated Cloud-RAN deployments. In Proceedings of the 2022 IEEE 19th Annual Consumer Communications & Networking Conference (CCNC), Las Vegas, NV, USA, 8–11 January 2022; pp. 1–6. [CrossRef]
30. Zhang, H.; Song, L.; Han, Z. *Unmanned Aerial Vehicle Applications over Cellular Networks for 5G and Beyond*; Springer: Berlin/Heidelberg, Germany, 2020.
31. Edmonds, J. Maximum matching and a polyhedron with 0, 1-vertices. *J. Res. Natl. Bur. Stand. B* **1965**, *69*, 55–56. [CrossRef]
32. Tran, T.N.; Nguyen, T.L.; Voznak, M. Approaching K-Means for Multiantenna UAV Positioning in Combination With a Max-SIC-Min-Rate Framework to Enable Aerial IoT Networks. *IEEE Access* **2022**, *10*, 115157–115178. [CrossRef]
33. Andrade Maciel, L.; Alcântara Souza, M.; Cota de Freitas, H. Reconfigurable FPGA-Based K-Means/K-Modes Architecture for Network Intrusion Detection. *IEEE Trans. Circuits Syst. II Express Briefs* **2020**, *67*, 1459–1463. [CrossRef]
34. Xu, X.; Shen, B.; Yin, X.; Khosravi, M.R.; Wu, H.; Qi, L.; Wan, S. Edge Server Quantification and Placement for Offloading Social Media Services in Industrial Cognitive IoV. *IEEE Trans. Ind. Inform.* **2021**, *17*, 2910–2918. [CrossRef]
35. Yao, R.; Zhang, Y.; Wang, S.; Qi, N.; Miridakis, N.I.; Tsiftsis, T.A. Deep Neural Network Assisted Approach for Antenna Selection in Untrusted Relay Networks. *IEEE Wirel. Commun. Lett.* **2019**, *8*, 1644–1647. [CrossRef]
36. Li, Y.; Zhang, H.; Long, K.; Nallanathan, A. Exploring Sum Rate Maximization in UAV-Based Multi-IRS Networks: IRS Association, UAV Altitude, and Phase Shift Design. *IEEE Trans. Commun.* **2022**, *70*, 7764–7774. [CrossRef]
37. Moraitis, N.; Tsipi, L.; Vouyioukas, D.; Gkioni, A.; Louvros, S. Performance evaluation of machine learning methods for path loss prediction in rural environment at 3.7 GHz. *Wirel. Netw.* **2021**, *27*, 4169–4188. [CrossRef]
38. Zhang, Y.D.; Zhang, Y.; Hou, X.X.; Chen, H.; Wang, S.H. Seven-layer deep neural network based on sparse autoencoder for voxelwise detection of cerebral microbleed. *Multimed. Tools Appl.* **2018**, *77*, 10521–10538. [CrossRef]
39. Amirabadi, M.; Kahaei, M.; Nezamalhosseini, S. Novel suboptimal approaches for hyperparameter tuning of deep neural network [under the shelf of optical communication]. *Phys. Commun.* **2020**, *41*, 101057. [CrossRef]
40. Moraitis, N.; Tsipi, L.; Vouyioukas, D.; Gkioni, A.; Louvros, S. On the Assessment of Ensemble Models for Propagation Loss Forecasts in Rural Environments. *IEEE Wirel. Commun. Lett.* **2022**, *11*, 1097–1101. [CrossRef]

41. Marinho, M.A.; da Costa, J.P.C.; Antreich, F.; de Freitas, E.P.; Vinel, A. Adaptive communication and cooperative MIMO cluster formation for improved lifetime in wireless sensor networks. In Proceedings of the 2016 IEEE International Conference on Wireless for Space and Extreme Environments (WiSEE), Aachen, Germany, 26–28 September 2016; pp. 190–195.
42. Maranhao, J.P.; da Costa, J.P.; de Freitas, E.P.; Marinho, M.A.; Del Galdo, G. Multi-hop cooperative XIXO transmission scheme for delay tolerant wireless sensor networks. In Proceedings of the WSA 2016; 20th International ITG Workshop on Smart Antennas, Munich, Germany, 9–11 March 2016; pp. 1–5.

Disclaimer/Publisher's Note: The statements, opinions and data contained in all publications are solely those of the individual author(s) and contributor(s) and not of MDPI and/or the editor(s). MDPI and/or the editor(s) disclaim responsibility for any injury to people or property resulting from any ideas, methods, instructions or products referred to in the content.

MDPI
St. Alban-Anlage 66
4052 Basel
Switzerland
www.mdpi.com

Sensors Editorial Office
E-mail: sensors@mdpi.com
www.mdpi.com/journal/sensors

Disclaimer/Publisher's Note: The statements, opinions and data contained in all publications are solely those of the individual author(s) and contributor(s) and not of MDPI and/or the editor(s). MDPI and/or the editor(s) disclaim responsibility for any injury to people or property resulting from any ideas, methods, instructions or products referred to in the content.

www.ingramcontent.com/pod-product-compliance
Lightning Source LLC
LaVergne TN
LVHW070431100526
838202LV00014B/1571